READING THE NEW LANDSCAPE: AN ECOLOGICAL AESTHETIC

RICHARD K. SUTTON

18.1 Copyright © 2020 Richard K Sutton
All rights reserved.
ISBN 9781722849580

Table of Contents

Acknowledgements iii

Foreword iv

Preface v

SECTION 1 Valuing Landscapes 2

    Chapter 1 Nature of Experience 3

    Chapter 2 Ecological Aesthetics 13

    Chapter 3 Valuing Farmland 29

    Chapter 4 Human and Landscape Scale 46

SECTION 2 Natural Landscapes 64

    Chapter 5 Influences on the Natural Vegetation of Nebraska ... 65

    Chapter 6 Nebraska's Plant Communities and Associations 88

SECTION 3 Cultural Landscapes 108

    Chapter 7 Nebraska's Agricultural Landscape 109

    Chapter 8 An Irrigated Landscape 121

    Chapter 9 Contested Ground: Plantings in the Image of a Garden 131

    Chapter 10 Placing Middle Ground: Cather's Divide Landscape 156

SECTION 4 Intentional Landscapes 170

    Chapter 11 Prairie Ecology and Conservation Design 171

    Chapter 12 Selfish Form, Selfless Nature 194

    Chapter 13 Pioneers Park: Landscape and Program Dynamics 207

SECTION 5 Future Landscapes 223

    Chapter 14 Sights (Sites) Worth Saving 223

    Chapter 15 Future Landscape; Eternity of Distance Meets the Illusion of Open Spaces 233

    Chapter 16 Reading the Nebraska Landscape 250

INDEX 260

Acknowledgements

Though the experience and work represented in this book span more than 50 years, it was not until the last several years, as it took form that many key individuals helped to make contributions. First, I must mention the support of my wife, Lisa. As well, my teachers and students have also contributed immensely to my intellectual growth in suggesting, challenging, and shaping my ideas on landscape and how to read it. For example, a good deal of Chapter 1 began as notes from Dr. Yi-Fu Tuan's class, Space and Place, at UW-Madison in 1991.

More recently, Amelia Jenson, budding landscape architect—only newly arrived in Nebraska, worked through and commented on earlier drafts of the book. It is entirely my fault if those comments were not as well implemented as she suggested. Lauryn Higgins gave the draft a thorough edit, but any errors in it still remain my responsibility. Frank Herbolsheimer another landscape architect crafted many of the Nebraska maps using his GIS skills. He worked to make color data readable in grayscale -- no mean feat. Kari Ronning, a Cather scholar graciously gave the book's Chapter 10 on the Divide landscape a detailed review but again I accept responsibility for any errors, misinterpretations, or mechanical defects. David Wishart, a historical/cultural geographer and long-time friend, encouraged me to write this book. He was key in commenting on many of the earlier articles before they were first published in academic journals; their content later became the grist for this book. David Murphy, architectural historian pointed to the importance of looking at cultural landscape structure in rural Nebraska. Thank-you to Martin Massengale for his foreword to this book.

I also thank many others: Reid Coffman, Editor, *Journal of Living Architecture*, for permission to use "Aesthetics for Green Roofs and Green Walls" as the basis for Chapter 2 (it appears here in an expanded and slightly difference form; Taylor and Francis Group, LLC, a division of Informa PLC allowed permission to reprint From *Under the Blade* (1998) Richard Olson and Thomas Lyson (Eds.) Chapter 6, Ethics and Aesthetics in the Loss of Farmland by Richard K. Sutton; The University of Nebraska press granted permission to reprint portions of my articles, "Landscape Ecology of Hedgerows and Fencerows in Panama Township, Lancaster County, Nebraska," which appeared in *Great Plains Research* 2:2, 1992 and, A Model of Human Scale Tested on Rural Landscape Scenes, which appeared in *Great Plains Research* 21:2, Fall 2011; UW Press granted permission to use portions of my article, Rural Planting Relicts in Eastern Nebraska, from *Landscape Journal. Vol. 4 No. 2,. 106-115 Winter*; the journal, *Material Culture* granted permission to include parts of my article, The Image of a Garden: Vernacular Conifer Plantings in Otoe County, Nebraska, published in its previous title, *Pioneer America Vol 14 pp. 93-113*. Chapter 14 includes parts of an article I published in *Prairie Fire* newspaper under the same title: "Sights (Sites) Worth Saving, Conversations Worth Having" and W. Don Nelson, Publisher, has given me permission to include them. The late, Walter T. Bagley collaborated with me on ideas about conservation easements used in Chapter 10;

Also, I would like to thank former Nebraska Poet Laureate, Twyla Hansen, painter, Keith Jacobshagen, and photographer, John Spence, for their willingness to be interviewed and for giving permission to share examples of their work. They create daily, for all of us, examples of aesthetic inspirations from the Nebraska landscape.

Foreword

Richard Sutton has spent his entire professional career studying, researching, evaluating and designing landscapes of all sizes. He prepared this book after retirement from his professorship at the University of Nebraska-Lincoln based on his observations and scholarly work. It is, undoubtedly, one of the most detailed descriptions available of the many different and common landscapes throughout Nebraska. In this book, Richard relates his own ideas, background and experiences recounting the different landscapes that can be seen.

Landscapes constantly change and become modified by numerous factors including humans. So, he shares some of the changes occurring in Nebraska landscapes during his lifetime. While his accounts project a highly personal viewpoint, he makes clear that each individual forms his or her own impression of different individual landscapes and, in turn, values them for many and various reasons.

Each person who observes and analyzes a landscape will form an opinion on that particular landscape depending on their background, the reason they are viewing it and the value they place on its different components. For example, someone with a rural background will see a landscape from a different perspective than someone from an urban background. Previous use and management impact landscapes, and we need to recognize that there may be many different viable options for use of an area of land with some uses more appropriate and better applied at different times and under different circumstances. All options need to be considered when making decisions on the use of a specific area.

Professor Sutton provides some interesting details and valuable information for those especially interested in history, agriculture, geology, flora and landscapes of Nebraska. All of us should give serious consideration to some of the author's ideas as we consider options that affect/alter our landscapes and their futures.

I am not aware of any other single source of information available with as much detail on different Nebraska landscapes as compiled in this book by Professor Sutton. If you have an interest in Nebraska and its landscapes, I recommend that you obtain a copy, read it and consider how you view its wide and varied spaces.

Martin A. Massengale

President Emeritus, University of Nebraska

Preface

> "When you think of a landscape, you think of romantic green gardens and hedges and flowers, right? . . . But a landscape is so much more than that – it encapsulates society, politics and our own existence on a planet where we're bound by natural forces. It's how we give form to our land and cities. Ultimately it's how we identify with places." —James Corner

> "The issue of landscape identity [or appreciation] is easily is bypassed, not because it is obvious, but because it is so complex. One could easily spend a lifetime trying to come to terms with a few square miles of the earth's surface, to understand why it appears as it does, to appreciate [understand] its histories and meanings, to grasp its patterns and associations that constitute the character of a region. But there is a danger of becoming lost in parochialism. The way to avoid this narrow focus is to recognize the universal truths are embedded in the unique identities of particular landscapes. To come to know the individuality of a landscape through careful seeing and reflection is a considerable achievement; but to identify broader principles implied in that landscape requires what Ruskin (a 19th Century British painter and art critic) called "a sort of farther vision," an effort of the imagination that makes it possible to grasp the whole nature of something of which we only know a fragment. Such farther vision works by means of the features of a particular landscape . . . we have to make the effort to see landscapes clearly, without bias and in their totality, and we must appreciate their aesthetic qualities and grasp their identities with all sensitivity we can muster. "-Ted Relph

Our family's Ford sped north on the curbed, two-lane US 77 and somewhere between the Crete Corner and Lincoln I shouted "Ah Hah! I can see the Capitol!" I rarely was first with this pronouncement punctuating the tedium of car trips in the early 1950's. In the days before the constraints of seatbelts my parents had invented a game to keep three rambunctious boys occupied while traveling. Being the youngest, I hadn't quite made the connection in this time/space game between the sequence of distant landmarks and specific topographic positions that produced the "Ah Hah" point-moment.

Later on when I began to hunt, looking and seeing took on a different meaning. Looking has always been a hunter's activity, but walking to hunt is quite different from manning a tree stand. When walking, your point of view changes and feeds a feeling of participation in the landscape. Carefully reading a landscape's structures was critical for finding pheasants and careful planning needed to minimize the steps and energy. Routinely I looked close for animal signs and then to the distance, plotting the most advantageous route to take—all the while keeping in position to cover the field of fire and tracking my hunting buddies.

When seeing things up close, in detail, then at a distance, the middle ground diminished in importance. (Unless it was suddenly filled with a flushing cock pheasant!) My attention swung from poles of closeness to distance. I believe this activity is a phenomenon of the Great Plains (and other open places) experience but morphs into claustrophobia in densely forested landscapes. My hunting encounters brought concrete examples of scale shifts, constructs of prospect, refuge, and hazard, first-hand experience of soils, plants, animals, and habitat, adaptation to changes of day, season, and decade, questions about values gained and lost over time and an interest in etching my own ideas into the landscape's pre-existing arrangement.

So, just what is landscape? To me it is the total dynamic, sensory environment which we interpret at one place at one time. It changes as we move and as it evolves. Because of our experiences, landscape or its interpretation lies inside our minds as well as in front of them.

It is interesting how an early exposure to looking and seeing landscapes could later have an important impact on my learning and seeking to understand the complex, ambient environment that surrounds us.

In this book I wish to share some of what I have learned about observing and thinking about what is seen and experienced in our shared environment generally and in many cases specifically, here in Nebraska. I do all of this with the implicit knowledge that people bring different ways of seeing and different experiences to bear, and that the reader may not agree with my interpretation of what is seen, how it is discussed, or ultimately what it means. Nevertheless, the landscape I once knew has changed or is rapidly changing so, in some measure this book helps document, explain, and examine that landscape before is has evolved into something very different.

This book and the sections and chapters it contains dwell on seeing and thinking about what is seen, how it came to be, and what the future might hold. It is a big order, though it's one that I have spent a lifetime contemplating, experiencing and writing about.

Creating landscape begins with humans. Section 1 examines our experiences, proposes an aesthetic approach to understanding landscapes, and balances that with an ethical dimension. Our aesthetic experiences of landscape require value judgments and I give examples of judging scale.

In Section 2, I give a natural history account of the forces that influenced Nebraska's natural landscape and still in many ways are at play today. In places where natural history rings true and in other places highly modified by humans, culture predominates but it nevertheless responds to the context provided by natural processes and forces.

Humans have unself-consciously created much of what we see in the Nebraska's landscape. So, Section 3 deals with cultural landscapes where continual husbandry and development largely based on science, technology, practice, or custom, form common, everyday arrangements and places. And the examples I discuss of my years of study of Nebraska's landscape begin to exhibit where ideas result in unique artifacts of land use and land cover patterns that we can begin to read.

Section 4 gives examples of intentional or designed landscapes and helps to portray the role of planning and design processes in creating a surrounding environment that supports humans and other living things. For landscape architects, process, form, and space become key aspects to designed landscapes. In the end, thoughtful design provides the connection required for our survival in climate-stressed places like Nebraska.

Drawing on the forces, concepts, features, and processes in the first four sections, I assert in Section 5 that scenery and open spaces found in Nebraska, while not grandiose, still impact human society and democracy. They are part of our national DNA. Meanwhile, our aesthetic values and responses need nurturing and training. In the future and open Nebraska landscape, time and space remain intertwined. I suggest that in a future landscape Nebraska might evolve and I give fictionalized examples of wind energy development, drought, and societal displacement as likely to radically change the quality and value of what and how we see when reading its landscape.

Finally, I extract 15 concepts which I think can be employed to aid one in reading the landscape. Then, following my own advice I chat with three creative people who read the Nebraska landscape daily as inspiration for their work and explain examples of that work by reading their landscapes.

SECTION 1   VALUING LANDSCAPES

> "What one thinks of any region while traveling through, is the result of at least three things: What one knows, what one imagines and how one is disposed. What one knows is either gathered first-hand or learned from books or indigenous observers. This information, however, is assembled differently by each individual, according to his cultural predispositions and his personality. ... Human beings, further, are inclined to favor visual information over the testimony of their other senses ... What one imagines in a new landscape consists of conjecture, for example, about what might lie beyond that near horizon. Often it consists of what one "hopes to see" during the trip . . . At a deeper level, however, imagination represents the desire to find what is unknown, unique, or farfetched . . . The way we are disposed toward the land is more nebulous, harder to define. The reluctant traveler, brooding about events at home, is oblivious to the landscape. . . The individual desire to understand, as much as any difference in acuity of the senses, brings each of us to find some thing in the land that others did not notice." --Barry Lopez

> "Landscape is the conception of a mature mind"- Yi-Fu Tuan

Landscapes do not exist without a viewer and participant. While we might choose to see and think of landscape as a list of objects like trees, rivers, mountains, and so on, it really exists as a reflection of our mind interacting with a specific place. And there are as many places existing on this Earth as human memories, actions, and thoughts can conceive, which is why we start a book on the Nebraska landscape with a section on humans thinking about landscape and not simply listing its physical features (see Section 2).

In this section I trace how humans make judgments about landscapes and bring values to bear in that process. Gregory Bateson, in *Mind and Nature*, points out that our minds grow to reflect the world of nature that surrounds us. All human events take from place. I use a couple of general examples to illustrate the role of our experiences in forming landscapes.

This book's subtitle, *An Ecological Aesthetic*, provides a unique framework to organize how we observe, acknowledge, enjoy, and value our broader world -- the phenomena I call landscape. By detailing specific examples from widely divergent Nebraska landscapes, I mold Bateson's expanded idea of aesthetics into *ecological* aesthetics as a basis for our moment-to-moment transactions with our surroundings.

Farms and ranches compose much of Nebraska's landscape so I focus next on our values and valuations found there. I compare and contrast aesthetic and ethical values about our productive lands and how we came to be vested in those ideas. As urban areas expand and radically and completely alter rural landscapes, the associated values we apply often change.

Scale has been evoked as a general Nebraska landscape descriptor, yet it too, is a value judgment. In the last chapter of this section I share detailed information I have garnered from my research. While definitions of scale rely on a list of physical parameters, it is our interpretation that matters. At certain scales, strong agreements occur amongst viewers. I argue that ways in which researchers (and viewers) have traditionally examined scale can be thought of as a series of interacting relationships, much like ecology.

1 Nature of Experience

"It takes a great deal of experience to become natural." Willa Cather

"[T]he way we experience and interpret the world obviously depends . . . on the kind of ideas that fill our minds." E. F. Schumacher

"Little by little . . . by experience we place not only ourselves but all things in their proper places in the universe." John G. Neihardt

Introduction

Travelers on the nearly 2200-mile Oregon Trail journey (part of which crosses what is now Nebraska) left accounts of weather, physical hardship, disease, and death. Though some of their experiences provide slices of aesthetic connection with the landscape through which they trudged: open distant vistas, blooming wildflowers, exotic (to them) animals like pronghorn antelope and buffalo. For those who came from forested regions in the eastern U. S. or from enclosed European landscapes, a daytime sky filled with light, clouds, and birds was only rivaled by the parade of night-time stars, planets, and the moon. They shared the commonality of the trail, but each reacted to it in his or her way.

While our experience of life, space, place, and landscape is intensely personal, we can still discuss and generalize about it. Furthermore, it is impossible to understand experience without knowing the landscape spaces we share that form part of that experience. We must also be aware that our size and speed, bias that experience. Even though the theory of relativity connects time and space along a continuum, changing spatial scales for humans comes more easily than changing temporal scales.

Movement through landscape brings a fundamentally different experience caused partly by a shift in scale. Furthermore, we cannot fully experience or create a change in movement, speed, or scale without a reference or starting point. Imposing such structure, like designing and building or a physical place, can be accomplished most efficiently by acknowledging the tension of our probing senses attached, strung, and tightened against it. Structure allows us the freedom to indulge in particular details and composed structures help communicate general experience. Likewise, the structure of our mind evolves in relation to our experience of the physical world of landscapes and vice versa. Connected by a shared experience, most likely those Oregon Trail travelers became more similar by their journeys' ends. Structure begets structure.

Yi-Fu Tuan, in *Space and Place*, suggests that human physiognomy – with its location of eyes to the front and ears to the side, yet cocked to the front – structures our normal means of movement. When combined with our upright stature, we are predisposed to certain interactions with the environment. Forward is future; behind is past. The elemental experience of body in the environment leads to assigning values and extrapolates into surrounding space. Just as our size and speed structure our interaction with the world, so does our basic anatomy.

However, I believe we share far more similarities than differences, so I start with an overview of experience and sensory perception of landscapes. Next, I provide three specific examples of experiences tied to ways of seeing, trees in the landscape, and earning the right to an experience in the first place. In these examples notice the importance of existing or imposed structure(s) on defining the experiences.

Experience

Experience is a coverall term for all the modes through which we apprehend reality and what changes it. However, this reality has been mediated by sensation, perception/cognition, learning, personality, culture, and worldview. How does the world surrounding us come into being? Reality describes and depicts a series of events conveniently packaged as stories; telling the story makes it more real. Naming the actors and their setting in the story directs our attention, though the name is not the actor or the setting and hence not the thing named. Naming requires our attention. Naming, though, unlike seeing, puts things at arm's length, generalizes, and makes the experience easier to share. Seeing, on the other hand, brings a phenomenon to the fore, structures it, and adds a contextual meaning. The seeming ease of this process does not, however, make experiences any more real. In fact, upon naming, much may be lost in translation. As John Berger notes in his book, *Ways of Seeing*, the differences between naming and seeing are never fully resolved. Directly seeing something as an experience can never be replaced by describing it. It's similar to the old game called "Gossip" where a couple of short sentences are sequentially whispered to a neighbor and travel around a circle. What comes out rarely resembles what the originator said. Any place created by naming can be destroyed by words lost or altered through time or simply misunderstood. Words must be repeated and maintained through oral transmittal or writing as a part of social discourse.

I ==> think. I ==> tell. I ==> write. I ==> transfer meaning.

I ==> see. I ==> draw. I ==> transfer meaning.

The upper sequence narrows and reifies; drawing communicates and expands meaning by relying more on the interpretation of the viewer and the context of the image. Drawing is directed also largely by the right hemisphere of the brain, language by the left. Structure begets structure.

The two basic qualities of a language are representation and description, and they aid communication. Nelson Goodman in *Languages of Art*, tells us that a multivariate environment needs a multitude of communication paths. Goodman's approach to a language of images versus a language of words lies in the image being a whole and thus irreducible into meaningful parts. To parse it damages meaning. Images or visual languages densely pack information whereas speaking and writing articulate and distill information. In a holistic, image-based system, each element relates to all others including its context, whereas an articulate, linguistic system relates to only a few or sequential relationships. While it is possible to relay emotional information by the practiced timbre, modulation, volume, and timing of voice, written, or spoken language connects partially, selectively, and socially, whereas an image over-connects and explodes with meaning.

Perhaps drawing what we see helps select and trace some of the structure and details we perceive. The late Alan Gussow, a painter, has declared that he didn't know whether a painting he created of the Kaaterskill Clove was a picture of the clove or a description of how experiencing that clove changed him. Yet the very act of drawing creates a separate reality. The result of that reality might be the residue of experience from drawing and often appears more subjective than objective. Anyone who has tried to capture a place or the experience of that place in a drawing knows any drawing takes on a life of its own. Epistemology – learning how we know what we know – seems to be a two-way flow. What we sense (and draw) of the world structures our senses and memory in a way that has meaning to us.

The role of the senses plays importantly on what we perceive. Connected, our senses interact as a multi-modal perceptual system (Table 1.1). Those senses not only act in concert, but also have physical, physiological, psychological, and cultural hierarchies. Again, structure begets structure.

Light activates the raw material of visual experience, without it, space collapses into isolated intimacies of sound, touch, taste, and smell. The quality and source of light in turn affects how we perceive a space. Filtered light beneath a forest canopy conjures an experience not unlike flickering firelight on a cave wall. Because human vision assumes the key role in perception of space, a large portion of our frontal cerebral lobe supports and processes it. Nevertheless, hearing supplements seeing by acknowledging and confirming distant phenomena. Sound energy attenuates with the square of its distance, and because it diffuses we must work hard to pinpoint its source in the distance. According to William Irwin Thompson, at its worst, sound becomes noise cutting one off from careful contemplation. We can close our eyes, but it is harder to plug one's ears.

Touch, taste, and smell bring more intimate knowledge. Sight also supplements touch since texture must be confirmed by seeing a surface. While smell can bring some distant information by way of the puny human nose, its chemistry intimately and tightly intertwines with taste. Sensory inputs can be distorted, filtered, ignored, categorized, and focused. What we know of the world comes from a narrow range of visible light, waves of sound, scant chemicals, and palpable contact. Humans have extended their given senses somewhat by creating instruments in order to see, hear, taste, and touch a wider swath of the world, but such extensions represent second-hand knowing that we experience indirectly. Seeing strongly biases our visual sense of the world, but in sum, our senses act as a multi-modal perceptual system, not independently.

Table 1.1 Our senses as an interacting multi-modal perceptual system

Input	Altered	Spatial Relationship	Multi-modal
Visible radiation	Reflected	Distant or close	See--> Eyes
	Refracted		
	Absorbed		
Infra-red radiation		Close	Feel-->Skin
Pressure		Close	Feel-->Touch
Sound waves	Reflected	Distant or close	Hear-->Ears
Gravity		Distant	Balance-->Inner Ear
Chemical	Absorbed	Distant or close	Smell-->Nose
Chemical	Diffused	Close	Taste-->Tongue

Environmental and other psychologists explore perception and conduct rigorous, often simple, experiments using human subjects. They try to understand the mechanism and sequence of how we process incoming sensory information and then how we react to it. A simple eye blink is pre-cognitive; we don't have to think about it and we just blink as a reflexive action However our cognition allows us to perceive, assess, and create a world. That world and an experience of it form the basis for being, interacting, and changing that world. Experience of the world provides a basic structure leading to knowledge and learning.

Learning in the proper context is the business of culture and in Western, post-industrial culture it means assuming the dominance of the scientific paradigm. Science represents a worldview that presupposes the system being studied can be disconnected from the observer and assumes that the observer is bias-free bringing no preconceptions, emotions, or involvement to his or her observations. Yet one cannot know anything without assuming an epistemological position as a starting point.

According to psychologist, Jean Piaget, children progress through identifiable mental stages as they develop cognitively and physically. Cultural initiation often marks the stage of sexual maturity as adolescent becomes adult. In Western societies, the child in us leaves when we lose our sense of a continuous, chaotic present, where everything sparkles, seems new and matches our innocence. Children's places lack most of the structure imposed by the adult mind and this changes how we (and they) experience the world. Such an idea led Yi-Fu Tuan to remark, "Landscape represents the construction of the mature mind." That is, children do not understand or appreciate the complexity of landscape: they simply do not have the necessary experience. Experience binds tightly with space and time as we mature. Adults rarely focus upon the present, but instead look backward with nostalgia or forward into the future with anxiety, anticipation, or resignation. Meanwhile, Ram Dass implores us to return to our childlike ways and, "Be here, now!"

For ill or good, we each remain captive to our experience; each of us encounters colors or shapes and then those impact what we have seen, heard, thought, done, and read. Otherwise, perhaps we have become submerged by routine. A beautiful winter sunrise tints and saturates a vanilla landscape, a rustle of wind kisses treetops, fragrance drifts from a springtime orchard, and a cool stream tickles our toes. These daily aesthetic experiences connect us to our world. They remind us that we are in and of this world, despite many of our photographs' attempts to freeze and capture such experiences. John Fowles warns us that such a snapshot attitude damages aesthetic connections by objectifying experiences, and relegating them into a "present pastness," . . . "as if have got beats having got."

Experience of Landscape: Some Examples

In the next three sections I give extended examples of deliberate landscape experiences, (not all of which are in Nebraska) such as understanding one's point-of-view, relating to important landscape elements like trees, and participating in a common landscape activity like earning the right to an experience.

An Experiment on Point of View

Worldview as a viewpoint of the world intertwines with presuppositions of a dominant culture, though a viewpoint may also be a point in space with a unique view of the world. Wishing to understand worldview I set out to explore and experiment with it and our experience of space. Optical illusions suggested a starting point and seemed to be of two general types. The first, which involves no movement, lies inside our cognitive system, and gains its effect when we rapidly reinterpret the meaning first inferred by the view. The Necker Cube (Figure 1.1) and the Crone/Maiden paradoxes are examples. Psychologists altering the physical location or angle of a viewpoint, which in turn causes paradox, indicate that in order for this shift to occur, the mind and the eye must be intensely focused, become bored with an unchanging image, and then cognitively alter its interpretation. Studying this type of internal viewpoint reveals how the mind understands and imposes structure on reality.

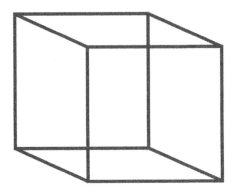

Figure 1.1 The Necker Cube

The second type, in fact, involves a change in our external context by altering the physical location or angle of a viewpoint, which in turn causes paradox in the observer's mind. Our understanding of physical reality is not arbitrary. Over the course of our lives, we gain long and deep experience from exploring (experimenting with) our physical environment. Due to our binocular vision, parallax[1] embeds within and informs our perception. J.J. Gibson suggests that additional knowledge also comes from an interactive process of muscular tension of the eyeball, face, neck, and body interplaying and feeding back movement with precision that creates new viewpoints that present new challenges and learning. For example, the toddler must be able to see, judge, and move from support to support. Spills lead to correction and increased competence in movement. Scientific method formalizes and expands this concept applying it to a series of rigorous observations from a controlled viewpoint. It then statistically compares observations from one viewpoint to another equally controlled viewpoint. The scientific observer hypothesizes he or she will be able to detect differences and create an explanation linking two or more viewpoints in a system generalized enough to predict future viewpoints.

Both of these changes of viewpoint, internal and external, have been explored by artist John Pfahl with regards to our understanding of landscape space and scale. He presents his observations of reality in the form of photographs. They include architectural and natural spaces and contain carefully composed and technically competent contexts. However, on these images of real places – ground planes, wall planes, and canopies – he imposes a simple and readily visible structure that represents a different viewpoint. When I first saw his scenes, it seemed to me that the artist had just drawn some lines that didn't even fit with the perspective structure of the photo. However, on closer examination, I noticed the lines were actually physically part of the scene being captured on film. Pfahl had interacted with and manipulated the scene using tape or string, creating the appearance of a line or a grid as counterpoint to the context.

My experiment drew from Pfahl's techniques. In a human-planted forest, I chose a space with a visible, structured foreground and extended middle ground with a physically delimited, though porous, wall plane. This context for my experimental photos necessarily contained clues to visual height and depth by the diminution of in size as in a perspective from my single

---

Parallax: From Greek, meaning apparent shift of an observed object due to a observer's change of location.

Figure 1.2 A point of view on a path in Leopold Woods, UW Madison-Arboretum

Figure 1.3 Another point of view on a path in Leopold Woods, UW Madison-Arboretum

camera viewpoint. With such a referential viewpoint from a camera on a tripod, I proceeded to place masking tape on the objects comprising the wall plane. I did so with two lines of tape in the photo. It was necessary to widen the strips of tape placed on more distant objects in such a way that their apparent right angles extended up and down and left to right. Since the effect was to show the inherent bias in any single viewpoint on the world, I also took a photograph from a viewpoint, two feet behind and three feet above and three feet to the right of the first viewpoint. The second photo reveals the apparent, fractured nature of the first photo by showing meaningless, unstructured, and disconnected strips of tape (Figure 1.3). I would have liked to have produced a photo of an actual right angle in the taped lines, but the darkness of the forest, slow shutter speed, and wide (f-1.4) aperture reduced my depth of field and resulted in a fuzzy foreground. The overlap between the lower left to upper right diagonal displayed an obvious discontinuity, which is exactly the kind of visual clue to which we clutch for indications of depth. The curved tree trunks also posed problems and perhaps using a stiff piece of cardboard in place of tape would have helped reduce the trunk's impact on line straightness.

This experiment into constructing an experience and winnowing its residue, re-enforces this comment from Gregory Bateson, "The division of the perceived universe into parts and wholes [viewpoints] is convenient and may be necessary, but no necessity determines how it shall be done . . . Explanation must always grow out of description, but description [viewpoints] from which it grows will still necessarily contain arbitrary characteristics. . ." Likewise description grows out of observation and experience.

Experiencing Trees as Landscape Places

One spring I visited a certain specimen of Amur corktree (*Phellodendron amurense*) planted by Charles Sprague Sargent a century ago in the Arnold Arboretum. From it, a graceful lateral limb extends horizontally and then arches up in a gentle curve like a gesturing arm. Its position also happens to be low to the ground, about the height of a high bench. Over the years this tree has served as a shady lap or refuge, and now its smooth brown bark belies a brocaded gray skin producing the quintessence of patina obtained through use as a human place. This encounter leads me to propose that trees, while natural objects in space, can in concert with people create special places. Thoreau described trees as places too in the opening paragraphs of the "Baker Farm" chapter of *Walden*, where cedar trees rose "fit to stand before Vallhala and the creeping juniper covers the ground with wreaths full of fruit." I argue trees become places insofar as they serve to even center human attachment to a locale or to nature in general.

Humans have an affinity for trees. Trees occupy the same space-time scale as humans. Popularized by Desmond Morris in, *The Naked Ape*, theories of human emergence has our precursors emerging from trees and onto a savanna landscape. Jay Appleton aptly confers on the tree a continuing importance of the term called, arboreal refuge. Omnipresent trees mothered our ancestors and welcomed them into their leafy arms when threatened by danger. The perfect tree still reveals itself to the simultaneous safe haven and distant prospect affording a view outward. Leading up to a scene in the movie, *Robin Hood Prince of Thieves*, the omniscient camera sweeps grand, open prospects. The setting contains fine physical dimensions, almost stage-like qualities of topography and a single tree. In the distance, a small figure rushes across open fields pursued by men on horseback. It is a boy for whom the tree was the only possible refuge. The viewer is led to experience the archetype of spatial terror, perhaps filled with ancient memories of a large saber-tooth tiger pursuing a small bipedal hominid caught in the open and away from his mother, the tree.

So, if trees are central to the functioning or definition of a place (and landscape) in which human activities happen, they must become part of that place and not simply be its furnishings. To people living in the company of trees, a place can become more or less defined by the addition or removal of trees. Very often however, trees simply reside in the background and only in their absence does their loss strike a chord. In regions of tree scarcity, like the Great Plains, even a few trees can transform an anonymous locale into a place. Willa Cather's description of Antonia's Divide farmstead recalls the human qualities of trees. Antonia talks about planting and caring for young trees as one would a child. Very few trees live where they do on the Great Plains without a human story attached to their placement or survival. On those open plains trees become highly visible symbols, and in such unrelieved places, embody central objects in a field of care. Trees become the most stable living elements of many habitable landscapes. (See Chapter 9)

Rooted in time and place, trees may extend several decades beyond human experience. This allows trees to merge with a place and often to symbolize its essence. And to the extent that trees become symbols they even more readily become places. Human symbols only grow out of conferred and shared meaning; trees are centers of meaning in diverse cultures and a myriad of ways. Native Americans identified sacred trees such as the ash and cedar that became artifacts of ceremony and story. Gardens in Japanese Imperial villas contain two consecrated trees—one a plum, the other a cherry always planted in a special location and in a special side-by-side relationship. As all fifty states attest, even those political entities have designated symbolic "State Trees"; the Cedar graces the flag of Lebanon, some schools still honor Arbor Day with ceremonial tree plantings, and The Ohio State University chose the Ohio buckeye as its mascot and so on.

Trees also move beyond the secular to the spiritual. Druids worshiped trees and primitive priests/shamans accorded a tree's spatial orientation with a simple structural cosmology: first, crowns reached into the heavens, noting the spirit from the first springtime flush of new leaves; second, trunks attached to the earth; and third, underground roots extended to the netherworld. Evergreen trees are brought inside to celebrate and symbolize the Christian Yule season and are found in most every temperate cemetery--planted to console those who have lost loved ones during the winter; purloined fruit from the tree of knowledge of good and evil precipitated Adam and Eve's expulsion from the Garden of Eden; planted fruit trees grace the Islamic paradise garden.

Being objects that define space, trees can too quickly be dismissed as lacking the qualities of place. Yet trees provide a unique experience providing physical and spiritual refuges perhaps offering a view out. Trees become fields of care, remaining static in space and abiding time, and thus finally serve as symbols for centers of meaning.

Earning the Right to an Experience

Above I referred to John Fowles' disavowal of the "snapshot aesthetic experience" that relegates our experiences into a present pastness. He elegantly and simply questions whether, "Have got beats having got." Fowles' dictum lies at the heart of earning the right to an experience, for it is in the process leading up to an experience that the full experience resides, not just its payoff.

For example, it was my intent over a six weeks' stay in Kyoto, to visit and experience Japanese gardens. I did three things to vary and widen the contexts of my visits: I visited several gardens more than once and at different times of day; I sought out obscure gardens; I spent many hours in a garden. In visiting those gardens in a widened context, two things struck me. First was the pivotal role of the gardener and second, that my experience of a garden really began before I entered it. Visiting Daisen-in early in the morning meant I could observe the gardener go about his or her work. In some ways, it was like seeing performance art resulting in living sculpture. The diligence and ease with which the gardeners swept moss carpets, sheared budding tables of azalea, combed and clipped the pine's tresses, and toted great bundles and baskets of residue, lent a startlingly realistic quality and bustle to a normally quiet tableau.

Second, my trips to and sojourns within gardens required that I do my homework:

background readings, studying garden diagrams and images. But also planning in detail what rail line and bus to take and using maps to find the entry gate. In the case of Imperial Gardens and several others I also needed to secure reservations. To find the lesser temples and their adjoining gardens required planning. Occasionally, I lost my way wandering into residential or suburban precincts rarely traveled by tourists, but I always found the garden I sought. I was struck by the quiet, solitude, and privacy they afforded me compared to the cackling polyphony of major tourist attractions like Ryoan-ji. Quiet gardens led me to sit, think, and sketch mostly undisturbed. I could luxuriate in the sights, sounds, textures and fragrances of a garden, spending an hour on a sketch, unbidden by an impatient tour bus driver. Like a za-zen student, I could drift in and out of reverie, drawing in if gaggles of visitors streamed by and back out to a peaceful reality when they left. I also moved about the gardens, relishing their spaces and the connections in between. The garden designers possessed skills often only attributed to sculptors; spatial ambiguity appeared. Perhaps the sculpted garden spaces possessed ambiguity because the garden designer intended it, but many cultural and natural places display spatial ambiguity. It makes them maddening and mysterious at the same time, and it also helps make them landscapes.

Such direct experiences of gardens need savoring in their approach and reminiscence. Memories take from a place and when they are recalled, instantly transport us in space and time. I recorded Kyoto and its gardens deeply through sketching and photography. The sketchbook became the more important, for it, like the gardens themselves, records a residue of earned, active experience in a dynamic, ambiguous environment. In the end, all the planning and observing and recording justified and earned me the right to the experience of these unique gardens. So, while structure begets structure, our experience must constantly account for the change and dynamism of the world. This accounting requires an investment in time and effort which is all part of earning the right to an experience.

Did other visitors arriving on tour busses earn the right to their brief encounters with gardens like Ryoan-ji? Certainly they paid a tour operator, but were their experiences part of a personally planned process? It is unlikely most had studied the garden beforehand. Loudspeakers in several different languages and the tourists' short visits belie the contemplative roots of a Zen garden.

Conclusion

Thoreau sought to use his exploration of the New England countryside and observations of nature therein as a means to self-knowledge. He believed that the wilderness he experienced out-of-doors reflected the wilderness inside his mind—what John Fowles called the "green man." We each have our own "green man or woman hidden inside" ready to present itself as we experience landscape. But without structure, experience confronts us with chaos, so we need to shun its apparent meaningless portions by first ignoring details. Starting with structure allows us a way to understand its very creation. If we were to see structure without detail, though, our experience of the world devolves into dissatisfaction. So much so when we lack, miss, ignore, or misunderstand creative clues in the world before us; we become less human.

Creation of meaning and ultimately creation of place turns on our ability to experience it first as space. Intensely personal space becomes something different and more important when leading with our imagination: we share it, explore it, and discuss it. The details important to us come to the fore. The ever-changing features of both the natural and human-made world require us to understand it as a dynamic system. Spatial ambiguity inherent in our landscape experience calls for our interpretation as a kind of active participation. As a leap of faith, those two key aspects ultimately force us to construct, value, and share place.

Further Reading

Bateson, G. 1979. *Mind and Nature: A Necessary Unity* (p. 238). New York: Dutton.

Cather, W., 1986. *Interviews, Speeches and Letters* edited by L Brent Bohlke (Lincoln.

Berger, J. 2008. *Ways of Seeing* Vol. 474. Penguin UK.

Dass, R. 2010. *Be Here Now*. Harmony Books.

Fowles, J. 2000. *The Tree*. Random House.

Gibson, J. J. 1966. *The Senses Considered as Perceptual Systems*.

Gibson, J. J. 2014. *The Ecological Approach to Visual Perception* Classic Edition. Psychology Press.

Goodman, N. 1968. *Languages of Art*: *An Approach to a Theory of Symbols*. Hackett publishing.

Gussow, A. 1972. *A Sense of Place: Artists and the American Land*. San Francisco: F*riends of the Earth,*

Pfahl, J., & Bunnell, P. C. 1981. *Altered Landscapes: The Photographs of John Pfahl*.

Piaget, J. 1964. Part I: Cognitive development in children: Piaget development and learning. *Journal of Research in Science Teaching*, 23, 176-186.

Neihardt, J.G., 1997. *The River and I*. U of Nebraska Press.

Schumacher, E. F. 2011. *Small is Beautiful: A Study of Economics as if People Mattered*. Random House.

Thoreau, H.D., 1981. *Walden and Other Writings*. Bantam Classics.

Thompson, W. I. 1985. *Pacific Shift*. San Francisco: Sierra Club Books.

Tuan, Y. F. 1977. *Space and Place: The Perspective of Experience*. U of Minnesota Press.

Tuan, Y. F. 2013. *Topophilia: A Study of Environmental Perceptions, Attitudes, and Values*. New York: Columbia University Press.

2 Ecological Aesthetics

"By aesthetic, I mean being responsive to the pattern which connects." Gregory Bateson

"Never think that the poetry of nature's moods in all their infinite variety is lost on the scientific observer, for the habit of observing refines our sense of beauty and adds a brighter hue to the richly colored background against which each particular fact is outlined. The connection between events and the relation between cause and effect in different parts of the landscape unite harmoniously what would otherwise be but a chain of unrelated scenes." - M. G. J. Minnaert

"I experience space as a dynamic relationship, sculptural, architectural, and temporal in nature rather than pictorial and arising diffusely from the whole body not just the eyes." –Frank Gohlke

Introduction

I exhale just as drops of rain begin falling on the canoe. The rain pit-pats on leaves, the Dismal River, and lightly drums the sides of my aluminum canoe. Rainwater accumulates in the canoe bottom washing about some recently swatted deer flies. Only a few moments earlier driven by the pressure drop of the approaching storm, the flies had bitten in frenzy and I had fought back. Bloody smears now decorate my bare legs. (Somehow a story about a Sandhills rancher's cows being driven through a boundary fence into a wildlife refuge by biting flies becomes more believable. Seems the trespassing cows plunged themselves into a lake up to their bellies to avoid biting flies. Then they stayed for weeks grazing in the forbidden pasture. The rancher paid a fine for their sins.)

The rain steadily picks-up, and although it does not chill we pull on ponchos anyway. We stop paddling and quietly float the river meanders, hearing just the falling rain. No other sounds, breezes, lightening, or thunder challenge us. The air smells fresh and grassy; as we drift, time evaporates.

Did I just describe an aesthetic experience? Or did I respond to my surroundings and become part of their pattern? If it is the latter, what was the pattern to which I connected? Do the two, brief opening paragraphs relate how my surroundings changed or how the surroundings changed me?

This book's subtitle, *An Ecological Aesthetic*, might seem like an odd juxtaposition of two, very different words and concepts. After all, ecology is a science, right? And aesthetics, is a humanity and deals with human judgments and reactions. Yet in its largest sense ecology makes connections between things and events. It, just like aesthetics, describes relationships. So the two concepts readily connect us with the world.

In the next chapter, I will discuss, trace, and differentiate the values we bring to our relationship with farmland, and in reality any landscape we care to experience. In it I talk about the aesthetics of engagement (Berleant 1997). But before doing so, I want to expand an understanding of aesthetics and extend it to Nebraska landscapes: natural, cultural, and intentionally designed.

Aesthetics

Our ethical worldview, determines whether an action we might take is right or wrong. Its sister valuation, aesthetics, evokes our judgment as to like or dislike. Ethics set rules and

Figure 2.1 A sunny day on the Dismal River in Hooker Co., NE

boundaries, determines who has standing, why, and their correct recourse. Ethics underpins religion and law. On the other hand, aesthetics taps our experience, learning, and moment-to-moment sensory awareness; aesthetics engages and binds us to the material world.

According to Webster's 7th Collegiate Dictionary, aesthetics has these meanings:

- branch of philosophy dealing with the nature of the beautiful and judgments concerning beauty
- description and explanation of artistic phenomena and aesthetic experience by means of social sciences such as psychology, sociology, ethnology, or history.

So philosophers and social scientists, not just critics, artists and designers, help us judge and understand beauty. Beauty covers a suite of human experiences, affects, emotions, and thoughts, and as we can gauge from the definitions; applied beauty fully integrates a process of description, interpretation, and evaluation. Make no mistake: when one talks about beauty or ugliness, the discussion broadly involves value judgments that we call aesthetic.

At least two aspects occur during that evaluation. First, there must be something describable that arouses a judgment; second, an evaluator offers judgment. Aesthetics allows us to judge our feelings and value our responses on a scale from value to disvalue; such judgment may not always be positive. Examining the disvalues below can help illustrate a broad range of concerns and interactions found in real situations. For example, below are some common disvalues (from Berleant 1997):

- Banal - acquiesces to conventional style, subject matter, or sentiment
- Dull - no invention, poor technique, shallow imagination
- Unfulfilled - something's missing; a good idea poorly executed

- Trite - ignores new possibilities
- Inappropriate - not suitable to its context
- Desensitizing - ignores a place's sensory richness or our perceptual completeness
- Deceptive - hiding faults; lacking truthfulness
- Destructive - degrades context or demeans user

Notice how some, but not all, of the listed disvalues involve only the feature being judged. Some disvalues call to question the skill and intention of the designer, or focus not just on the feature or creation, but its context. Others begin to describe harmful impacts on the evaluator.

Much of what people seek when they travel and experience landscapes falls under the broad guise of making (or remaking) their connections with the world around them. While, biologist, John Janovy, Jr. (2018) does not expressly use the word, aesthetic, to describe his exploration of Africa, its landscapes and inhabitants, he does suggest that his *Africa Notes* represents a, "quest for an explanation for why sights, sounds, smells, and qualities of light engage us in ways that words and deeds cannot. If successful, I will have made a contribution to what makes us human." Awe and a sense of other worldly connections often mark our aesthetic connection to our world. On Skaerling Island in the high arctic Barry Lopez (2019), a writer and inveterate traveler, describes what I would call an aesthetic experience: "As I walked the Alexandra lowland, I was brought to a heightened sense of the "beauty" within it, a particular integration of color, line, proportionality, sound, smell and texture. I was aware of its effect on me, and of how my vulnerability to it enhanced a feeling of health in me, of being in harmony with the world that existed outside my own thoughts and beyond my understanding."

Describing and detailing beauty has occupied humans since at least the Ancient Greeks. Alder (1981) in his book, *Six Great Ideas*, proposes that beauty as studied by philosophers and our responses to it can be reduced and summarized into the simple categories of enjoyable beauty and admirable beauty. Given the last several hundred years of philosophical study and debate, those two concepts work well to understand and interpret the beauty arising from human creations. But a problem occurs when nature specifically or the non-human environment in general, becomes the focus of aesthetic inquiry simply because, it is beyond human control or understanding.

There is not enough room here to fully trace how interest has risen and fallen in aesthetics when applied to the environment. If the reader wishes more depth, Carlson (2012) has completed such a review. In brief, Carlson's explication of environmental aesthetics goes beyond what Adler (see below) called enjoyable beauty and admirable beauty. Carlson describes and discusses the recent interest in environmental beauty as paralleling concern regarding the deterioration of our environment starting in the last part of the 20th century (though Morton (2007) notes it started much earlier during the rise of the Romantics). Aestheticians (e.g. Hepburn 1966) working on the characteristics of the environment or nature relationships showed interest in our everyday environments and our interaction and response to natural elements and ecological processes. According to Carlson, cognitive views of environmental aesthetics use knowledge of nature, while non-cognitive views rely on some other aspect such as nature's engagement of humans (Berleant 1997). Most recently, Carlson notes that some scholars of environmental aesthetics (e.g., Nassauer 1997) and ecological-based beauty are attempting to include multiple viewpoints and explain multiple interconnections.

Below I describe Adler's simple, but useful and accurate explanations of enjoyable beauty and admirable beauty, because those concepts fit and are widely espoused by many who envision the aesthetics of natural, cultural or designed environments. I then bring forward a wider and more useful concept of ecological aesthetics.

Enjoyable Beauty

St. Thomas Aquinas (1274) adroitly stated that beauty is, "that which being perceived, pleases." Such an idea of beauty, while it may be true, is unfortunately strongly subjective. It is one's opinion and no one else can confirm or deny that personal response. Its basis cannot be accessed; so therefore, it is not really open to dialog or persuasion. Much of the subjectivity of enjoyable beauty (Adler 1981) may be the result of cultural learning not shared by others. "Beauty is in the eye of the beholder," as a shallow, self-contained and self-referential approach tends to separate one from what catalyzed the aesthetic experience in the first place. Finally, its focus on immediate gratification, also fails to deal with a wider, older, and more complex contexts for the experience.

Admirable Beauty

Turning to what brought on the experience provides no more complete an explanation to an aesthetic experience either, since it focuses solely upon the stimulus', physical, and admirable properties. This object-oriented approach, favored by art critics and many designers, may also be culturally learned and must acknowledge the intention of the artist. According to Kant (1792), contemplation or interpretation of an aesthetic experience must be a disinterested act. And just as enjoyable beauty requires separation of a subject and object, so does admirable beauty (Adler 1981). Often based solely on formal, visual elements such as color, texture, and form, and the design principles of variety, unity, and proportion, this approach can become superficial and focus narrowly on pleasure derived from object's shallow surfaces. This pleasure or affect most often ignores the surrounding context in favor of a designed object.

Explaining an aesthetic experience based upon admirable beauty brings several problems. First, not all critics agree that some object may be worthy of admiration or use widely different criteria to judge it. Cold, calculated criticism fails to account for human emotions and may be often biased in favor of only the sense of sight. Trapped in a static field, objects often belie and deny their changing context.

These arguments seem fairly obvious when dealing with solely human -created phenomena like a sculpture, painting, or even a building, but things become more complicated when natural phenomena (e.g., scenery or landscapes) come into play. When an ecological system, however much it was designed and initiated by a human, takes on a life of its own, we need a different more encompassing approach to beauty.

Ecological Beauty (Ecological Aesthetics)

Ecological beauty arises from the subject (individual user), object, (landscape) and their higher order connection (Individual-landscape-context) (Gobster 1999). In this approach, subject, object, and context become unified. Focusing on interaction frames ecological beauty hierarchically, much like nature herself. Beauty and its perception emerge from these underlying properties and interactions. An ecological approach to beauty thus extends beyond mere surface properties and embraces unseen forms and processes, deeply and holistically engaging our personal experience. This deep experience simultaneously draws upon our

Table 2.1 Three types of beauty

Enjoyable	Admirable	Ecological
Subjective	Objective	Object/Subject Interact
Cultural Model (Learned)	Art Model	Biological/Cognitive Model
All about ones experience	Product of intentional creative act	Interactive; hierarchical
Sensory-based pleasure	Requires disinterested interpretation	Pleasure requires interpretation or knowledge
Separates viewer & object	Separation of viewer from context	Object/Subject/Context unified
Opinion; not discussable	Judged in isolation of context	Evidence-based; emergent properties
Internalized	Superficial; shallow-surfaced	Based on formal characteristics
		Deeply engages one's experience
Descriptive	Normative	Multi-modal, uses all senses and movement
		Primarily visual
		Teaches about and bonds with place
Criticism	**Criticism**	**Criticism**
Shallow; self-contained	Critics disagree of use different criteria	Will never have enough knowledge
Does not deal with context	How to access and apply human emotion?	Can't control context or viewer
		Too often only visual
		Static; denies change

knowledge and teaches us about our general environment. Over time, experience bonds us to specific places. Unlike enjoyable or admirable beauty, ecological beauty makes no attempt to control the subject with esoteric cultural knowledge or the object with precise description. Those who desire perfection in aesthetic experience will be disappointed with ecological beauty, because humans will never have enough knowledge to perfectly describe or specify all natural features, contexts, and processes. (Table 2.1)

Aldo Leopold (1949) in his classic book, *A Sand County Almanac*, developed the well-known valuation system called the "Land Ethic." His dictum below is also quoted at the being of the next chapter:

> "Quit thinking about decent land use as solely an economic problem. Examine each question in terms of what is it ethically and aesthetically right as well as what is economically expedient. A thing is right when it tends to preserve the integrity, stability, and beauty of the biotic community. It is wrong when it tends otherwise."

Morton (2007) claims that integrity, stability, and beauty are all features of aesthetics.

In the same book Leopold also sketched out another valuation system he called the "Conservation Esthetic"(sic). Callicott (1983) recounts the differences and similarities in Leopold's valuation systems. The Conservation Esthetic recognizes the more common, directly visible, and less scenic (i.e., non-superficial); it emphasizes benefits such as psychic and spiritual rewards. Unlike the Land Ethic, the Conservation Esthetic is non-consumptive and applies to private not just public places; it does not focus on obligations and responsibilities, but offers spiritual rewards. The major connection between the two interactive relationships, derives from ecology, albeit for the Conservation Esthetic it is more conceptual; it includes ideas of diversity, complexity, species rarity, nativity, their interactions, and so on. Another key feature of the Conservation Esthetic encourages individuals over time to cultivate sensibilities and acquire knowledge about specific environments. In short, it evokes learning and ecological awareness which takes a lifetime to acquire (Kovacs 2006; see Lopez 2019).

Leopold's Conservation Esthetic embraces many of the aspects described earlier for ecological beauty such as interaction between subject and object with the subject capturing information that is beyond a "pretty" surface. As well, it allows a deep and knowledgeable experience to bond us with place over time. And as alluded earlier, ecological science's, *raison d'être*, seeks to unlock and explain how the ecological world works. However, with regards to an ecological aesthetic, ecological science becomes propelled by lack of knowledge dampened neither by control of viewer nor by context. The essence of ecological beauty means that we will always be engaged and learning about it.

Natural Environment

Because of his diverse study of biology, human systems, mental illness, and cybernetics, Gregory Bateson has become a quintessential 20th century discoverer. His work was based on an aesthetic philosophy not tied to the ethics and its boundaries of right or wrong. His application of ideas such as a "difference that makes a difference" brings quality and not quantity to the foreground. Bateson (1979) in his seminal book, *Mind and Nature: A Necessary Unity*, argued that our mind and its structure and connections emerged from contact with our environment – our social and ecological natures. More simply stated: interconnected synapses of our brain reflect the nature of the environments which we have experienced.

Aesthetics

Just what do we mean by nature and environment? Are humans part of or separate from those concepts? Interest in nature and aesthetics appeared in the Romantic Period, the first time in western culture that the impacts on our surroundings claimed a voice (Morton 2007). Morton goes on to say that the concept of nature "collapses into objectivity and subjectivity." Thus, nature's dual connection makes it elusive and difficult to articulate and describe what comprises it. ...[N]ature and its analogue[s] the local, [and] the sense of place. . . disappear when you try to look . . ."

> "The environment is that which cannot be indicated directly. ... It is not in the foreground. It is the background caught in a relationship with the foreground. As soon as we concentrate on it [background], it turns into the foreground. [So] in ecological terms [when] nature becomes bunny rabbits, trees, rivers and mountains—we lose its environmental quality, though this is what we want to convey... we are compelled to rely on a list that gestures toward infinity. ... And the list is perilous in this regard, because it will necessarily exclude something (cities, pylons, races, classes, genders). Simply adding something to the list that ends in an ellipsis and the word nature is wrong from the start." (Morton 2007)

Nature has not been nor cannot be simply a list of things (object) or a list of our thoughts and relationships to it (subject). Chinese philosophers had such a list and referred to it as the "ten-thousand things" (Hinton 2012). Indeed, a list so long so as to make it infinitesimal. It is more ecological, more about relationships e.g., "the foreground caught in a relationship with the background." Our subjective experiences hold, but not in the way we might think. When our subjective experiences and interactions with objects in our daily work truly engross us, we dissolve within that environment and become part of it (Morton 2007). And if we carried the idea of dissolving into our environment into society at large, perhaps we might truly care for the environment.

Next, as application and example I describe, interpret and evaluate a few of Nebraska's natural, cultural and designed landscapes so that the reader might further understand ecological aesthetics.

Figure 2.2 Deciduous forest at The Nature Conservancy's Rulo Bluffs Preserve, Richardson Co., NE

Natural Landscapes

Rulo Bluffs

Rulo Bluffs (Figure 2.2) occupy several hundred acres in extreme southeast Nebraska where The Nature Conservancy (TNC) manages the land on a small portion of them. Visiting Rulo Bluffs Preserve in late spring after a rain was the closest thing to a rainforest that I had experienced since visiting years ago the tropical "high bush" in Liberia, West Africa.

Moisture, lush plant growth, and large trees graced both those woodlands. At Rulo Bluffs' small parking area, paw-paws and redbuds greeted me dripping with dew. From there, I followed a small trail of sorts in a narrow gully bottom raising hordes of mosquitoes. Moving upward, I traversed a steep slope in waist to chest deep underbrush, the vines and brambles constantly trying to trip me. Wavering to catch my breath and balance, I grabbed and easily dislodged thin saplings. Upon closer examination, I could see that they had been burned at their bases by the TNC's managed fire program. Looking below, I could no longer make out where I had parked, but noticed around me some of the tallest, straightest, and most massive trees that I have seen in Nebraska. Sycamores creeping up the gullies 80-feet tall with 40-inch in diameter trunks -- also red, black, and chinquapin oaks, ironwood, red mulberry, hickories, and linden -- invaders and refugees from different plant communities all mixed and squeezed together. All of them growing straight-boled and for Nebraska, above average in size. The smells of scuffed duff, soil, and crushed leaves bathed me in natural perfume. Out of breath after a nearly 200-foot vertical ascent, I broke out of the shade through a clump of rough-leaved dogwood and scrambled onto a narrow sunlit opening filled with prairie grasses and forbs. In the background along the narrow ridge, a wind-gnarled bur oak stood, and behind it still further in the distance spread the Missouri River floodplain. In the span of a mere 10-feet, I had breached the boundary between dense deciduous forest and prairie, between mass and space, between enclosure and vista, and between object and subject.

Rowe Sanctuary

On the Great Plains for at least 10,000 years and maybe longer, bison, neo-tropical songbirds, and waterfowl like Sandhill cranes (Figure 2.3), have migrated north in the spring and south in the fall taking advantage of seasonal food resources and weather. The cranes pause and congregate along the central Platte landscape in their spring flight north. Here they stock-up on the needed nutrients for nesting in the arctic spring where and when no food is available.

In the past 50 years, this migration, a massive, visible, and stirring, ecological process has become one of the great wonders of the natural world to behold, and an important human aesthetic experience. The Audubon Society, true to its mission of protecting and educating about birds and other wildlife, created a special viewing location called the Rowe Sanctuary in the thick of crane habitat along the central Platte River's "Big Bend."

We arrive at Rowe before the appointed time in a dark, rocked parking lot. Following subdued lighting and shivering in the early morning cold of late winter, we make our way to the interpretive center, sign-in, and congregate in designated groups much like the cranes. An interpreter/volunteer goes over the protocol: blinds are optimally placed, but there is no guarantee cranes will be densely packed around ours, use the restroom now, keep voices quiet and move carefully and soundlessly. She then leads us along a dirt path, several hundred yards to the viewing blinds. With about two-dozen others, we shuffle (quietly!) into the plywood blind, and continue shivering in the predawn darkness – still too dark to see our foggy breaths.

A few visitors fiddle with their muted cell phones or high-end cameras, even fewer hazard whispers. To the east, a slightest tinge of light gray appears, then darker gray clouds mottle the sky. Nearby, outside and unseen, cranes eerily trill to themselves. Warm clothing protects the wise against sitting motionless in blinds with small open windows facing the river and a slight prevailing westerly breeze. The cranes' ample plumage keeps them warm, even with their feet resting in cold water.

Figure 2.3 Sandhill cranes at Rowe Sanctuary, Buffalo Co., NE

The eastern light gives way to a dirty, yellow patch and from the eastern blind window, black knots of cranes appear standing downstream. We can see the light glistening off the river, and the enclosing trees appear beyond it. Closer crane groups become visible as they shuffle about in the shallow river shoals and submerged sandbars; the trill raises an octave. Then at an unseen, but on an apparently orchestrated cue, one crane then, nearly all launch upward with a deafening cry and wing flap. Groups of cranes further up or down the river now launch skyward. Overhead their dark bodies silhouette against the light gray sky, legs stiffly stretched behind them. Now singing, swirling and gaining altitude cranes by the pair, by the scores, by the hundreds and by the thousands on their way to another day before the sun has fully risen.

Cultural Landscapes

Cultural landscapes do not attend to overt aesthetic goals; such landscapes like those of Nebraska's agricultural landscape make no pretense of beauty. Nevertheless, blending human (subject) and the familiar nature list (object), they organize by the objects of nature, (streams and their corridors, undulating topography and bits of woodland, prairie and weedy waste ground) and the subjective structure of roadway grids, circular pivot fields, conservation waterways and terraces, repetitive crop covers (corn and beans, beans and corn) and they open up space with distance views and close in on foreground objects. *Nebraskaland* magazine's wild and scenic issues, contain mostly images of vistas (sky, sunsets, storms, forests, prairie, hills, valleys, etc.) or close-ups (flowers, animals, trees, campers, hunting dogs, rusty farm equipment, wind mills etc.) Images of or from the middleground have mostly gone missing.

Meanwhile, people on the land, and working it, become a big part of the definition of cultural. Their very use of land and manipulation of land cover in repetitious spatial and temporal patterns displays culture. Almost as ritual, they begin to blur the difference between subject and object. According to Morton (2007):

> "When people are involved in their work, they experience, and produce, as experience, a dissolution of the reified object and for that matter, the reified subject. Involvement in the world is a negation process, a dissolving; there is no such thing as an environment, since, being involved in it already, we are not separate from it."

Peter Harries-Jones (2005 p.65) notes Gregory Bateson's ecological aesthetic examined, "epistemological propositions that arose from and were expressive of forms of nature...patterns of recurrence; the perceptual abilities of all organisms engendered through their capacity for anticipatory response; a way in which the evident interconnectedness of nature is not simply a phenomena of physical interaction but is mediated through communication." Nassauer (1997) says that seeing and understanding connectedness is critical for humans; essentially making connections makes us human. For example, to Nassauer, common or cultural landscapes communicate the owner's knowledge and may apply an aesthetic of care seen as intention and involvement. Naturalized landscapes "without a clear human intention seem unoccupied and invite human presence whatever its intention."

Intelligent care (Nassauer 1997) of landscapes calls on human understanding of ecological parts, their relationships, and systems as best we can understand them. It also requires that we be modest and humble when deciphering natural systems. Nassauer's (1997) concept of vivid care, occurs when we "suppl[y] the visual framework of human presence," and intent with requisite knowledge about what constitutes ecological health. Nassauer talks about vivid care for natural and agricultural landscapes including lawn care. In the end, we must realize that care (and abuse) of agricultural landscapes dissolved the boundaries between human and nature, subject and object, background and foreground.

Cottonwood Allees

I catalogue and describe in detail the Holt County cultural landscape with its tree claims and windbreaks in a later chapter. However, now, traveling through the Elkhorn River headwaters of Holt County in late October, I encounter the protracted openness of wet meadows and hayfields, interrupted by occasional tree claims and long rows of roadside cottonwoods. These cottonwood rows (Figure 2.4) date to the time of 19th Century tree claims, but their openings with trees spaced about 30 to 40-feet apart (or a bit less) do not configure into bonafide windbreaks. More likely these tree lines demarcated property boundaries parallel to the county roads of the one-mile grid. In some cases, they occupy both sides of the road creating dramatic, cathedral-like spaces.

Figure 2.4 Cottonwood Allees, Holt Co., NE

Just before this October visit, northern Nebraska has already experienced cold and snow, and while the snow quickly melted, the cottonwoods hold many of their bright yellow leaves and flutter in the breeze on loose petioles. These massive, craggy trees thrust to 70 to 80-feet tall; their girth in most cases splayed three to four-feet clad by gray and almost plank-like sections of thick bark. Further up, toward their tops, thinner branches gleam in cool gray-white. Leaves, a few still yellow, but mostly brown, deeply litter the lightly used roadway. (Don't expect to find these roads displayed on a ground view from Google Maps™. They are off the beaten track.)

The leafy canopy on the other hand, is still dense enough to create a dappled flicker of sun and shade as we travel down the road. These roads reminded me of great French allees plotted by Andre' LeNotre. They are of the same magnitude—miles in length, though lack the formal aesthetic intent of a French garden. These Nebraska-style allees intend function, but not necessarily overt beauty. They would shade and cool a hay crew traveling down them in July, as would an allee' placed by Napoleon shade his marching troops. The experiences of the hay crew and soldiers no doubt dissolve each group into their environment, as subject incorporating object.

Dreams Gone Bust

A week before Christmas and while hunting for places to hunt pheasants in Furnas County we pulled into farmyard and found the owner with two pigs loaded in trailer ready to head to market. We asked him for permission to hunt an abandoned farmstead one-half mile south on the same section. He agreed, we thanked him and left. I couldn't help but think those pigs were his bank account and their sale (with-drawl) should bring him some Christmas cash. I also couldn't help thinking that he lived hand to mouth, and after doing his best in raising his fattened hogs, the farmer was still a captive of the global market

Bare fields or close-cropped pasturage lined both sides of the road, and stretched as far as the eye could see as we made our way south. We liked to hunt abandoned farmsteads since they offered some of the only cover left for pheasants after harvest and concentrated their numbers in one location. We checked the wind direction, presence of food (picked dryland corn), livestock (none), the density and lay of the heavy cover. All these factored into making our plan to hunt the abandoned place and associated fields. The house, a bungalow dated from around 1920, still stood upright, but the old farmstead lacked most of the typical accouterment of sheds and barns. The house would have been a stylish showplace in its heyday, but now it sat paint-less, with punched out windows, holey roof, and sagging siding. A large open area between the road and the house was most likely an unused cattle pen with a light cover of kochia. West, beyond the house and wrapping around to its right, coming all the way back to the north-south road was a western and northern windbreak planted in eastern redcedar. A few overgrown ash and Siberian elms occupied the front yard. Two of us walked the east-west windbreak to its corner, and the driver and I walked the west windbreak, meeting them at the intersection to circle back along the house to the vehicle parked on the road.

The house site had been abandoned; though let go, it sported many cedars with broken-out tops untouched by shears. Judging the age of naturalized Siberian elms, in what was probably the garden west of the house, the place had been abandoned 20 to 25-years earlier. A couple of half-dead apple trees jostled for sunlight with the elms; overgrown lilacs half-hid windows of the front porch. The site's lack of care (lack of pheasants too) made a dreary, depressing statement. "Dreams gone bust!" muttered the driver out loud as we departed.

Designed Landscapes

The most successful designed landscapes intend, at minimum, to bring subject and object together. Landscape architect, Robert Thayer (1989) conceptually defines sustainability; to him, sustainability "symbolize[s] resource preservation through visual, spatial and sensory means to produce a positive affective response." Sustainable landscape features like green infrastructure also exemplify Thayer's idea that, "visibility and imageability of the sustainable landscape is critical to its experiential impact and the rate at which it will be adopted and emulated in common use" (p. 108). This means that for an ecological aesthetic to become understood and appreciated by the public, it must be seen and experienced. Accordingly, "conspicuous experiential quality" should help speed the diffusion of change in aesthetic expectations (Thayer 1989).

Arnold Berleant (1997) has offered new insight to this participatory aesthetics that he calls "aesthetics of engagement." It jibes with Gregory Bateson's (1979), statement about aesthetics as "be[ing] responsive to the pattern which connects." Because the design process allows for input from the client and potentially the user, an ecological aesthetic would capture such activity as a chance to educate, and thus participate more fully in the design's intent and implementation. We must be able to interact with a design's natural elements to draw out information that conveys content as well as form, and meaning beyond just surface appeal.

The result of response and participation, Thayer (1989) claims is, "People who are able to comprehend how and why a sustainable landscape functions will respond differently to that landscape than those who are uninformed... environmental knowing heightens landscape experience." This cumulative, educated effect comes from ". . . creating new associations between place and perception and displacing the old normative meanings of landscape context."

Complexity and diversity in content take time, training, and experience to discern however. Thus in using ecological aesthetics, we add the ecologist's knowledge with the artist's intent, raising our level of participation and interaction with the environment and ultimately improving our sense of connectedness. For example, Dunnett (2010) concludes that biodiversity designed onto accessible green roofs has been guided by neither aesthetics nor studies of people's preferences. He argues that nativity of individual species, ecotypes, or communities and substrates in support of green roof plantings is at best misplaced. Though acknowledging biodiversity for its own sake, cannot be sustained by a public unaware of esoteric and largely scientific concepts of ecology, Dunnett fails to probe more deeply into educating people about what they see planted on green roofs and how it interacts and how gardeners seeking maximized color effects.

As suggested above, planted landscapes that grow, change, and become more self-organizing may on their surface look disheveled, rough, and unpolished. Harries-Jones (2005) notes an, "[e]cological aesthetic ... registers a relation between the parts and the whole in a manner very different from an observer pretending to be outside the setting engaged in an exercise of eco-management." Likewise, Nassauer (1995) points out, "A neat, orderly landscape seldom enhances ecological function"; they "require control and domination." Horticultural gardens, indeed entire landscapes, maintained with an eco-management mindset often lack biodiversity, ecological structure, and require excessive, costly outside inputs such as water, fertilizer, and labor (Sutton 2013b).

Nassauer (1995) identifies this nexus of design and an ecological aesthetic as "translating... ecological patterns into cultural language." To do this, Koh (1988) suggests revising long-held design principles by remaking unity into inclusive unity, seeing balance as dynamic balance, and adding complementarity (Pattee 1967) as a third principle. Inclusive unity brings together the participant and the environment; dynamic balance acknowledges an ecological and biological system that self-organizes and permutes over time and is always changing; complementarity revises the dualistic view from "either-or" to a qualitative, "both-and" approach thus gives a designer other ways to communicate knowing. Suzi Gablik as quoted in Harries-Jones (2005) might agree saying, "the sub-text of all art [and design] should therefore be restoring the balance, attunement to nature, together with the idea that all things are linked together in the cyclical processes of nature."

The two examples described below fall at the opposite ends of the design intervention and intention continuum. The first, a very natural landscape where intent comes from the layout of a trail leading the viewer (subject) through a non-arbitrary route as a participant, not simply a follower. The second, a green roof, is 100 percent human-made from its location on top of a building to the very substrate and plant selection, but seeks to satisfy multiple intentions.

Scotts Bluff National Monument

Aesthetic experience of the environment may be as simple as moving through it with intentions for learning and recreating. America has an immense, diverse system of parks, monuments, seashores, trails, and recreation areas that display our environmental and historical heritage. Americans share, preserve, and hold these places in common because they tell us who we have been as Americans. These places are held in trust and many are managed by the National Park Service (NPS) including places like the 3000-acre Scotts Bluff National Monument (SBNM) in western Nebraska (Figure 2.5).

In order for more visitors to learn and experience the landscape of the Overland Trail (Oregon Trail + Pony Express Trail + Mormon Trail) SBNM embarked on a multi-disciplinary project to expand its trails and access. Their intent for experiential learning flows from the NPS 1916 Organic Act. Professor Bret Betnar and a cadre of third and fourth year landscape architecture students from the University of Nebraska-Lincoln did much of the analysis and synthesis on the SBNM trail project (Betnar 2013). Their design intention was to create educational and aesthetic experiences on the entire 3,000 acres of SBNM, much of which has not been traveled upon or seldom seen up close. One such low-use area lies south of the SBNM visitors' center across County Road K (aka Oregon Trail Road) in the rugged South Bluffs area. Their proposed trail for it was not as you would expect; it eschewed graded edges, with water-bars, switchbacks, and benches at resting stations. After thoroughly investigating the area, the landscape architects designed an E-trail, where the hiker is guided via GPS waypoints, to various points of interest like geologic formations, typical plant and animal communities, and scenic overlooks. The trail follows digital bread crumbs and lacks obvious structural features; these low use trails can evolve and be easily rerouted, thus giving the manager flexibility in dispersing the trampling impacts of feet, calling the hiker's attention to new interpretive material over different seasons or years. It empowers the user to really gain a sense of an untouched and unmitigated setting, much like the pioneers on the Overland Trail.

Figure 2.5 Figure Scotts Bluff National Monument, Scottsbluff Co., NE

Larson Building Green Roof

Green roofs cover and protect building waterproof membranes with layers that ameliorate water runoff, temperature fluctuations, trap particles, house insects, and welcome birds. These intentions require extreme artifice, technical knowledge about materials, and understanding of ecological processes.

Lincoln's Larson building (Sutton 2013a) has a swath of prairie grasses and forbs partially covering its eighth floor (Figure 2.6). It is a de facto roof top prairie buffeted by high winds, intense solar radiation, and thin substrate layers. Over two-dozen native and adapted plant species cover its surface and make an attractive background for residents of the apartment complex surrounding it.

On the green roof, windy day during July, the temperatures easily can reach 100° F or more, and the swirling winds regularly gust to 30-mile-per-hour. Its specialized, highly permeable substrate slows down rainfall infiltration and runoff, but allows little to remain for sustaining its layer of living plants. The plants protect the green roof from wind scour and substrate loss, as well as, intercept rainfall, cool the surroundings through evapotranspiration, and provide a home to living organisms like soil microbes, invertebrates and birds. Its covering largely depends on native grasses and those plants provide a visual connection to natural features due to season changes, wind dynamics, and seasonal flower displays.

Figure 2.6. Green roof on Lincoln's Larson Building, Lancaster, Co., NE

Summary

Aesthetics deals with the sensory experiences that make us value and become part of the material world, and is non-trivial because it taps our senses and links us to the landscape around us. Chenoweth and Gobster (1990) in their study of student diaries that compiled daily aesthetic experiences, found that such experiences were common and did not need exotic or highly designed places, and occurred regularly in the course of daily life. They found that these brief encounters were important, personal connections to a place. In other words, the subjects and their surroundings formed a relationship which could be described as ecological.

However, when embracing ecological aesthetics, the designer must have goals to conspicuously engage the user as partner and participant, to communicate the client's intentions, to educate the user about the place's unique ecology, to allow for dynamics of growth, change and self-organization, and to design differently moving beyond the static, visual, and shallow in the creation. Doing so will reduce or eliminate the disvalues brought by the banal, dull, unfulfilled, and trite in design.

Further Reading

Adler, M. 1981. *Six Great Ideas*. New York: Macmillan.

Aquinas, T. 1274. *Summa Theologica*.

Bateson, G. 1979. *Mind and Nature; A Necessary Unity*. New York: Bantam.

Berleant, A. 1997. *Living in the Landscape; Toward an Aesthetics of Environment*. Lawrence, KS: U of Kansas Press.

Betnar, B, 2013 Scotts Bluff National Monument Trail Development Plan & E. A. http://parkplanning.nps.gov/projectHome.cfm?projectID=44254

Callicott, J. 1983. Leopold's land aesthetic. *Journal of Soil and Water Conservation*. July –Aug.

Carlson, A. 2012 "Environmental Aesthetics", *The Stanford Encyclopedia of Philosophy* (Summer 2012 Edition), E. Zalta (ed.), http://plato.stanford.edu/archives/sum2012/entries/environmental-aesthetics.

Chenoweth, R.E. and Gobster, P.H., 1990. The nature and ecology of aesthetic experiences in the landscape. *Landscape Journal*, 9(1), pp.1-8.

Dunnett, N. 2010. People and nature: Integrating aesthetics and ecology on accessible green roofs. In, Proc. 2nd Intl Conference on Landscape and Urban Horticulture. G . P. Gianquinto and F Orsini (eds.). *ISHA Acta Horticulturae 881*.

Gobster, P. 1999. An ecological aesthetic for forest landscape management. *Landscape Journal* 18 (1) 54–64.

Gohlke, F., 2009. *Thoughts on landscape: collected writings and interviews*. Hol Art Books.

GRHC. 2006. *Biodiversity Workshop Participant's Manual*. Toronto: Green Roofs for Healthy Cities.

Harries-Jones, P. 2005. Understanding Ecological Aesthetics. *Cybernetics & Human Knowing*, 12 (1-2) 61-74.

Hinton, D. 2012. *Hunger Mountain: A Field Guide to Mind and Landscape*. Boston:Shambala

Janovy Jr, J. 2018 *Africa Notes: Reflections of an Ecotourist*. Center for Great Plains Studies

Kant, Immanuel, 1790. *Critique of Judgment*, Translated by J. H. Bernard, New York: Hafner Publishing, 1951. (Original publication date 1892)

Koh, J. 1988. Ecological Aesthetics. *Journal of Landscape Architecture*. 7(2)177-191.

Kovacs, Z, et al. How do aesthetics affect our ecology? *J of Ecol Anthropology* 10.1 (2006): 61-65.

Leopold, A. 1966. *A Sand County Almanac*. New York:Balantine Books.

Lopez, Barry 2019 *Horizons* New York: Random House

Minnaert, M. 1995. *Light and Color in the Outdoors* (Vol. 17). Springer Science & Business Media.

Morton, T.. 2007. *Ecology without Nature: Rethinking Environmental Aesthetics*. Harvard: Cambridge.

Nassauer, J. 1995. Messy Ecosystems, Orderly Frames. *Landscape Journal*. 14(2) 161-170.

Nassauer, J. 1997. Cultural sustainability: Aligning aesthetics and ecology. In *Placing Nature: Culture and Landscape Ecology,* J. Nassauer (ed.) pp. 67-83. Washington, DC:Island Press.

Pattee, H. 1979. The complementarity principle in biological and social structure. *Journal of Biological and Social Structures*. 1:191-200.

Sutton. R. 2013a. Seeding green roofs with native grasses. *Journal of Living Arch*. 1 (1) 23p. http://livingarchitecturemonitor.com/index.php/journal/research

Sutton. R. 2013b Rethinking extensive green roofs to lessen emphasis on above-ground biomass. *Journal of Living Arch*. 1 (1) 3p. http://livingarchitecturemonitor.com/index.php/journal/research

Thayer, R. L. (1989). The experience of sustainable landscapes. *Landscape Journal*, 8(2), 101-110.

3 Valuing Farmland

"Quit thinking about decent land use as solely an economic problem. Examine each question in terms of what is it ethically and aesthetically right as well as what is economically expedient. A thing is right when it tends to preserve the integrity, stability, and beauty of the biotic community. It is wrong when it tends otherwise." Aldo Leopold

Introduction

Lorna Jacobs Doolittle inherited a half section farm. Once Iowa Prairie, it was long ago converted to cropland. That is, all except a 40-acre parcel of potholes, prairie grasses, and wildflowers. The Doolittle Prairie is now a tiny patch in a quilt of corn, soybeans, and pasture. She left it as prairie, and forewent a sizable yearly income because this place of tillable soils was also a container of fond childhood memories. Her decision was irrational to some, yet to Lorna, the land had value other than money. She is now a memory too, but the tiny prairie lives on as a relic that provides a place of memories for hundreds of Story County school children who visit it regularly.

Half a continent away, New York City expanded across the west end of Long Island, replacing farms with housing, roads, and retail developments. All but one, two-acre parcel, the Klein Farm, which in 1990 was the only land in New York City still zoned for agricultural use, and the last working family farm within the city limits (Hiss 1990). Here, too, school children visit for a glimpse of the past. When asked why Mr. Klein had never accepted the lucrative offers of developers, his daughter replied, "Well, it still feels like country, and he didn't want to part with it."

These examples, exceptions to the normal course of events, hint at both the ethical and aesthetic aspects of landscape and its use (Figure 3.1):

• Ethics are formal systems of human values that allow and require certain attitudes and actions. Van Rensselaer Potter (1977) defines ethics as, "a set of culturally accepted beliefs and guidelines for decisions affecting the course of human activity, with idealistic goals in mind usually involving the adjustment of competing claims without resorting to the use of coercion, unless mutually agreed upon by members of the culture."

• Aesthetics, according to Arnold Berleant (1997), "concerns itself with the special values found in making and appreciating art and in the enjoyment of natural beauty," and it also concerns itself with "human well-being and the intrinsic satisfaction that are the living heart of experience."

Ethics and aesthetics are both useful in analyzing the relationships between humans and the land. In the context of this chapter, ethics applies to the right and wrong of permanently committing farmland to urbanization, and aesthetics applies to the resulting good or bad experiences inhabitants have before, during, and after changing farmland into cities.

Values go beyond the mere objective recitation of facts to tap the subject and emotional side of human experiences. So, while we can examine the loss of farmland from many different perspectives, we should first identify and explain the impact of human values on the land in general, and farmland in particular. Below, I identify what I believe to be the driving human values that lead to wasteful land-use and urban sprawl, and in doing so, describe the loss of farmland in aesthetic terms.

Figure 3.1 We can value shared rural landscapes for their ethical and aesthetic impacts Washington, Co. NE

Because the loss of farmland is tightly bound with the dominant values Americans hold, the first objective traces how these values have come about, and considers some less well-known ethical systems that might be more supportive of the preservation of rural landscapes. A second objective is to explain the relevance and importance of agricultural land to the quality of our individual and shared aesthetic experiences. Intertwining the first two objectives, I wish to show how ethics and aesthetics are inextricably linked. Finally, to do so, I will be talking in generalities about values, farmland, and relationships with cities. You might be surprised that Nebraska is an urban state with about 70 percent of its citizens living in cities and towns. Nebraska certainly has plenty of productive countryside and urban nodes, and though the ideas discussed and advocated here point to landscapes everywhere, they still can be readily applied to real Nebraska places.

Land Ethics

Historical Roots of American Land Ethics

Although the North American continent was already densely settled prior to European colonization, the rapid subjugation, and in many cases extermination of its resident Native Americans by Europeans, ensured that the ethical systems of the Native Americans has had little influence on land use in the United States. Instead, European ethical systems, expressed in a new environment of abundant resources and increased personal freedoms, formed the foundation of our current land use policies and laws.

Resettlement of Europeans to North America in a period roughly from 1500 to 1800, was affected by the radical and portentous changes in the religion, economy, moral ideals, and science of northwestern Europe. The renewed religious beliefs of the Reformationists, the economic morality of Locke and Smith, and the rational science of Descartes, all influenced the idea of land in America was simply an exploitable commodity.

Religiosity in Value Decisions

Where people and cultures subscribe to religious teachings, they project its tenets into their ethical relationships with the land. Western Christianity has had an important influence on the development of a European, and subsequently an American land ethic (White 1967). The replacement of pantheism in Europe by Christianity was a major step toward eliminating the view of nature as sacred (Jackson 1987). Once the gods or spirits that inhabited specific groves, lakes, or mountains were banished, their former residences were much more likely to be viewed solely as sources of lumber, irrigation water, and metal ores.

This is not to imply that Christianity preaches only an exploitative view of the land. The biblical evidence is mixed, and one can find admonishment to "dress the garden and keep it" as well as to "subdue the earth." Gottfried (1995) traces back to the Old Testament the ancient Hebrew relationship the natural world that is reflected, for example, in biblical teachings, that the Sabbath be applied to the land, which was to be fallowed every seventh year. The Dominican priest, Matthew Fox (1991), points out that creation spirituality, which stresses a spiritual relationship between people and the land, is endemic to the Old Testament and carries through into the New Testament.

Nascent creation spirituality advanced in the 13th century beginning with the writings of St. Francis of Assisi and St. Thomas Aquinas, but the church soon after officially renounced this mysticism. Reformationist thinking and theology in 16th century Europe largely overlooked the importance placed by the Bible on the care of God's creation. The subduing of the earth was emphasized, particularly in the attitudes of Calvinists, Lutherans, and Puritans. To the Puritans settling in New England, the place was in reality a "howling wilderness" - a place in which the true nature of human morality and superiority was tested (Nash 1973, Thayer 1994).

Rise of Utilitarian Thinking

Concomitantly with the final demystification of the church, rose modern science and a reductionist worldview. Renée Descartes, the French philosopher of the early 1600's, advocated the solution of problems by disassembly into smaller, manageable pieces. However, the method was soon perceived as synonymous with the actual structure of the world: things really are no more than the sum of their parts (Jackson 1987). We now know that the whole is often greater than, or at least different from, the sum of its parts, but Descartes provided support for the approach of making land use decisions on a parcel-by-parcel basis.

Furthering this concept, John Locke published in 1690 his seminal essay, "Of Property," an interweaving of religion, morals, and economics (Wood 1984). To Locke, land only had value if it was used and improved by the labor of an individual. In the same time period that American colonists began to push back the wilderness and improve it with their labor by cutting trees and draining swamps, the common lands of England, referred to by Locke as wastes and compared with the trackless American wilderness, were being enclosed and improved. This philosophical position was the underlying moral basis used by English colonists to justify dispossessing the Native Americans of commonly held tribal lands and appropriating them as farms.

Improvement for one winner, results in irreplaceable losses for others. What is called improvement then and now most often means changing the natural organization of the landscape to shorten nutrient cycles, simplifying the community of living things and directing the flow of energy into short-term economic gain. And such a process leaves much behind.

Locke influenced English utilitarians, Jeremy Bentham (1748-1832) and John Stuart Mill (1806-1873) in asserting that land is only useful if it is improved by man's labor and produces something of utility. Much of the neoclassical economic theory espoused by Adam Smith and later 19th century industrialists, builds upon utilitarian principles, so much so that it could be called economic utilitarianism. In his classic book, *The Wealth of Nations*, Smith (1776) firmly adopts for economics the Cartesian, reductionist viewpoint, by stressing that the annual output or revenue of the society is precisely equal to the sum of the revenues of its individual entrepreneurs. So, each businessman seeking to maximize his own profits maximizes the benefit to society as a whole. This is the famous invisible hand that guides the pursuit of individual gain into the promotion of the common good.

Thus, when Europeans arrived in America, the church had ensured that the land would not be perceived as sacred, and Descartes had ensured that it would be treated as more than the sum of its parts or parcels. Locke made it clear that the land had no value until "improved" by the settlers, and Adam Smith assured them that their ignorance regarding how to treat the land would not detract from the common good, if each person simply acted in their own self-interest. These are the primary values European immigrants brought to America and the interaction of these values with the American landscape has shaped land use decisions (and the land) from colonial times until today.

Coming to America

Jackson (1987) writes that, "how we look at the world is how it becomes," and so values are translated into changes on the land. Yet, the exchange is not uni-directional. Interplay occurs between people and the landscape in which they live; each is changed due to the presence of the other. The values developed in Europe were transplanted to another continent, where the immigrants were faced with both an abundance of land and the opportunity to own land—two characteristics absent in their homelands.

Unfortunately, freed from the physical constraints of Europe, the value systems held by the settlers proved inadequate to prevent destructive use of the land. The pioneers followed a pattern of development, exploitation, and abandonment. Left in their wake, were vast areas of degraded lands such as the cut over forest lands in Michigan, Wisconsin, and Minnesota, eroded farms of the Appalachian uplands, and later the drought stricken Dust Bowl in the southern Great Plains. In the 1790s, a new settler described Albemarle County, Virginia, the home of Thomas Jefferson, as "a scene of desolation that baffles description-- farm after farm worn-out, washed and gully, so that's scarcely an acre could be found in a place fit for cultivating" (McEwan 1991). Jefferson stayed and made an effort to improve his farms, but many others simply moved south or west.

The dominant tendency in American history according to Wendell Berry (1977) has been to conquer and move on, while the tendency to stay and prosper in one place has been much weaker and less successful. This dominant tendency has been called a "Vandal ideology" (Paradise 1969). It's an attitude toward the land which necessarily reflects an attitude toward certain groups of people—those who occupy the land that the exploiters wish to "improve." "If there is any law that has been consistently operative in American history, it is that the members of any established people or group or community sooner or later become 'redskins' – that is, they become the designated victims of an utterly ruthless, officially sanctioned and subsidized exploitation" (Berry 1977).

In the earliest application of this ethic, Native Americans were dispossessed from their communal and tribal lands for the establishment of private farms. Now, the same thing occurs in areas of urban expansion. Farmers and other rural residents are displaced by a wave of suburbanites. The developer does not stay in the place he built and continue to develop it as a community; he moves on to the next piece of exploitable ground.

As cities expand in concentric rings, the inner rings tend to decay as the well-to-do and their businesses move to the new developments. When revitalization of the inner city is undertaken, the poor are pushed aside by gentrification, another form of conquest and exploitation.

Here we see the impact of Locke and the Utilitarians leading to an important part of America's land ethic. It describes our view of the land as merely a form of capital or monetary wealth. Farmland is viewed in the same way in which Locke viewed the unimproved English commons – it has low relative utility and monetary value and thus, simply awaits the entrepreneurial labor to convert it to a "higher" urban use. In capital-poor and low-population colonial and early America, land substituted for lack of the first two. The trans-American railway system, laid in the shadow of Civil War debt, relied on the substitution of tens of millions of acres of public land in place of capital given to private railway companies.

As a corollary to this ethic, land speculation has been a traditional and honored method to gain personal wealth. The speculator buys at the fringe, and simply waits, often with agricultural production filling the time and paying the taxes until the land is converted to a more lucrative economic purpose. Ironically, speculation rarely fits Locke's vision of profits accrued from one's labor, because the value of land, "is largely created by things unrelated to the actions of the owner . . ." (Lincoln 1996). Increases in land value often result from public expenditures for roads and other infrastructure, and Lincoln suggests that windfall profits "should accrue to the community as a whole, not to individuals. . . ."

Toward a Viable American Land Ethic

D. C. Lincoln is far from alone in offering suggestions for alternative, ethical views. As early as the mid 1800's, George Perkins Marsh examined the tendency to develop, destroy, and then move on. Other 19th-Century figures such as John Muir, Frederick Law Olmsted, and Gifford Pinchot, argued for the preservation of the public's common interest in the resources of the American West. Furthermore, Matthew Fox (1991) refers to the writings of Walt Whitman, Emily Dickinson, Robert Frost, Wendell Berry, John Muir, Rachel Carson, and Annie Dillard as evidence that a creation-centered spirituality still retains some hold in North America.

Many examples of individual actions (for example, the Doolittle Prairie and the Klein Farm) and other societal actions provide further evidence that economic utilitarianism is not the only principle guiding American land-use decisions. Many of our public goods and shared democratic values in the form of land found in National Parks, state school lands, county conservation areas, and municipal watersheds came about and will continue to be preserved, not simply because of the quantifiable recreation user days, rent, wildlife harvested, or acre feet of water that these public areas supply. These lands endure because they also provide intangible goods and shared, meaningful memories as a kind of American pride.

Elizabeth Anderson (1993) describes public spaces such as parks or open-space as shared goods which cannot be accurately valued only as private goods in a free market.

> "In a democratic society we are free to participate in collective decisions that affect everyone. This is the freedom to be included rather than exclude others. When exit is impossible, when decisions concern shared goods, or where freedom can be effectively exercised by all only in public spaces of free and equal association, democratic freedom supersedes market freedom."

This is the political and ethical basis for local elective bodies debating and approving or denying land-use changes. Economist Daniel Bromley (1991) states that, "The fundamental policy problem in any economy is to determine the location of the boundary that divides the proper domain for collective choice from the proper domain of atomistic choice (the market)." So how might we determine this boundary as we consider the loss of farmland?

Ethical systems beyond economic utilitarianism

Theologian John Cobb (1993) looks beyond the economic utilitarian viewpoint and suggests that an ethical system should contain answers to two basic questions: (1) what is good or desirable? And knowing that, (2) what are the principles of "right action" that must follow? With regard to land use decisions, these questions might be answered from one of four perspectives:

- For yourself in the present
- For yourself for the rest of your life
- For all humans for the indefinite future
- In general

Perspectives one and two dominate classical economics, and indeed the theories of Adam Smith suggest that these are the only proper approaches for maximizing the public good. The third perspective sets up an artificial dichotomy between humans and the environment, missing the essential place of humans in the environment. The fourth is the only approach that Cobb thinks is "stable and acceptable" through time and space. Anything is right when it maximizes value in general.

"In general," refers to all landscape functions, including habitat for other species, water supply, waste assimilation, aesthetics, and of course agricultural production. For example, land use decisions that do not consider relationships among different neighboring parcels of land, lead to degradation of landscape function. Aldo Leopold (1949) addressed the "in general" in *A Sand County Almanac*, where he encourages humans to take a bio-centric view of ethical relationships. Leopold's land ethic is a radical holistic approach to human interaction with the environment and recognition that humans are an integral part of the biotic community. According to him, "ecologically, an ethic is the limitation on freedom in the human quest for survival. It is the setting aside of instinct in competition in favor of cooperation." Leopold goes on to say, "philosophically, an ethic is the distinction between social and anti-social conduct." Ethics and ecology are related through their common emphasis on the relationships among members of the biotic community.

The simple words, "in general", raise the stakes in the human-environment relationship. The first three explicitly list the parameters of who and for how long, but, "in general" opens up the very complex world, asking us to include other living things (even processes like global warming) and expanding our time frame to gage impacts. This has been difficult for western cultures to accept. Relationships between people and the land are the foundation of farming and the preservation of farmland, but it is essential to realize that these relationships include both farmers and non-farmers. Farming isn't just an ecological endeavor, it is also a cultural undertaking that involves all people. "If you eat, you're involved in agriculture," reads a popular bumper sticker. Wendell Berry (1990), when asked what city people can do to the reverse the decline of American farming and rural life, replied, "eat responsibly."

This may sound at first like a flippant answer, but of course it is not. Eating responsibly acknowledges the unbreakable bond between all people and the land. Consuming the bodies of other creatures is one of the most profound indications of our membership in the biotic community, and a clear reminder of the need to consider the effects of our actions "in general." Responsibility requires knowledge of the implications of one's actions and demands modification of those actions to produce a right outcome.

Unfortunately, many Americans lack the knowledge that is required for taking true responsibility. Berry (1990) writes, "most urban shopkeepers would tell you that food is produced on farms but most of them do not know on what farms, or what kinds of farms, where the farms are, or what knowledge or skills are involved in farming. They apparently have little doubt that farms will continue to produce, but they do not know how or over what obstacles." One of those obstacles of course is the paving-over of those farms, largely subsidized by taxpayer funding of roads and sewers. Another is the consumer preference for highly processed foods that help to put $0.93 of every food dollar in a pocket, other than the farmer's. Yet another is the acquiescence of taxpayers to the funding of agricultural research that supports the food industry rather than farmers. However, most Americans eat their Big Macs™ in blissful ignorance of their contribution to these problems.

Such profound ignorance of a relationship that is absolutely essential to our existence and well-being is truly irresponsible and unethical. A viable land ethic would recognize the interrelationships of all people, all land, and all life; it would demand personal understanding and accountability for the effect of one's actions on these relationships; it would emphasize the preservation of "the integrity, stability, and beauty" (Leopold 1949) of these relationships.

The rationale for this land ethic derives not just from concern for our own well-being but what Burkhardt (1989) argues is, "a general obligation we have to respect and secure rights of future generations." Some would argue that future generations do not exist and therefore, do not have rights. This logic is antithetical to the continuity of biology and human culture. One can simply look backward and ask: is the quality of our lives affected by previous generations? And because it obviously is, we can ask: have they diminished our options and our rights to clean, productive, and healthy environment through their decisions regarding the land and resource use? As we look backwards, the answer is yes. Looking forward, how will our descendants judge us?

Land Aesthetics

"No matter how important such resources as prime agricultural soil, clean water, and wildlife habitat may be, they rarely have the emotional appeal of a beautiful countryside setting. A love for scenic beauty often provides the common bond among people who work for the protection of wetlands, historic houses, and farmland. A community leader may strive to protect the economic well-being of local farmers, realizing that this is the key to farmland retention, but may be motivated—consciously or not—by the pleasure of observing scenic farmland and farming activity" (Stokes 1989).

Much of the discussion so far about the ethics of farmland preservation has been related to the future availability of resources to meet the basic needs of our descendants. Yet, we live our lives in the present, and assuming our needs are met, much of the quality of our lives depends on the quality of the landscape of which we are part. Jean Giorno illustrated in his classic fable, The Man Who Planted Trees, that ugly, degraded, dysfunctional landscapes result in ugly, degraded, dysfunctional people. But landscapes can be restored and healed to hold soil, water, plants, animals, and people. Better yet, humans can plan their interactions with landscapes to avoid degradation in the first place, and to enhance the structures and functions that make life more meaningful (Figure 3.2).

Dysfunctional landscapes are no different than the people who inhabit them; we can tell when a working landscape is properly designed. People show significant agreement in their evaluations of what makes a landscape look good, and often these are the same characteristics that promote necessary landscape functions. Our ethics and values, through their influence on our actions, determine the quality of the landscape, and the aesthetic is a guide to the right form and function. Ethics and aesthetics are inextricably linked, and aesthetics are far more than just trivial consideration of artistic taste. Yi-Fu Tuan (1993) links ethical and aesthetic issues in the agricultural landscape when he says, "agricultural land is good, hence also desirable and pleasing. Americans share this view. However when Americans appraise in landscape, they use the word good in an explicitly moral sense." In a larger sense, Tuan (1979) says, "Yearning for an ideal and humane habitat is perhaps universal. Such a habitat must be able to support a livelihood and yet cater to our moral-aesthetic nature."

Landscape development that has a form that supports good function will be more aesthetically pleasing than development that detracts from good function. Some examples of this include the following:

• Water is essential to life, and humans have an innate attraction to it. In studies of visual preferences, views incorporating water are universally popular (Smardon et al 1986). However, most housing developments deal with accelerated runoff from impervious services by channeling the water quickly off-site, often in underground storm water systems. This piping strategy contributes to downstream flooding, reduces water quality and costs more. Developments that deal with water by preserving or constructing ponds, wetlands, bio-swales, rain water gardens, green roofs, and floodplains mitigate many of the hydrologic and hydraulic problems, while creating functional open spaces that residents enjoy at less cost.

• In mountainous and hilly regions of the United States, homes are frequently built on ridge tops in order to provide the owner with excellent views, but in the process they degrade the views of all other residents-- a result referred to in Europe as "cropping public value." These exposed houses also have higher heating and cooling costs, and the steeper, longer access roads accelerate erosion and fragment habitat. Municipalities that zone against ridge-top homes improve landscape function and retain a landscape that all people enjoy.

• New developments often have no large trees and present a sterile, uninviting look. Vegetation moderates local climate, and a single mature tree can provide the same cooling

Figure 3.2 Rural landscapes depict productive relationships between humans and nature, Lancaster Co., NE

effect as 10 room-size air conditioners working 20-hours-per-day (Lyle 1994). A residential landscape with trees is not only more aesthetically pleasing, it is more energy efficient.

Knowledgeable landscape design can substitute ecological and aesthetic intelligence for energy, materials, and dollars: an approach I will revisit in Chapter 11. For now, I will address three particular aesthetic problems caused by the loss of farmland, each stemming from the ways in which we alter these rural landscapes: (1) loss of or reduced contact with nature, (2) loss of a sense of place and shared community, and (3) additional noise and cluttered spaces.

Loss of contact with nature

Environmental psychologists Rachel and Stephen Kaplan (Kaplan and Kaplan 1989) have explored the importance of nearby nature to human well-being. Their research showed that city apartment-dwellers were more satisfied with their lives if they could see or visit nearby nature on a daily basis – if only a shade tree, a patch of shrubs, or a tiny flower garden. E. O. Wilson (Kellert and Wilson 1993) suggests that humans have an innate need, which he calls biophilia, for contact with a variety of species. This need is derived from an evolutionary history as a member of a diverse global ecosystem, where such contact was both constant and essential. Lewis (1996) concludes, "Homo sapiens learned to survive by listening to and learning from nature. Acknowledging its reverberations within us beyond the symbols of our apparent success as a Twenty-First-Century civilization to the basic truth that we are still creatures dependent on earth; whatever we inflict on the planet, we inflict on ourselves."

When we replace farmland with urban sprawl, we are eliminating our most prevalent remaining connection to nature. Renée Dubois (1980) declares, "Over much of the world, farmland has become the most distinctive feature of the scenery. It constitutes the 'nature' that has replaced wilderness in the minds of both rural and urban people." Joan Nassauer (1997) in her article, "Agricultural Landscapes in Harmony with Nature," describes an ideal scene: "where elevated viewpoints create opportunities for panoramic views over rolling hills, new landscape patterns that create more small fields, more crop variety, more hedgerows, and more wooded patches will help the public see nature in the countryside." (Figure 3.3).

What people see helps them not only to meet a need for nature contact, but also to refine their understanding of and appreciation for the non-urban world. This could be as simple, but critical as understanding that food comes from farms, not supermarkets. At a deeper level, it involves the development of what Aldo Leopold referred to as a "conservation aesthetic" (Callicott 1983). Leopold suggested that this aesthetic, like the formal aesthetics of art objects, must be developed both from study and first hand experience. Green (1981) claims that the aesthetic importance of open land and the preservation of productive farmland are demonstrated by the large numbers of recreationists who use it for such diverse activities, as hunting or nature and bird study.

Loss of Place and Shared Community

Driving on Route 1 along the east coast of Florida, you pass through Juno Beach, North Palm Beach, Lake Park, and other towns. But unless you catch the "Welcome to . . ." signs, the continuous band of strip sprawl provides no clues that you have left one place and entered another. Berleant (1997) observes that, "Where cities once had protective boundaries, there is now neither boundary nor any protection." As cities merge into amorphous, monotonous blurs of suburban development, the inhabitants lose their ability to discern social units such as neighborhoods and towns or ecological units such as watersheds. Loss of identity exacerbates ignorance and indifference to shared social and environmental problems.

The erasure of natural phenomena in landmarks all happens in the guise of short-term economic self-interest. Berleant points out, "Cities that succumbed to the exclusiveness of economic values are like opportunists, people who put a price on their integrity and lose their identity in the process."

Noise and Cluttered Space

William Irwin Thompson (1991), a cultural historian, has described noise as the solvent of modern civilization. It pervasively enters our minds and our relationships, slowly dissolving and changing their quality and meaning and ultimately their outcomes. Green belts appeal to the urbanites' needs for respite from the dreary, cluttered, and noisy city—an all encompassing assault on our perceptions of our immediate, daily environment (Whyte 1968). Radio advertisements extol the peace and quiet of rural subdivisions, playing on our experiences of the city as noisy. Yet, implicit in these ads is that one would be, presumably far enough away from one's rural neighbor not to hear his riding mower putting acres of lawn under the blade. In rural areas, one is also presumably buffered by space from feedlots, hog factory farms, freeways, landfills, sewerage lagoons, rail corridors, and airport approach patterns.

But is not only what we hear and smell that affects our sensitivities. Sullivan (1994) examined resident's preferences for scenes of the urbanizing fringe of rural Washentaw County, Michigan, near Ann Arbor, in order to understand the aesthetic and non-economic values that residents found there. He states that, "preference can be viewed as an expression of bias toward adaptively suitable environments, environments that include elements and spaces that are useful and supportive for human functioning." His survey of preferences for a range of

Figure 3.3 Farming on the contour creates harmony with the land's topography Lancaster Co., NE

Landscape scenes found that regardless of the type of resident (farmer, county official, homeowner, or multi family occupant), views of trees or farmland with defined edges of trees were highly rated. Other scene groupings that contained more built elements and fewer trees were rated lower. His explanation for the impact of trees is that their spatial definition creates a pleasant feeling of mystery in the observer.

Stemming the Loss of Farmland at the City's Edge

The movement of people into our rural landscapes is a push-pull phenomenon operating within a trend of an overall increase in the population of the United States. The push of urban problems, like threats of violence and lack of shared public spaces, repels, while the pull of quiet, serene nature in suburbia attracts. However, only the economically advantaged can participate in this exodus, leaving an even more impoverished group within the city and reinforcing the incentives for flight by those who are able. Suburban and exurban immigrants find that the quiet, the serene, and the natural, soon disappear under the relentless march of urbanization, and another wave of people pushes further into the countryside.

To stem the tide, cities must get denser, but land must be used in a way that maximizes productive human relationships and supports shared community values. Cities must become more civil and livable. At the same time, the inherent productivity, pattern, character, and process of the countryside must be preserved and indeed strengthened. Recognizing the duality of the push-pull phenomenon, LaGro (1996) suggests "a prudent strategy, therefore, would be to couple rural growth management programs with efforts to improve the quality of life in existing urban communities, thereby reducing the push factors that stimulate migration from urban to rural areas." However, if the strategy is to be successful, it requires a third component: a significant change in the ethics of the American people.

Reimagining Linkages Between City and Country

One way to rethink the "us versus them" mentality of city versus country might start with the redefinition of their vital linkages. As it stands, the low value per acre of farmland cannot compete with that of developed land, and as noted above, denser cities need less land. Still, that alone is not enough. Linkages in the form of water and drainage corridors, transportation corridors, utility and energy corridors, and movement of food, all have rural versus urban implications. People need access to food, open spaces, nearby nature, and must be able to move about, visit nature, and consume food while disposing of stormwater. All of these things currently happen in a city, but mostly as single predominant uses.

Federal lands are managed using the concept of multiple use. With careful design and planning, our cities can also integrate and coordinate multiple uses. These happen now, but often without an overall plan. For example, a city park has a drainage swale turned into a bio-swale, a vacant lot supports neighborhood gardens, or a new bike trail piggy-backs on boulevard design. What would happen if more uses were programmed alongside? One outcome would be the interpenetration of desirable land uses with the places people live.

Unless experienced on a regular basis, our perceptions of natural seasons, sights, and sounds atrophy. A city's green infrastructure, its gardens, parks, schoolyards, cemeteries, golf courses, drainage-ways, and undeveloped open spaces, bring natural aesthetic values daily to lives of its inhabitants. Cities must do more to preserve, link, and expand their systems of public open spaces. This does not mean narrowing those spaces' uses to heavily programmed and single-purpose active recreation, such as lighted ballfields with bleachers, domed tennis courts, and parking lots — these simply encourage users to drive in from a distance. Nor does it mean that all of these open spaces should be publicly owned and maintained.

It does mean that expanded space and enhanced care will both be needed. Within the most urban areas, there are many opportunities for establishing bits of nature. Hiss (1990) describes how a local group created Brooklyn Bridge Meadow" by planting native wildflowers — many of them collected from vacant lots in Brooklyn — on a small triangle of once dusty land between City Hall and the entrance ramps to the Brooklyn Bridge." Just as important, new buildings need to be regulated, so as to not to block views of natural features, and public access to natural areas needs to be promoted. The Brooklyn Queens Greenway, a 40-mile bicycle and pedestrian path, is not only an open space itself, but links many city parks and botanical gardens. In doing so, it increases the effective natural area for millions of residents.

Conversion of vacant lots into community gardens provides both green space and green goods. The National Gardening Association estimated in 1989 eighteen billion dollars worth of food is produced each year in the United States by household and community gardens (Joseph 1996) — an amount greater than the wholesale value of all vegetables produced by U.S. commercial farms (USDC 1996). Gardens improve the health and nutrition of the community, and strengthen the bonds among the residents and between the residents and the land.

As an added incentive, a community that is permeated by open space not only gains an improvement in quality of life, but in real estate values. Public investment in green spaces, by increasing the property values of adjacent lots, may result in overall economic benefits to the community including increased property tax revenues.

As planning for needed urban expansion moved forward, the connections would be identified and included. Meanwhile, large, close-in areas of farmland with fertile soil might be kept in the design of housing or commercial land uses. Such areas make natural locations for community supported agriculture (CSA) with users drawn from the same nearby development. CSAs then support open spaces, nearby nature, food production, and people interacting. A major feature in many existing urban residential developments and high property value urban neighborhoods is the golf course. In the next decade, millions of acres are projected to be converted to golf courses with adjacent homes. This is in spite of the fact that about half of those purchasing homes near a course have no intention of playing golf. They are interested in the protected open-space. Though now in the process of changing their image and management practices, golf courses have traditionally been sources of excessive chemical and water usage, far more on a per-acre basis than the farmland they supplanted.

Randall Arendt (1996), in his book *Conservation Design for Subdivisions*, proposes that the golf course be replaced by community controlled open-space. This is accomplished by building nearly the same number of houses on smaller lots, while protecting natural or sensitive features. If a large enough area is left undeveloped, it could be maintained as productive farmland. This could be anything from a community pasture or hayfield, to truck farming, orchards or nursery production. Perhaps this common space could be a focus for community-supported agriculture, where the bulk of the produce grown goes to the residents.

Natural networks of drainage swales intertwine with hiker-biker trails with nodes of recreation space and perhaps stormwater storage. Perhaps cities need natural open space standards applied to them, just as planners apply park and recreation standards to cities showing 11 to 20 acres per 100 residents (see Chapter 11).

Population density in cities and towns must increase. Suburban patterns spawned by the postwar love affair with the automobile must be abandoned, while blighted inner city areas and abandoned industrial complexes must be redeveloped. Large-scale urban renewal has largely been a failure, but small-scale, lot-by-lot or block-by-block rebuilding can replace a portion of the development occurring at the urban fringe. As commercial and residential developments occur, new standards of design care should be applied. For example, each site must have, for lack of a better word, conservation easements within them that address at minimum runoff quality and quantity, soil preservation, open spaces and views, and multi-modal transportation connections.

Cities have the advantage of existing utilities and services that can reduce development costs. Should a community decide to achieve growth through infill, reuse, and rebuilding, it will need political will, leadership, and vision. It will also need to ensure that poorer residents will not be displaced as property values increase.

The Portland, Oregon, urban growth boundary has largely been a failure in controlling sprawl. It simply moved across the river into Washington. Lately Denver has seen increased economic vitality and density go hand in hand with carefully planned deployment of its light rail system. In his book, *Finding Lost Space*, Roger Trancik (1986) points out that our existing cities have a variety of spaces that are underutilized and can be used more efficiently. But doing so will require that outmoded ordinances and practices regarding street widths, setbacks, and minimal lot size be revamped. More careful land subdivision and design, prescribed building footprints, zero lot lines, and careful placement of indoor and outdoor functions are needed. Most of our subdivisions have carelessly placed homes in which split-level designs are foisted upon flat sites or oriented with thoughtless placement of windows. This precludes privacy or stymies a potential view of nearby open-space. Every window, room, doorway, curb-cut, tree, and fence must be conceptualized as part of an overall planning process and not left to whim or happenstance. Developers, engineers, and surveyors alone are simply not up to this task; they must be required to team with architects, landscape architects, and interior designers. But most importantly the future residents must be full partners in the design process. If all this becomes so, denser living patterns can correspond with an improved quality of life.

At best, opportunities exist for the intentional use of good design to teach people about natural systems and functions. Seeing the ecological function of the urban world around us is vitally important for an informed citizenry. This approach has been termed visual ecology (Thayer 1976) and promotes designed environments that:

- Help us to see to become more aware of the abstractions we superimpose on the land
- Make complex natural processes visible and understandable
- Unmask systems and processes that remain hidden from view
- Emphasize our unrecognized connections to nature.

Strengthening the rural community and landscape

Improving the city will help to preserve the countryside, but by itself will not be sufficient to prevent its exploitation. To achieve that will require first a vision of the type of rural community, economy, and landscape we want, and then a set of actions crafted specifically to achieve that vision. It is a tired cliché, but if you don't know where you want to go, you probably won't get there. Each community needs to undertake a planning process to develop a vision for its countryside. Once a common vision is developed, then the necessary laws and policies can be determined. Laws frequently turn out to be insufficient or even counterproductive to meet desirable goals, so a thorough evaluation of the likely effect of proposed laws or policies is essential as are opportunities for midcourse corrections, after new rules have been implemented. Although goals and strategies will vary in different locales, the successful approach will likely be a coordinated mix of public and private actions including:

1. Agricultural zoning

If a city's vision includes a boundary with a large area of predominately agricultural land, the only way to achieve that goal is through zoning of the land for exclusive agricultural use. Given the effect of urban proximity on land prices for development, agriculture can never compete economically at the urban edge. No municipality can afford to purchase the development rights to more than a small fraction of the land needed to maintain a critical mass for a viable agricultural economy and infrastructure. A majority of the citizenry will have to be willing to deny certain developers and landowners the right to maximize short-term profits in order to promote the long-term public good. (In Chapter 11, I will talk more about conservation easements supplementing zoning.

2. Land trusts

In an era of stretched fiscal resources and mistrust of government, it is unrealistic to think that local governments can purchase or control all the lands that need protection. The land trust represents a way to privately keep substantial areas from urban development (Daniels and Bowers 1997). It simply requires private owners who come together under a common goal (or threat) to pledge their lands for a larger, more common weal. These landholders may or may not be farmers, but in the best sense of Leopold's (1949) land ethic, they're "putting a limitation on their economic freedom," in exchange for preservation of the landscape. They're "setting aside an instinct for self-interest in competing land development in favor of cooperation and preservation." A corollary to land trusts is the conservation easement. Like any legally binding easement, the landowner places things which should be saved, like trees, views, or even fertile farmground into the hands of a third party steward, who receives a tax break, but still controls access to the land cover by the easement.

3. Community supported agriculture

Rural landscapes are not, nor should they be museums. They are living, changing communities and even if some restrictions are placed on the economic uses of land, landowners need to be able to earn a living from their land. Rather than simply dictating land-use policies, urban residents can be non-exploitative partners in the rural economy by direct purchase of produce from farmers rather than heavily processed "value added" food from the supermarket. Arrangements vary from roadside produce stands to farmers' markets to subscriptions or community supported agriculture (Lapping and Pfeffer 1997).

In community supported agriculture arrangements, city dwellers subscribe to the produce or animals raised on smaller, more intensively managed farms. These small, specialized farms are quite unlike the traditional industrial farm with its large inputs, extensive fields, large machinery, and anonymous distant markets. The subscriber may be required to contribute some labor to the farm and may also be involved with the year-to-year planning. The farmer owns the land and is the day-to-day supervisor and marketer. Instead of visiting the bank for a production loan, the farmer may ask for an advance payment on what is to bring produced the next season. In all of these various arrangements, the consumers are more involved in the production of their food, and begin to have a personal connection and a stake in the use in future of a piece of productive land.

Conclusion: Changing Values

It is fine and good to describe policies and actions that would slow or stop exploitation and destruction of farmland and the farm landscape, but there are some major changes required before we are likely to embrace these actions. Earlier I stated that values precede actions, and that somewhere during our long history as a humans and shorter history as Americans, we have acquired some values that have led to short-term thinking and misuse of the land. So, how can we make the changes within ourselves that will lead to a more equitable and ecological treatment of the land? At the beginning of this essay, I discussed the important, even dominant role of Christianity in the evolution of our western ethics with regard to farmland or the environment at large. It is not that we don't understand the problem, we just have trouble doing what is in the best interests for every person and thing involved for now and in the future.

Fox (1991) says that "letting go is at the heart of spiritual growth and of economic and ecological justice . . . In the Gospel of Matthew, letting go—repentance—precedes justice." The idea of letting go is not just a Christian one. Buddhism for example has as central tenant to let go and not grasp. It also preaches mindfulness, a concept sorely lacking in our consumer-oriented life. Our current western philosophy engenders poor land use and allows us to acquire some poor values. We also need to be mindful of the consequences of our actions. If we are to survive, we need to let go of some of those values so that they can be replaced by ethics and actions that will promote our (and future generations') survival and well-being. These ethics guide us in the judgment of right and wrong and lead us to valuing the everyday world our senses enjoy. Therefore we need to exchange:

- The ethic of unending growth for an ethic of limits
- The ethic of consumption for an ethic of sufficiency

- The ethic of conquest for an ethic of nurturing
- The aesthetic of detachment for an aesthetic of engagement
- The aesthetic of the abstract for an aesthetic of real places
- The aesthetic of the visual for an aesthetic including all our senses.

Annie Dillard (1974) wrote that letting go is one way to understand, and "when I see this way I sway transfixed and empty." Once emptied, perhaps we can see and follow a path to a future in which our actions damage neither land nor people. Poet, Gary Snyder (2010), noted that, "An ethical life is one that is mindful, mannerly, and has style." Humans can call on their unique ability to value the morality and aesthetics of the places they make and for which they care.

Further Reading

Anderson, E. 1993 *Value in Ethics and Economics*. Harvard: Cambridge.

Arendt R. 1996 *Conservation Design for Subdivisions*. Island Press: Washington, DC.

Bateson, G. 1976 *Mind and Nature: A Necessary Unity*. Batam: New York

Berleant, A. 1997 *Living in the landscape: Toward an aesthetics of environment*. University of Kansas Press: Lawrence.

Berry, W. 1990 The pleasures of eating, pp 125-131 In: R Clark ed. *Our Sustainable Table*. North Point Press: San Francisco.

Callicott, B. 1983 Leopold's land aesthetic. *Journal of Soil and Water Conservation* 38:329-332.

Cobb, J. 1993 Ecology, ethics and theology. In: Daly and Townsend (eds.) *Valuing the Earth*. MIT Cambridge.

Daniels, T. and D. Bowers 1997 *Holding Our ground: Protecting America's Farmland*. Island Press: Washington, DC.

Dillard, A 1974 *A Pilgrim at Tinker Creek*. Harpers Magazine Press: New York.

Dubois, R. 1980 *The Wooing of Earth*. Scribner: New York.

Fox, M. 1991 *Creation Spirituality: Liberating Gifts for Peoples of the Earth*. Harper Collins: New York.

Green, B. 1981 Why should the countryside be conserved? pp 8-25 In: B. Green (ed.) *Countryside Conservation*. Allen & Unwin: London.

Hiss, T, 1990 *The Experience of Place*. Knopf: New York.

Jackson, J. B. 1977 Changing rural landscapes. In: E. Zube, & Zube, M. J. (eds.). *Changing Rural Landscapes*. Second Edition Univ of Massachusetts Press.

Jackson, W. 1987 *Alters of Unhewn Stone*. North Point Press: San Francisco.

Joseph, H. M. 1996 *Community Food Security, Agriculture and the Environment: A Massachusetts Example*. pp 245-253 in W. Lockhertz (ed). Environmental enhancement through agriculture. Center for Ag, Food and Env.: Tufts University Medford, MA.

Kaplan, S and R. Kaplan 1989 *The Experience of Nature: A Psychological Perspective*. Cambridge Press: New York

Kellert, S. 1993 The biological basis for human values of nature. pp 42-72 In: Kellert and Wilson (eds.) *The Biophilia Hypothesis*. Island Press: Washington, DC.

LaGro, J. Jr. 1996 Designing Without Nature: Unsewered residential development in rural Wisconsin. *Landscape and Urban Planning* 35:1-9.

Lapping, M and M. Pfeffer 1997 City and country: Forging new connections though agriculture. pp 91-104 In: Lockertz ed. *Visions of American Agriculture*. Iowa State University Press: Ames.

Leopold, A 1949 *A Sand County Almanac*. Oxford Press: New York.

Lewis, C. 1996 *Green Nature, Human Nature*. University of Illinois Press:Urbana

Lincoln, D. C. 1996 Ethics, business and land. *Line Lines* 8, No 6.

Lyle, J. 1994 *Regenerative design for sustainable development*. Wiley: New York.

McEwen, B. 1991 *Thomas Jefferson, Farmer*. McFarland Publishing: Jefferson, NC

Nash, R. 1973 *Wilderness and the American Mind*. Yale University Press: New Haven

Nassauer, J. 1997 Agricultural landscapes in harmony with nature. pp 59-76. In: Lockertz (ed.) *Visions of American Agriculture*. Iowa State University Press: Ames.

Potter, V. R. 1977 Evolving ethical concepts. *BioScience* 27: 251-253.

Smardon, R., J. Palmer and J. Felleman (eds.) 1986 *Foundations for Visual Project Analysis*. John Wiley and Sons: New York.

Snyder, G. 2010. *The Practice of the Wild*. Counterpoint Press.

Stokes, S. 1989 *Saving America's Countryside: A Guide to Rural Conservation*. John Hopkins University Press: Baltimore

Sullivan, W. III, 1994 Perceptions of the rural-urban fringe: Citizens' preferences for natural and developed setting. *Landscape and Urban Planning* 29: 85-101.

Thayer Robert J, Jr. 1976 Visual ecology: Revitalizing the aesthetics of landscape architecture. *Landscape* 20(2): 37-43

Thayer Robert J, Jr. 1994 *Gray World, Green Heart: Technology, Nature and the Sustainable Landscape*. John Wiley and Sons: New York.

Thompson, W 1991 *The American Replacement of Nature*. Dell: New York.

Trancik, R. 1986 *Finding Lost Space: Theories of Urban Design*. Van Nostrand Reinhold: New York

Tuan, Y. 1979 Thought and landscape. pp 89-102 In: D. W. Meinig (ed.) *Interpretation of Ordinary Landscapes*. Oxford Press: New York.

Tuan, Y. 1993 *Passing, Strange and Wonderful: Aesthetics, Nature and Culture*. Island Press: Washington DC.

USDC 1996 *Statistical abstract of the United States:1996* 116th Edition US Bureau of the Census. Washington DC.

Van der Ryn, S and S. Cowan 1996 *Ecological Design*. Island Press: Washington DC.

White, L, 1967 Historical Roots of Our Ecological Crisis. *Science* 155:1203-1207

Whyte, W. 1968 *The Last Landscape*. Anchor Books: New York.

Wood, N. 1984 *John Locke and Agrarian Capitalis*m. UC Berkeley Press: Berkeley.

4 Human and Landscape Scale

"Size determines an object, but scale determines art . . . Scale depends on one's capacity to be conscious of the actualities of perception."- Robert Smithson

"[T]he landscape is not a collection of fixed objects on a static grid but a fluid and dynamic set of relationships. Its appearance is the result of a multitude of forces acting in time on the land itself and its human accretions."- Frank Gohlke

"To look upon that landscape in the early morning with the sun at your back, is to lose the sense of proportion." – N. Scott Momaday

Introduction

In the preface to my dissertation, I related the change in my perceptual scale of a mountain landscape in a storm, but what I experienced there could also easily happen in Nebraska and its expansive Great Plains landscape. For example, imagine a view from a Platte River bluff with a grain elevator in the distance on the western horizon, and an accouterment of intervening objects such as farmsteads, groves, fields, etc.—all fixed objects. As an early evening thunderstorm sweeps across the space toward you, the viewer, those objects become hidden or highlighted due to the burgeoning storm clouds. What was once far, appears nearer as the storm obscures distance. At one point the clouds and hanging sheets of rain collapse on you, then move past, revealing the distant elevator strongly backlit just like a Steven Spielberg movie scene. Meanwhile, the grove and farmstead lie in murky gloom. In just the few minutes that the imaginary storm swept through, it has changed perceptions of an apparently fixed, immutable landscape by stretching, shrinking, and rearranging it. Our aesthetic experience of the stormy landscape's pattern leaves us torn between contemplating a distant prospect and venturing forth to explore it (Figure 4.1). Thinking back, what we have perceived and experienced is scale and its shifts.

Human perception and experience of landscape are important because as the dominant species on most of the earth, we rely on our perceptions and experiences in making judgments about the existing landscape's structure, function, and future changes. These judgments affect our understanding and decisions regarding use and management of landscapes.

Humans are biological and ecological creatures as well as cognitive, social, and intellectual beings. We respond to the structure and scale of landscapes, and thus are affected by it. Scale is a feature of the landscape, a component of visual organization, and interactive process, all of which engage and relay to us information about our ambient environment.

So, with those over-arching ideas in mind, I recount below two studies I completed on landscape scale. The first seeks to understand what human scale might mean to folks familiar with the countryside in southeastern Nebraska. The second, expands the use of scale more widely, comparing and contrasting its use by landscape ecologists and by visual resource managers. First, let's start with definitions of scale.

Definitions of Scale

Scale connects humans to their environment. Absolute scale (Figure 4.2a) relates "the size of any object to a definitely designated standard" (in this case a human) and relative scale (Figure 4.2b) refers to "the size [comparison]... between landscape components and their surroundings" (Grinde and Kopf 1986: 329). In other words absolute scale is definitional and relative scale is observational (Allen 1998). Both types of scale interest an array of researchers: landscape ecologists, archaeologists, geographers, psychologists, landscape architects, and also artists.

The perceived quality of landscape has been systematically studied for nearly 50 years, including scale of landscape structure and its impact on quality of life. Landscape quality studies support environmental assessments mandated by the U. S. National Environmental Policy Act (NEPA 1969), and in 2000, the European Landscape Convention also bolstered assessment of rural landscapes and aesthetic quality.

Figure 4.1 Greenwood, NE as view from I-80. Watercolor by the author

Scale is a familiar term to landscape architects. It is one of many visual relationships taught in introductory design studios to help designers perceive, explain, and order the structure of landscapes. Moving between scales, such as the region and the site is one of four requirements for a general theory of landscape assessment. Concomitantly, scale emerges as a central organizing theme in landscape ecology. As studies attempt to connect visual quality of landscapes with their ecological structure, it becomes more important to understand the role of scale.

Forman and Godron (1986: 15) state that scale is "the level of spatial resolution perceived or considered," while Allen and Hoekstra (1992) declare, "scale-independent entities do not change their qualities when perceived at different scales." While these ideas seem contradictory, human scaling of landscapes appears to use both. Scale relates the size of objects, but because of the optics of the human eye, the apparent size of objects diminishes with distance, and it is easy to interchange clues about size (Figure 4.2a & 4.2b) with clues about distance (Iverson, 1985; Coeterier, 1994) (Figure 4.3). Therefore, human scale also applies to perception of relative distance. Montello (1993) verbally described a hierarchy of four human scales: 1) figural scale – smaller than a human and containing objects manipulated them; 2) vista scale – as viewed from one point; 3) environmental scale – understanding of this scale requires movement and multiple view points; and 4) geographic scale – can only be assessed indirectly via maps or remotely-sensed media.

Ahl and Allen (1996) explained spatial scale as hierarchical and rather like fishing with a net. Everything not captured by the net is merely background. That is, the smallest thing captured is a function of the size of the mesh, and the largest by the size of the net. Mesh size is the grain, and the net size is the extent. Scale relates the size of objects. An observer of a landscape in Montello's vista scale casts his or her view rather like a net, but in the interactive process of perception, likely makes a decision about what constitutes the smallest space in which he or she resides. Visible landscape beyond (to as far as he or she can see) would then become the viewer's extent. The process is similar to fishing with a net, except for two potentially conflicting differences: 1) not every observer may use the same size grain; and 2) the very structure of boundaries in the landscape work to suggest a grain and an extent. Landform, vegetative walls, or breaks in surface texture can trigger a boundary designation, and if one focuses upon the grain, then the extent becomes background (Figure 4.4). Two basic features that affect scale are landscape structure and what humans interpret from this space as visual structure.

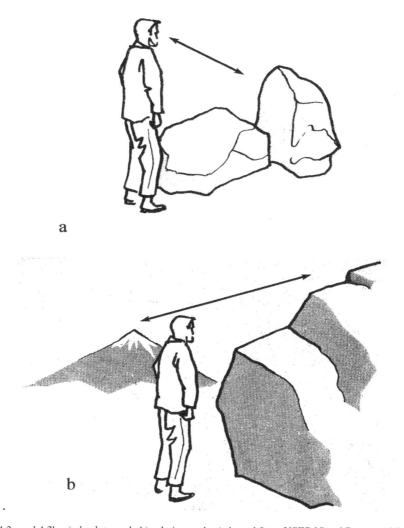

Figures 4.2a and 4.2b. a) absolute scale b) relative scale. (adapted from USFS-Visual Resource Mgt.

Landscape Structure

Landscape structure is the arrangement, organization, and physical juxtaposition of fixed biological, abiotic, and cultural entities; for example, most dominant in the rural landscape are: vegetation, landform, and land cover. Scale becomes a way to describe the relative size and distances inherent in landscape structure. Landscape structure as a fixed pattern, becomes similar to Gibson's (1986) "invariant structure," which operates as a limit or boundary. Examples of invariant structure are horizons, vertical topographic breaks, and vegetation barriers. Such structure contains, halts, or slows flows of species, energy, nutrients, and information. And for humans, visible information is a critical aspect of the informational theory of landscape preference.

For the landscape ecologist, physical processes such as erosion and ecological processes, such as species succession, respond to structure over space and time. Yet, if we take the idea of landscape structure further to examine how humans act on and react to landscapes, then

Figure 4.3 Same-sized hay bales diminish in the distance. Relating size gives this scene depth.

structure becomes a basis for studies of both visual and ecological processes. Visual structure is an anthropocentric construct representing a viewer's interpretation of arrangement, importance, and meaning of landscape structure.

Visual structure is tied to a place and arises from landscape structure, yet it obviously does not occur without an observer. So, visual structure could be examined as aggregations of basic human perceptions and responses. Thus, when humans visually perceive, consider, and act on the structure of a landscape, it is transformed into visual structure. Gobster et al. (2007: 960) call this "perceptible structure" and as perception is multi-modal, they include other senses besides sight.

Perceiving Scale

Size and distance are not the same things as scale, merely clues to it. Importantly, the number and quality of the relationships both contributed to perceiving size and distance. Coeterier (1994: 333) concluded that to humans, size and distance (view depth) represented unique processes and used different cues or the same cues differently. Space perception integrates distance and size because, as Gibson (1986) theorizes, our perceptual faculties appear to automatically integrate visible landscapes, and scale is one of those integrative mechanisms. Sculptor and artist, the late Robert Smithson, had said something similar and I started this chapter with his quote: "Size determines an object, but scale determines art… Scale depends on one's capacity to be conscious of the actualities of perception" (Holt 1979).

Allen and Hoekstra (1992, p. 87), note that, "human perception of landscapes is probably the result of selective pressures. It is reasonable to suppose we have been selected to perceive the world in a way that allows prediction. Prediction comes easier in familiar circumstances. Since changes in scale change perception radically, it would be of advantage [to humans] to perceive in a way that recognizes patterns that occur at multiple scales; then *the world remains familiar even under scale changes*" (emphasis added). Thus, humans readily and easily make judgments about the perceived sizes of individual parts or features of landscapes, and most likely have adapted to quick, perhaps sub-conscious reaction to our physical context to survive in an uncertain world.

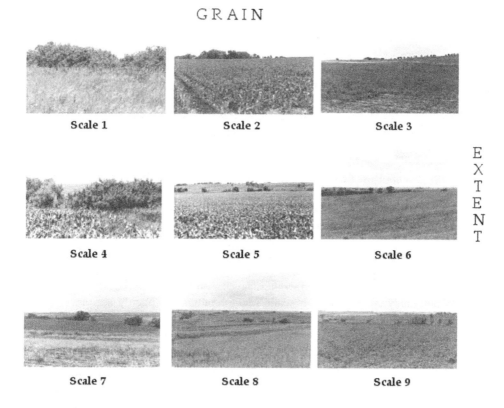

Figure. 4.4 Grain and extent form a matrix of landscape structure interpreted as classes of scale.

In many environmental perception and visual landscape studies, scaling applies to the observer's ability to subconsciously understand different relationships within a landscape, and his or her tendency to quickly rescale as a normal act of perception. This is borne out by Gibson's (1986) explanation of seeing in perspective.

Seeing Hierarchically

Gibson observed that scale came from two broad concepts. The first explains how we see hierarchically in a hierarchical world. The second involves invariants in the visual array that humans use to understand where they are and then how we use invariants to find our way around.

A place is contained within a larger place and differs from that of a Cartesian coordinate point. Gibson explains that surfaces of boundaries affect visibility, and thus, control and filter information from the surrounding ambient array. These surfaces can be detailed in texture, and "…units of texture are generally nested [e.g., hierarchical] within one another at different levels of size." (Gibson 1986: 28).

Not only does he describe the physical world as nested, but also how our eyes, head, and body move and adjust to give us additional information about distance. What we see of the earth's surface occurs in a range of sizes, deriving from the visual angles of those features, and not the same as earthly features. According to Gibson, we innately see hierarchically and derive information about the landscape by interpreting and using nested optical angles.

Gibson also describes the concepts of variant and invariant structure in the environment. The most common and critical invariants are the horizon and the texture of the earth's surface, which become evident in movement in what he called optical or perspective flow. Using relative comparison, he explains that hierarchically nested objects have constant size relationships, as does an individual object. For example, he stated, "equal amounts of texture for equal amounts of terrain suggests that both size and distance are perceived directly" (p. 162). That is, a distant land surface appears smaller, as does its surface texture.

Basically, we apply scale hierarchically. For example, when hierarchical size constancy (scale continuity) abruptly breaks, the landscape view becomes less harmonious. Since naturally occurring patterns display a visual hierarchy, they become important features of visual scaling; seeing in scale requires us to include surrounding objects or spaces as context.

Hierarchy theory attempts to describe and explain relationships between objects, spaces, time, and processes in the context of their complex human, ecological, and physical systems. Landscape ecologists are concerned with scale and hierarchies, because the objects and processes they study may vary with scale. Most ecologists explicitly set the scale for an investigation or sampling of physical landscape early in their research design and researchers who use scale as an investigative scheme in landscape ecological analyses, apply hierarchy theory to order the scale changes.

Tveit et al. (2006), proposed a scheme of visual scale, dimensions (visibility, openness and grain size), attributes (topography, vegetation, and man-made obstacle), and indicators. (viewshed size, viewshed form, depth of view, degree of openness, grain size and number of obstructing objects) These could be thought of as a nested hierarchy. Because human perception of landscape is an ecological, hierarchical, multi-scalar process, it requires us to constantly scale up and scale down.

Grain and Extent

By identifying structural boundaries, we can use the concepts of grain, and extent in a hierarchy to examine human scale.

Boundaries

In both the landscape structure and visual structure of a particular place, scale can be identified as a combination of grain and extent (also sometimes called resolution and scope). Regarding visual structure, grain is the smallest area of interest to the observer (i.e., the mesh size of the net); extent defines all else that can be seen beyond, thus offering a context for grain (i.e., the size of the net). The observer however, decides upon what to focus and what to call grain and extent.

Boundaries mark contrasting edges between contiguous areas. Cadenasso et al. (2003) propose a theory of boundary functioning, categorizing impacts on movements across open space into: 1) type of flow, 2) patch contrast, and 3) boundary structure. Boundaries represent structural constraints on visual information, separating surfaces and defining what and how much is perceivable of the landscape spaces. Thus, these spaces become visual entities or wholes determined by the homogeneity of adjacent surfaces: often the ground plane. One unique aspect of landscape as a visual phenomenon, arises in the variability in composition and location of its boundaries. The longest, tallest, and most dense boundaries have greatest power to constrain our visual information, enclose a space, and most strongly fix a perceived grain, described by Tveit et al. (2006) as a "grain-space" (Figure 4.5). The relative order of assessed boundary strength is linked first to how tightly any given homogeneous space or grain holds together visually to form a whole, and second to the relative importance of the boundaries delimiting it. Topographic breaks, vegetative barriers, and ground pattern represent basic classes of landscape boundaries found in rural landscapes.

Figure 4.5. A rural landscape scene that depicts the concept of space-grain.

Viewers determine boundary's importance; boundaries vary in their capacity to hold attention and filter information. Nevertheless, one often becomes aware of the larger landscape beyond a primary space stretching to other visible but less dominant boundaries in the distance. Distant boundaries would then most likely form the context or extent, and suggest visual relationships beyond a primary space of interest.

To illustrate what grain and extent mean in relation to visual structure, imagine a person at some point in a landscape (see Figures 4.6 and 4.7). Figure 4.6 is reproduced from the Elmwood, Nebraska quadrangle (USGS 1966) and depicts a planimetric view of a landscape's topographic structure. Projected on this map is a portion of the limits to a stationary observer's vision cone looking northwest from the designated viewpoint. Figure 4.7 shows what might be interpreted about the landscape's boundaries moving sequentially out from his or her location. (Boundaries for each corresponding horizontal limit of view in Figure 6 are marked by letters and are shown and noted similarly in Figure 4.6).

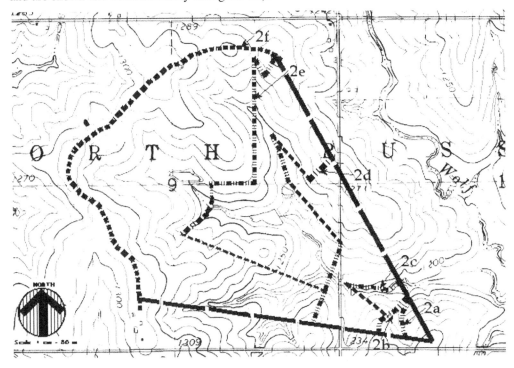

Figure 4.6. Planview landscape boundaries delineated on a portion of North Russell Township on the Elmwood, Nebraska 7-1/2 minute USGS quadrangle.

First, it is likely that the viewer might unconsciously and quickly expand his or her focus to a visual boundary — one that offered enough contrast, density, and enclosure to stop the eye and stabilize the focused view, say to one such noted as the Boundary 2b. Doing so, the viewer would 'scale-up' to fit the grain suggested by the landscape structure. Continuing outward to Boundary c, we see Boundary 2b nested within it. So, arranged hierarchically, the cornfield's stubble edge (2b) is more easily seen and understood, because a true boundary's structure shows the differences between areas. All information is news of a difference. The arc shown in each scene represents an imaginary border (2a) of an arbitrary circular plot surrounding the viewpoint. As we continue to deconstruct what is seen from the observer's viewpoint and move out through Boundaries 2d, 2e, and 2f, we can see the roles that landscape structure, formed from breaks in the topography and barriers of vegetation, play in revealing and enclosing the visual landscape.

The viewer may look outward through a series of nested landscape spaces, quickly collapsing the view inward, and expanding it again outward several times. At the completion of this process, the view will have become fixed in the viewer's mind, and one of the boundaries will dominate. It could be the horizon (Boundary 2f), the riparian vegetation (Boundary 2d), or the edge of the corn stubble (Boundary 2b). The viewer will have settled upon a primary boundary; other perceived boundaries beyond, thus form its context. The primary boundary defines the viewer's grain; boundaries more distant than the dominant one are a measure of the viewer's extent. Thus, for purposes of understanding the visual landscape's scale, we must consider both grain and extent.

Figure 4.7. Horizontal views of boundaries depicted in Figure 4.6.

Distance of View

Measures of grain and extent make it possible to quantify scale. Researchers have often employed distance of view (DOV) as a variable to describe a scene's scale, where DOV defines the distance a viewer could see. This approach does not account for a viewer affixing on one of a number of boundaries. Modification of the DOV where the viewer identifies boundaries better indicates scale, especially relative scale. It would convey more information about the observer's interpretation, and once marked on a photo, it could readily be measured in the field or from maps or aerial photographs. However, neither distance of view (DOV), nor distance of view to a primary boundary (DOV-Prime) alone, determines scale. We also need a measure of extent, without which no reliable determination of a scene's context is possible. Boundaries identified by the viewer beyond DOV-Prime can be used to determine the degree of nesting of grain within a given context. This nested relationship between DOV-Prime and number of boundaries beyond become relative, contextual, and hierarchical.

Testing a Model of Visual Scale Via Pictures from a Watershed in Otoe County, NE

Using the model below, selected grains and extents present in photographs of rural scenes were tested to determine how well the selected scales agreed with those determined by a set of viewers. Full description of the study which followed Institutional Review Board protocols can be found at Sutton (2011).

A Model Depicting Human Scale

Physical landscape structure can be defined as a function of its boundaries where in rural landscapes, boundaries are a function of the horizon defined by topography breaks, vegetative barriers, and textural surfaces. Vegetative boundaries occur as changes in land cover, enclosing walls, or overhead canopies. Large masses are readily identified whether near or far. Topographic breaks vary in size, but are easily recognized even at a distance, for example, the horizon. Textural surfaces of the ground plane weakly define edges. Although these boundaries are fixed and measurable physical elements, they are still open to interpretation (see Figure 4.5). When a viewer selects a boundary, he or she selects a scale where grain is a function of the grain and extent. Grain and extent relate and interpret landscape structural boundaries. Scale can be defined by its grain and extent cued by boundaries that form its context.

Grain and extent can be delimited in sample photographic scenes of the landscape by two visual structure variables: (1) distance of view (DOV) to the critical, viewer-identified primary boundary (DOV-Prime); and (2) the number of boundaries identified beyond the DOV-Prime in the scene by the viewer (Figure 4.4). So, for definitional purposes, grain is a function of the distance to the primary boundary identified by the viewer. Extent sets the context for grain and can be measured by the number of viewer-identified boundaries beyond the viewer identified primary boundary i.e., the more boundaries beyond the primary boundary, the greater the perceived extent.

Again, just as for grain, other factors are involved, such as the prominence of the horizon and orientation of the boundaries to the viewer. Where the existing boundaries cross perpendicular to the view, a greater extent is possible because of more potential boundaries being seen. Where boundaries tend to be parallel to the direction of view, the boundaries do not function as effectively as edges, but function as visual corridors. Visual corridors tend to expand one's distance of view and thus increase the perceived scale of a landscape, just as a drainage corridor links and more closely connects nutrient flows in a landscape. Likewise, a prominent horizon means less enclosure, thus increasing the likelihood of viewing at larger scale.

Conclusions About the Model of Human Scale

While it is good to have described what I think is a useful model of human scale, how well does it work? To test the model (Sutton 2011), viewers were asked to indicate where the space indicated by a photographic landscape scene ended by marking it on a photo. Comparing relationships between the model and perceived scale from respondents suggest that scalar characteristics, grain, and extent can be described and tied to a human scale. However, significantly more respondents agreed with the model on close, well-defined spaces. This suggests the restrictions from enclosure by structures on the view beyond them were successful in constraining responses. However, as extent and/or grain increased, the opportunity for different interpretations also increased and predictability waned. At the middle ranges of grain and extent, many respondents simply did not perceive large, distinct differences in boundaries.

Departures from the model included a:

- "Foreground Effect" where extent shifts up due to seeing a closer boundary. Most likely ground textural differences come into play presenting a variable foreground.
- "Mid-ground Extent Effect" where extent shifts up due to selecting a closer boundary or shifts down selecting a more distant boundary.
- "Mid-ground Grain Effect" where grain shifts up due to selecting a farther boundary, since more boundaries are available, possibly due to ground textural differences.
- "Background Effect" where complex interaction of both mid-ground extent and mid-ground grain effects probably occurred. Here the number and variety of scene grains and extents make prediction harder. The viewer simply has too many possibilities from which to choose.

In management of landscape resources and their attending visual consequences, Litton (1968) has noted the importance of what he called "middle ground views." The middle ground links close and distant impressions of a landscape. As a viewer's attention moves from fore- to-middle-to-background views, (a process that is tantamount to scaling) his or her ability to recognize changes in the landscape diminishes. The visual structure and associated human scale responses to middle ground landscape may also fall into a class of middle number systems. Allen and Hoekstra (1992) note that middle number systems often defy prediction because they contain too many variables to model and too few to average.

Thinking back to the opening of this chapter and the view from a bluff in a storm, it is possible to see how the grain and extent effects noted above, sparked by storm clouds and occluded lighting, restructured relationships between the scene's objects. While it appears that nearby changes in landscapes bring some similar human responses, if changes in landscape do not account for our penchant for a human scale, then such changes may fail to gain acceptance (see Chapter 14). But this is a two-edged sword, since humans have and will continue to restructure the pattern of landscape to preclude a scale of structure appropriate for other organisms.

Linking Landscape Ecology, Scale, and Visual Studies

Many of the changes revising and reducing the Nebraska landscape, have visual and ecological impacts. Being able to conflate those two approaches helps the viewer anticipate those changes. So, the second of my studies I wish to relate here applies scale to the broader concept of visual resource assessments, but to do so using landscape ecologists' parameters of scale.

Landscape ecologists Wu and Li (2006) summarize the scale and briefly discuss three aspects of scale: characteristic scale, scale effects, and scaling. Characteristic scale is part of a phenomenon's essential nature. As observed by humans, scale effects are changes in outcomes based on changes in scale, and scaling extrapolates information from one scale to another. Wu and Li break scale into a hierarchy of (1) dimensions, (2) kinds, and (3) components. The discussion below reframes Wu and Li's concepts for the visual landscape.

The most basic level of their conceptual hierarchy deals with the dimensions of scale, that is, space, time, and organizational level. Space and time scale studies are straightforward, connected, and widely used and understood. Any organizational level perceived by a researcher has inherent space and time scales. Large events cover more space and return more slowly, whereas smaller events are contained within and often constrained by larger events in time and space as nested hierarchies (for more examples of hierarchies see the discussion of panarchy in Chapter 11).

When an individual confronts landscape, selection of organizational level may occur quickly and subconsciously. For example, moving down a hierarchical level brings more detail and smaller temporal or spatial units. Movement, whether it is the scanning eye or the walking body, essentially activates and links humans, their perceptive minds, and the environment. Assuming an elevated view (what Litton (1968) called "observer superior position") shifts the observer up in level and scale, allowing comprehension of larger units of landscape.

Next Wu and Li describe what they call kinds of scale. First, intrinsic scale is "the scale on which pattern or process actually operates." In the case of visual landscape studies, intrinsic scale may closely match their second kind of scale – observational scale – because "the observed scale of a given phenomenon is the result of the interaction between the observer and the inherent scale of the phenomenon" (p. 7).

As was shown in the first study in this chapter about scale, humans showed the tendency to make similar scale conditions close-up, but as distance increased the opportunities for different interpretation occurred. Whyte (1969, p. 32) in his discussion of hierarchies, (and scale is certainly a hierarchical concept) reinforces this human penchant to choose an observational scale, "Selection of the strata [levels] in which a given system is described depends upon the observer, his knowledge and interest in the operation of the system . . . stratification is an interpretation of the system."

Although hierarchies can be conceptualized as levels that decompose into subordinate levels or compose into super-ordinate levels, they are not mere aggregations, but holistic, identifiable units interpreted or defined by the observer. The role of the observer is central to understanding scale. His or her decision may be long and deliberate in a research study, or quick and subconscious by a casual observer.

Wu and Li's observational scale often coincides with the scale at which samples are measured or data is modeled or analyzed. They describe these as experimental scale and modeling/analysis scale. Of importance to visual landscape studies is what they call the policy scale that acknowledges the context of local, regional, and national planning regulation. For visual landscape studies, it might be a region or a discrete public land management unit. Summarizing these ideas about kinds of scale: they note a sequence in which proper observation and analysis allow detection of the phenomenon's characteristic scale, in turn allowing appropriate scale of experimentation and modeling, and resulting in planning and management at a scale of the problem at hand.

At a more detailed, basic level Wu and Li discuss components of scale that include: cartographic scale, grain, extent, coverage, and spacing. Cartographic scale is familiar as a ratio of a map's distance to that same distance in the real world and applies absolute scale (see Silbernagel, 1997). They use a definition for relative scale from Meentemeyer (1989) where "relative scale [is] the relationship between the smallest distinguishable unit and the extent of the map, which can be expressed simply as the ratio between grain and extent." However, sole reliance on map extent, unnecessarily restricts the concept of relative scale, and for studies of the visual landscape compromises observational and intrinsic scales.

Coverage and spacing have to do with sampling in time and space affecting capture of the appropriate characteristic scale. Grain and extent are basic elements of scale represented by the net size and mesh size described earlier. Wu and Li note that the grain size must be smaller than the phenomenon of interest and include its range (cf. net to mesh-net size). Observation of an environment can be thought of as a quick, subconscious, and ongoing visual sampling.

Comparing Visual Studies to Concepts of Scale

With those carefully considered and logically defined concepts in mind, let's turn to what is known and practiced about scale in visual studies. Visual landscape studies examine the landscape as an environment visible to and valued by humans. Human reactions may be functional (way-finding, Kaplan and Kaplan, 1989; sustenance or safety, Appleton, 1975), ethical (stewardship, Nassauer 1995), and/or aesthetic (Gobster and Chenoweth, 1989; Hammitt et al. 1994), and they imply an interest in and judgment of quality (Daniel and Boster, 1976; Palmer, 2003).

I reviewed 21 visual landscape studies with strong conceptions of space for how they addressed scale linkage and their correspondence with Wu and Li's concepts of scale. Some of the 21 selected were more conceptual than applied; I only used detailed, published studies in which scale, hierarchy, or space featured prominently (Table 4.1).

What do the dimensions, kinds, and components of scale tell us about scale when examining the 21 visual landscape assessments? Since all of the studies chosen for review had a spatial component, it is not surprising that all had implicit or explicit concepts of space. Eight of the studies implied a connection with time, and three specifically controlled for seasonal landscape effects. Eight studies employed hierarchies with some type of nesting: six of the studies used Background-Middleground-Foreground (B-M-F), three used Close-Far, two used Small-Transitional-Large, one used three unspecified distance zones, and one implied an unspecified hierarchy.

The reviewed visual studies utilized mostly intrinsic, observational approaches, though some had an experimental aspect tied to kinds of scale. As applied experiments, 15 of the studies used or tested hypotheses or models, and 19 attempted to use their findings for design, planning, or management policies. As with much of biological landscape ecology work, visual landscape studies are strongly applied. While the dimensions and kinds of scale were widely utilized by researchers in the visual studies, components of scale, especially grain and extent, were explicitly used by only a few, though 11 of the studies or implied grain or extent. European researchers have begun to define and use more specific components of scale and are now spurred on by EU policies aimed at preserving rural landscape structure and amenity.

Conclusions About Human Scale and Visual Landscape Scale.

In addition to placing the studies within Wu and Li's (2006) larger framework as noted above, my review also identified other scale-based issues important for visual assessments of landscape and needing further study. As suggested by studies, the five points below are recommended for further research to define, recognize, and more fully incorporate scale into visual landscape studies:

- explicate use of absolute and relative scale

- compare traditional and multi-scalar, hierarchical approaches

Table 4.1 Concepts in twenty-one visual assessment studies sorted by components of scale.

Citation	Dimensions of Scale			Kinds of Scale					Components of Scale				
	Space	Time	Hierarchical Organization	Intrinsic	Observational	Experimental	Modeling	Policy	Grain	Extent	Coverage	Sample Spacing	Map Scaling
Dramstad et al. (2006)	✓		Nested	✓	✓	✓	✓	✓	✓		✓		✓
Fuente de Val et al. (2005)	✓		Nested	✓	✓	✓	✓	✓	✓	✓	✓	✓	✓
Palmer (2004)	✓	✓	Nested	✓	✓		✓	✓	✓	✓	✓		
Coeterier & Dijkstra (1976)	✓	Implied	Small-Transitional-Large	✓	✓	✓	Implied	✓					
Palmer & Lankhorst (1998)	✓	Implied	Nested	✓	✓		✓	✓	Implied	Implied	Implied		
Zube, Pitt & Anderson (1975)	✓		Implied	✓	✓		✓	✓		Implied		✓	
Gemino et al. (2001)	✓		3 Distance Zones	✓	✓	✓	✓	✓	Implied	Implied	✓	✓	
Hammitt (1988)	✓	Implied	B-M-F	✓	✓	✓	✓	✓	Implied	Implied	✓	✓	
Hammitt et al. (1994)	✓	Implied	B-M-F	✓	✓		✓	✓	Implied	Implied			
Litton (1968)	✓	Implied	B-M-F	✓	✓			✓	Implied	Implied			
Coeterier (1994)	✓		Small-Transitional-Large	✓		✓	✓		Implied				
Hull & Buhyoff (1983)	✓		Close-Distant	✓	✓	✓	✓	✓	Implied	Implied			
De Veer & Burrough (1978)	✓	Implied	Nested	✓	✓	✓		✓		Implied			
Gimblett et al. (1985)	✓		B-M-F	✓	✓			✓		Implied			
Litton & Tetlow (1978)	✓	Implied	Nested	✓	✓		✓	✓			Implied		
Schafer et al (1969)	✓		B-M-F	✓	✓		✓	✓					
Ruddell et al (1989)	✓	✓	Near-Far	✓	✓		✓	✓			✓	✓	
S Kaplan, R Kaplan, & Associates 1972-1989	✓	Implied	Close-Far	✓	✓		✓	✓					
Higuchi (1983)	✓	Implied	B-M-F	✓	✓		✓	✓					
Litton et al (1974)	✓		Nested	✓	✓			✓					
Iverson (1985)	✓		Nested	✓	✓			✓					

- examine and revise the current reliance on use of distance for extent or scale
- compare space/mass interactions, not simply masses, to determine visual grain
- design research protocols with psycho-physical metrics correlated with eco-physical metrics.

The review of linking landscape ecology, scale, and visual studies found that since the 1960's, visual landscape studies have indeed become more ecological. They are, in fact, simultaneously ecological and psychological, because humans inhabit and respond to landscape structure, function, and change. Future theory, studies, and siting practices must continue to become more cognizant of scale factors. This is because the hierarchical structure of the landscape interacts with a hierarchical system of human sensory perception to create information, much of it dealing with environmental and landscape quality.

Conclusions

These studies of human scale suggest that plans for major manipulations in rural landscapes in and beyond Nebraska, such as windbreak and hedgerow clearance (Chapter 9) or planting, field consolidation, conservation structures (Chapter 11), new roads, rural electrical transmission line siting (Chapter 14), wind turbine location (Chapter 14), among others, are subject to the filter of human response to scale. This filter is implicit in visual preference studies that are a part of studies on major environmental impacts. It is quite possible that a portion of visual preference assigned to the quality of landscape results from our predilection for human scale.

Further Reading

Ahl, V. and T.H.F. Allen. 1996. *Hierarchy Theory: A Vision, Vocabulary and Epistemology*. New York: Columbia Press.

Allen, T.H.F., A.W. King, B.T. Milne, A. Johnson and S. Turner. 1993. The problem of scaling in ecology. *Evolutionary Trends in Plants* 7(1): 3-8.

Allen, T.H.F. and T. Hoekstra. 1992. *Toward a Unified Ecology*. New York: Columbia Press.

Allen, T.H.F. (1998) The landscape level is dead: Persuading the family to take it off the respirator. In, Peterson, D. L., & Parker, V. T. (eds.). *Ecological Scale: Theory and Applications* pp 35-54. New York:Columbia University Press.

Brown, T. T. Keane, and S. Kaplan. 1986. Aesthetics and management: Bridging the gap. *Lands. Urban Plan*. 13, 1-10.

Cadenasso, M.L., S.T.A. Pickett, K.C. Weaver, and C.G. Jones. 2003. A framework for a theory of ecological boundaries. *BioScience* 53(8):750-58.

Coeterier, J. and H. Dijkstra. 1976. Research on the visual perception and appreciation of, and visual changes in a hedgerow landscape. *Landscape Planning* 34, 421-452.

Coeterier J. F. 1994. Cues for the perception of the size of space in landscapes. *Journal of Environmental Management*. 42(4):333-47.

Coeterier, J. F. 1996. Dominant attributes in the perception and evaluation of the Dutch landscape. *Landscape and Urban Planning*, 34(1):27-44.

Daniel, T. C. 2001. Whither scenic beauty? Visual landscape quality assessment in the 21st Century. *Landscape and Urban Planning* 54:267-81.

Déjeant-Pons M. 2007. The European Landscape Convention. *Landscape Research* 31(4)363-84. DOI: 10.1080/01426390601004343.

De Veer, A. and P. Burrough. 1978. Physiognomic landscape mapping in The Netherlands, *Landscape Planning* 51, 49-62.

Dramstad, W., M. Tveit, W. Fjellstad, and G. L. A. Fry. 2006. Relationships between visual landscape preferences and map-based indicators of landscape structure, *Lands. Urban Plan.* 78, 465-474.

Forman, R. T. T. and M. Godron. 1986. *Landscape Ecology.* New York:Wiley.

Fuente de Val, Gonzalo de la, J. Atauri, and J. de Lucio. 2005. Relationship between landscape visual attributes and spatial pattern indices: A test study in Mediterranean climate landscapes. *Lands. Urban Plan.* 774, 393-407.

Germino, M. and W. Reiners, B. Blasko, D. McLeod, and C. Bastian 2001. Estimating Visual properties of Rocky Mountain landscapes using GIS. *Lands. Urban Plan.* 53, 2001 71-83.

Gibson, J. J. 1986. *The Ecological Approach to Visual Perception.* Hillsdale, NJ:Lawrence Erlbaum Associates, Inc. (originally published 1979).

Gimblett, H. Itami, R. and J. Fitzgibbon. 1985. Mystery in an information-processing model of landscape preference, *Landscape Journal*, 4 (2), 87-95.

Gobster, P. 1987. Properties of Aesthetic Preference for Rural Landscapes. PhD. diss., University of Wisconsin-Madison.

Gobster, P., 1993. "The aesthetic experience of forest ecosystems", In, *Sustainable Ecological Systems: Implementing an Ecological Approach to Land Management*, W.W. Covington and L. F. DeBano Eds. 246-255. USDA:USFS General Technical Report RM 237 July 12-15, Flagstaff, AZ.

Gobster, P., J Nassauer, T. Daniel, and G. Fry. 2007. The shared landscape: what does aesthetics have to do with ecology? *Landscape Ecol.* 22:959–72.

Gohlke, F. 2009 *Thoughts on Landscape.* Hol Art Books

Grinde, K and A. Kopf. 1986. Illustrated Glossary. In, *Foundations for Visual Project Analysis*, ed. R. Smardon, J. Palmer and J. Felleman, 307-34. New York:Wiley.

Hammitt, W., M. Patterson, and F. Noe. 1994. Identifying and predicting visual preference of southern Appalachian forest recreation vistas, *Lands. Urban Plan.* 29, 171-183.

Hammitt, W. 1988. Visual and management preferences of sightseers, in: F. Noe and W. Hammitt Eds. *Visual Preferences of Travelers Along the Blue Ridge Parkway.* Scientific Monograph Series No. 18. USDI-NPS, Washington D.C.

Higuchi, T. 1983. *The Visual and Spatial Structure of Landscapes.* MIT Press, Boston.

Holt, N. (1979) *The Writings of Robert Smithson* .NYU Press

Hull R., and G. Buhyoff 1983. Distance and beauty: A non-monotonic relationship, *Environment and Behavior.* 153, 77-91.

Iverson, W. D. 1985. And that's about the size of it, Visual magnitude as a measurement of the physical landscape. *Landscape Journal* 4(1):14-22.

Kaplan, R. and Kaplan, S. 1989. *The Experience of Nature: A Psychological Perspective.* Cambridge:Cambridge University Press.

Kaplan, R. 1985. The analysis of perception via preference: A strategy for studying how the environment is experienced, *Landscape Planning.* 12, 161-176.

Kaplan, R., S. Kaplan and T. C. Brown. 1989. Environmental preference: Comparison of four domains. *Environ. Behav.* 21, 509-527.

Kaplan, R, S. Kaplan and R. Ryan. 1998. *With People in Mind: Design and Management of Everyday Nature.* Island Press, Washington, DC.

Kaplan, S. 1979. Concerning the power of content-identifying methodologies. in: T. Daniel, E. Zube and B. Driver Eds. *Assessing Amenity Resource Values* Gen. Tech. Report RM-68 Ft. Collins, CO: USDA-USFS.

Kaplan, S. 1987. Aesthetics, Affect and *Cognition: Environmental Preferences from an Evolutionary perspective.* Environment and Behavior. 19, 3-32..

Kaplan, S., R. Kaplan and J. Wendt. 1972. Rated preference and complexity for natural and urban visual material. *Perception and Psychophysics.* 12, 354-356.

Kosslyn, S. M. 1994. *Image and Brain*. Boston:MIT Press.

Litton, B.R. 1968. *Forest Landscape Description and Inventories-A Basis for Land Planning and Design*. USDA Forest Service Research Paper PSW-49. Berkeley.

Litton, B. and R. Tetlow. 1978. *A Landscape Inventory Framework: Scenic Analysis of The Northern Great Plains* Research Paper PSW-135 Berkeley, CA: USDA-USFS.

Lyle, J. 1985. *Design for Human Ecosystems*. New York: VNR.

Meentemeyer, V. and E. O. Box. 1987. Scale effects in landscape studies. In, *Landscapes, Heterogeneity and Disturbance*, ed. M. Turner, 15-34. New York:Springer-Verlag.

Momaday, N. S. (1966) *House Made of Dawn*. Harper and Row

Montello, D. R. 1993. Lecture Notes in Computer Science. In, *Spatial Information Theory A Theoretical Basis for GIS*, ed. Frank, A.U and I. Compari, 312-21. Berlin/Heidelberg :Springer.

Montello D. R. 2001. Scale in Geography. In, *International Encyclopedia of the Social and Behavioral Sciences*, ed. Smelser N.J. and P.B. Baltes. Oxford:Pergamon.

Nassauer, J. 1995. Culture and changing landscape structure. *Landscape Ecology* 10(4):229-38.

Palmer, J. and J. Lankhorst. 1998. Evaluating visible spatial diversity in the landscape, *Lands. Urban Plan*. 431, 65-78.

Palmer, J. 2004. Using spatial metrics to predict scenic perception in a changing landscape: Dennis, Massachusetts, *Lands. Urban Plan*. 341, 201-218.

Ruddell, E., J. Gramann, V. Rudis, and J. Westphal. 1989. The psychological utility of visual penetration in near-view forest scenic-beauty models, *Environment and Behavior*. 214, 393- 412.

Shafer, E., S. Hamilton, and E. Schmidt 1969. Natural landscape preferences: A predictive model. *Journal of Leisure Research*. 11, 1-19

Silbernagel, J. 1997. Scale perception - from cartography to ecology. *Bulletin of the Ecological Society of America*. January, 166-169.

Sutton, R. K. 1997. Scale in the Aesthetic Assessment of Landscapes. PhD. Diss., University of Wisconsin-Madison.

Sutton, R. K. 2011. A Model of Human Scale Tested on Rural Landscape scenes. Great Plains Research Fall 21:215-230.

Sutton, R. K. 2018. The Ecology of Scale in Visual Assessments In, Visual Resource Stewardship Conference Proceedings. USFS General Technical Report NRS-P 183 December.

Talbot, J. F. and R. Kaplan. 1986. Judging the sizes of urban open areas: Is bigger always better? *Landscape Journal*. 5, 83-92.

Tveit M., A. Ode, and G. Fry. 2006. Key concepts in a framework for analysing visual landscape character. *Landscape Research*. 31:229–55.

USDA. 1995. *Landscape Aesthetics, A Handbook for Scenery Management Agriculture Handbook* Number 701 Washington, DC: USDA-USFS.

USGS. 1966. Elmwood, Nebraska Quadrangle. N4045-W9615/7.5.

Whyte, L. L. 1969. Hierarchy in concept. in: L. L. Whyte, A. Wilson, and D. Wilson Eds., *Hierarchical Structures*. Elsevier, New York.

Wiens, J. 1989. Spatial scaling in ecology. *Func. Ecology* (3):385-97.

Zube, E. H., D. Pitt, and T. W. Anderson. 1974. Perception and Measurement of Scenic Resource in the Southern Connecticut River Valley. Institute for Man Environment, University of Massachusetts, Amherst, MA.

Zube, E., D. Pitt, and T. Anderson. 1975. Perception and measurement of scenic resource values of the northeast in: E. H. Zube, R. O. Brush and J. G. Fabos Eds. *Landscape Assessment* 151-167. Dowden Hutchinson and Ross, Stroudsburg, PA. USA.

Zube, E.H., J.L. Sell, J.G. Taylor, 1982. Landscape perception: Research, application and theory. *Landscape Planning* 9(1):1-33.

SECTION 2   NATURAL LANDSCAPES

"The physical landscape is baffling in its ability to transcend what we would make of it. It is as subtle in its expression as turns to the mind, and larger than our grasp; yet it is still knowable. The mind, full of curiosity and analysis disassembles a landscape and then reassembles the pieces-the nod of the flower, the color of the sky, the murmur of an animal-trying to fathom its geography. At the same time the mind is trying to find its place within the land, to discover a way to dispel its own sense of estrangement."--Barry Lopez

"Surface appearances are only that; topography grows, shrinks, compresses, spreads, disintegrates, and disappears; every scene is temporary, and is composed of fragments from other scenes." — John McPhee

Much of what we know about landscape in general and the Nebraska landscape specifically resides in the catalogue of its static physical dimensions. The two chapters in this section could fall under the labels of physical geography and natural history. First, I provide broad evolutionary and historical descriptions of Nebraska's physical features. Details about geological fundamentals lead into and connect with discussions of soils, waters, and plants as they have come to be over time and space. Several maps depict and locate physical features and give an overview of their configurations in the state.

Next, I describe plant communities in more detail. Plants and plant communities evince and display the background impacts of geology, microclimate, soils, and water. By comparing several scholarly approaches to describing and parsing plant communities I lead the reader to understand that such systems have been artificially created as convenient pigeonholes from human judgments. Many of Nebraska's native plants show great fluidity and flexibility in where they grow. Adding to that, after 150-years of our remolding Nebraska' topography and soil and extirpation of many local native plant communities, we are experiencing the impact of naturalized Asian and Eurasian species. I am not being xenophobic because now much of Nebraska's apparently natural vegetative cover is an amalgam and admixture of native and introduced plants.

5 Influences on the Native Vegetation of Nebraska

"The vast prairie in summer is a land of waving grasses. Except for its grandeur of expanse and the abundance of its varicolored flowers, it appears almost monotonous in the general uniformity of its cover. The dominance of grasses, paucity of shrubs, the absence of trees, except along rivers and streams and a characteristic drought enduring flora constitute its main features."-- John E. Weaver

Introduction

In the late 1880's, eminent Professor of Botany at the University of Nebraska, Charles Bessey, upon visiting the Niobrara Valley near Long Pine remarked with amazement that ponderosa pine grew nearby black walnut. (Overfield 1993). Bessey, born in Ohio, educated in Michigan and just arrived in Nebraska from Iowa, had never seen natural stands of eastern hardwoods within a stone's throw of western conifers. He labeled Nebraska a "transition zone" for the meeting of eastern and western plants. While the eastern species grow on the south side of the Niobrara along the protected north-facing slope, members of the western coniferous forest populate the warmer and drier south-facing slopes of the north bank and spill out over the tops of both. Though less noticeable, western herbaceous ground layer plants creep east along the Platte and some eastern forest ground layer plants move west. Nebraska forms a biological crossroads in the slow movement of plants around and across North America. A handful of species from the eastern deciduous forest cling to the narrow riparian environment of Nebraska's Niobrara River valley and spread westward to the Black Hills.

The anecdote above illustrates the deep and immense understanding of environment, which can be gained from knowing a plant and its membership in a community, environmental requisites, growth habits, and natural history. Understanding plants and their communities is a basic lesson of reading the landscape. Plants and their communities respond to background environmental influences and structure like climate, geology, soils, and topography. Knowledge about a stand of plants can tell the careful observer the important features of that place. This chapter provides critical background on the physical conditions that support and challenge both plants and humans now making a living in the Nebraska landscape. It is a lesson drawn upon deeply and often for many of the later chapters in this book.

Ornithologist and writer, Paul Johnsgard's (2001) book, *The Nature of Nebraska*, follows and uses some of the same sources for identifying plant communities as this book does. He gives short natural histories of individual plants and animals that he deems as "keystone and typical species", though offers no definition of what constitutes a keystone or typical species. His passages, while eloquent, only occasionally talk about the critical relationships like food and responses to the abiotic environment like soils, drought, and fire. What are the critical interactions for dominant species? He corroborates fire as a key for ponderosa pines, but misses other important ones. For example, though the mule and whitetail deer both browse on woody material nothing is said of the devastating impacts of whitetails on the young seedlings of bur oak in eastern Nebraska's woodlands.

Johnsgard's *Nature of Nebraska* cleaves humans from the picture, except for our impacts. His one paean to people is acknowledgment of protection of relict community sites by The Nature Conservancy, the Nebraska Game and Parks Commission, Natural Resource Districts, National Monuments, and National Wildlife Refuges. He states, "[Nebraska's natural bounty] has freely bestowed on us either to keep or destroy. May we choose to keep it."

In the debate between whether humans are part of or separate from nature, Johnsgard comes down squarely on the side of castigating humans who overstep and cause irreparable damage. However, it should be pointed out here that humans have the capacity to understand natural influences and species, (if not always the willpower) to move beyond preservation, adapting their plans to Nebraska's natural contexts and species.

During the ebb and flow of Pleistocene glaciations, spruce-dominated taiga and oak woodlands came and went from the area we call Nebraska. Though only a portion of eastern Nebraska succumbed to glaciers, vast areas completely changed plant communities over the millennia as the climate chilled or warmed and moistened or dried. More recently on regular, though shorter intervals, epic droughts have occurred denuding and revegetating in cycles. The plant-covered dunes of the Nebraska Sandhills may have been revegetated only as plants from the northwest, southwest, and east, moved into a vacuum stabilizing them in the last seven thousand to ten thousand years. A prime example and remnant of this multi-directional movement occurs in Oak Canyon of southwest Nebraska a few miles north of the Kansas-Nebraska border (aka 40th Parallel). The oaks protected there represent a hybrid swarm of post oak (*Quercus stellata*) now found to the south, Gambel's oak (*Quercus gambelii*) now found to the west, and bur oak (*Quercus macrocarpa*) to the east. Nearly all the oaks in the canyon reside hundreds of miles from populations of any of their genetic ancestors and their leaves and fruits represent morphological intergrades between the three species.

Excepting the Missouri River, a natural feature hugging and defining Nebraska's eastern border, the rest of the state's boundaries extend artificially, arbitrarily, and politically north to south or east to west as imposed by the geometry of the Public Land Survey System. Vegetation, however, like all natural features follows natural boundaries. Individual plants and conglomerations of communities spread opportunistically and dynamically, responding to environmental gradients.

Native Americans lived off the land which supplied the raw material and food their culture needed. Their use of fire and hunting of large mammals for hundreds years no doubt impacted the area now known as Nebraska, as has been noted for other places in North America (Cronon 1973). Impacts by indigenous people on the land, however, pale in comparison with those wrought by the plow, the fence, the windmill, and road of our modern industrial culture. It is impossible to fully understand Nebraska's vegetation without knowing the environmental, ecological, and anthropogenic contexts that have shaped it over the last 6,000 years and especially the last nearly 200 years of Euro-American exploration, exploitation, and settlement.

While years of settlement have seen (and caused) dramatic changes in the extent and composition of the vegetation of Nebraska, that vegetation and its background environment have always been dynamic. Plants respond to past environmental changes and gradients. Plants and plant communities simply and predictably react but do not presage the future. Their individual health and community composition can be read as a physical and historical integration of environmental conditions and ecological relationships. Plants relate most closely to moisture, light, and mineral nutrient gradients. Yet, we must remember that those three basic abiotic plant needs also interact and inter-grade.

Soil depth and makeup become the important locus of plant growth and activity: soil supplies physical anchorage, stores water and air within its pores, creates chemical context, and juxtaposes the biological interface with helpful and harmful biota. Somewhat set off from these main three, the abiotic factors are the interplay of seasonal and diurnal temperatures that strongly impact the timing of biotic functions like seed germination, carbohydrate production, shoot and root growth, and flower phenology. Plant-water relationships do not simply mean water, per se; humidity, temperature, and wind amplify those impacts. Merely moving a plant to the opposite side of a low hill affects not only the impact of sun angle and thus radiation and heat, but also wind flow, humidity, and the exposure to evapo-transpiration (ET) from surfaces of soil and plant alike. Vegetation and our experience of it can be dynamic in more than one way. The state of Nebraska lies in the center of North America and as seen from space its surface appears largely a flat, undifferentiated color gradient: tan to green to tan through the seasons of spring, summer and fall; sometimes tan to white if winter brings snow. Were we to look from a lower point, say the 35,000-foot altitude of a trans-continental air flight, the landscape's seemingly two-dimensional homogeneity becomes speckled and lined with textures. Descending and landing in an airplane at night, we see the lights from farmsteads and towns collapse to the horizon, displaying a lighted rim. During daylight we see plants, bare ground, and human roadways and habitations ranging from single tracks and buildings to towns, but rarely open water (Though hundreds of reservoirs, lakes and ponds dot the depressions of the Nebraska landscape, they are not as readily seen from the ground as the air). Finally in the lower and slower view perhaps traveling along Interstate 80, we no longer see the land as a planar surface as from above. Through the windshield these features do not form a single point perspective. Vegetation and human structures arise in the wall plane, drape rolling topography, and aggregate like the night lights along the horizon line. In a kind of landscape scale shift, we experience Nebraska's vegetation differently depending on the season and our viewpoint impacted by our relative distance and speed.

Geology, Glaciations, and Soils

The geology of Nebraska matters in so far as much of the state's underlying bedrock dates back hundreds of millions of years. It arose variously as shale, sandstone, and limestone from the sediments of an ancient bed of a shallow inland sea. (Figure 5.2). Thus, Nebraska's typical soils come from those parent rocks and periods of glacial sedimentation in the eastern quarter of the state and the alternating climate changes with wind deposition westward. Over millennia, while the gravels and cobbles of the ancient forerunner to the Platte River – derived from the mountains that preceded today's Rockies – remained in place, finer quartz sands blew north forming the basis of the Nebraska Sandhills. Glacial outfalls and blockages created favored runoff routes that have become the relatively young Elkhorn, Blue, and Nemaha Rivers that drain into an older Missouri River. Even the Platte River in its lower reaches diverted south near North Bend, Nebraska. The Missouri River carved high bluffs and deposited a broad floodplain from melt-water. At one point, the Niobrara River was a short, minor stream emptying into the Missouri, until its headwaters cut into and captured the upper drainage of the Elkhorn at a spot north and west of Newport in northern Rock County; it now accepts flows all the way from Wyoming. Westward, in the Nebraska Panhandle, sedimentary rock layers uplifted and then worn down creating buttes, escarpments, and rocky ridges: what we see today as the Rocky Mountain foothills. Several ancient proto-Platte and contemporary Platte Rivers dried up during droughts, and their sandy floodplains time and again blew north depositing the fine sands now in Sandhills dunes. As northwestern winter winds blew south and east, the heavier sand particles formed east to west ridges and the finer silty (loess) particles deposited to the south and east of the Sandhills forming the central loess hills with distinctive vegetation.

Eastern Nebraska with its access to moist Gulf of Mexico storm fronts receives more than double the annual rainfall compared to areas west of the 100th Meridian (Figure 5.3). The higher rainfall made river valleys and smaller creeks moister and allowed them to constantly rework and modify their underlying soils creating very young soils with little or no

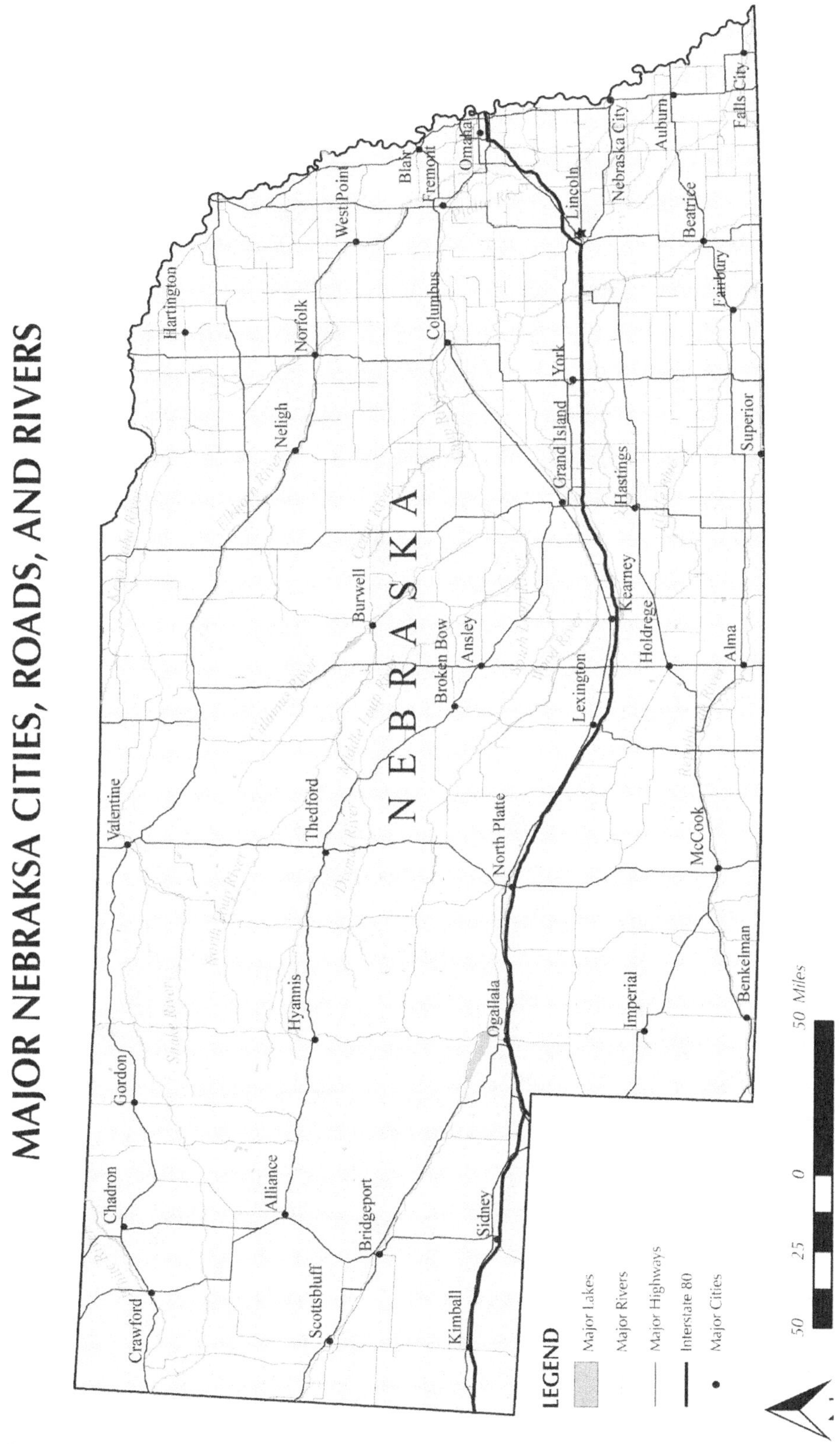

Figure 5.1 Nebraska's major roads and political subdivisions Source: http://www.nebraskamap.gov/

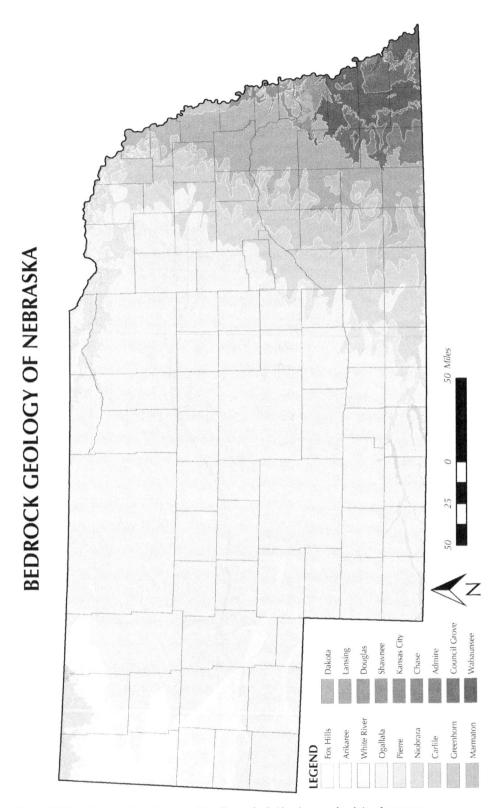

Figure 5.2 Underlying bedrock Sources: http://snr.unl.edu/data/geographygis/geology.aspx

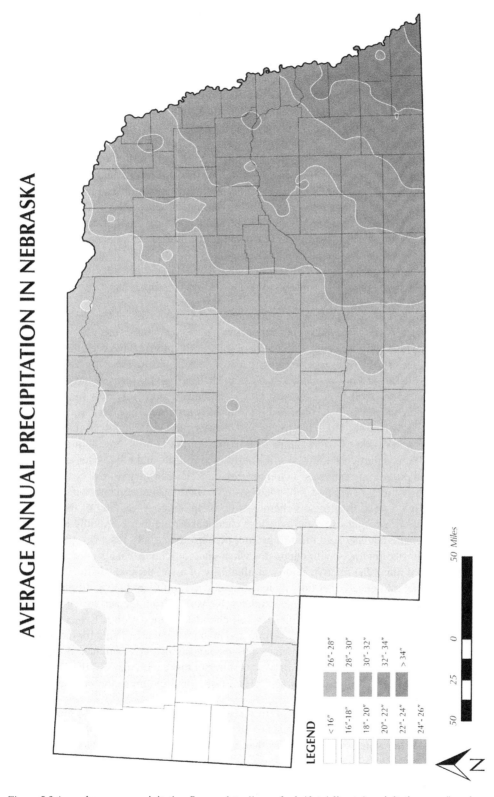

Figure 5.3 Annual average precipitation Source: http://snr.unl.edu/data/climate/precipitation.aspx#precip

differentiated structure. The higher moisture allowed forests of deciduous trees to produce more above ground biomass.

Intervals of glaciers and drought produced layers of loess (Figure 5.4) (a windblown, silt-sized parent material) over 50 feet deep along both sides of the Missouri in Nebraska and in Iowa. Loess blown south and east from the Sandhills accumulated in central Nebraska, creating a large relatively homogeneous area called the Loess Hills covering all or part of 13 Nebraska counties. As the silty loess weathered, it produced soils different from the sands of the Nebraska Sandhills and the clays derived from glacial tills. More rain also meant leaching of soils and parent materials to a greater depth, making them slightly acidic. In eastern Nebraska drought, fire, soil depth, and negative water balance constrained forests and favored tallgrass prairie. Meanwhile, near and west of the 100th Meridian, lower rainfall and humidity created by the rain shadow of the uplifting Rocky Mountains formed shallow mollisols with less plant organic matter and reduced internal leaching of nutrients – making them droughty, but fertile. At a finer scale, permutations of soil types occur where the slope steepness and slope position formed subtle layers of soil gradients with differing depths, with variable amounts and layers of sand, silt, or clay. Where lenses of impervious clay formed under hillsides, they intercepted percolating water, diverting it horizontally to create springs or seeps.

Over time, deep prairie roots, with nearly 50% yearly turnover of root hairs and small roots, deposited tons of organic matter per acre many feet deep creating soils through a process known as melanization. These deep, dark mollisol soils of the prairie have been under creation since the last glaciers. In Nebraska, mollisols also underlie the forests along the Missouri Bluffs. These soils are a kind of natural bank deposit from which farmers have withdrawn the fertile principal for well over a century. Our latest bank statements show many areas are overdrawn in their soil fertility account and no interest is accumulating. Soils form over long periods of time and can be understood in terms of their physical, chemical, and biological properties. The proportion of sand (2mm to 0.06mm), silt (0.06mm to .004mm) and clay (.004mm to 0098mm) particles affects a soil's ability to infiltrate and hold water and air, resist compaction, and provide strong roots anchorage. Silt particles can vary from about 50% to 5%, the thickness of a human hair. Sand, silt, and clay have chemical constituents which influence soil chemistry, but a good deal of soil chemicals lie in an aqueous solution of the soil water found in its pores or coating its particles. These chemicals can either be rapidly absorbed by plant roots or leached deeper into the soil profile, perhaps eventually reaching ground water. Physical particle size interacts with chemistry when charged clay particles attract oppositely charged chemical ions. The relative acidity or alkalinity of a soil depends on the chemistry of its parent material influenced over time by leaching due to rainfall and the addition of organic compounds from root decomposition and exudates, as well as from the activity of soil micro-organisms. In those cases, biology influences soil chemistry, since high pH soils restrict the availability of some chemical elements like iron and manganese that are vital for the formation of chlorophyll molecules needed for plants' photosynthesis of carbohydrates. As a general rule, soils become more alkaline as one moves west in Nebraska with many of the young sands of the Sandhills tending toward slightly acid pH and stream alluvium nearer neutral.

Biology also affects the physical properties of soil especially its structure. As root exudates and micro-organisms interact in the presence of soil particles they coagulate particles into larger meta-particles which form structures that are prismatic, block-like, or spheroidal. This structural soil hierarchy allows deeper, more systematic pore space to develop in aid of root, water, and air penetration, even in tight, clay-based soils.

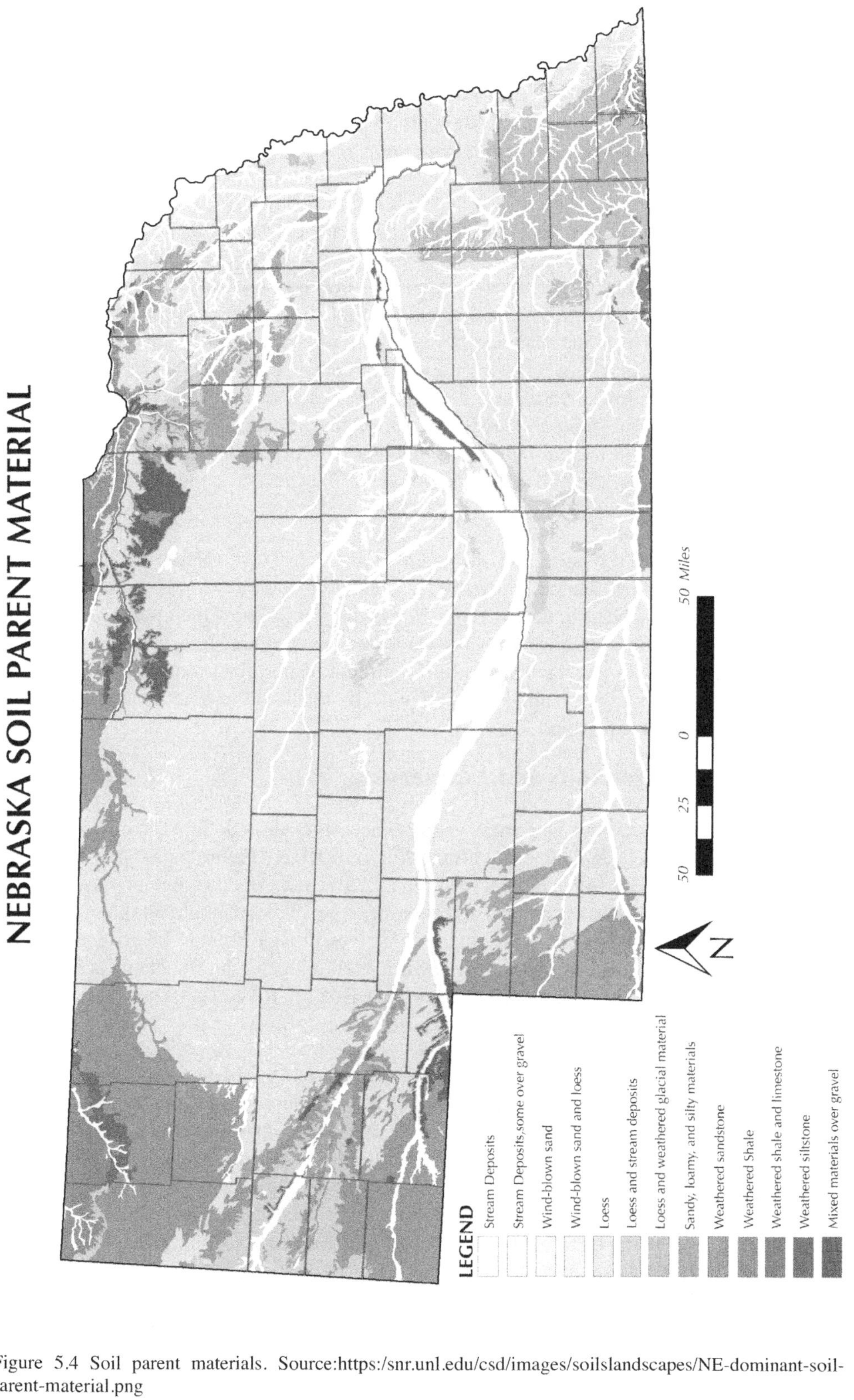

Figure 5.4 Soil parent materials. Source:https://snr.unl.edu/csd/images/soilslandscapes/NE-dominant-soil-parent-material.png

Climate cycles in the form of rainfall and freezing-thawing impacts soil and plants growing in it. Heat and drought from the variable Great Plains' climate exacerbate natural (and anthropogenic) wildfires. Wildfires, in turn, favor the prairie grasses, forbs, and shrubs that can initiate growth following fire. Fire penalizes trees invested in above ground buds and biomass. Climate change currently is a topic of interest, but broad and violent swings in Nebraska's climate have been common for thousands of years due to its location in the semi-arid Great Plains environment.

If we examine the timing and qualities of Nebraska's climate changes, the following factors come into play for plants, individually and in concert: wind speed, direction, and season, precipitation intensity and season, humidity, and light intensity. Where the potential evaporation (PET) from bare soil and transpiration (Figure 5.5) from plants exceeds precipitation, a negative water balance defines semiarid conditions. Traveling east from Nebraska, a zero PET point between semiarid and humid happens about midway between Des Moines and Iowa City, Iowa. And while deciduous trees can and do survive to the west and beyond, their tall stature and broad leaves lose enormous amounts of water often not readily resupplied. Trees become increasingly disadvantaged and often restricted to stream valleys and corridors with ample alluvial soil moisture where they garner some protection from the relentless wind.

For example, I-80 rest stops on the open plains near York, Nebraska display oaks, maples, lindens, and pines planted in the 1960's. Stunted to one-half to two-thirds of the sizes expected for the same species in nearby river valleys, they aptly show the impact of the prairie environment, and especially the impact of water and wind stress. Prairie plants resist this climatic "one-two punch" by staying low to the ground, using plant morphologies aimed at reducing water loss, going dormant, and growing deep roots to draw water from the depths of soil profiles unobtainable by trees.

Rivers Streams, Wetlands and Aquifers

The surface of Nebraska's land mass gently tilts east resulting in most rivers and streams flowing downhill to their confluences with the Missouri River (Figure 5.6). The Platte River for example flows at an average gradient of around 1.25%, amounting to about 66 feet drop per mile; though in some sections it flattens and becomes a braided stream. Most major Nebraska rivers have dams and reservoirs whose main objectives include storage for irrigation, flood control, and recreation. Dam-free exceptions within Nebraska are: the Big Nemaha River, Big Blue River, the North, South and Loup Rivers and the Elkhorn River. Dams on rivers affect the amount and timing of runoff from spring melts and large storms.

The Republican River flood of late May 1935 was fed by 24 inches of rain falling in 24 hours along the upper reaches of the Republican in Colorado on crop ground with little cover. The resulting flood, uncontrolled by dams, swept 200 miles eastward destroying lives, towns, and farms. The aftermath included major flood control dams and such catastrophic floods have ceased. While a flooding river no longer sweeps structures away it does not thin adjacent forests, so an extra dense riparian forest has sprouted in the years since the flood. In 2005, because of legal conflicts between Nebraska and Kansas concerning water flows in the Republican River, it was suggested that all riparian forest be removed. Its trees represented phraetophytic (high water using) vegetation that some said transpired and wasted dear water resources.

Figure 5.5 Potential evapo-transpiration Source: https://snr.unl.edu/data/climate/evapotranspiration.aspx

Impacts on vegetation also can be seen in the Central Platte Valley and its heavily vegetated islands. Upstream dams impeded this natural vegetation removal action and prompted the Platte River Crane Trust to use real bulldozers to keep channels and islands clear of dense vegetation. The Platte riparian forest now results largely from loss of the natural bulldozing affect of spring floods combined with ice chunks that formerly opened it up. Importantly, dense vegetation deters migratory cranes from roosting, because they fear predator ambushes.

Impressions of a densely forested river as seen by today's travelers on I-80 adjacent to the Platte from Grand Island to North Platte belie its previous natural state. Photographs from the late 1890's depict a thin covering of cottonwoods and willows, with no eastern redcedars and few shrubs. The Platte River's channel appears as a band varying in width from one-quarter to one mile wide. While it may be true that the Platte's riparian forest was recovering in 1890 from overuse forty years earlier by nearly one-half million settlers traveling along it needing firewood, it was never really densely wooded until the cessation of floods, prairie fires, and westward migration.

Water and wood were the two most valued resources by permanent or migrating settlers. Where that need was coupled with the burgeoning use for wood ties in railroad expansion, many of Nebraska's river valleys were stripped of tie-sized timber. Even in a remote section of the Sandhills a stream was virtually clear-cut of cottonwood, hackberry, green ash and eastern redcedar to supply the railroad passing through in the 1880's. Because of its denuded landscape, it earned the name Dismal River — looking as dismal as the "cutover lands" of northern Minnesota, Wisconsin, and Michigan during the same era. But settled improvements brought not just clear-cuts. Where some streams such as the Big and Little Nemaha meandered through wide fertile valleys and made agricultural field size and shape subject to the whims of naturally changing river courses, those streams were straighten and lined with levees. This was also true for the lower reaches of the Elkhorn and Salt Creeks before they empty into the Platte River. The lower Platte itself has many miles of levees, once placed to protect agriculture and industry. Those levies now protect cabins and recreational activities. So while they appear natural, most rivers in Nebraska and their riparian vegetation have been manipulated and radically changed by domestication of the earth and the needs of agriculture.

Open water or lakes and streams appear occasionally in the Nebraska landscape, but wetlands are more abundant. They consist of four general types. The first, with open water, includes the bayous, oxbows, cutoff channels, and shorelines of streams. The second type is ephemeral and occurs when melt water or runoff from spring storms accumulates in shallow, but enclosed basins lacking lateral drainage and subsequent connection to rivers and streams. The third occurs when the water table rises close to or above the surface. Finally the fourth type occurs where excess moisture seeps or flows from a spring into a drier plant community.

Standing water or high water tables are not hard to imagine along streams. There, within a few feet of the channel and beneath the banks, the availability of water allows plants which thrive in wet places such quiet, shallow waters harboring floating, submerged, and emergent plants. For perennial streams these wetland plants can be found year-round, but on seasonally flowing streams they become restricted in number and diversity.

Several areas occur in the state possessing very flat topography and no defined drainage outflows. Perhaps the most extensive and well known is the Rainwater Basin at the headwaters of the Big and Little Blue Rivers in Clay, Hamilton, York, Fillmore and Adams Counties. Over time, fine clay particles have settled into these shallow, seasonal basins effectively sealing

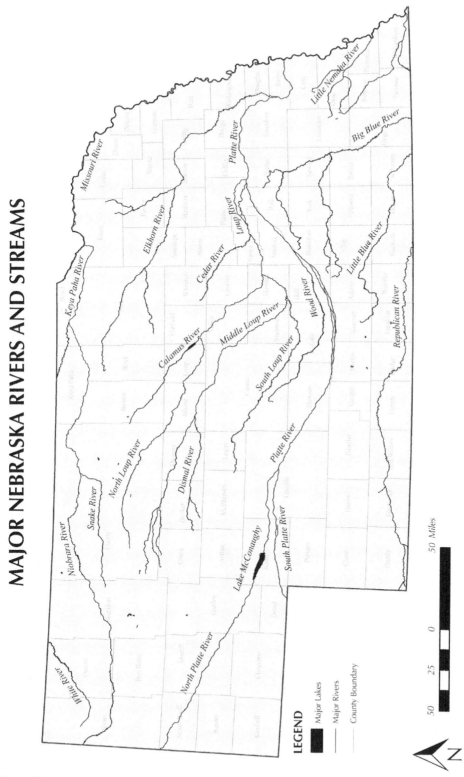

Figure 5.6 Major rivers Source: https://watercenter.unl.edu/resources/publications/NebraskaMain.pdf

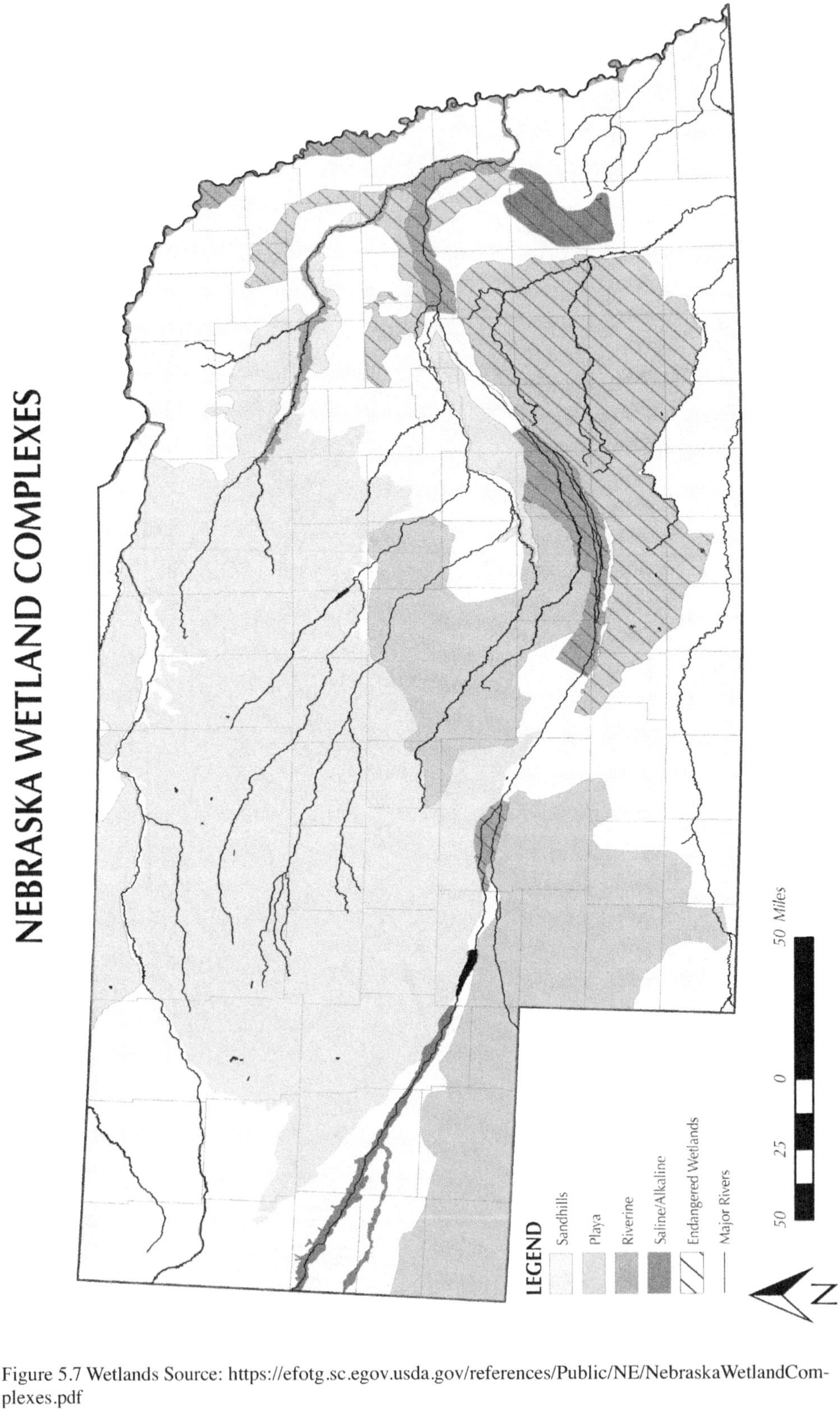

Figure 5.7 Wetlands Source: https://efotg.sc.egov.usda.gov/references/Public/NE/NebraskaWetlandComplexes.pdf

them from water percolation. During most spring seasons these basins attract migrating waterfowl and also provide nesting habitat in summer. In wet years, deeper ones can maintain wet soils or even display open water into the fall.

A unique type of wetland occurs in Lancaster and Saunders Counties based not only on captured seasonal precipitation, but also on the upwelling of saline groundwater once trapped in the sedimentary rock of the ancient seabed. The water moves north from Kansas and comes to the surface in Nebraska as springs and seeps. Over the years the salt deposits accumulated on the surface and in the late 1880's spawned commercial salt collection on the west side of Lincoln. These wetlands contain local rare plants like seablite and saltwort found normally near the ocean. This unique ecosystem also contains the rare and endangered Salt Creek Tiger Beetle (*Cicindela nevadica lincolniana*).

The next type of wetland, formed by a high water table, can be found widely in the central and western Sandhills. The Ogallala aquifer underlies most of western and central Nebraska, but is many feet below the surface and many feet below even the most penetrating plant roots. Only in the Sandhills, where the aquifer is deepest does it widely come to the surface in the bottoms of valleys between the dunes and often remains for decades. This wet substrate supports emergent plants like sedges, cattails, reeds, and hydrophilic plants such as willows. Where the water table extends a bit deeper, wet meadows occur. Two large Federal Wildlife Refuges overlay portions of those wetlands and support tens of thousands of resident and migrating waterfowl.

The last wetland type may or may not have typical wetland vegetation, but instead supports plants from moister communities. This happens when seeps or springs occur on dry prairie hillsides and supply enough moisture for taller prairie woody shrubs and even trees to gain a foothold and grow miles from the nearest stream or deep soil and its water resources. For small seeps, woody or more moisture demanding plants can easily transpire all the excess seepage in a very small area. Settlers quickly learned not to rely on such minor local water sources as they often quit flowing in drought years.

Plant Communities

Plant communities are important to read and understand the Nebraska landscape. (Figure 5.8) However, because plant communities change along their boundary gradients (ecotones), in size, and membership, they do not always occur as perfect, concrete examples. So structure becomes an important feature of a community and because it has physical boundaries, a community can be located and mapped, though any community boundary is most likely neither stationary nor well defined and that fact often confounds our conceptual communities.

Conceptually, plant communities are a product first of environmental conditions but also rely on an element of chance. If the environmental conditions remain favorable, similar groupings of plants provide structure that in turn modifies those conditions. For example, a shrubby margin growing at the edge of forest and prairie, and serendipitously planted by birds, shades out grasses. Meanwhile, tree seeds find a start there with less competition for water and if tree seedlings find enough moisture, they can overtop and shade out shrubs and grasses. Competition for light defines forest communities and competition for water defines prairie. Shrubs aid tree establishment, but then grasses respond favorably to fires that set back trees. Both the presence and impact of shrubs and fire rely on chance. Larger, fairly obvious groupings of dominant plants are called formations or biomes. They are relatively easy to identify because they are composed of the same or similar life-forms. Like the tree dominated forest formation and the grass dominated prairie formation. Within formations a wider variety of specific species can be identified as the dominants, such as bluestem prairie or oak-hickory forest. Reoccurring species associations within a formation such as an oak-hickory community allow us to be more specific with our categories. Furthermore, identifying dominant plant communities allow us to infer other information about a site: for instance, a bur oak-bitternut hickory association tends to grow on drier sites and in a variety of loamy soils.

For example, closed canopy forests with large, well-established trees provide shade from sun, block winds, and deposit ample leaf insulation that also produces an enriched soil. These factors, in turn, favor trees with seedlings and saplings that can grow in shade until released when a gap forms in the forest's canopy. Communities are comprised of dominant species that provide the important structure that resists and modifies the environment. At its edge within a canopy's hierarchy one can find a vertical layering of understory plants, ground layer plants and, of course, soil and animal biota dependent on the community's structure and species.

Communities are loose conceptual containers where the various interactions of its members take place; some good, some bad, depending on which organism is favored. However, moment-to-moment details of the interactions are open-ended involving randomness and happenstance. That squirrels plant acorns is a given, from whether they are retrieved and where they are planted and less so. Just as in a human community, different plants and animals interact daily. Some insects feed on certain tree's leaves, some feed on the cambium layer of a tree's bark and eventually kill it, opening a gap for another tree seedling to grow. (In forests, if the need for moisture is satisfied, the real competition is for sunlight.) Soil microorganisms such as mycorrhizal fungi can form win-win liaisons in symbiosis with tree roots. This physical intertwining multiplies a tree's ability to absorb water and nutrients while the tree supplies carbohydrates to the fungi. Many animals such as squirrels eat tree fruits. Take for example the oak's acorns planted by the scores in the forest duff for future use, but with some forgotten each winter left to sprout in the future, perhaps several dozen meters beyond the boundary of the existing forest — potentially expanding its coverage.

Rules that assign a plant membership in a community have good foundations, but plants don't read the rules. They confound experts by occurring outside their customary community. Plants are plastic and some can survive better than others in less favorable conditions. Often, close examination of past changes in the soils, microclimate, land use, or management of a site can explain such disjuncture. In the preceding section, an example of plant communities described a small woody plant community miles into the prairie fed by seeps — an anomaly indeed, until understanding the site's underlying hydrology allows an explanation. First, since the soils derived from glacial till occasionally have clayey layers impermeable to percolating water, these small lenses (usually in the hundreds of square feet or less) store and divert water to the surface in enough volume to support woody plants. One might ask how woody plants made it miles from their sources? Wind carries winged seeds easily which then grow into perches useful for birds. Next, visiting birds deposit a rain of seeds scarified by their gizzard and seedlings sprout. Once woody plants have established and grown taller they, in turn, produce more fruit and become attractive perches and hence, recruitment and even nesting sites. Larger trees also affect the existing microclimate, reducing wind, encouraging snowdrifts and shading soil.

Plants often have a broad ability to adapt to a site if protected from major catastrophe, and may be able to survive in hostile conditions. Again, re-examine the example of deciduous forest trees planted at the I-80 prairie rest-stop which were watered for establishment and

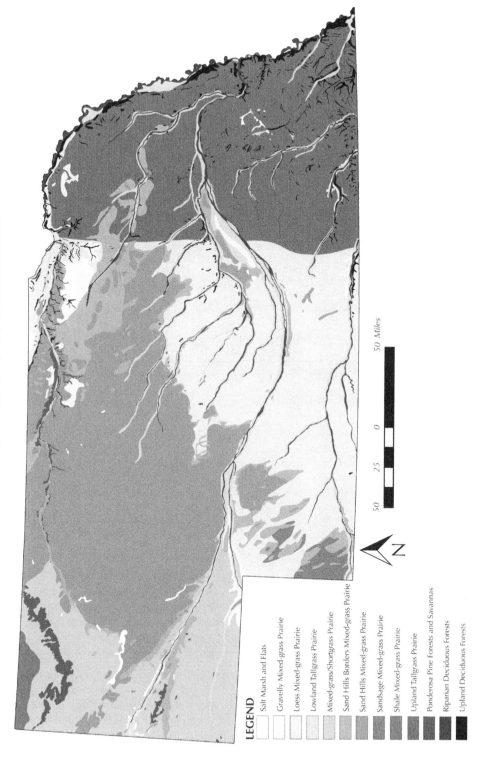

Figure 5. 8 Native vegetation of Nebraska Source: https://snr.unl.edu/data/geographygis/land.aspx

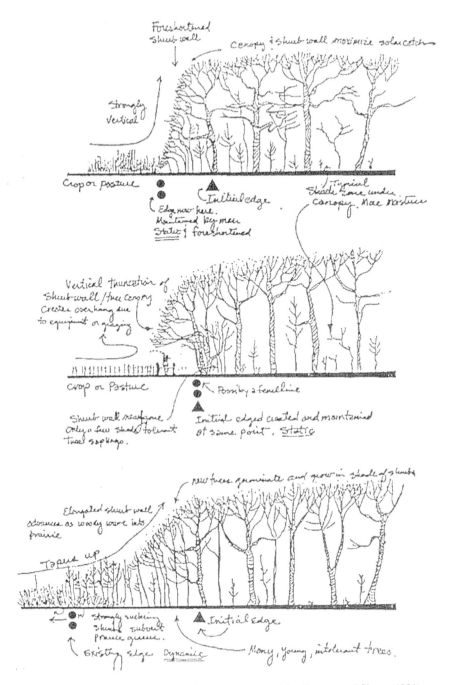

Figure 5.9 Forest, shrub and prairie edges differ with management. (After Burgess and Sharpe 1981)

survived. For bird-planted tree seed left on its own away from readily available water, any germinated tree seedling would most likely not survive drought or the fiercely water-competitive prairie species as neighbors. Our human plantings at rest-stops have grown large enough now that even a wildfire would neither destroy the older bark-thickened trees nor the prairie plants. In the now vanished, fire-created savannas of Illinois, Wisconsin, and Iowa, bur oak once dominated dispersed tree stands because of its fire tolerant bark and ability to compete better than other trees with prairie.

Describing and Locating Nebraska Plant Communities

Discrete lists of species membership tied to soils, microclimate, topography, and aspect best describe plant communities. They also have more utility if communities can be mapped in space and compared over time. John E. Weaver in *Native Vegetation of Nebraska* relied on botanical records of Charles Bessey and his students, but also brought into play his decades of ecological experience from across Nebraska and the Great Plains. His written characterizations of dominant and other species are extensive and detailed. That work, however, contains a dearth of maps. Botanists Kaul and Rolfsmeier have extensive taxonomic experience and in 1993 produced a revision of an earlier map of Nebraska's pre-settlement vegetation (Figure 5.8) based on numerous site visits, field notes, and aerial photos. They did indicate the emergence of one new community type, the cedar forest and savanna, which evolved largely from human control of wildfires. Their map also locates detailed subareas within the Sandhills based on wetland type. One anomaly between Kaul and Rolfsmeier's map and Weaver is a very narrow band of eastern deciduous forest following the Missouri River, where Weaver's redraft of Aikman's map[2] for the bur oak shows a much broader swath of perhaps 20 to 25 miles.

Rolfsmeier and Steinauer (2010) produced a publication detailing the membership and condition of Nebraska plant communities citing example locations. Merchant and Henebry relied on 1991-1993 (Figure 5.10) satellite data from the LandSat Thematic Mapper plus some of Kaul and Rolfsmeier's community categories as a guide, to create a map with photo quality detail. However, their photo interpretation is not without problems. For example, their designation of a Western Wheatgrass-Mixed Prairie community defies Weaver's published work and Kaul and Rolfsmeier's map. The wheatgrass designation may have come from reliance on and misinterpretation of the LandSat spectral bands. Weaver and Kaul and Rolfsmeier all relied on ground-truthing their work and thus are more reliable. Merchant and Henebry's map was produced for the USGS and EPA GAP Analysis program and has become the basis for the current 2001 Level III AND IV Eco-regions maps for Nebraska (Figure 5.11). The eco-regions mapping process for the entire USA came about because of the need to document impacts from the North American Free Trade Agreement, improve natural resource management, and enhance the study of ecosystems and their constituent plant communities.

Environmental characteristics such as geology, water bodies, topography, climate, land usage, soils, and endangered species played a dominant role in describing eco-regions and their boundaries. Thus the eco-regions map cuts across plant communities and its most detailed boundaries at levels III and IV. Also, the names of these areas are more based on topographic and soil factors than plant communities. Comparisons of Weaver, Kaul and Rolfsmeier, Henebry and Merchant, and Eco-regions communities can be seen in Table 5.1.Nebraska Game and Parks Comm. has created a map of the unique biological landscapes (Figure 5.12

Conclusion

This natural history account of the forces that influenced and impacted Nebraska's natural landscape communities continues in many ways to play out today. The preceding discussion and examples show my biases toward plants and people as a potential positive force in an evolving landscape. But, because plants don't readily move, they absorb and reflect environmental changes. Many plants have lifespans within our range of understanding and

---

2 an exception is the bur oak distribution map in NVN redrawn from Aikman (1926).

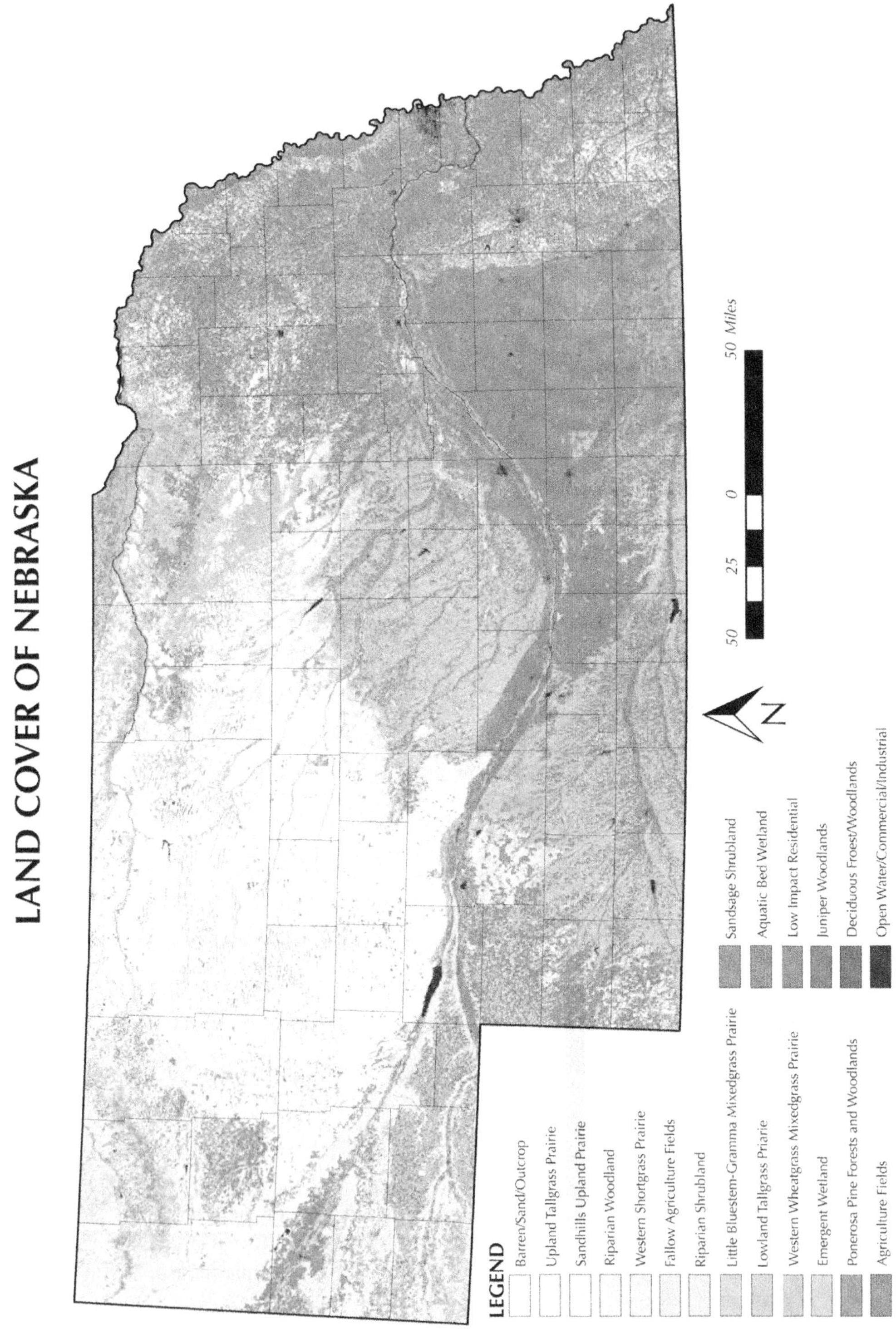

Figure 5.10 Nebraska land cover (Merchant and Henebry) Source: http://snr.unl.edu/data/

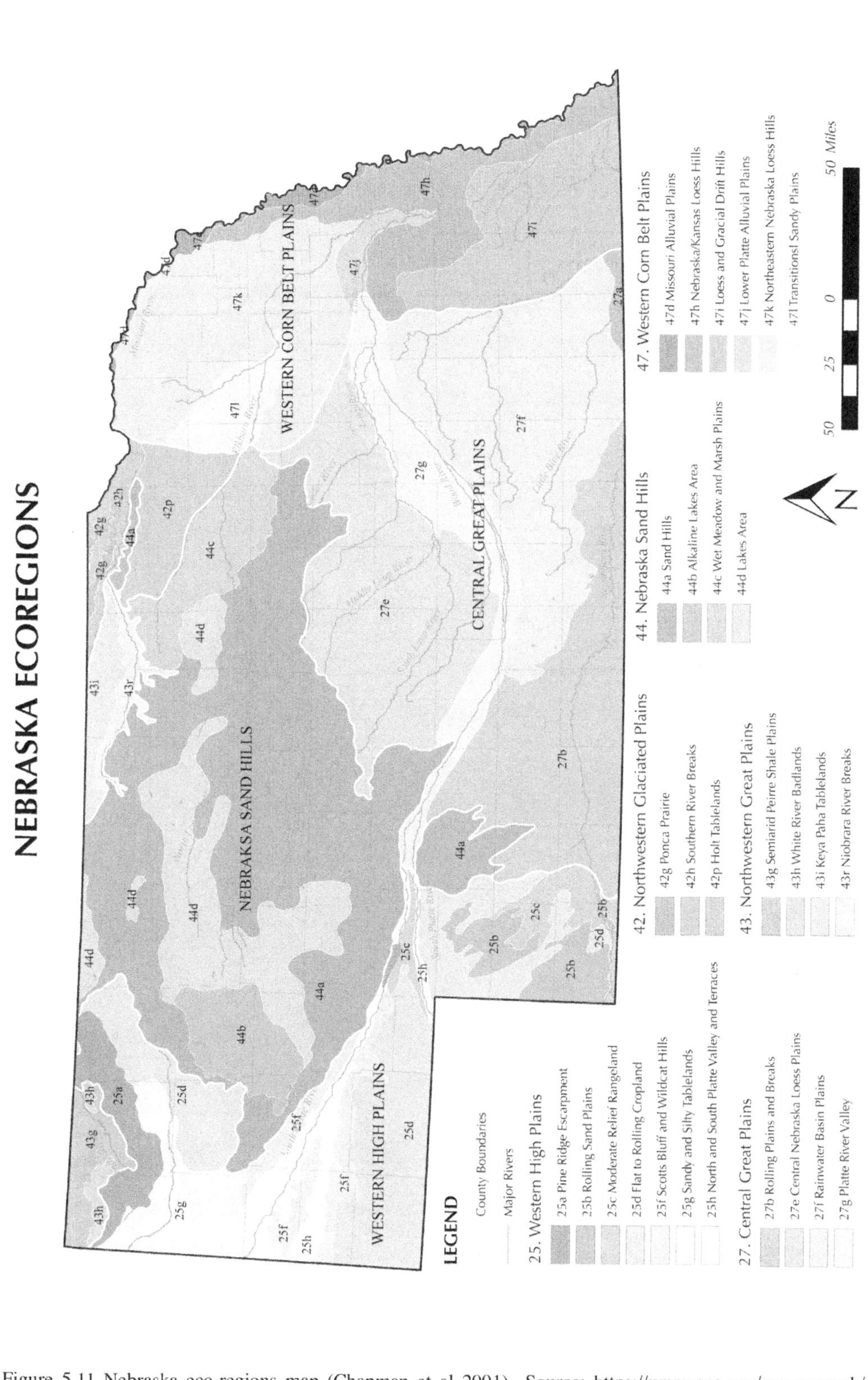

Figure 5.11 Nebraska eco-regions map (Chapman et al 2001) Source: https://www.epa.gov/eco-research/ecoregion-download-files-state-region-7

84

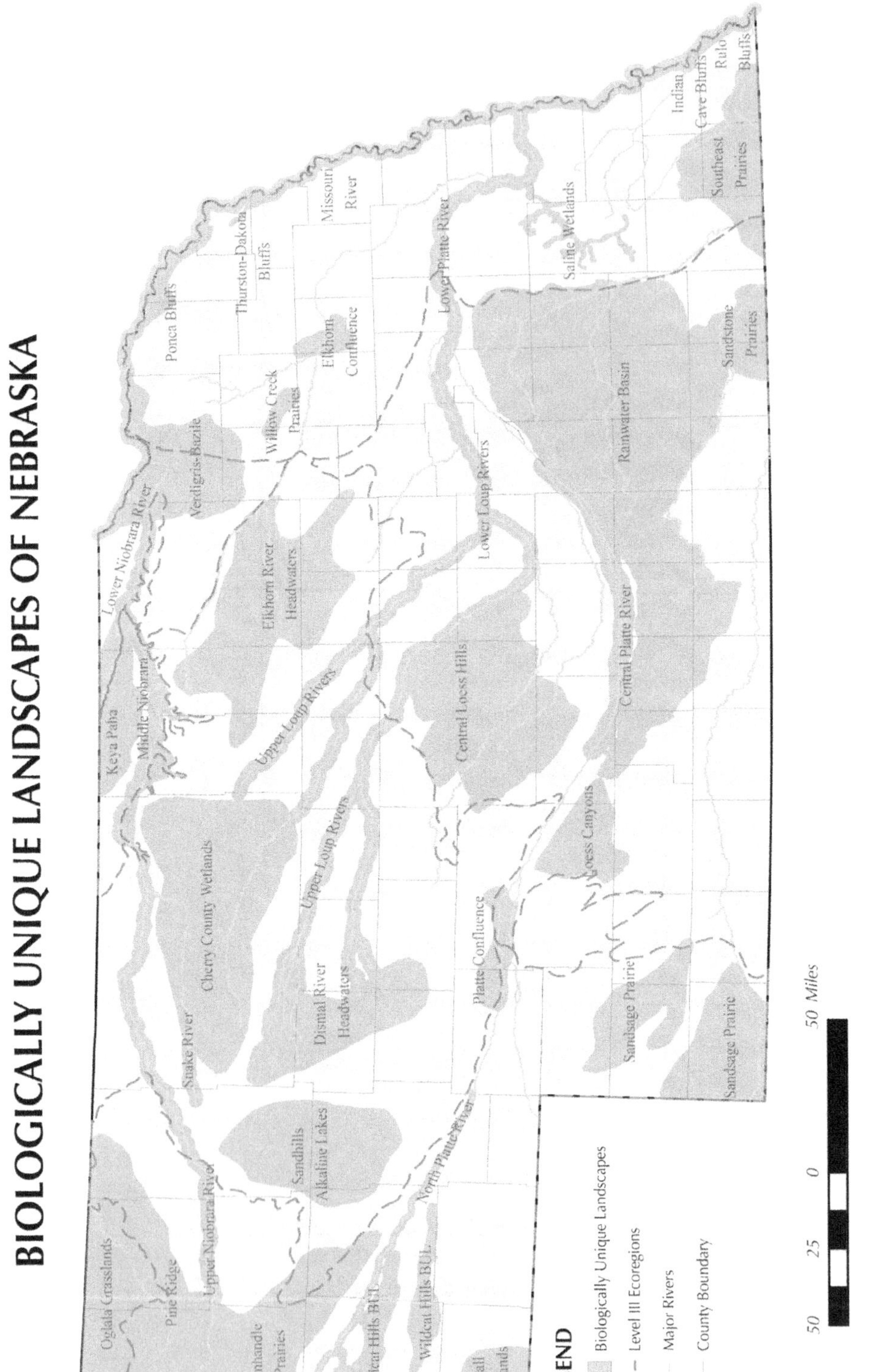

Figure 5.12 Nebraska's Biologically Unique Landscapes Source:https://wind-energy-wildlife.unl.edu/toolsBUL.aspx

exhibit clues to the broader environment if one knows where and how to look. In places natural history rings true as seen in the size, number, membership, quality, and resilience of a plant community. Even plantings initiated by humans or highly modified by us, still respond to natural processes and forces. Our knowledge of those forces remains the key to creating a synthesized landscape reflecting both humans and nature.

The environmental conditions that led to the actual and conceptual plant communities described above give important clues and provide understanding needed to use our native plants, predict their interactions, manage their growth, and perhaps aid knowledge to restore of Nebraska's native vegetation. Without such contextual knowledge, human management of natural plant communities and even intentionally designed plantings will result in them faltering or requiring additional resources to thrive.

Further Reading

Aikman, J. M. 1926. *Distribution and Structure of the Forests of Eastern Nebraska.*

Bagley, W. T and R. K. Sutton 2002 *Woody Plants of the Northern and Central Prairies* Caldwell, NJ: Blackburn

Burgess, R. L., & Sharpe, D. M. 1981. *Forest Island Dynamics in Man-dominated Landscapes.* Springer-Verlag..

Chapman, S. S., Omernik, J. M., Freeouf, J. A., Huggins, D. G., McCauley, J. R., Freeman, C. C., ... & Schlepp, R. L. 2001. *Eco-regions of Nebraska and Kansas* (color poster with map, descriptive text, summary tables, and photographs): Reston, Virginia. US Geological Survey (map scale 1: 1,950,000).

Cronon, W., 2011. *Changes in the Land: Indians, Colonists, and the Ecology of New England.* Hill and Wang.

Henebry, G. M. and James W. Merchant. 1993. *Land Cover Map of Nebraska.* UNL CALMIT-SNR

Henebry, G. M., M. R. Vaitkus, and James W. Merchant. 2008" Nebraska Gap Analysis Project." UNL CALMIT-SNR

Johnsgard,P. 2001 *The Nature of Nebraska.* Lincoln:UNebraska Press

Kaul, R. B., and S. B. Rolfsmeier. 1993. *Native Vegetation of Nebraska* [map 1: 1,000,000]." Lincoln, University of Nebraska Conservation and Survey Division .

Kaul, R. B., D. Sutherland, D., & S. Rolfsmeier. 2006. *Flora of Nebraska: Keys, Descriptions and Distributional Maps of All Native and Introduced Species that Grow Outside Cultivation: with Observations About Their Past, Present and Future Status.* Lincoln, Neb.: School of Natural resources, University of Nebraska-Lincoln 966 p. ISBN, 1921077090.

Overfield, R. A. 1993. *Science with Practice: Charles E. Bessey and the Maturing of American Botany.* Ames:Iowa State University Press.

Rolfsmeier, S. B., and Steinauer, G. 2010. *Terrestrial Ecological Systems and Natural Communities of Nebraska.* Version IV. Nebraska Game and Parks Commission

Table 5.1 Nebraska Plant Communities according to various authors

Weaver (1965)*	Kaul & Rolfsmeier (1993)	Merchant & Henebry (1998)	Chapman et al Ecoregion (2001)
Not Noted	Not Noted	Not Noted	43r Niobrara River Breaks
Not Noted	Not Noted	Not Noted	47h Kansas-Nebraska Loess Hills
Deciduous Forest	Upland Deciduous Forests	Deciduous Forest/Woodland	7d Missouri Alluvial Plain
			47j Lower Platte Alluvial Plain
Floodplain Forest	Riparian Forests		25h N & S Platte Valleys
			27g Platte Valley
Evergreen Forests	Ponderosa Pine Forests & Savanna	Ponderosa Pine Forests & Woodland	43r Niobrara River Breaks
			25b Pine Ridge Escarpment
			25f Scotts Bluff & Wildcat Hills
	Redcedar Forests & Savannas	Juniper Woodlands	27b Rolling Plains and Breaks
	Mosaic Mixed & Shortgrass Prairie	Western Shortgrass Prairie	25d Flat to Rolling Cropland
			25g Sandy and Silty Tableland
Bluestem Lowlands	Lowland Tallgrass Prairie	Lowland Tallgrass Prairie	47j Lower Platte Alluvial Plain
			25h N & S Platte Valleys
Uplands*	Upland Tallgrass Prairie	Upland Tallgrass Prairie	47i Loess and Glacial Drift Hills
			47k NE Nebraska Loess Hills
			47l Transitional Sand Plain
Sand Hills	Sandhills Mixed Grass Prairie	Sandhills Upland Prairie	44a Sandhills
		Sandsage Shrubland	25b Rolling Sand Plains
	Sandhills Border Mixed Prairie		44a Sandhills
Transition to Loess Hills	Loess-Mixed Grass Prairie	Little Bluestem- Gramma Mixed Prairie	27a Smoky Hills
		Western Wheatgrass Mixed Prairie	27b Rolling Plains & Breaks
			27e Central Nebraska Loess Hills
			27f Rainwater Basin
			42h South River Breaks
			42g Ponca Plains
			42p Holt Tablelands
Transition to Loess Hills	Gravelly Mixed Grass Prairies		43i Keya Paha Tablelands
	Shale Mixed Grass Prairies	Western Shortgrass Prairies	43g Semiarid Pierre Shale Plains
			43h White River Badlands
	Sand Hills Lakes, Ponds & Fens	Aquatic Bed Wetland	44c Wet Meadow/Marsh
			44d Lakes
Lakes & Wetlands	Rainwater Basin	Emergent Wetland	27f Rainwater Basin
	Scattered salt Marshes and Flats	Open Water	44b Alkaline Lakes
Not Noted	Not Noted	Fallow Agriculture	Not Noted
Not Noted	Not Noted	Agricultural Fields	Not Noted
Not Noted	Not Noted	Urban/Transportation	Not Noted

*Treats forbs & grasses separately

6 Nebraska's Plant Communities and Associations

"It's etiquette to know the names of at least some of the plants that grow in your area and some of the birds that come through. And to be able to say hello to them when they come by... neighborly awareness toward the natural world. That's just one part of the exercise of making ourselves good Americans... you should love your country, [but] your country isn't just your human public."-

Gary Snyder

Introduction

This chapter gives more information on specific plant communities, their major plant associations, composition, and structure with many examples appearing as images. The chapter focuses on the more important plant communities and identifies their dominant associative members. It gives a view of the Nebraska landscape through a lens depicting whether a place is pristine, impacted, unraveling, invaded or remade. Knowing plant community membership gives us insight as to what may be evolving in the face of changing climate, depauperate soils, and human management and neglect. Knowledge about a plant community suggests habitat protection needs for animals and other animals including humans. Understanding the communities and plants highlighted here helps pinpoint their wider use for creating gardens, parks, urban green infrastructure, and wildlife habitat. And when taken as a whole, a plant community's structure and function, set the changes for its future landscapes.

First some details — the brief descriptions and plant listings below follow from Kaul and Rolfsmeier (1993) Native Vegetation of Nebraska (NVN) map (Figure 5.8) introduced in Chapter 5. The descriptions generalize, summarize, and closely follow its expanded key (Table 5.1). Also a later narrative (Rolfsmeier & Steinauer, 2010) gives good community descriptions and a complete list of example sites. Where appropriate, some reference will be made to Weaver (NVN). Merchant and Henebry's map (Figure 5.10) represents the existing land cover including agriculture, urban areas, and large reservoirs, but are only remnants of pre-existing vegetation as they exist today. The Ecoregions Levels III and IV map (Figure 5.11), in my experience, does not parse plant communities in a useful way, so it is ignored. For more detailed information and reference in the field, consult Kaul and Rolfmeier's and Merchant and Henebry's full-sized, detailed maps available on line at https://snr.unl.edu/data/geographygis/land.aspx

For more details about species mentioned, refer to *Woody Plants of the Northern and Central Prairies* by Bagley and Sutton (2002) and the *Flora of Nebraska* by Kaul, Sutherland, and Rolfsmeier (2006). Nowick's (2014) book on the historical Great Plains plant names may also be useful.

Deciduous Forest Community

Nebraska is not a forested state, as only about three percent of it was covered with communities dominated by trees. Forests and woodlands must have favorable moisture and protection from wind and fire to thrive. Trees fight a constant and tenuous battle to grow in Nebraska. We find most of Nebraska forests' combinations of canopy, understory, and ground layer species are fewer than those in Pennsylvania, Ohio, or even eastern Iowa, and the species number continues to shrink as we move into woodlands of northern and western Nebraska.

Upland Forest Association

Forest uplands can be broadly grouped based on mesic (moist) to xeric (dry) conditions. Along the Missouri River and its bluffs, an upland border of the oak-hickory association gradually changes its membership as one travels upstream from the Kansas border (Rolfsmeier & Steinauer 2010). Chinkapin and red oak-shagbark hickory associations become black oak and bur oak-bitternut hickory associations north and west from the Platte River's confluence with the Missouri River. Out away from there and above it in drier reaches above Omaha, bur oak and red oak become the lone oak dominants. Bur Oak stretches even more widely and grows in the uplands above streams westward to the middle of Custer County in the state's center, and to south central Nebraska past the 98th meridian into Franklin County. Bur oak accompanied by a minor component of American linden and ironwood also continues along

Figure 6.1 Fontenelle Forest, Bellevue, Sarpy CO., NE with closed canopy of the upland deciduous forest.

the Niobrara River into South Dakota and the Black Hills. Bitternut hickory goes no further west than Saline County along the Blue River near Milford and where it grows in Lincoln's Wilderness Park (Lancaster County).

In Richardson, Nemaha, and Otoe Counties of southeast Nebraska, the upland forest contains American linden, black walnut, green and white ash, hackberry and Kentucky coffeetree. The understory consists of smaller trees like redbud, serviceberry, ironwood, paw-paw, and black cherry. Shrubs include coralberry, bladdernut, chokecherry, Missouri gooseberry, prickly-ash, hazelnut, and rough-leaved dogwood. Where they are afforded more light, this woody understory can be quite dense. Vines clinging to over-story trees include Virginia creeper, woodbine, and poison-ivy, with virgin's bower, wild grape, and bittersweet at the forest edge and in sunny openings. Ground layer plants rarely venture into the prairie and include numbers of species that decrease as the forest community moves west and north. These herbaceous plants include woods nettle, woods vervain, white snakeroot, white avens, sweet cicely, bedstraw, beggar's ticks, blue phlox, false solomon's seal, great bellflower, and horsemint to name a few. In the mesic oak-hickory woodland along the Missouri River, a seasonal aspect with spring flowers reveals itself for a short time appearing before the leafy canopy expands and casts dense shade. It includes Dutchman's breeches, columbine, spring lily, spring beauty, culver's-root, Mayapple, jack-in-the-pulpit, and bloodroot.

Riparian Woodland Association

Since streams collect and harbor moisture, their banks, benches, and valleys can also support trees well into the prairies and drier portions of the state. Just as with the upland, forest species of trees, understory, and ground layer species become fewer. Protection from flooding in streams with dams combined with fire suppression has benefited woody riparian species. In many areas, this association appears in an earlier to middle succession and in later succession stands some upland woodland species begin to appear. At the beginning succession, stage trees like cottonwood and a couple willow species quickly give way to box elder, green ash, elm, and hackberry. Introduced plants such as white mulberry and catalpa also grow there along with the native eastern redcedar. Shrubs include black currant, false indigo, redosier dogwood, roughleaf dogwood, and Missouri gooseberry. Vines include virginsbower, woodbine, poison-ivy, and wild grape. Open areas near the top of the watershed might include wild plum, chokecherry, and elderberry.

Along the lower Platte River from North Bend to the Missouri River and in its flood plain to the Kansas border, the riparian forest associations occurring in later succession stages contain black walnut, a few remnant elms, silver maple, and honeylocust. Sycamore is found mostly along the Missouri. All these floodplain trees can withstand lengthy inundation and low soil oxygen levels—precisely the feature which makes them good street trees in our compacted urban soils. Shrubby members of the association include pale and roughleaf dogwood, plus many members of the upland forest association and earlier riparian succession stages. Herbaceous ground layer plants include a wide complement of more sun-loving and drought tolerant herbs from the forest. Where the riparian community has gaps, lowland prairie forbs grow.

Moving into the central and western parts of Nebraska, along streams, we find fewer overstory, understory, and ground layer species, and those stands growing at a younger stage of succession. Willows and cottonwood abound with hackberry and green ash locally common (Figure 6.3). Eastern redcedar also grows as an understory plant and in the central Platte Valley and westward. Also introduced, naturalized plants such as Russian-olive and tamarisk can be found there.

Evergreen Forest Community

Scant evergreen forest exists in Nebraska and it is mostly the ponderosa pine association of the western coniferous forest community that has moved east from the Pine Ridge escarpment along the Niobrara River. Ponderosa Pine forest associations can also be found in the Wildcat Hills of the Nebraska Panhandle. Rocky mountain juniper intermixes with the western stands of ponderosa pine, but is replaced with a hybrid between it, and eastern redcedar, and then

Figure 6.2 A riparian (floodplain) forest at Desoto Bend National Wildlife Refuge, Washington CO, NE.

to the east and north by eastern redcedar itself, in the Niobrara valley. Small outliers of ponderosa occur on the south side of Sandhills and an outlier of limber pine grows in the extreme southwest corner of the panhandle at the Wyoming line.

Cedar Woodlands and Savanna Associations

The eastern redcedar grows from Virginia west to Nebraska (Figure 6.4). In pre-settlement times occasional large specimens could be found in shallow or rocky soil, or as isolated specimens atop the Missouri River Bluffs. When settlers looked for useful native plants, the cedar filled an important need for windbreaks and even ornament. The tree is dioecious, meaning that it has individual specimens that are either male or female. Its small, berry-like cone about the diameter of a pea provides an attractive food source for birds nearly year round. The spread of eastern redcedar was originally kept in check by fire, but as thousands of farmsteads and their complement of fences, buildings, and roads proliferated, redcedar spread

Figure 6.3 Willows pioneering the top of a drainage in Lancaster County, NE

Cedars now densely crowd the understory of central Platte River with an overstory of cottonwoods. They also invade shelterbelts, hedgerows, and any other place that provided structure and perches for birds; cedar has spread more widely than ever. Cedar seedlings can germinate and grow in the shade for many years, waiting for canopy gaps to open. Once they fill in an area, nearly all other plants become excluded. In addition to shading out other plants, redcedar deploys allelopathic roots that chemically dissuade other plants from growing.

Major wildfires have been controlled in the Nebraska landscape since settlement, thus favoring the emergence of an anthropocentric plant association called the redcedar forest or its more open version as savanna. A large area south of the Platte River in southwestern Lincoln County, the upper Dismal River, and a swath of the loess hills in Custer County, on the southeast fringe of the Sandhills have extensive and expanding redcedar forests and savannas. Range and pasture managers fight a continual war against the spread of eastern redcedar using controlled burning. It is important for the managers to burn often enough to short circuit the growth of larger more fire resistant trees and extirpate more susceptible seedlings and saplings.

A few of the plants which can be found with the redcedars are boxelder, fragrant sumac, green ash, western poison-ivy, and woodbine. In some places, a few single-seed ricegrass or fragile and woodsia fern can be found in the dense shade beneath the cedars.

Ponderosa Pine and Savanna Associations

Ponderosa pine grows on dry rocky outcrops readily sprouting from seed on banks and hillsides with exposed mineral soil. The species can form park-like settings of uneven-aged stands, but is prone to fire when young, or in dense stands. After fires, it often seeds in thickly and forms "dog-hair" stands. Before settlement, fires kept the ponderosa pine association confined to rocky hills and thinned. Spreading on to the adjacent tablelands, ponderosa pine can have 10 to 100 times the number of trees per acre. When growing in canyons, ponderosa can be found along side of riparian woodland plants like elm, cottonwood, green ash, hackberry and in some localized canyons even bur oak, (Figure 6. 5) aspen, and mountain maple. In more open stands, the shrub complement includes spreading common juniper, fragrant sumac, and

Figure 6.4 The start of a cedar savanna in Jefferson County, NE

needle-and-thread, prairie sandreed, and threadleaf sedge. Eastward shrubs found in the ponderosa pine association include yucca, chokecherry, sumac and prairie rose. Amongst openings, grasses and forbs from the adjacent Sandhills become most common in the open herbaceous understory.

Grassland and Prairie Community

The prairie community and its associations dominated Nebraska's landscape until settlement. Since then, except for the Nebraska Sandhills, 98 percent has been converted to row crop agriculture or pasture. Some prairie remains in eastern Nebraska where steep slopes or glacial soils laden with boulders discouraged cultivation. In many unplowed pastures, the complement of native prairie plants has been greatly reduced by long-time and intensive grazing or by foolish managers spraying the forbs (wildflowers) and errantly thinking it will increase palatable grasses.

Grasses interspersed with forbs and a few shrubs dominate prairies. Prairie occupies drier areas where trees can not compete for moisture, thus the much shorter prairie plants get all the sunlight they need, but fight a never-ending battle for subsurface moisture. Much has been made of the deepness of many prairie plants' roots, however, the bulk of those roots remain in the top 12-18 inches of soil and only a few penetrate deeply to 4-feet or more for moisture needed in the hot, dry months of a July and August. Prairies also have a strong phenological structure that corresponds with the cooler, moister spring, giving way to the warm, dry summer. Most prairie plants utilize C3 or C4 photosynthetic pathways. C3 photosynthesis becomes most useful for growth in spring and to some extent fall) when the temperatures cool and the humidity rises, whereas the C4 photosynthesis conserves moisture and is most active in the summer.

Prairies have adapted to not only drought, but also fire. In fact, in addition to accumulating organic matter in the soil, prairies build up so much above-ground biomass, that it can smother

Figure 6.5 Ponderosa pine, green ash, hackberry, black walnut and bur oak mingle near Long Pine Creek Brown County, NE,

itself if unconsumed by grazing or fire. Grazers fertilize the soil's surface and scuff the ground preparing a seedbed. Fire recycles nutrients and retards or eliminates the growth of shading from over-story plants. True prairie plants position their growing points and buds, at or beneath the earth's surface, largely protecting them from grazing or fire damage. In the spring, a burned prairie greens up quickly—a fact not lost on grazing buffalo or the Native Americans who set fires to ease their hunting.

Tallgrass Prairie Upland Association

Grass species' heights dwindle westward. Eastern Nebraska supports tallgrass associations often over 6-feet in height (Figure 6.7), while mixed grasses with midgrasses and short grasses grow in central Nebraska, and short grasses dominate in the southwest and panhandle. But microclimate and soil moisture conditions can apparently move tall grasses east in drought or into moist niches in the west. Weaver's detailed plant records showed the domination of short and mid grasses moved 30 miles eastward during the drought of the 1930's. It should be noted that the shorter grasses always grew as a small complement of the association and became more apparent and dominant in drier and warmer conditions.

As far to the east as Illinois and northwest Indiana, tallgrass prairie appears in close relationship with deciduous forest. Some species of grass drop out where the association occurs in eastern Nebraska as well as, many species of forbs. Nevertheless, upland tallgrass prairie may have dozens of mostly perennial species packed into a small area. Weaver notes that 40-60 acres of upland tallgrass prairie in eastern

Nebraska contained 65-90 species, whereas the mixed grass association further west might contain only 25-40 species. Along with the grass family, legumes and sunflower families remain abundant. The legumes supply nitrogen to the soil by a symbiotic relationship with the

Figure 6.6 Ponderosa pine, and eastern redcedar on a rocky hillside in southeastern Banner County, NE

Rhizobium bacteria. Nitrogen, like water, always limits the growth of grasses. In the 1930's, Weaver noted seeing deeply rooted grasses turning yellow with nitrogen deficiency symptoms when leguminous forbs died back from drought, and what little nitrogen remained in the soil could not be absorbed by grass roots since scarce rainfall provided little solution for uptake.

The dominant grasses commonly found in the uplands of the eastern third of Nebraska are big and little bluestem, Indiangrass, porcupinegrass, rough and prairie dropseed, sideoats grama, and switchgrass. Legumes include bushclover, ground-plum, leadplant, purple and white prairieclovers, wild indigo, baptisia, and scurfpea. Sunflowers include asters, several sunflowers, blazing star, compassplant, goldenrod, purple coneflower, native thistles, and white sage. Many other species of forbs grow in the matrix of grasses and most have active growth during either cool-seasons or warm-seasons, thus spreading the prairie's bloom phenology across the entire growing season and supporting a wide variety of native pollinators and other insects.

Tallgrass Prairie Lowland Association

The lowlands that support this association of prairie plants occur throughout Nebraska in river valleys and along broad floodplains with moist or sub-irrigated sands or sandy loam soil (Figure 6.8). Mostly these areas now have been converted to crops, pastures, or hay meadows. Lack of fire may have doomed many to an onslaught of shrubs and trees, especially eastern redcedar, the exotic, naturalized white mulberry, Siberian elm, and in southeastern counties, Osage-orange. Many of the same dominant upland grasses belong to this lowland association, but the more xeric members such as little bluestem and sideoats grama are rare. Additional

Figure 6.7 Spring Creek Prairie Lancaster County, NE

plants such as sedges, scouring rush, prairie cordgrass, and Virginia wild-rye appear along with Maximillian sunflower, meadow anemone, Illinois bundleflower, and prairie phlox. In western lowlands, gentian and lance-leaved blazing star are found, and in the eastern lowlands prairie fringed-orchid and white lady's slipper orchid and shooting star are rare members.

Mixedgrass Prairie Association

Mixed-grass prairie is sometimes called midgrass prairie. Both are apt descriptions: where "mix" refers to the presence of taller and shorter grasses and forbs growing intertwined with one another, midgrass refers to the visual dominance of middle-sized grasses – those more xeric members of the tallgrass upland association including big and little bluestem, sideoats grama, western wheatgrass, needle-and-thread, Junegrass, plains muhly, and dropseed. Because of drier conditions, the species intermix and the reduction in height of the mixedgrass prairie association occurs mostly west of the 98th meridian roughly in a line from Neligh to Superior.

Loess Hills

Weaver describes in detail the "catsteps" of the Loess Hills mixed grass prairie. The catsteps literally look like steps rising several inches to over a foot high perpendicular to the slope (Figure 6.9). This sharp vertical relief occurs because of loess soil's ability to lock particles and resist slumping. Shorter grasses, buffalograss and blue grama cover the hilltops and move down dry slopes. Along slopes, on the catsteps, midgrasses such as little bluestem, sideoats grama and western wheatgrass intersperse with the lower-growing buffalo and blue grama grasses. At the base of the slopes the finer soil collects and holds more water, so taller grasses such as big and little bluestem, sideoats grama, plains muhly or western wheatgrass dominate and largely shade out the lower sod-forming grasses.

Figure 6.8 Tallgrass lowland prairie at Squaw Creek National Wildlife Refuge, Iowa. Nebraska's Rulo bluffs rim the horizon.

Figure 6.9 Cat-steps in the mixed prairie of the Central Loess Hills, Howard County, NE.

Important forbs of the midgrass prairie include leadplant and psoreala. Sparse vines and shrubs occupy moist areas at slope bottom or in ravines including poison ivy, wild grape, wild plum, western chokecherry, wild rose, wolfberry and currant. In the wettest of ravines American elm, boxelder, green ash and cottonwood tenuously grow much like the upper woody plant stands of the riparian forest association.

Yet, in spite of Leoss soil's ability to lock it particles, erosion can be very severe in the Loess Hills and thus a good portion of it remains in hay, pasture, or government programs to keep it out of rowcrop cultivation.

Sandhills

The 18,000 square miles of the Nebraska Sandhills form the largest area of stabilized sand dunes in the western hemisphere. From high points one can easily see its typical dune topography (Loope and Swinehart 2000). Abrupt ridges or hilltops look like large ocean swells in stop-action photographs. The valley bottoms between the ridge top swells may be 150-feet lower and one-half to one and a third miles wide, though the distance between ridges becomes shorter as one moves east. Because of the prevailing winds, the valleys generally lie in a southeast to northwest axis. In the western Sandhills, these lower valleys harbor lakes or wetlands. The latest round of dunes formed 6,000-7,000 years ago and little or no soil formation has occurred, though the bases of many large dunes have been dated as far back as 18,000 years BP. Weaver notes the extreme monotony and sameness of the topography and vegetation with very little to distinguish one place from another. Occasional blowouts, stock tanks, and windmills can standout as landmarks, but without keen local knowledge (or GPS tracking), getting lost in the Sandhills is always very strong possibility.

Blowouts

A curious feature of the stabilized dunes occurs when they lose vegetative cover at or just below the ridges, destabilize and open to form blowouts (Figure 6.10). Rangeland conservation practices are important in reducing the incidence of blowouts, but the drought of the 1930's created many blowouts, which have taken 40 to 50 years to revegetate and stabilize. Blowouts create a specialized niche with several pioneering grasses like blowout grass. Its strong, far-reaching rhizomes with both vertical shoots and deep, moisture-seeking roots, stabilizes an open blowout bottom for sand lovegrass, needle and thread, Indian ricegrass, and sand reed. Nebraska's only endangered species, the blowout penstemon, and the sandhills begonia pioneer blowouts with many forbs like tooth-leaved primrose, spiderwort, annual umbrellaplant, rattlepod, white-flowered spurge, wooly and yellow hymenopappus, and lance-leaved psoralea. These forbs' very deep roots often grow to depths of five or even 10-feet, and many often have tough wide-spreading rhizomes. Shrubs like wild rose, poison-ivy and sandcherry, all of which can withstand sandblasting, thrive in blowouts with little competition.

Bunchgrasses

The visual monotony of Sandhills vegetation comes from the ubiquitous bunchgrasses (Figure 6.11). The major grass species are little bluestem, sand bluestem, sand reed, and needle and thread. Weaver details the rise and fall of the importance of little bluestem, sand lovegrass, and sand bluestem due to drought and grazing pressure. These bunch grasses have some deep

Figure 6.10. Sandhills blowout in Thomas County, NE

Figure 6.11 Bunchgrass Sandhills prairie north of Thedford, NE in Cherry County.

moisture seeking roots to six or seven-feet and short rhizomes that slowly spread the bunches of grass. Little bluestem occupies many of the ridge tops with the other bunch grasses on the slopes or in valleys. The open to sparse overstory supports lower understory grasses like Junegrass, sand dropseed, hairy grama, blue grama, and dryland sedges such as sun sedge. Many different forbs can be found amongst the bunchgrasses, but never make up a majority of the cover. The perennial forb species list is quite variable and includes purple and silky prairieclovers, lanceleaf psoralea, western spiderwort, sand milkweed, bractless mentzelia, evening primrose, pucoon, slenderbush eriogonum, blazing star, and bush morning-glory. Shrubs or sub-shrubs include leadplant, sandcherry, western poison ivy, pricklypear cactus, prairie rose, and soapweed yucca remain with few stems.

Transitions from Sandhills Mixed Prairie

Several transition zones from predominantly sandy soil to finer or coarser soils, occur on the margins of the Sandhills. In these transition areas those species which grow best on pure sand dropout are replaced locally by other species. One such area in southwestern Nebraska and westward into Colorado south of the South Platte River that becomes dominant and visually prominent, is the sandsage (Figure 6.12).

Figure 6.12 Sandsage prairie transition in southwest Dundy County, NE

The clayey hardlands north of the Pine Ridge Escarpment, host droughty forb species from the west such as locoweeds, milkvetch, psoraleas, with shrubs such as broom snakeweed, rubber rabbitbrush, pricklypear cactus, big sagebrush, and winterfat. These forbs and shrubs grow sparsely among blue grama, thickspike, and western wheatgrasses.

Shortgrass Prairie Association

Shortgrass prairie occurs on finer soils, and much of it in the Nebraska Panhandle (Figure 6.13) has been converted to wheat farming. Some still remains as rangeland supporting cattle. Beneath its finer, calcareous, but fertile soils, a hardpan or caliche layer often occurs. Because shortgrass prairies occur in low rainfall areas, the dissolved carbonates percolate only 1 to 1-1/2 feet, then harden. Thus this prairie community and its co-dominant species, buffalo and blue grama, spread their roots widely to absorb shallow penetrations of moisture. During summer dry periods, blue grama can actually go in and out of dormancy many times a growing season, as shallow soils dry and then become resaturated by summer thunderstorms.

Figure 6.13 Shortgrass prairie Kimball County, NE

Buffalograss becomes less common moving north from Colorado into Nebraska where blue grama becomes the dominant. Threadleaf sedge mixes with buffalograss and blue grama in the northern and central Panhandle and sun sedge in the southern panhandle. Wetter areas at slope bottom or in swales support western wheatgrass, little bluestem, and needle-and-thread. Some swales support lemonade sumac, sandcherry, and soapweed yucca.

Wetlands Communities

Wetlands are natural lands exhibiting permanent or temporary excess moisture (Figure 6.14). Wetland communities are important environments varying in their structure and species composition in contrast with communities in Nebraska's subhumid to semiarid climate. Now recognized for the environmental services they provide, wetlands sequester nutrients, trap sediment, and supply patches and corridors for plant and animal movement both locally and globally.

Lakes, Marshes, and Fen Associations

Some plants float freely in open water, others anchor themselves at different bottom depths then emerge above the water surface, and yet others grow above the shoreline but need moisture to permanently wet root zones. The Platte Valley and its wetlands have been particularly hard hit by invasives. Boaters who fail to sanitize their crafts when moving between lakes also transport invasive floating plants like Eurasian milfoil and curly pondweed.

Just as with soils, the pH of the water can affect the plant association. Alkaline Sandhills lakes (Figure 6.15) tend to have less vegetation, consisting mostly of bulrushes and cattails with some areas of saltgrass on the shores. In larger lakes with long wind reaches, wetland plants grow mostly in protected coves. Less alkaline lakes have emergents such as arrowheads, common reed, cattails, and softstem bulrush. Some of these plants may also be present in clear, free-flowing streams. Floating lake plants include duckweeds, pondweeds, bladderpod, stoneworts, and water milfoil; over time, water lilies have diminished in this plant association. Sandhills lake shorelines and very wet meadows support sedges, rushes, spiked bulrush, and water-loving grasses such as reed canarygrass and rice cutgrass along with forbs such as iris, water hemlock, smartweeds, and mints. Willows and cottonwoods also grow nearby.

Figure 6.14 Wetland at Spring Creek Prairie, Lancaster County, NE

A very few fens (also know as bogs) have formed in Cherry County where excessive amounts of wetland vegetation such as sedges or wetland grasses have died and their biomass has accumulated. These fens support plants typically found further north such as marsh marigold, bogbean, cottongrass, and swamp lousewort. Because of the Sandhills' mostly unplowed rangeland, the majority of its lakes and marshes still remain. However, wet meadows can be important sources of hay and many have been subjected to regular mowing.

Rainwater Basin

The Rainwater Basin lies atop a broad ridge separating the Platte, Little Blue, Big Blue, and Republican Rivers, and was once traversed by the Oregon Trail. In those older times seasonal lakes and marshes formed in depressions after winter thaws and spring rains. However, unless the depression was quite large, the water would have evaporated by late summer, so these wetlands experienced frequent dry cycles that limited the types of plants. Though clays mostly seal the depression bottoms, enough seepage occurred to keep them from becoming saline. Most of these wetlands now have been drained and placed in row crops or pasturage. The federal and state governments have protected some to serve as migratory waterfowl habitat.

Where enough perennial water remains, we find tall bulrush and spike-rush. These two plants are joined in other less moist sites prone to drying out by cattails and smartweeds. Because the Rainwater Basin wetlands straddle the tallgrass prairie and midgrass prairie divide, they have grasses from lowland tallgrass prairie, often growing in a transition zone near the wetlands. In them one may find grasses such as prairie cordgrass and reed, and perhaps switchgrass and big bluestem in their margins.

Figure 6.15 Wetlands and wet meadows at the Valentine National Wildlife Refuge, Cherry County, NE. Sandhills bunchgrass prairie stabilizes the distant dunes.

Saltmarshes

Salt marshes occur when salt accumulates in the soil, saturates it, and is not flushed out. Areas of the North Platte Valley and Central Platte Valley have a few salt marshes. The most unique salt marsh association (Figure 6.16), however, occupies a small portion of southwestern and central Lancaster County, and a few acres at the Lancaster and Saunders County line along Rock Creek. These salt marshes arose because salty ground water upwelled in springs and seeps. The salt water came from ancient sea deposits of Dakota sandstone that migrates all the way from Kansas and reaches the surface in Lancaster County. Overtime, the soils surrounding the springs and seeps, have become saline and support plants able to tolerate high salinity. These areas also support an endemic, endangered insect called the Salt Creek tiger beetle. This rare species has led to the public purchase, protection, and management of a few of the surviving salt marsh remnants near Lincoln.

Some of the plants found growing in the Salt Creek, Little Salt Creek, and Rock Creek salt marshes include: marsh elder, saltgrass, saltmarsh aster, saltwort, seablite, spearscale, Texas dropseed, and rarely alkali sacaton. No alkali plantain or arrowgrass occur there.

Saltmarshes in the North Platte Valley typically support alkali plantain, alkali cordgrass, alkali sacaton, arrowgrass, poverty weed, saltgrass, seablite, and spearscale. The Central Platte Valley has similar plants with less alkali cordgrass and alkali sacaton; few untouched areas remain.

Anthropogenic Influenced Groupings

The cedar savanna has emerged as a plant grouping of highly anthropogenic influence due to agricultural land use changes coupled with wildfire suppression. It would not exist without humans. Other groupings of mixed native and exotic plants also can now be found in Nebraska's human-dominated landscape of city and farm.

Figure 6.16 Saline wetland at the Little Salt Wildlife Management Area, Lancaster County, NE

In addition to native plants found in Nebraska towns, farms and ranches, exotic ornamentals, and exotic invasive weeds, appear where their requisite growing needs are met, propagules occur, and the environment provides the opportunity to naturalize. For example, Sandhills lakes have permanent open water, but their shoreline structure and depth, support different types of plants. Unfortunately stream corridors also easily conduct invasive species such as tamarisk, lythrum, and Eurasian phragmites. Exotic plants will not be leaving the Nebraska landscape any time soon, particularly those which can withstand the state's dry climate and soils, and utilize methods like the ubiquitous wind or birds for their seed dispersal. They will make themselves at home, but because of drought in central and western Nebraska, most eastern exotics are restricted to moist valleys and river courses.

Exotic trees including Siberian elm, Russian-olive, tree-of-heaven, Russian mulberry, Callery pear, blacklocust, and Osage-orange, readily naturalize and grow in eastern Nebraska. Pioneer native tree species such as boxelder, hackberry, silver maple, eastern redcedar, American elm, and green ash often intersperse with the invasives. Exotic shrubs such as multi flora rose, Amur honeysuckle, Tatarian honeysuckle, Japanese honeysuckle, autumnolive, European buckthorn, including the vine, wintercreeper, all can be found in human modified niches in eastern Nebraska, while tamarisk invades along stream courses from the west.

As a sign of organism interaction, Russian-olive is listed now as a noxious weed in Colorado, but has also been beset by diseases such as soil-borne fungi and twig cankers. These biotic interactions have limited its spread in some areas in the Central Platte Valley. In addition to the woody invasives mentioned above, a whole host of herbaceous annual and perennial plants like Johnsongrass, bindweed, musk thistle, leafy spurge, lythrum, Eurasian phragmites, and others, adapt themselves to agricultural activities and often invade stream corridors, pastures, and native woodlands.

Urban Lands

Cities represent quintessentially human-dominated landscapes. For example, a 1-mile walk along the MoPac Trail (Figure 6.17) in central Lincoln finds a mix of exotic and native plants (Table 6.1). Several interesting features occur in studying this list. First, species from local landscape plantings in yards and streetscapes are represented, native plants are largely pioneer species, and not all plants have the same abundance.

Overstory, understory, and shrub layers provide bird habitat and absorb a rain of seed that recruits plants from nearby yards and gardens due to bird foraging. Structure of the plant assemblage provides nesting and recruiting foci for plants, whose fruits support neotropical migratory songbirds, such as swallows, wrens, robins, vireos, sparrows, blackbirds, flycatchers, kingbirds, and warblers. Squirrels also play a dispersion role for some plants with large fruits such as black walnut and oaks.

Figure 6.17 A mix of exotic and native plants grow along the MOPAC Trail in Lincoln, NE (see Table 6.1)

Human planted hedgerows, windbreaks, and timber claims are discussed in another chapter. The plant abundances and specific actors involved in hedgerow plant communities may be different, yet the script is the same and relays the importance of abiotic and biotic impacts in their successful establishment and growth. These types of human landscape plantings surprisingly produce membership plant lists similar to the example (Table 6.1) of an urban trail.

Further Reading

Bagley, W. T and R. K. Sutton (2002) *Woody Plants of the Northern and Central Prairies* Caldwell, NJ: Blackburn Press

Del Tredici, P. (2010) Spontaneous urban vegetation: reflections of change in a globalized world. *Nature and Culture* 5(3): 299–315.

Henebry, G. M. and James W. Merchant. (1993) Land Cover Map of Nebraska. UNL CALMIT-SNR

Henebry, G. M., M. R. Vaitkus, and James W. Merchant. "Nebraska Gap Analysis Project." (2008).

Kaul, R. B., and S. B. Rolfsmeier. *Native Vegetation of Nebraska* [map 1: 1,000,000]." Lincoln, University of Nebraska Conservation and Survey Division (1993).

Kaul, R. B., D. Sutherland, D., & S. Rolfsmeier. (2006). *Flora of Nebraska: Keys, Descriptions and Distributional Maps of All Native and Introduced Species that Grow Outside Cultivation: with Observations About their Past, Present and Future Statu*s. Lincoln, Neb.: School of Natural resources, University of Nebraska-Lincoln 966 p. ISBN, 1921077090.

Loope, D. B., & Swinehart, J. B. (2000). Thinking like a dune field: Geologic history in the Nebraska Sand Hills. *Great Plains Research*, 5-35.

Nowick, E. (2014). Historical Common Names of Great Plains Plants, with Scientific. Names Index: Volume II: Scientific Names Index (Vol. 2). Lulu. com.

Rolfsmeier, S. B., & Steinauer, G. (2010). Terrestrial ecological systems and natural communities of Nebraska. Version IV. Nebraska Game and Parks Commission.

Weaver, John Ernest. (1965). Native Vegetation of Nebraska. Lincoln;UNebraska Press

Table 6.1 Exotic and native woody plants along a 1-mile stretch of the MOPAC Trail

		Overstory	**Understory**	**Shrubs**	**Vines**
Native					
Animal spread					
		black walnut	black cherry	chokecherry	bristly catbrier
		bur oak	hackberry	wild plum	wild grape
		eastern redcedar	American elm	elderberry	Virginia-creeper
		pin oak		smooth sumac	moonseed
		hackberry			
Wind spread					
		green ash	Redbud		
		silver maple			
		boxelder			
Exotic					
Animal spread					
		mulberry	mulberry	Amur honeysuckle	wintercreeper
		Osage-orange		cotoneaster	Hall's honeysuckle
				Nanking cherry	
				Quince	
				cranberrybush viburnum	
Wind spread					
		catalpa			
		tree-of-heaven			
		Siberian elm			

SECTION 3 CULTURAL LANDSCAPES

"The way to learn about the human [cultural] landscape is to study it in terms of the people in a place . . .[and as] a matter of social and physical context."- Robert Riley

While the Nebraska Game and Parks Commission has identified and delineated several biologically unique Nebraska landscapes (Figure 5.12), such places enmesh with farm and ranch lands. Agricultural production systems', layout, supportive services, its operators, and their tenure play a major role in what we see in rural Nebraska landscape. In many cases and counties such an interacting system overrides the physical conditions of soil, water and weather.

Nebraska's landscape spans the climate transition of sub-humid (in the east) to semi-arid (in the west), and often becomes subjected to periodic droughts during the growing season. However, most of it is blessed with an abundant underlying aquifer and adequate system of rivers and streams. These factors have led to a more productive and stable irrigated landscape set within the agricultural production system. Yet it looks different -- dams and reservoirs spawning canals which trace the topographic contours and circles of crops within a square General Land Survey pattern.

Also interwoven into those agricultural production systems reside artifacts of early intentions and land use systems, such as hedgerows, windbreaks, tree claims, shelterbelts and other conservation programs. These integrated layers have come and gone based on the need for food, fiber and fuel.

These extensive, albeit dynamic, cultural Nebraska landscapes remind viewers of the past and represent preserved backdrops for stories of the settling and making of America. What happens when those nostalgic, storied landscapes change and we are confronted with incongruity of memory and today's economic survival?

7 Nebraska's Agricultural Landscape

"In addition to contributing to erosion, pollution, food poisoning, and the dead zone, corn requires huge amounts of fossil fuel - it takes a half-gallon of fossil fuel to produce a bushel of corn." –Michael Pollan

"The countryside just doesn't look like the countryside is supposed to anymore. The ax, plow, horse, and rifle have been displaced by the mobile home, propane tank, satellite dish and pickup."-Robert Riley

Introduction

I'm on a summer road trip through Nebraska, and it's a late July evening. I angle north and east off the Divide between the Republican and Blue Rivers into productive irrigated farmland southeast of Hastings. A setting sun casts an orange glow over tens of thousands of acres of corn as I pass them speeding north on Nebraska Highway 14. Center pivot irrigation systems abound and deliver some of the 3,000 gallons of water needed to grow a bushel of corn. With the windows rolled down, the smell of corn pollen pervades the air; it's hot, sticky, and bugs regularly splat against my windshield. Occasionally the end sprinkler gun of a center pivot, splashes the windshield and I have to use my wipers. They smear until I eject enough wiper fluid to make the road visible again. Lights wink on in the few farmhouses I pass while neither taillights nor headlights mark the road ahead or behind. Enclosed by darkening eight-foot high edges along the right-of-way, I am alone, plowing through a green sea of corn.

Agriculture makes up the dominant land use in Nebraska and thus is responsible not only for the state's tremendous abundance and one-third of its jobs, but ultimately what we see of, in, and on its landscape. Yet agriculture's long, dynamic history has caused and continues to cause impacts like habitat depletion, erosion, sedimentation, and now chemical-laced groundwater, greenhouse gas emissions, invasive weeds, and empty streambeds in a dry year, some of which are palpable and others we can only imagine.

In Chapter 3, I discussed farmland in a general way emphasizing the human values of ethics and aesthetics which we can associate with it. This chapter will present a more specific and descriptive narrative of how Nebraska's agriculture operates today as an industrial system to grow corn and soybeans as exportable commodities and raw materials. It is important to remember that while Nebraska farmers proudly declare they grow food to feed a hungry world, much of their corn and soybean yields merely become industrial products, like ethanol, high fructose corn syrup, distiller's grain, and biodiesel. Furthermore, in the following narrative, the way the agricultural landscape is structured affects how it looks; how it looks has come about with little conscious thought about either ethics or aesthetics.

It is hard to imagine what the Nebraska landscape once looked like and nearly as difficult to understand what we see there today. The rolling prairies with wooded stream courses are now gridded into the one-square mile, quarter section General Land Survey (GLS) system proposed by Thomas Jefferson to aid the Federal government's disposal of land. Later, checker-boarded sections of railroad land and public domain Nebraska's hugged the railroad rights-of-way, fulfilling that penchant. Counties claimed thin interstices for the road network devoted to access for settlers. Saddled with the human and financial wastes of Civil War, late 19th century America was short on capital, but long on land. United States government policies known around the world opened millions of acres to an immigration floodgate. And to this day, the General Land Survey grid which structured and ordered the give away of land, remains the dominant feature and artifact of a settled and civilized Nebraska landscape.

True, the Sandhills remain seemingly natural under the stewardship of ranchers who rely on its perennial bunch grasses to fuel a pastoral economy. Its extent remains devoid of the relentless grid of large one-square mile divisions. Some forested landscapes remain on the rocky Pine Ridge escarpment and in the Wildcat Hills. In eastern Nebraska, forests, prairies, and wetlands are mostly gone, depleted or converted to intensive row-crop agriculture subdividing the grid. A few dozen square miles of deciduous forest fragments cling to steep slopes near the Missouri River and adjacent streams. Prairie remnants occur on rocky soil left by glaciers now used for pasturage or hay. Minor amounts of prairie can be found in some cemeteries, along a few railroad rights of ways, and other areas missed by the agricultural boom of the 1950's, 60's, and 70's.

The Post-World War II era ushered in fossil-fuel-powered agricultural equipment that converted and farmed more Nebraska acreage and did it faster (Powell 2015). This motomechanization and energy-driven agriculture came to the fore in 1973 with then Secretary of Agriculture Earl Butz's call for farmers to, "Get big or get out." His statement resulted in countless remnant pockets of prairie and trees being swept from the agricultural landscape. In Nebraska, tens of thousands of highly erodible acres, broken from grass, helped fan a corn boom. An echo of which occurred in the 2010's as highly erodible acreage in the Conservation Reserve Program (CRP), were plowed and planted to corn. The result of these accelerated plow-downs by farmers is, however, merely a blip in America's long-standing drive to produce more and cheaper crops by substituting energy and land for labor and capital.

Agriculture applies ecological thinking in the simplest ways and as it is most widely practiced, agriculture pays minimal service to the conservation of resources like soil and water. Government programs attempt to assuage eroding farmland using best management practices (FACT 1990), while the prairie model of a natural, self-sustaining ecosystem (Jackson 2011) receives scant attention in the design of farms, watersheds, foodsheds and the aglandscape. I'll cover that more in Chapter 11.

Agriculture

Agriculture appeared around 10,000 years B. P. and arose in several widely dispersed and unconnected places. Historians debate how it happened, but the move from Paleolithic hunter/gatherer cultures to Neolithic farmers created sedentary villages dependent on food produced from the land and its longer-term storage. Such permanent agricultural settlements however, did not preclude hunting, gathering, and herding; those pursuits for food continued and fit easily into a village's calendar and nearby natural habitats unsuitable for crops.

J B Jackson (1980) describes the organization of a Neolithic village not so much in differences between hunters, gatherers, herdsmen, and farmers but in differences between the garden and the field. He suggests that small gardens grew inside private enclosures, close to the dwelling, possessed plant and insect diversity, were intensively nurtured by women requiring detailed knowledge of annual and perennial plant growth cycles and cultivation practices, and required many specialized tools. Large fields spread out away from the village standing unenclosed. These communal fields required a strict calendar and an organizational hierarchy of men to plan, plant, and cultivate them. These extensive fields grew only few different crops high in calories, were rotated, and included a fallow period. So, the garden and the field have always lay juxtaposed yet opposed: intensive versus extensive, private versus communal, bio-diverse versus monoculture; small versus large, detailed specialized knowledge held by women versus simple crop cultivation by men.

Pawnee and Omaha agriculturists in what is now Nebraska, were in fact, women horticulturists growing corn in small gardens intertwined with beans and squash--the three sisters. The women practiced a form of subsistence farming supplemented by harvesting wild plants, and men hunted for small game and bison. Crops were not grown for trade. Theirs was subsistence farming, which by definition means that crops or domesticated animals raised were to sustain the farmer and the farmer's family, with little, if any surplus to trade or sell.

Today, worldwide, poor agricultural peoples practice subsistence farming. Interestingly the subsistence farmers in areas of South America have provided the world with distinct varieties of beans, many of which possess genetic resistance to diseases. Ironically as Western agriculturists look askance at those subsistence farmers, many farmers leave the land and migrate to large urban barrios where they can neither support their families nor maintain the biodiversity of plant germplasm valuable to the entire world. Half a world away, that diversity in the form of genetic resistance to white mold and other diseases underpins the dry bean production in western Nebraska.

Today's Techniques and Materials

What follows are descriptions of modern farming techniques and materials that create much of the ecological and visual experience in Nebraska's aglandscape. While what I describe may seem fragmented, it is basic to current agricultural production and underlies the structure and function of the Nebraska landscape (Figure 7.1). These practices also foster a degradation of the pre-existing soils, plants, and animals sustained (or not) by those practices. Selection of crops and methods of arranging and managing the land include knowledge and use of soils and fertility, pest control, field size, and layout. Planted crops survive, grow, and mature by satisfying their basic needs for environmental conditions such as climate, water, and nutrients. Because most crops are grown as monocultures, they are at risk for insects and pathogens as well as competition from annual and perennial weeds.

Farmers selecting species and cultivars for planting must keep in mind the number of frost-free days and the growing degree-days needed for the crop to mature. They also need to gauge the amount and timing of natural precipitation or resort to irrigating the crop. An ancient technique, decrue farming, relies on planting just above seasonal flood levels as they recede. Pawnee gardeners may have made use of it, and only a few changes bring such a farmer to direct irrigation.

Gravity fed irrigation through a network of stream diversions, canals, and field furrows has been a part of agriculture for 4,000 to 5,000 years and was important in the Mesopotamian Fertile Crescent, Egypt's Lower Nile, and elsewhere. As agricultural technology has become more advanced, large diesel or electric pumps now can move reservoir water or groundwater into gigantic circular systems with wheeled towers supporting pipes and sprinklers above the crop being irrigated. These center pivot irrigation (CPI) systems, unlike the nearly level irrigation canals and field furrows, easily deploy water on to crops planted on hilly lands. Irrigation has had and continues to have such an impact on the landscape, I devote the next chapter to its impact on the Nebraska landscape.

Fertile soil contains all the nutrients a plant needs, which along with air and water in the presence of chlorophyll and sunlight photosynthesize carbohydrates, much of which is deposited in harvestable seeds, roots, or leaves. Nitrogen (N), phosphorus (P), and potassium (K) supply major parts of the elements needed for plant growth. Plants need these macronutrients but also must have smaller, important traces of micronutrients available to create all the biological compounds for growth. Beginning in the 1930's and then rapidly increasing after WW II, the technology and energy that had been used to make munitions based on phosphorus and nitrogen were unleashed on croplands. Reasonably inexpensive nitrogen and phosphorus became available and widely applied to cropland resulting in impressive yield increases.

Figure 7.1 Both natural and cultural influences underlie the structure and configuration of this Lancaster County, Nebraska agricultural landscape. Property boundaries are an artifact of the Jeffersonian Grid.

These chemical elements have always been more or less available but depended on microorganisms breaking down plant organic matter in a slow recycling process that makes limited amounts available. Legume roots have the ability, in concert with microorganisms, to fix nitrogen. Thus, legumes are often rotated in sequence with grains or used as cover-crops and plowed down into green manure to enrich soil with nitrogen.

This is important because corn yield is especially sensitive to timely applications of increased N; fertilizer use has increased along with corn acreage. However, as the increased cost of energy has driven up the cost of nitrogen and phosphorus fertilizers and groundwater contamination has also occurred, thus rates of fertilizers usage have leveled off. For example, nitrogen fertilizers have been switched from ammonium nitrate to anhydrous ammonia to urea. Ammonium nitrate, and the tonnage used in Nebraska leveled off starting in 1975 at 661,000 tons, growing only about 9% to 725,000 tons in 2014. The landscape of corn which dominates the eastern and southern thirds of Nebraska won't disappear any time soon as farmers find ways to manage soil fertility and its costs.

Chemical-based fertilizer has been dissolved into irrigation water, a process referred to as "chemigation" or "fertigation." And on Nebraska farms and elsewhere, the amount of relatively inexpensive chemical fertilizer has too often exceeded the ability of crops (especially corn roots) to absorb it. Unfortunately, this led to many years of nitrogen leaching below the root zone into the ground water beneath. The problem has been especially troubling in permeable sandy loam soils in the Central Platte Valley. Because of this, some Natural Resource Districts

(NRDs) now limit the amount of nitrogen fertilizer that can be applied. Deep irrigation wells can tap the nitrogen-laden groundwater and bring it to crops on the surface. While this creates large, quasi-hydroponic farms, nitrates in ground water damage many potable rural community and farm wells. Blue baby syndrome appears from methemoglobinemia caused by nitrate contamination in groundwater that depletes the oxygen carrying capacity of hemoglobin in babies, leading to death. Mature animals do not seem as susceptible, but even dairy cows drinking ground water high in nitrates produce milk that could threaten infants.

Protection of crops is a part of being a farmer. This includes cultivation (and now use of herbicides) to reduce or eliminate competition with weeds. Genetically modified crops may have a gene or genes inserted to confer herbicide resistance for glyphosate (e.g., "Round-up Ready" soybeans) or other herbicides, so they alone survive under repeated application. Traditionally, rotating crops and fallow has reduced buildups of weeds, insects, and pathogens, though it reduces yields. Attempts to completely eliminate those biological pests (weeds, insects, and diseases) with GMO cultivars can and has led to weed resistance against herbicides, and insect resistance against insecticides. Many of the crops have pests that have dogged them for millennia, but invasive pests now present, provide new challenges to the plants commonly used for crops.

Crops that cover the vast majority of Nebraska's aglandscape can be just about counted on two hands: corn, soybeans, alfalfa, wheat, sorghum, dry beans, potatoes, sugarbeets, and oats. For Nebraska, it has been estimated that for crop value, not acreage, marijuana is worth two and one-half times more than oats – but lies hidden inside urban "growhouses." A closely related plant, called hemp has many uses for fiber and oilseeds, but is illegal to grow. Growing hemp would diversify Nebraska's crop coverage. Minor acreage can be found for crops like sunflowers, canola, millet, fruits and vegetables, grapes, nursery crops, and Christmas trees. However, in 2016, corn (9.5 million acres) and soybeans (5.3 million acres) made up well over three-fourths of Nebraska's crop acreage. The growth in acreage of soybeans is startling since in 1940 only 5,000 acres grew in all of Nebraska, and it was used largely as a forage crop.

Genetically modified organisms (GMOs) represent a major input of agricultural biotechnology. They differ from traditional crop cultivars as bred in the last half of the twentieth century in two connected ways. First, GMOs often have incorporated genes with no basis in the original organism's genetic profile. For example, the addition of a genetic component from the bacteria *Bacillus thuringensis* (Bt) into corn is responsible for killing the larvae of insect pests like the European corn borer. Seed companies who own patents on Bt-corn suggest that it is best managed by the farmer planting some non Bt-resistant cultivars adjacent, so that non-resistant insects are available to inter-breed with those that become resistant, setting their progeny up for elimination. Of course the farmer will get the disincentive of lessened yields on those non-resistant cultivars. Second, the speed and novelty of GMOs added to a complex agro-ecosystem that has never experienced them, does not account for unforeseen problems like interference with natural food-webs. Farmers who do not grow GMO crops worry about being sued if GMO characteristics get transferred to what was originally a non-GMO crop. They do represent the march of technology that increases grain output and reduce labor and energy. The issues with GMO crops are complex (Zhang et al 2016) and can't be addressed in the space and focus of this chapter.

Farming systems

Animal agriculture has been tightly intertwined with crop farming since its beginning. This type of system is called mixed farming. Animals as herbivores supplemented or supplied the energy needed for plowing, harvesting, processing, and transporting crops. In turn, draft animals could be fed from the forage on nearby less productive land and as with all stable animals, their waste could be gathered and placed onto croplands to replace nitrogen and other nutrients. Animal products can be considered as added value to the primary productivity of crops. Other animals supply needed dietary protein in the form of milk, eggs, or flesh. Bees, while supplying high calorie honey, also provide the service of pollination required by some crops. Today, with the wide use of insecticides and exotic pests like mites and fungi, native and domestic pollinators have been impacted.

As fossil fuel and moto-mechanization reshape agriculture, mixed farming has segregated into livestock-raising or row-crops. Concentration of cattle or other farm animals also concentrates their effluent, and causes problems unless carefully planned and handled. Crowding animals into feedlots, barns, or cages brings a need for antibiotics to keep them healthy. Some livestock operations also add growth hormones to increase the rate of weight gain and the animal's final weight. Since the need for draft horses has vanished, some of those animals' former grazing sites on poorer land, often with highly erodible soils, have been pressed into row crop use with limited success and excessive erosion.

Nebraska is well situated to link the raising of cattle on rangeland and finishing on grain in feedlots. Sandhills ranches supply the calves, while a short distance away corn is available for feeding. About 60 percent of Nebraska's corn fuels the fattened cattle market and the other 40 percent fuels vehicles. Except for minor acreage in popcorn or specialized white corn hybrids, Nebraska's corn crop directly feeds few humans.

A different approach to animal agriculture uses the extensive Nebraska rangelands not simply to produce calves for feedlots, but to feed cattle on intensively-managed native grass pastures (Figure 7.2). While this brings less and slower weight gain, some say it improves meat quality and allows for less crowding and minimal use of antibiotics. The meat from such animals brings a higher price from a consumer market more interested in meat quality and humane animal treatment.

Based on the soil conditions, topography, and climate, row-crop farmers must decide on the crop, where to plant it, when to plant it, and what will follow. Two major tillage methods can be used. The first method uses mechanical implements to plow (often in the fall after harvest), disk, and plant. Fall plowing exposes soil to winter erosion and requires major soil disturbance, resulting in loss of organic nutrients. It also means more fuel for three equipment passes over the soil. Traditional fallowed croplands and meaningful crop rotation have largely faded from today's farming techniques. Coupled with ever increasingly expensive applications of chemical fertilizer and irrigation in the hopeful (but unrealistic) drive for maximizing and continuously increasing yields, in fact means that profit margins become slimmer or disappear. Fallow and crop rotation have been successful in keeping pests at bay without pesticides. During a year's fallow period, soil microbes have time to break down waste organic matter into usable nutrients. About the only rotation used today in Nebraska is some trading off between corn and soybeans (Figure 7.3) and minor rotations between alfalfa and corn. Interestingly, farmers in other parts of the world have developed pairings of a high calorie crop with a rotation mate of a leguminous, nitrogen-fixing crop: rice and soybeans in Asia; wheat and

Figure 7.2 A Richardson County cow-calf ranch utilizes extensive pasturage.

lentils or chickpeas in the Middle-east; oats, barley, or rye and peas in Europe; and corn and beans in the Americas. The Pawnee's use of corn and beans comes from that last tradition. Thus Nebraska's agriculture combines New World corn with Asian soybeans.

No-till is the second major type of tillage; with it, a crop is planted directly into the stubble of the previous season's crop. A hybrid between traditional tillage and no till is strip-till. No-till mimics a shortened fallow period, and protects the soil from exposure to wind and water erosion somewhat better than traditional fall plowing. It may also increase soil microbial diversity and vigor important for the biological health of soil. No-till only works well if the stalks and leaves (stover) stay in the field, however, many mixed farming operators will cut and bale stalks as a winter feed for cattle. Less starch and more fiber found in the corn stover provides less energy than corn silage or grain. Because corn is a grass, its forage components remain low in protein, but it can add energy and fiber to ruminants' diets. Cattle can also be put on corn stalks to graze for the fall. A second way that stover has been targeted for use is raw fiber for paper mills. Of course, this completely removes about 40 to 50 percent of the organic matter each year corn is grown. The balance remains below the surface as roots. Unfortunately, over time this process mines the nutrients from soil unless it is fortified with additives.

Cover crops are now gaining attention as part of no-till. They protect the soil from winter erosion, impact soil structure, fix nitrogen, feed microbes like arbuscular mycorrhizal fungi, and maintain soil moisture. A wide and biodiverse group of cover crop plants can be matched to the flow of crops slated for a field and often get planted in mixtures. Typical cover crops to name a few include winter wheat, oats, brassicas like canola even turnips, and clovers. No-till systems with or without cover crops require an herbicide application in the spring before planting crops.

Figure 7.3 A field of soybeans in Salt Creek Valley of Lancaster County with Waverly and Greenwood beyond. Watercolor by the author.

Using herbicides and other chemicals in agricultural production limits their marketability, as consumers have shown willingness to pay more for grains, other crops, and animals products that do not have undue traces of chemicals. When growing corn and soybeans for use as industrial components this is less of an issue. Organic farming grows such crops and animals with little or no chemical inputs, but must undergo a lengthy application and certification process. Unfortunately, a specific farm surrounded by neighbors who use chemicals, or which relies on surface or well water contaminated by such chemicals, may fail to gain certification.

Grazing pasture and rangeland cover 23 million acres in Nebraska, about one-fifth more area than cropland. The bulk, about two thirds of that grazing land lies in the Nebraska Sandhills, while in the rest of the state 6.6 million acres of pasture intermixes with 19 million acres of cropland. Steep topography, poor soil, or wet drainage-ways, and wooded creek bottoms have long been assigned to feed cattle and horses, but with the change from mixed farming, pastures remain unused, rented out to cattle, or possibly hayed. In Nebraska's eastern and southern counties, pastures represent the lowest land values, yet are the most heavily grazed and weed infested land use and land cover in the state. Making pastures productive requires careful thought, analysis, and investment in fencing, water, and day-to-day management. Too often those human inputs are lavished on cropland, but not grazing land or maintenance of soil conservation structures (see Chapter 10). Poor grazing land management in the Sandhills quickly brings blowing and drifting sand as immediate feedback, but many other pastures in Nebraska are little more than large corrals or holding yards for livestock and represent some of the most abused land in the state.

Permaculture is a type of agriculture that relies on perennial plantings of grass or woody plants which do not require annual plowing, planting or chemical applications. Sandhills cattle ranches are one example, and specialty crops like grapes and Christmas trees are another. Agroforestry is a special type of permaculture where trees are grown not necessarily for lumber, but to supplement and improve the structure and function of the rural landscape. Field shelterbelts, center pivot corners with trees, shrubs for wildlife, and home or feedlot windbreaks all use trees and shrubs as an accessory to improve structure and micro-climates on agricultural landscapes. Field windbreaks, for example, make up for the yield lost to space by reducing crop stress and improving overall yields in the field they protect (Quam et al 1991)

This section on farming systems found in Nebraska may seem overly detailed, however nearly 15 million acres of corn and soybean are a major part of what we see in the aglandscape. Those crops' reach beyond their fields and impact communities, transportation structures and power transmission lines. They spawn isolated grain elevators, feedlots, ethanol distilleries, fertilizer plants, machinery sales lots, and center pivot irrigation systems while sweeping away many rural dwellings.

Economic Organization

Today, the economics of farming and ranching clearly requires complex and technical knowledge to select, grow, protect, and harvest crops. However, those who make a living by farming and ranching must also know the local and world markets, daily and yearly costs, and cost structure of loans, whether for this year's production or long-term equipment purchase. Local and state laws regulate farms and ranches. If participating in federal crop insurance, conservation cost sharing, or acreage allotments, a farmer must be aware of deadlines, prices, and operational constraints that accompany many of those programs. All of these factors feed back into how a farm or ranch is operated.

Farm income can vary widely from year to year. Many farmers have handled this via seasonal or full-time off-farm employment. Diversification allows a farm to change traditional farming by adding new income sources. This could be as simple as leasing farmland to hunters for seasonal use or as complicated as offering bed and breakfast accommodations or attracting farm tourists.

Because farming has high labor and capital needs, expanding an individual farm's size (i.e. its land base) helps to balance cost though an economy of scale and this can be summed up rather simply by the Nixon's Secretary of Agriculture Earl Butz's maxim: "Get big or get out."

Like all maxims however, some limitations apply. Even with the most modern, large-scale equipment, one farmer can only cover a certain number of acres or manage a certain number of animals. The quality and location of additional land must always be considered; simply finding additional land nearby at a manageable price can prove very problematic. Many who lost their farms in the 1980's farm crisis, over-extended their ability to meet mortgage payments for additional land when the price boom of the 1970's slid into the bust of the 1980's. Despite those pitfalls, the number of farms in Nebraska from 1950 to 2012 more than doubled in size, going from an average of 425 acres per farm to 900, while their numbers dwindled from 108,000 to 50,000. Often, as farms consolidate under an individual, the owner will enlarge fields by removing interior and former boundary fencelines or hedgerows, thus further reducing landscape structure.

As alluded to above, buying more land is not the only way to create a more balanced and profitable farm or ranch. Just as many business owners do not own their stores or factories, some farmland can be rented through banks, trusts, or farm agencies.

Maximizing the system output

In the face of uncertain weather and markets, maximizing and increasing the yield of crop or animal products each year represents the Holy Grail for farmers and ranchers. With fits and starts caused by weather or pests, the average yield per acre of cropland in the US has

Figure 7.4 Modern agriculture relies more on inputs from chemicals than inputs from God.

increased due to inputs: fossil fueled equipment, better genetics, adding chemical fertilizers, more irrigation, and better pest control. The costs and markets have not been as predictable or malleable. This often leaves farmers with a version of cognitive dissonance: they tend to be overly conservative and at the same time overly optimistic.

A "yield-growth trap" occurs when a farmer or rancher assumes that each coming year will bring more production and better prices. Philosopher and organic farmer, Fred Kirschenmann, calls this a "dreamy belief." It is not based in reality and does not follow the second law of thermodynamics. Nothing can grow or increase continuously forever. And while the costs and limits of energy work their way through agriculture, options for increasing yields without further damaging its very resource base have closed or are now quickly closing.

Importantly, personal property taxes on farms fund rural counties. This "tax driver" may be a big reason that farmers need to have continual beliefs in "yield-growth" and/or higher prices. Unfortunately, with the tax bill directly tied to the productivity of the land, farmers abuse highly erodible land and drive the ecology of agriculture to an unsustainable and unstable maximum.

George Marshall, 4th Chief Justice of the US Supreme Court, has said, "The power to tax is the power to destroy." Though he meant that taxation could destroy the equity and estates of men, it surely also means that heavy tax burdens on farmers get passed down to the land, the basic resource on which agricultural production depends. So, at least part of the intention to produce, produce, produce, comes from having to meet obligations via property taxes for police, courts, roads, schools and other community and government functions. Nebraska planner and professor, the late Emiel Christensen, has noted that the cities and small towns embedded in the rural landscape become parasitic through taxing the countryside, and are well-versed in ways to re-appropriate the economic value of rural land. This squeezes the

Figure 7.5 A farmstead factory, Lancaster County. Watercolor by the author

farmer trying to make a living, not only between low market prices and high input costs, but also among those ever-increasing property taxes.

Conclusions

In the agricultural landscape field size and the use of corn and soybeans changes very little, but using no-till, strip-till, and cover crops, create a different land cover with different colors, textures, and spatial and temporal patterns. As these more complex agro-ecosystem become more widely adopted, the landscape may become more interesting and visually varied.

Meanwhile, farmers endure, then fight back against taxes in small and probably unconscious ways that become readily apparent in the landscape. For example, in Cheyenne County and other western Nebraska counties that grow wheat and where the topography is suitably flat, farmers will farm very close to the county road edge. Power poles marking the edges of rights-of-way become slalom posts for equipment as the edge of the wheatfield weaves in and out (Figure 7.6) of private and public land long the road. In corn country of Polk County, the commissioners have been known to order a farmer to cut his corn in the county right-of-way because its encroachment created a safety hazard at intersections. Using rights-of-way, how ever illegal, helps farmers grow more crops, the value of which could be upwards of $1,000 dollars along a mile of field expanded boundary. This produces a situation where the structure of farm debt and taxes become visible in the structure of the landscape largely played out in changing technology.

Unfortunately, ag-producers attempting to balance output and inputs have been seduced by short-term thinking to a focus largely on markets, costs, and taxes. A more sustainable and ecological view requires long-term thinking into the distant future, and considers more than the next quarterly loan payment, more than next year's harvest, more than the 10-year county comprehensive plan, more than a 30-year mortgage, more than the three score and ten of a human life. It may be in the realm of 100-year floodplain, the Pioneer Family Farm or the 7-generation Iroquois' (110 years) decision horizon, but probably is longer. Ecological activities that work on soil formation and nutrient build-up occur in the timeframe of millennia. Those are the long-term characteristics which portend a productive, sustainable, and beautiful landscape (see Chapter 11)

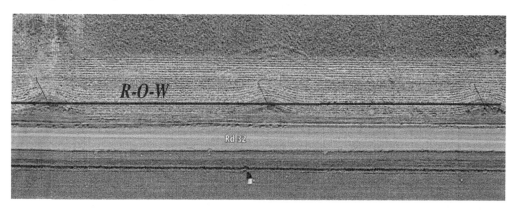

Figure 7.6 Field edges slip on to the public right of way in Cheyenne County, NE. (Image Source Google Earth).

Further Reading

Hiller, T., L. Powell, T. McCoy, and J. Lusk, 2009. Long-term agricultural land use trends in Nebraska 1866–2007. *Great Plains Research*, 225-237.

Jackson, J. B. 1980. "Nearer than Eden?". *The Necessity for Ruins and Other Topics*, 19-36.

Jackson, W. (2011). *Consulting the Genius of the Place: An Ecological Approach to a New Agriculture*. Counterpoint Press.

Kirschenmann, F. 2014. Redefining Wealth. *Leopold Letter Leopold Center for Sustainable Agriculture* Spring 2014.

Linklater, A. 2003. *Measuring America: How the United States Was Shaped by the Greatest Land Sale in History*. Plume Books.

Mazoyer, M., & Roudart, L. 2006. *A History of World Agriculture: From the Neolithic Age to the Current Crisis*. NYU Press.

Pollan, M., 2006. *The Omnivore's Dilemma: A Natural History of Four Meals*. Penguin.

Powell, L. 2015. Hitler's Effect on Wildlife in Nebraska: World War II and Farmed Landscapes. *Great Plains Quarterly*, 35(1), 1-26.

Public Law 101-624 1990. Food, Agriculture, Conservation, & Trade Act

Quam, V. J. Gardener and J. Brandle 1991. *Windbreaks in Sustainable Agricultural Systems* EC91-1765

Vasey, D. E. 2002. *An Ecological History of Agriculture 10,000 BC to AD 10,000*. Purdue University Press.

Zhang, C., Wohlhueter, R. and Zhang, H., 2016. Genetically modified foods: A critical review of their promise and problems. *Food, Science and Human Wellness*, 5(3), pp.116-123.

8 An Irrigated Landscape

"It so happens that the American rural landscape is composed not only of forests and lakes and mountains, but of farms and feedlots and irrigation ditches and orchards and tractor agencies and rangeland. It is a place of work and because it is a place of work, hard and not always rewarding, it is at present undergoing a revolution in its way as radical as a revolution in the urban environment." —J. B. Jackson, 1966

Introduction

The swiftly moving waters grab my fishing lure and sweep it down the large irrigation supply canal. Unlike a similarly sized swift mountain river, the Keystone to Sutherland Canal has a uniform rock edge and a geometric engineered appearance, utterly lacking any bottom or edge structure. It has no riffles and pools to step it down as it travels east along the base of the narrow bluffs separating it from the South Platte Valley. I'm fishing here in hopes of landing a lake trout rumored to have been sucked into the canal from the stilling pool (Lake Ogallala) below Kingsley Dam. Parked on the Central Platte Public Power and Irrigation District canal service road I can see to the north, the narrow North Platte River Valley still with some water in it. A few miles east, the supply canal makes a hard-right turn just beyond Paxton and flows south into the broad valley and under I-80. Finally catching the contours again, it continues east at the bluffs containing the South Platte Valley, and then on to Sutherland Lake and a series of over two-dozen smaller reservoirs. Looking south, I imagine Native Americans sitting atop the dry ridge between the two rivers among the few scattered eastern redcedars as they studied and worried over the westward flow of explorers, wagon trains, and settlers.

Ever since humans entered the semiarid plains and used fire as a part of nomadic hunting culture, we have been altering its landscape. Relatively recent settlement by Euro-Americans speeded and enlarged the process. Those settlers unleashed the industrial revolution to remold the landscape with mass-produced plows, windmills, trees, barbed wire, the one-mile square grid system of the General land survey, and irrigation for croplands. The resulting landscape has changed in structure and scale. The use of water for crops stabilizes yields and the rural economy, however using water as a connector and resource change its quality and quantity.

Nebraska prairies, which sit astride the 100th meridian transitioning from humid east to semiarid in the west, evolved in cyclic droughts. Such reoccurring events now stress crops and farmers alike, making some form of irrigation almost inevitable. In the hundred years following settlement and the initiation of large scale farming, the Great Plains has had at least five severe, prolonged droughts occurring in cycles of about 20 years. However, even in years of average rainfall, critical growth and development stages in crops can be retarded by short periods without rain.

Irrigation

Farmers who settled the more arid fringes of the Great Plains near the 100th meridian dreamed of irrigation as a panacea that would bring reliable moisture and stable growing conditions. However, the technology, capital, and energy needed to irrigate very large acreages have come about only since the 1930's. Like agriculture in general, irrigated agriculture in Nebraska started small. The first version was the traditional gravity fed system to deploy water onto nearly level cropland. Local creeks, rivers, and floodplains supplied irrigation water to Native Americans and later to settlers, but those sources failed in the face of severe droughts.

In 1882, The Platte River became the focus of irrigation activity when builders of the Kearney Canal diverted some of the central Platte River's flow into 24 miles of canal. Further west in 1899, the Scottsbluff County Farmer's Canal Cooperative diverted and dispersed water from the North Platte River into its surrounding flat dry landscape, irrigating 150,000 acres. Later in 1902, with the aid from the "New Lands Act" (aka Reclamation Act) canal irrigation again expanded in the North Platte Valley. Here, irrigation and commercial farming's success can be traced to the sugar beet. H. G. Leavitt, a sugar entrepreneur, attracted Great Western Sugar to Scottsbluff and started a boom that ran from 1910 to 1920.

Both the Kearney Canal and the Farmers Canal Cooperative worked well in most years capturing the runoff from melted Rocky Mountain snows flowing down the North and South Platte Rivers, but they became nearly useless in late summer droughts and especially extended droughts, because those systems lacked storage. One of the first storage projects was Lake Helen above Gothenburg, which not only supplied irrigation for an extended season, but also had a tailrace release for producing hydro-electric power -- the first of its kind on the plains. Several shrewd local entrepreneurs purchased a used hydro-system from a Massachusetts mill town, brought it to Gothenburg and produced electricity for several associated manufacturing plants. All these early projects validated cropland irrigation, foreshadowed electrical power generation and set in motion the identification, appropriation, and dedication of senior water rights along the Platte River.

By 1894, most of the Platte Valley, Eastern Nebraska, and south-central Nebraska had been parceled off into farms by either homesteaders or settlers who purchased railroad land grants. That year and several after saw drought, low humidity, high winds, and heat. Locals called on rainmakers and paid well for poor results. The multi-year drought distressed city and county governments and thousands of settlers packed up and headed east. Some counties lost up to 10 percent of their population. Many days the temperature climbed over 100 degrees Fahrenheit; dust storms became common as fields baked to the ground and tree groves lost their leaves. All the while a vision of bringing water to parched ground haunted those who stayed.

A few years later in 1910, another drought prodded Holdrege grain merchant and mayor, C.W. McConaughy, into a 25-year quest to create a major project to irrigate parts of three counties south of the Platte River: Gosper, Phelps, and Kearney with the Tri-County Project. It followed closely on the heels of the less successful Thirty-mile Canal project which in 1926-1928 lacked storage reservoirs. McConaughy's plan was the first to make extensive use of storage reservoirs linked to canals. Water was to be supplied from a proposed reservoir damming the North Platte Valley and diverted from several places on the south side of the Platte River between North Platte and Gothenburg. Canals angled south and east to the bluffs and fed into and linked reservoirs fashioned from dammed, drowned canyons. In 1930, the entirety of Nebraska had only 500,000 acres under irrigation. In 1933, the Nebraska legislature created the Central Platte Public Power and Irrigation District to spur use of publicly owned electricity and irrigation, though not until the severe drought of the mid-1930's did Federal aid became available to supplement that from the state of Nebraska. It took $43 million dollars to build the second largest hydraulic earthen filled dam in the world. The pool backing up behind it was to be called Lake McConaughy and holds at maximum storage nearly 1.75 million acre-feet of water, irrigates 170,000 acres, stretches 22 miles, plunges to over 140 feet deep at the dam. Hydro-electric generation at the 4-mile long dame was also part of the project and other reservoir sites along the canal system. G. P. Kingsley, a Minden banker for whom the dam was named, had aided McConaughy in his quest. The $43 million dollars in loans was finally paid off in 1973 with interest just 31-years after the project opened.

Ditch-fed gravity irrigation in the Tri-County project, however, required area farmers to learn new ways of farming. In 1941, a popular slogan, "Irrigate or Immigrate," was heard around the Tri-County area. With water, corn yields stabilized and improved 250 percent from 28 bushels per acre on dry land to 100-bushels on irrigated land. Today, beneath farmer's fields in the Tri-County project area, 80 years of irrigation has raised the groundwater table at least 50-feet, and in some areas 100-feet (Figure 8.2).

In the first gravity-irrigated fields, water was transferred into furrow by shoveling open feeder ditches at the furrow heads. Future techniques included siphon tubes or specially sectioned pipe with multiple valves called gated pipe that opened in sections. These systems were extremely labor-intensive and required constant monitoring and adjusting during the irrigation cycle. Also, large amounts of water ran off the field without being absorbed. Recent development of deep wastewater return ponds to capture the unused irrigation runoff has vastly improved the system's efficiency, but the need for land leveling was still a problem. Ditch irrigation remains unsuitable on steeper slopes, because water moves too quickly to percolate into the root zone and erodes furrows.

The next major change brought movable systems with sprinkler nozzles. These reduce the tedious labor involved with gravity systems and opened up more sloping land for irrigation. The systems can be moved by hand or skidded by tractor to dry areas in the field, but they have an important drawback: the pipe can damage tall crops such as corn, wheat, and beans. Most are used mainly with pasture and hay crops.

The sprinkler nozzles represented another technological advance leading to improved water utilization efficiency. Because soils easily absorb fine droplets put out by sprinklers, the threat of water erosion is reduced, particularly on sandy soils. One of the more recent developments in this relentless progression of technology is center pivot irrigation (CPI) (Figure 8.1). On the plains, it manifests itself usually as a circle with the radius of a-quarter-of-a-mile and an area of approximately 133 acres. This conveniently fits four pivots per square mile of the General Land Survey.

The latest advance in irrigation technology just now in its nascence, consists of small diameter perforated plastic tubing from a central water source. This subsurface irrigation eliminates the problem of excessive evaporation from finely dispersed droplets that occurs with sprinkler systems, and the runoff that occurs with gravity fed ditch irrigation. Some farmers who currently use gravity irrigation, and needing to reduce total water use and with fields that don't conform to pivot arcs, are now trying subsurface drip irrigation (SDI). SDI can deliver similar corn and soybean yields with 65 to 75 percent less water. Payback is around five years. The biggest issue with SDI is not machine damage to buried lines, but operating a filter system to keep lines from clogging. Precision farming techniques that use tractor-guided GPS make it possible to rip and plant between the drip lines. As slopes increase on rolling land that could be irrigated by CPI, SDI becomes unworkable, so buried drip lines will not completely replace center pivots.

The big move to CPI came with the high corn prices of 1974 just as technology was making it economically possible to grow crops on marginal, formerly non-irrigatable lands. Briefly, a CPI system consists of sections of quarter-mile long metal pipe supported by eight to 11 wheeled towers. The pipe, which has a sophisticated system of emanating sprinkler nozzles, sits eight to 10 feet above the ground, so it can clear taller crops. Drop nozzles, now in use, place the spray closer to the ground reducing evaporation losses. The water supply usually comes from a well, but occasionally it is piped in from a stream, river, or reservoir to the stationary end of the pipe. Areas formerly irrigated with gravity-fed canals and ditches have evolved, and laterals now supply CPI.

In operation, the length of the pipe circumscribes an arc, not unlike a clock's hand. The end furthest from the water source travels the greatest distance, so end sprinklers receive and disburse the largest volume of water. Towers closest to the center move more slowly and discharge less water. This system is fully automatic and propelled either by electric or hydraulic drive wheels on each tower. The end pipe follows along the approximately one-and-a-half-mile circumference in as few as 20 hours or as many as 200 hours. The system's enormous flexibility allows the irrigator to adapt to a range of weather conditions and crop moisture needs.

Technology helped farmers deal with uncertainty and expanded yields and CPI as a prime example. A CPI system is a large and expensive piece of farm machinery; it is anchored to a field lacking mobility of tractors and combines, so CPI becomes a capitalized land improvement. Capitalization binds CPI to corporate agribusiness, since its location and operation requirements strongly depend upon the organization of capital (and lots of it) plus, land and labor.

Dr. Leslie Sheffield, a specialist in the economics of irrigation from the University of Nebraska-Lincoln Institute of Agricultural and Natural Resources, outlined the system's main advantages in a paper given at the B. A. C. Christopher Agribusiness Conference in Kansas City in September 1976. He estimated that CPI eliminates 90 percent of the labor required

Figure 8.1 Center pivot irrigation with an end gun sprinkler on rolling land in Webster County.

for traditional gravity irrigation and from 25 percent to 75 percent of the labor required by other methods of sprinkler irrigation. CPI also simplifies management so that one person can supervise as many as eight to 12 center pivot systems covering as many as one to two thousand acres. With traditional gravity type irrigation one person can handle a maximum of 240 to 480 acres. With modern communication systems, each pivot can be monitored, turned off, or turned on at the touch of a smartphone. Moisture applications can be tied to buried sensors which in turn regulate the flow from nozzles.

Sheffield pointed out the CPI allows irrigators to match application to actual water requirements of crops throughout the entire growing season. The system offers wide flexibility in the rate of application of water and by varying the speed of travel, irrigators can apply as little or as much as much as they wish in a single revolution. As a rule of thumb, CPI places one-inch of water in a three-day sweep.

This control increases water and energy efficiency although the system is still energy intensive. With better water distribution, pivots average 85 percent efficiency, applying water more uniformly. Farmers can get the equivalent or better crop yields with half to two thirds of the water required in traditional gravity irrigation. Furthermore, fertilizer solutions (nitrogen), some herbicides and some insecticides (depends on EPA clearance) are easily and more uniformly applied when injected into the water.

The system can be adapted to a wide variety of topographies, since the flexible self-propelled towers can negotiate steep slopes. CPI has opened literally millions of acres of land with sandy soils and uneven topography for irrigation, with minimum land shaping required.

Economics

Sheffield has estimated the annual fixed costs for new center pivot irrigation on rolling land in 1974 for southwest Nebraska at $10,375 per 133-acre pivot, or about $78 per acre. It is difficult to compare these figures to costs for other forms of crop irrigation on rolling land, because the land leveling necessary for a gravity system may not be feasible. The fixed-costs per acre based on 1974 dollars have remained relatively steady. For example, in 2007 fixed costs ran about $130 per acre (about $30 in 1974 dollars) and 2016 the fixed cost ran about $435 per acre (about $85 in 1974 dollars).

On the other hand, any cost comparison must consider that CPI has opened up hundreds of thousands of relatively inexpensive, unimproved acres of rangeland, making them a prime target for corporate land purchases. The low initial cost yields a higher rate of return on capital invested when compared to capital costs of more expensive bottomland. In 1976, according to estimates from *Irrigation Journal*, Nebraska ranked third in the United States for total irrigated land, at 6,301,440 acres and about 11 percent of the entire country's irrigated land. Even more interestingly, CPI irrigated 1,000,762 acres of Nebraska farmland: about 33 percent of the country's total acreage under CPI. Moreover, center pivot irrigation systems accounted for 75 percent of the increase in irrigated land in Nebraska in 1976. In 2016 in the state of Nebraska alone, CPI covered 80 percent of over 8.29 million irrigated acres. It peaked at 8.58 million acres in 2011 and in 2016 Nebraska ranked first in irrigated acres and fourth in water use efficiency.

One other possible reason for Nebraska's high percentage of center pivots deserves mentioning. Frank Zybach, who developed the system, is a Nebraska native and with the help of local capital, he started a manufacturing company to produce the pivot in 1952. He and his partner, A. E. Trowbridge, sold the manufacturing rights in 1953. By 1970, of the over two-dozen U.S. firms manufacturing center pivot irrigation systems, seven were in Nebraska.

Implications

The advantages of CPI explain its phenomenal acceptance, but they also suggest some future problems. First, center pivot irrigation relies on a large aquifer, which has its limits. Nebraska experienced this phenomenal growth in center pivot irrigation because of the system's many advantages but largely because of a fortuitous balance between supply and demand for water. Ample and available aquifer water, an artifact from ancient times, propelled this boom. The one third of the state that is the Sandhills region, where moisture stress during the growing season is frequent, overlays the deepest portion of the aquifer. The Conservation and Survey Division of the University of Nebraska-Lincoln estimates that Nebraska has 2,000,000,000 acre-feet of groundwater, enough to cover the entire state to a depth of 40-feet or fill Lake McConaughy 1,142 times.

Second, center pivot irrigation is rapidly dissecting and altering existing natural and human land use patterns. Though interestingly, the legal structure of the General Land Survey (GLS) still holds sway over what Nebraskans see of irrigated landscape, though that has changed in some locations where a pivot corner was sub-divided, thus leaving a long circular arc to become a property line. Other irrigation types also tie to the GLS. For example, except for some supply canals from the Tri-County reservoirs flowing along the natural topography of the Platte River bluffs, most gravity fed canals follow the north to south, east to west grid. Gravity irrigation feeds into fields lying on gentle slopes deceiving human eye into seeing flatness. Meanwhile, the lateral canals and runoff returns, often fill the road ditches and flow into wastewater return ponds, or shallowly-filled low areas. These ephemeral wetlands and canals support riparian vegetation like cottonwoods, willow, and cattails miles from the river. The plants become another maintenance chore forcing periodically removal, much like the canal's inevitable sediment deposits. The canals have evolved over time from earthen channels to concrete-lined gutters, margined with rock and punctuated with concrete gated drop inlets or diversion outlets.

Power poles often march lockstep along the canal-lined roads as reminders of the interconnection of water and hydropower in the Tri-County Irrigation District. Another reminder is farms with lavishly irrigated lawns, gardens, and plantings around their farmsteads. Because flat, irrigatable land is valuable, dwelling and working areas often occur on fragments unsuitable for farming—places like adjacent bluffs, broken ground, and pivot corners. The cumulative impact of this irrigated rural landscape presents a picture very different from nearby landscapes based on rain-feed cropping systems.

A quasi-public reservoir system of a half dozen medium-sized permanent pools (Ogallala, Sutherland, Maloney, Jeffrey, Johnson, and Elwood) and another nineteen smaller lakes) link the main supply canal from Lake McConaughy. The six reservoirs offer thousands of people a place to recreate, swim, boat, and fish, as well as, offering long-term leases for 1,100 homes and cabins. If a lake is near enough to a larger town and nearby land is privately owned, it attracts permanent residents, and modern - even upscale - residences get built. Lake McConaughy attracts tens of thousands of summer visitors from as far away as Denver, CO.

Some maintain the Ogallala Aquifer in Nebraska is so vast it will always be there for man's benefit. Other resources, such as the nation's forests, were once described likewise. The explosion of center pivot irrigation has, however, led to areas of drawdown in the aquifer (8.2). As early as 1975, groundwater depletion as evidenced by lowering water tables in several areas of the state prompted legislative inquiry. This concern lead Nebraska's Unicameral enacted LB577 to set the framework for local natural resource districts to apply groundwater controls.

The Center for Rural Affairs, a nonprofit corporation, was conceived to study and disseminate information about impacts of corporate agricultural development on rural areas. According to a Center report, in 1975, Dundy County, Nebraska, had a total of 3,500 acres under corporate CPI on class IV land, almost exclusively on the sandy Valentine soil association. These soils produce good crops under fertilization, but it is unknown how fertilization and subsequent leaching are affecting the quality of groundwater also used for domestic and livestock water supplies. Starting in 2013, the Upper Republican River NRD began buying and decommissioning wells in the Rock Creek drainage of Dundy County, then began using that water to make-up the water owed to Kansas under the 1949 Republican River Compact.

Light rangeland soils opened up to the tillage of row crops by CPI are particularly susceptible to wind erosion on rangeland. The existing native vegetation has been removed, and replaced with sugar beets, dry beans, or commodity crops particularly corn. Many areas under CPI development have existing patterns of shelterbelts. Where CPI development has come into conflict with shelterbelts, hundreds of miles of trees have been removed or the belts truncated, thereby reducing or eliminating resistance to wind erosion. Cutting down these trees also reduces the psychologically important sense of spatial enclosure provided by windbreaks on treeless prairie (see Chapter 9). Other existing systems have also been altered. For example, where a CPI system comes into contact with major natural barriers such as a stream, bridge-like terrace tracks can be built along its margins or over top to accommodate the wheel towers. The circular arcs have gouged woodland borders along stream courses; nonconforming shrub pockets have been swept from view.

In an aerial view, the impact of CPI is spectacular. At ground level, it is subtle except where circles interact with an established grid. These interstices are used for alfalfa, trees, pasture, feedlots and crop, and machinery storage, as well as, farm residence buildings and wildlife habitat. All these uses diversify what we see in the rural landscape and if a trailing boom arm irrigates the corners, other land uses get swept away and the monotony of cropland prevails.

Human land use patterns can serve as a gauge of existing attitudes toward the environment. Since the 1940s, the traditional pattern of four farms per section has been disappearing. Still, the numerous small towns and abandoned farmsteads scattered throughout rural Nebraska, kept the illusion of density. The residents did not need to confront the anonymity of the urban scene. Nebraska no longer reflects the promise of the individual farm. Instead, it shows a pattern of absentee landlords and large corporate holdings, where farm families often do not know, nor have they met who owns the adjacent land.

Future Irrigated Landscapes

The forces that are weakening the visual sense of community are also depopulating the rural landscape. Young people from family farms have always moved to the city for jobs, since the family homestead could not provide livelihoods for all heirs. But on large corporate farms with highly mechanized operations, farming jobs are becoming even scarcer. The result is fewer people on land and more in the city.

What has emerged is a new Nebraska farmstead. Dwellings and accouterments for the large factory farms that use CPI are nestled into non-irrigated corners. The landscape is becoming

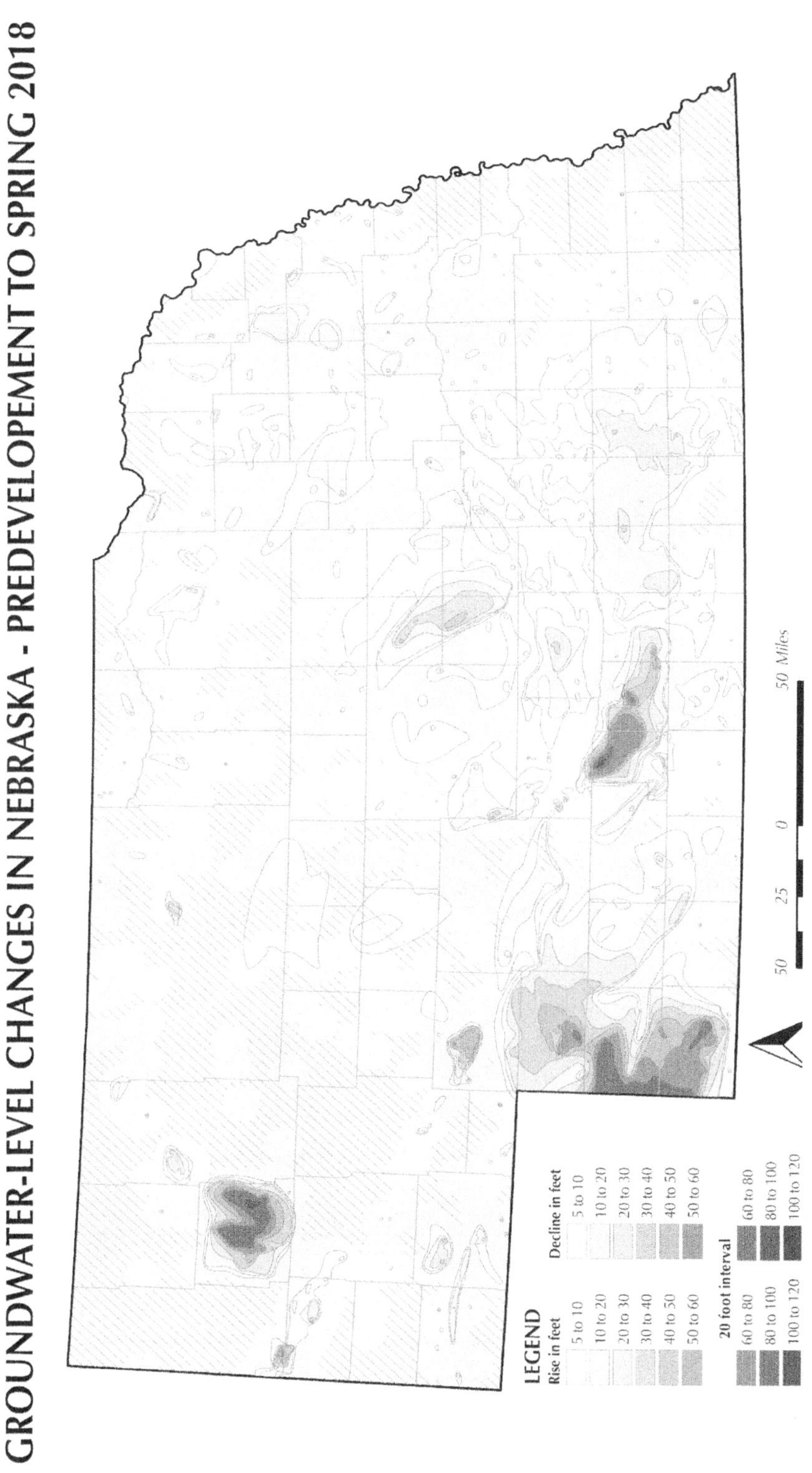

Figure 8.2 Groundwater changes in Nebraska. Source: http://snr.unl.edu/data/water/groundwater/gwlevelchangemaps.aspx

a study in rural impermanence: glass and steel silos, prefab metal barns, and double-wide house trailers. Impersonal mobile environments like those fostered by agribusiness speak of the American quest for mobility while long visible in cities and suburbs, now diminishes opportunities for lasting ties to the land.

Center pivot irrigation should be of interest to students of the landscape—planners, geographers, and landscape architects—because it marks the physical change from the previous landscape of the Yeoman Farmer to that of the corporation. Historically, irrigated landscapes have had strongly centralized land tenure systems. Probably in no other place rather than rural Nebraska, can the full contrast between the earlier Jeffersonian ideal of the citizen farmer (GLS grid) and the corporate farming operation (CPI circles) be seen so immediately and clearly (Sutton 1977). The cooperative Tri-county irrigation project with gravity fed cropland, is rapidly changing to one dominated by center pivots. Center pivot irrigation did not precipitate corporate agricultural patterns in Nebraska, yet it is a highly visible artifact of that phenomenon. Corporate-backed center pivot irrigation –millions of acres owned by a few and work for pay for those displaced from the land. The changes stamped on the landscape by the rise of CPI indicate the current attitude toward the environment in general and to the rural environment specifically. Depopulation and mobility ensure that land is not thought of as a place to live, but rather an economic base for making profit. CPI could represent the rural counterpart to urban dehumanization and its monotonous anonymity.

Although the circles are still spreading over more acres each year in Nebraska, they will probably have a lifespan much shorter than the grid. That timing could be part of the future problem. Center pivot irrigation is a highly complex and radical departure from traditional cropping systems, which represents a working accommodation between human adaptability and environmental adaptability. The natural environment, while extremely flexible, adapts to changes in much longer rhythms than humans seem capable of maintaining. Since it is composed of natural systems of microbes, soils, plants, and animals, the rural landscape needs more time than man does to accommodate the rapid and massive change. But there may not be time. Finite supplies of groundwater and the tremendous amounts of energy required for CPI are already suggesting its limits. It is just a matter of time before new patterns, perhaps subsurface drip irrigation, interact with the circles to continue the complex history of humans and the landscape.

Further Reading

Appleton, Jay. (1975) *The Experience of Landscape*. New York: Wiley.

About the Central Platte Public Power and Irrigation District. http://www.cnppid.com/about-cnppid/ . Accessed December 20, 2016.

Center for Rural Affairs (1976) *Wheels of Fortune*. Walthill, NE.

Henkes, R. (1977) Team farming. *The Furrow*. 82(1):2-5.

Green Circles. (1976) *Landscape* 20(2):1.

Hoskins, W. G. (1956) *The Making of the English Landscape*. London:Hodder and Stroughton.

Irrigation Survey –1976. (1976) *Irrigation Journal* Nov-Dec pp. 25-30.

Jackson, J. B. (1966) The New American Countryside: An Engineered Environment. *Landscape* 16(1):16-20.

Johnson, B., C Thompson, A. Giri, and S. Van NewKirk. (2011) Nebraska Irrigation Fact Sheet. UNL Department of Agricultural Economics. Report 190. September.

Mattern, H. (1966) Growth of landscape consciousness. *Landscape* 15(3):14-20.

Meinig, D. (1976) The beholding eye. *Landscape Architecture*. 66(1) 44-54.

Sauer, C. (1962) Homestead and community on the middle border. *Landscape* 20(2):44-47

Sheffield, L. (1976) Some facts and figures about groundwater availability and irrigation in Nebraska. UNL AgEcon Dept. Mimeographed.

Sheffield, L. (1975) The cost of center pivot irrigation now. *Irrigation Age*. January pp.12-15.

Sheffield, L. (1976).Advantages of center pivot irrigation. Paper B. C. Christopher Agri-business Conference. September. Mimeographed.

Splinter, W. (1976) Center Pivot Irrigation. *Scientific American*. 234. June. pp 90-99.

Sutton, R.K. 1977. "The Round Peg in the Square Hole: Center Pivot Irrigation in the Nebraska Landscape. *Landscape* Vol. 22 No. 1 pp. 3-10.

Taylor, C. (1975) *Fields in the English Landscape*. London:J.M. Dent & Sons.

Wagner, P. (1963) America Emerging. *Landscape* 13(1):22-26.

Wagner, P. and M. Mikesell. (1962) *Readings in Cultural Geography*. Chicago:University of Chicago Press.

Zube, E. et al (eds) *Landscape Assessment: Values, Perceptions and Resources*. Stroudsburg, PA:Dowden, Hutchinson and Ross.

9 Contested Ground: Plantings in the Image of a Garden

> "Children reared among trees and flowers [and] growing up with them will be better in mind and in heart than children reared among hogs and cattle." J Sterling Morton

Introduction

The tree is a valuable indicator of how the pioneer interacted with the environment and as well, a symbol of their feelings toward that landscape as a garden habitat and as a place to live. Cather partially captures those feelings at the end of *My Antonia* describing Antonia's garden enclosed with trees (Cather 1954 p. 340):

> "At some distance behind the house were an ash grove and two orchards; a cherry orchard, with gooseberry bushes between the rows and an apple orchard, sheltered by a high hedge for the hot winds. As we walked through the apple orchard, grown up in tall bluegrass Antonia kept stopping to tell me about one tree or another. 'I love them as if they were people,' she said rubbing her hand over the bark. 'There wasn't a tree here when we first came. We planted every one and used to carry water for them too- after we'd been working in the fields all day'."

Described as an awesome space, the Great Plains was once noted for its lack of trees. Today as one travels its many sections, trees are more commonplace. Large trees become an event in a landscape dominated by prairie. Since the time of human introduction of strongly formed masses of living material into a "limitless" space, a unique rural landscape has evolved delimiting spaces with masses of plant communities assembled by the pioneer planter.

Trees punctuate prairie, enrich our image of the events that have occurred there, and symbolize the fashioning of a garden in the prairie wilderness. The image is not trivial, for belief in the garden archetype (Jackson 1977) transformed prairie's harsh reality. And as Jackson says, "The garden is where we have to be."

Few writers have observed and recorded that microcosmic garden habitat which surrounds the rural, vernacular dwelling, but their omission is more an indication of a lack of understanding than lack of importance (Watson 1978, Droze 1977, Watts 1963, Reardon, 1977). What can these garden landscapes and their tree groupings tell us about the pioneers? Various individuals have looked at fences or houses, and Pierce F. Lewis has stated that he feels that the vernacular house exemplifies "man etching his culture in the landscape" (Meredith, 1951, Zelinsky 1959, Welsch 1979, Kniffen, 1965, Lewis 1972). What of plants? Do they reflect the agency of mankind as well? Do they indicate a cultural response to the environment? Do they show learning and adaptation or failure and abandonment?

Over the years, I have traveled and studied the rural landscape within the Great Plains and specifically eastern Nebraska. Four counties in particular, reveal a vernacular landscape created by different pioneer tree-planting schemes. Before I get to those examples, I would like to give an historical overview of human intentions behind the tree planting on the Great Plains, then comment on the changes in events and intentions producing the relicts we see today. I will then describe visual patterns and plant communities so you can understand the visual diversity and cultural history planted into a landscape. Finally, I will give my sense of how the plantings have changed or disappeared and what might be expect of a future, planted cultural landscape.

Intent and Events in Nebraska Tree-planting

During settlement of the Great Plains, trees most importantly represented a crucial resource for creating and maintaining a frontier economy and pioneer habitat. Local timber however was not of sufficient quality or quantity to supply such an economy for a long period of time. With the exception of areas along the few wooded watercourses, the pioneer depended upon wood imported at great cost and difficulty for fuel, housing, and fencing (Dale 1948). To remedy this, planting of woodlots in upland areas was strongly encouraged by the 1861 Nebraska Legislature which offered a $50 tax exemption for tree planting; in 1869 the exemption was raised to $100 (Maxwell 1951). Saw-timber for housing was scarce and mostly expensive and imported. Rather than a log cabin, a soddy or dugout more often provided shelter. After initial settlement and adequate crop yields, most farmers built homes from lumber shipped in from the mills of Wisconsin (Nebraska Historical Society 1872) and Chicago (Cronon 2009).

Self-sufficiency for the farmer engaging in mixed crop and livestock production required the field enclosure for practical reasons. Between 1850 and 1880, ruined crops and lost stock caused by insufficient fencing, spurred the use of hedges. Adoption of the hedge as a practical landscape feature by settlers in eastern Nebraska required considerable amount of adaptation. Since many exotic European and eastern American plants proved unfit to survive on the Great Plains, any plant that showed potential as a hedge was tried (Nebraska Horticulture Society 1880). Many plants failed as hedging, some escaped and naturalized, but the Osage-orange (*Maclura pomifera*) became the dominant hedge plant lining thousands of miles of fields.

Post Civil War Nebraska continued to be a conduit for settlers moving west, but also became a destination. The Nebraska Horticulture Society Proceedings focused on discussion of trees, orchards, flowers, and vegetables. Trees in particular garnered interest, and it was the planting of trees that captured the spirit of the day. Most of the early tree planting in Nebraska was done by zealous individuals and strongly promoted by such men as J. Sterling Morton, Gov. Robert W. Furnas and Prof. Charles E. Bessey. In 1872 for example, Morton's efforts culminated in the establishment of Arbor Day -- a day on which more than three million trees were planted in Nebraska, (Maxwell 1951) which was about 10 trees for every man, woman, and child in the young state. He preached the gospel of trees for the last 25 years of the 19th century and was responsible for the establishment of Arbor Day. Furnas created a profitable nursery at Brownville largely based on his production of Osage-orange hedge plants. Bessey applied scientific botany and native plant exploration that resulted in his grand idea for afforesting the Nebraska Sandhills. Buoyed by early success of conifer planting near Swan Lake in Holt County, Bessey pushed for planting the public domain near Halsey in Thomas County, creating the hand-planted Nebraska National Forest.

However, as dreams of afforesting the entire region wilted in face of events such as cyclic drought, grasshopper plagues, neglect, and the decline of poorly adapted species, the federal government stepped in to boost planting and to aid the settlement of the prairie. Beginning in 1873, successive governmental attempts intended to dispense federal land, using tree planting as an enticement to settlers. According to C. Baron McIntosh (1975 p. 347):

> "[T]he timber culture act [1873] was one aspect of the total adjustment necessitated in the settlers occupants of the central gap grasslands of United States where rainfall decreases rapidly westward; tying the planting of trees to gift of 160 acres of land was intended to increase the tree cover in order to modify the climate and much needed supply of lumber and fuel."

Subsequently, in 1911 as an amendment to the 1904 Kincaid Act, the US Forest Service provided free trees to Nebraska homesteaders near the 100th meridian. A United States Department of Agriculture publication describing the Kincaid Act stated:

> "The main objective of the tree distribution by the government is to stimulate interest in forest tree growing chiefly for the production of fuel and fence posts and the establishment of windbreaks ... Furthermore, the establishment of windbreaks and woodlots make living conditions pleasanter and adds much to the value of the property." (USDA 1925 p. 4).

The Kincaid Act ended in 1917 after dispersing nearly 9 million acres of public domain. When early plantings declined as a result of age, harvest, or poor management, another tree-planting program was launched that is still in operation today. Under a portion of the broad 1924 Clark–McNary forestry bill, the US Congress authorized that trees be distributed at cost in rural areas. Section 4 of the law, "Provides for the procurement and distribution of forest trees for the planting of windbreaks shelterbelts and woodlots on farms" Maxwell 1951 p. 3.

Concurrent with the Clark–McNary program and in response to the severe wind erosion of the Dustbowl, President Franklin Delano Roosevelt launched the Prairie States Forest Program in 1935 (Droze 1965, Karle and Karle 2016). While it is chiefly remembered as a soil conservation program it also provided employment to jobless men. In my opinion, shelterbelt remnants are as important human landscape artifacts of the Depression Era rural landscape as a WPA Road or a CCC picnic shelter.

Commonly referred to as the "shelterbelt project," the program was a highly controversial, yet carefully designed effort carried out by the US Forest Service. It first focused on an exhaustive regional study of soil, climate, existing planting successes, possible shelterbelt configuration, species availability, and previous windbreak research (Wessel 1967). As the project unfolded, trained crews planted on land provided by cooperating farmers. The entire process controlled by the Forest Service, involved a thorough site analysis and detailed planting recommendations prepared by a forester. Between 1935 and 1942, a total of 200 million trees were planted from Texas to North Dakota, thereby providing 18,500 miles of shelterbelts and covering 238,000 acres (Ferber 1964).

While the emphases of earlier individual and governmental planning programs have changed, overall intent has remained strongly functional. To the vernacular planter-immigrant however, trees also represented familiar masses that were to be found in the wooded landscapes of western and central Europe and in the eastern United States. In many cases, plantings provided psychological relief from the harsh climate and unending space of the Great Plains (Shelford 1944).

Relicts in Four Nebraska Counties

Christmas vacations during my youth were often spent on snowy pheasant and quail hunts. To deploy our manpower and take advantage of the dense cover holding birds, meant we needed to read the landscape. Two hunters could handle hedgerows, but the larger windbreaks needed at least three or four. Those walking in the center rarely got clear shots because of the dense canopy. On particularly snowy days with reduced visibility, nearby farmsteads often became visible only because of large old conifers planted near houses. These human-planted masses structured our hunts, provided shelter for our prey and served as landmarks in the rural Nebraska landscape.

Below, I describe in some detail three distinctive types of planting relics each within a specific geographic area, but they can be found elsewhere and intermixed throughout eastern Nebraska counties. These relicts are: 1) the ornamental conifers as found in Otoe County, NE; 2) the woodlot windbreak and shelterbelt plantings of Holt County, NE; and 3) the Hedgerow plantings growing in Pawnee County and Lancaster Counties, NE (Figure 9.1).

Otoe County Ornamental Conifers

Pioneer planters often started with landscape beautification efforts directly adjacent to their dwellings (Sutton 1982) (Figure 8.2). Today one often finds early farmsteads and public areas such as church grounds, cemeteries, and schools yards, associated with ornamental plantings of both familiar and experimental species (Sutton 1982). Nonetheless, even beautification had a functional basis as noted by an excerpt from a farm forestry press release published in *The Nebraska Ruralist*:

> "If we can have beautiful things [landscape plantings] to detract the mind while we are performing our daily toil we will live longer happier lives. This improvement could be accomplished according to the publication by a planters careful placement of shade trees of a better class arranged about the lawn and premises in such a way that they give ample shade for recreation . . [so] that he does not entirely cut off the view from the public highway. . . " (Jenkins 1918 p. 13)

Largely rural, Otoe County, NE, is particularly rich in ornamental pioneer plantings. It straddles the gradual ecotone between the eastern deciduous forest along the Missouri River and the tall grass prairie in the county's central and western parts; it stretches from an environment suitable for trees, to one hostile to them. The prairie environment is hostile to trees because of endemic natural forces including fire, hot summer winds, and periodic droughts (Clements 1937). Otoe County pioneers first settled mostly on prairie sites, except at the eastern fringes and along with a few wooded streams.

Two important socio-cultural factors influenced the first pioneer tree planting in this area: J. Sterling Morton and the Fort Kearney wagon road. Morton, a key businessman and politician strongly advocated tree planting. The grounds and arboretum at his home (aptly named Arbor Lodge) overlooked the Missouri River near Nebraska City, and were laid out in the style of the English landscape Garden School. His attitudes about trees and his example in planting them were widely known in the county. Secondly, the county straddles the important pre-rail supply road from the Missouri River to Fort Kearney. The road provided constant flow of goods services and especially information throughout the county during its early settlement. One of the first nurseries in Nebraska was located on this road at "Nursery Hill" near Syracuse, NE in the center of the county.

While records indicate that a variety of evergreen species were planted in eastern Nebraska for ornamental purposes (Pool 1951), a definite pattern of species distribution appears in Otoe County (Sutton 1982). On the drier, western portions of the county, Austrian pine Scotch pine and the native eastern redcedar were most common as examples of older plants. At the time of my 1982 study and survey, many old coniferous plantings were at least 100-years-old, and the moister areas closer to the Missouri River appeared richer in old plantings of Norway spruce, blue spruce, and white pine. Since then many have succumbed to age, insects, and farmstead removal. Below is a sort of tree roster highlighting the important arboreal players.

Eastern redcedar (*Juniperus virginiana*).

This is a medium-sized conifer native to Nebraska and the eastern United States where

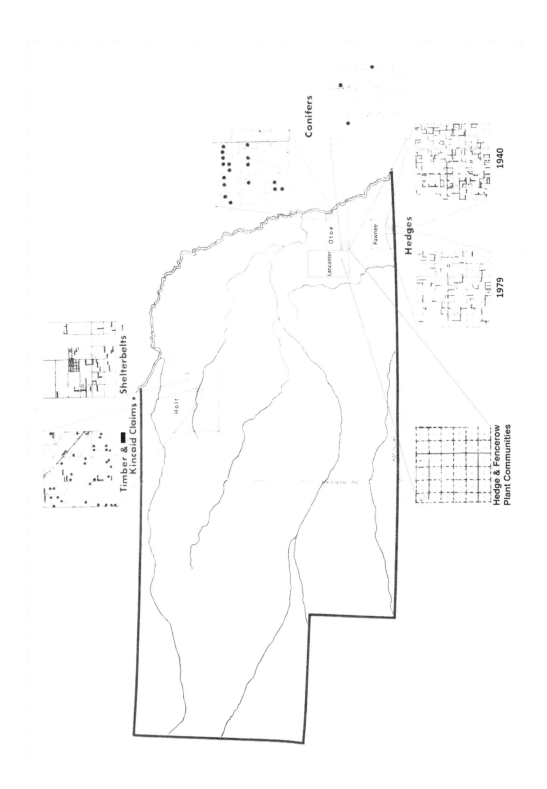

Figure 9.1 Study areas in four Nebraska Counties: Lancaster, Otoe, Pawnee and Holt

it was widely ignored in 19th century plantings. It survives in a variety of soil, light, and moisture conditions and primarily sees use in Otoe County for windbreaks. However, there it is also widely used in ornamental arrangements (9.2). Eastern redcedar takes shearing well, but tends to lose the top of its crown in old age. It may live to 150 to 175-years, if given proper care. Since the tree is indigenous to Otoe County, it can be deduced that many of the old cedars around the farmsteads are wildlings dug from pastures and waste places or volunteers in place. Settlers adapted this tree to their needs.

Ponderosa pine (*Pinus ponderosa*)

This tree is native to the northern and western parts of Nebraska, but was not used to any great extent in early plantings (1860 - 1920). Propagation and distribution of this tree was not undertaken until the early 1900's, however, it has been one of the main constituents of the Clark McNary tree distribution program and planted extensively in the windbreaks since the 1920's (Droze 1977). Few ponderosa pines are seen as ornamentals near older buildings except for what appears to have been an occasional "left over" from windbreak planting efforts. Planters of new rural dwellings on new sites, however, commonly employ ponderosa pine as an ornamental in close proximity to the home. It is a long-lived tree and takes wind and drought well. Young ponderosa pine may look similar to Austrian pine, but will lack the same broadly flattened crown at maturity.

Jack pine (*Pinus banksiana*)

This tree of the coniferous forests of the Canadian Shield has been widely available to local residents through the Clark McNary program. It is used as a windbreak planting, but is not long-lived in southeastern Nebraska. The few specimens observed were found to be in poor condition. The pine wilt nematode which arrived in Nebraska at the turn of the 21st century continues to kill jack pine, and tree's occurrence has been much reduced in the landscape as the disease progresses north and west. Jack pine was not made available until the early 1900's and was not a constituent of ornamental conifer plantings.

Norway spruce (*Picea abies*)

Norway spruce arrived from the coniferous forest of Northern Europe with Scandinavian immigrants, and is one of the most prized ornamentals of the 19th century landscape gardeners. It requires a cool moist climate and soil. It was most likely widely planted in eastern Nebraska as a windbreak, but has not thrived except in extreme southeastern Nebraska (Pool 1951). Norway spruce can be observed as a windbreak planting throughout the Midwest as near to Otoe County as Missouri and in central Iowa (Reardon 1977). It is found mostly next to homes and occasionally in well-attended cemeteries in Otoe County. Evidence of its relatively moderate-lived nature is seen in many declining specimens.

Blue Spruce (*Picea pungens*)

The blue spruce is intermediate, between Austria and scotch pines, and the White Pine in its tolerance of dry windy conditions. Native to the Rocky Mountains, it was quickly adopted by the nursery trades both in Europe and United States because of its handsome blue-green foliage. This ornamental quality made and continues to make blue spruce highly prized as a tree for planting in proximity to a home or in cemeteries, though it is occasionally used in younger windbreak plantings.

Austrian pine (*Pinus nigra*)

This is a hardy, adaptable exotic tree from Europe, which withstands a variety of soil and drought conditions. Most often seen in Otoe County as a picturesque, broadly flattened ornamental in close proximity to old dwellings, it is used to some degree as a windbreak. It may live at least 150 years under good care, but can suffer from needle-cast and tip-blight. Many of the oldest specimens have reached their lifespan limit and have disappeared from the Otoe County landscape.

Eastern white pine (*Pinus strobus*)

Eastern white pine is native to light loamy soil and moist forests of the northeastern United States with a natural range as far west as northeastern Iowa. It does not do well outside of southeastern Nebraska where it is still very susceptible to the drought and wind damage. It is used occasionally as an ornamental next to dwellings where it receives irrigation. Today, Eastern white pine is rarely seen as a windbreak planting on the Prairie. Planters have learned that it declines during drought.

Arborvitae (*Thuja occidentalis*)

Arborvitae has a range similar to that of Eastern white pine but occupies an ecological niche that is more moist. This tree has an attractive columnar shape and originally was planted in southeastern Nebraska as a windbreak, screen/hedge, and as an ornamental next to the house (Pool 1951). A severe freeze on Armistice Day 1940 (after 10 years of drought) nearly eradicated the arborvitae from this area. Occasionally, large old specimens exist where they had received plenty of moisture or irrigation since the impact of the freeze was most severe on drought stricken specimens. In Nemaha County, the next county south of Otoe County, a specimen of arborvitae shelters a plot in the Nemaha Cemetery dated 1879.

Scotch pine (*Pinus sylvestris*)

Scotch pine, a widely distributed native of Europe, most often was planted as an ornamental next to the house. Like the Austrian pine, it was brought to America in the Colonial Period withstanding a variety of soil and moisture conditions. Scotch and Austrian Pines were popular in the early 1880's (Watson 1978). Originally noted as not being long-lived as Austrian pine, it appears to have withstood the ravages of nature, as well as Austrian pine. These two trees are often seen side-by-side as ornamental groups (Pool 1951). Some of Pool's comments must be considered as resulting from observations of Scotch pine growing from less adaptable seeds sources, probably Scotland and England. Beginning in the 2010's, the pine wilt nematode began and continues to kill Scotch pine so it has been much reduced in the landscape.

Other ornamental conifers Pool (1951) noted in Nebraska that may have been present in my 1982 survey area, but are unrecorded, were American and European larch (*Larix laricina* and *L. decidua*) and Black Hills spruce (*Picea glauca densata*) (Pool 1951). One Otoe County farm site did contain Rocky Mountain junipers (*Juniperus scopulorum*) symmetrically framing the entrance to a home, while another contained a single Rocky Mountain Douglas-fir (*Pseudotsuga menziesii glauca*).

Distribution of conifers by type

The conifers in Otoe County, except for the indigenous redcedar, have rarely been able to reproduce naturally, and thus have required the conscious intervention of man for their

Figure 9.2 A Farm road allee' of sheared eastern redcedar in Otoe County, Nebraska photographed in 1981

presence. Interestingly, on I-80 from mile marker 390 to 380, Austrian and Scotch pines planted for highway landscaping have naturalized on the north-facing road cuts some time after 2002.

My 1982 transect surveys indicated that conifer plantings were widely distributed throughout Otoe County. The heaviest concentrations were along the eastern border, although plantings were found in most sections of the county. The Scotch/Austrian Pines, demonstrating their hardy character, by surviving in every section of the county, and were the most widely distributed species, though few plantings grew near the Missouri River. The less adaptable White Pine/Norway/blue spruce complex was much more restricted in its distribution. These species tended to be found most commonly in the eastern or protected sections of the county. Although several plantings in western Otoe County demonstrate they could be grown in any section of the study area if sufficient effort and irrigation was expended. This latter complex probably was once more extensively planted in western Otoe County, but is gone today.

Most of the conifers I tabulated in transects, functioned as windbreaks with the remaining used as ornamental conifers. Pioneers sought protection from the severe northwest winter winds by site selection, and site arrangement. Windbreaks are usually found on the north and west sides of farmsteads, though some pioneers also protected their orchards and gardens from searing summer winds with rows of cedars, planted as windbreaks to the south. The future landscape will most likely progress toward increased numbers of windbreaks with correspondingly less ornamental plantings.

Planting Patterns

In my 1982 survey, two patterns of ornamental groupings were noted of special interest: 5 percent of the sites contained what may be called an allee' (Figure 9.3), and 4 percent of the sites contained what might be termed a bosque. The term allee' is used here to describe the linear plantings beside pedestrian paths leading to the public road in front of dwellings. The patterns were symbols of the formal processional space in the French garden known as allee'. The bosque pattern is one where trees are planted around the house closing it off to develop a canopy or bosque over the space adjacent to the dwelling.

The allee' plantings were primarily of eastern redcedar, eastern white Pine, Austrian pine, Scotch pine, or Blue spruce. Two species were occasionally mixed together, most notably Scotch and Austrian Pines. The allee' planting represented a symmetrical layout which was not typical of the late 19th century landscape styles. Most of the literature of the period extols the virtues of the informal curvilinear English landscape Garden School style, used by A. J. Downing and others (Downing 1959, Westgate 1905, Card 1897).

Architectural historian, David Murphy feels that a common mistake in understanding central European adaptation of architectural forms to the Great Plains, is over reliance on the dominant Anglo-American culture and its architectural forms (Murphy 1979). Murphy's assertion may be valid. In relating the strong, formal allee's to the French influence on landscapes in central Europe, in the 18th and 19th centuries, and consequently immigrants to Nebraska from that region, is difficult. One would need to establish this link by documenting the planters and their national heritages. Such documentation could however lead to the conclusion that the central European immigrants perceived his homestead on the plains as a *de facto* kingdom, needing a touch of the old formal grandeur of the European nobility's garden allee'.

If this theory has any merit, then it along with the ecological adaptability of the Scotch and Austrian pine, may account for the preponderance of those two species as over mature, ornamental plantings and particularly found as allees'. The immigrants from central Europe may simply have been more familiar with species native to their homeland than the others (Watson 1978).

Two broadly defined groups of allees' were identified in this study: formal and informal, and the formal arrangement predominates. The major axis in both was either a north south or east west in orientation. The formal outlay is an excellent artifact to gauge species mortality, since if the outlay were of one species, the gaps would indicate the number of trees that fail to survive. Also noted was one allee' with two rows of trees, each of the different species on either side of the central axis.

The allee' is primarily confined to the northern section of Otoe County today. Only three of the 26 sites containing allees' were noted in the southern half of the county. There is no clear pattern in the distribution of allees' in the area where they are found, although the presence of four sites in a row containing allees' north of Syracuse may give that impression to the casual viewer.

The bosque is the second major ornamental planting formation characteristic of Otoe County conifers. This formation consists of a row of eastern redcedars closely grown together at a site near the house and totally surrounding it. Cedars were the only trees that were seen in this pattern and in most cases were quite old (in the 90+ years age range) and they were carefully limbed to above head height. This artifact is called a bosque here because the trees have grown so large and are still in close proximity to the house, that a strong overhead canopy still exists. Bosques are widely scattered in small numbers throughout Otoe County.

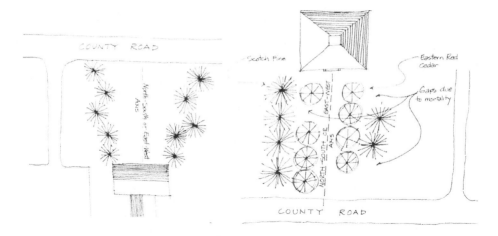

Figure 9.3 Formal (right) and informal (left) conifer allee's lead to a dwelling's door.

This formation cannot be considered a home windbreak because the closeness of the trees to the home does not meet the desired distance standards for effective wind reduction. Bosques could have originated as windbreaks, but the snow and wind are effectively controlled or managed only when trees were smaller. With the older, larger trees, snow driven by the wind would be trapped and allowed to drift into place around the house. This drifting may provide sound insulation, but it most certainly causes foundation, rot, and drainage problems. It might be theorized that the pioneer planter who utilized this type of planting did not fully realize the force of the prairie wind and the size and configuration of snowdrifts caused as these redcedars grew. The best wind and drift protection is two-to-five times the height of the windbreak, dependent up on density. The cedar bosque also may be overgrown consequences of the desire for immediate spatial enclosure on windy, exposed prairie sites. The eastern redcedar plantings may have been hastily installed and never redesigned or removed after reaching maturity. The ornamental effect occurred when the lower limbs were removed to reduce problems arising from snow drifting. What began as a functional planting evolved into one that is now ornamental.

An early pioneer remarks, show use and adaptation of native trees (NHS 1877, p. 78-9):

> "In April, 1868, I obtained from the Bluffs on Mission Creek near the Otoe Indian reservation, about 700 young eastern redcedar trees, the most of them being from 2 to 3 inches high--some were 6 to 8-inches. . . To partly enclose my perspective lawn and garden, being set 6 feet apart in a single row."

Holt County: Trees from Government Programs

Between 1873 and 1941, over 10 million trees were planted in Nebraska under the Timber Culture Acts, Kincaid Act, Clark McNary Act, and the Prairie States Forestry Program (PSFP). Each of these different programs and each of their different intentions–land dispersal, wildlife habitat, and fuel or wind protection – have resulted in a mosaic of planting relicts.

In the summer of 1982 I made a survey of Holt County (Figure 9.4), NE to view and note its pattern of woodlots and windbreaks. It was chosen for study because it is especially rich in a broad spectrum of woodlot (Figure 9.5) and wind protection plantings (Figure 9.6) (excepting hedgerows). The Elkhorn River dissects the county diagonally from the northwest to the southeast; to the north and east lie hardland soils conducive to row crop farming; and to the south and west lie the Sandhills, unsuitable for row crops. The broad Elkhorn Valley contains a floodplain forest along its margins, and the eastern section of the county is a transition zone from tallgrass prairie to mixed prairie (Kaul 1975). The southwestern half of the county is ranchland with scattered groves of human planted trees. Within Holt County are concentrations of remnants of the nearly 1,100 timber claims and later plantings under the Kincaid Act. To the north and east of the river are examples of shelterbelt (PSFP) and the more recently Clark-McNary plantings. In administering the 1904 Kincaid Act, the US Forest service drew on previous experience in the survival of plantings. They supplied not only trees, but also planting information and strict guidelines. Interest and learning continued in the selection of the planting site in the care of the trees (USDA 1925). While the configuration of the plantings was left to the discretion of the planter, a limitation on the number of trees supplied to an applicant often reduced the size of the woodlot plantings. Trees, after all, are forest species and benefit from growing together. So less of them meant wider spacing, and they could not reach the density of a self-protective grove. Stories abound of sticks stuck in the ground and called plantings to meet the acreage requirements (Welsch 1982).

The Kincaid Act also placed emphasis on windbreaks that were ideally narrower than woodlots and contained a mixture of both deciduous and coniferous species for summer and winter protection. Recommended species include: ponderosa pine (Pinus ponderosa), Scotch pine (*Pinus sylvestris*), Austrian pine (*Pinus nigra*), jack pine (*Pinus banksiana*), and eastern redcedar (*Juniperus virginiana*) as coniferous trees; and cottonwood (*Populous deltoides*), American elm (*Ulmus americana*), green ash (*Fraxinus pennsylvanica*), honeylocust (*Gleditsia triacanthos*), hackberry (*Celtis occidentals*) and black walnut (*Juglans nigra*), but also newly suggested exotics: Russian-olive (*Eleagnus angustifolia*), Siberian elm (*Ulmus pumila*), as deciduous trees (USDA 1925).

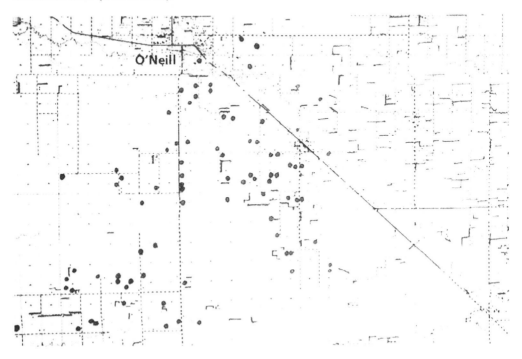

Figure 9.4 The central part of Holt County, NE with dots indicating woodlots and bars shelterbelts. Diagonal is US 20 Paralleling the Elkhorn River.

In Holt County, northeast of the Elkhorn River where large concentrations of neither Kincaid nor timber reclaims existed, the soil was damaged by wind during the early 1930's. This area was identified for planting in the Shelterbelt (PSFP) Project. Shelterbelts differ somewhat in their function from windbreaks. Mainly planted to protect fields as opposed to farmsteads, shelterbelts must be carefully coordinated with surrounding plantings. Since their planting, all such windbreaks have not remained as static, linear landscape features. For example, the highly mobile seeds of Siberian elm dispersed on southerly summer breezes help it quickly to invade pastures north of a shelterbelt. Species selection and spacing were based on 1) silvacultural value 2) economic value 3) susceptibility to damage 4) aesthetic value 5) wildlife value 6) cultivation requirements and 7) special values (Olsen 1935).

Figure 9.5 The interior of a Holt County woodlot.

According to Kaylor (1935), the timber claim woodlots measured either about 10 by 160 or 20 x 80 rods in size. This is approximately 10-acres or one-quarter-of-a -forty-acre claim. These areas form rectilinear blocks or masses in the landscape and now resemble remnants of a pre-existing forest. By noting tree size, evenness of age-class, and seemingly random spacing of the trees, we can estimate the age of a timber claim. This unevenness in age and spacing is due to the natural biological interplay of mortality and reproduction. The canopies, however, are well-developed and nearly uniform. Probably the most striking feature of these block-shape plantings is the lack of species diversity. This is because normally they were planted to as a monoculture of one of the following species (Listed in order of the most common occurrence): green ash (Fraxinus pennsylvanica), cottonwood (*Populus deltoides*), boxelder (*Acer negundo*), mulberry (*Morus alba*), American elm (*Ulmus americana*), blacklocust (*Robinia pseudo-acacia*), catalpa (*Catalpa speciosa*), eastern redcedar (*Juniperus virginiana*) (Kaylor 1935) In Holt County cottonwood is the most common and dominates woodlot canopies. A lack of nurseries often forced landowners to use native plants gathered locally for most of these early plantations. Ash, cottonwood, boxelder, American elm, and eastern redcedar are all native trees found along permanent, nearby stream courses. Pines and other conifers with the exception of redcedar are conspicuous by their absence. Shelterbelts unlike woodlots were designed to have width ranging from three to 30 rows wide (20 to 180-feet), though most were 10 to 20 rows wide (60-to-120-feet) (Olson and Stoeckler 1935). Conceptually their length was modified to be at least one mile, but they often were reduced to one half-mile because not all landowners participated.

While many plantings observed in the rural Nebraska landscape have been intended for beauty and living enclosures, in Holt County they primarily fulfilled the need for fuel and wind protection. Wind reduction can be best accomplished by placing belts at right angles to the prevailing winds. In Holt County, this configuration would make the long axis of the belt following an east to west line. To maximize wind protection the belts moving from south to north were spaced every one-half to one-fourth mile apart; this practice, again, was modified by land ownership and the extent to which farmers cooperated in the program Such a broad agenda indicated by these factors coupled with the 70 years of tree planting experience on the Great Plains, led to a large and varied plant list which included shrubs, deciduous trees, conifers, native, and exotic plants.

Figure 9.6 A multi-species windbreak protects a field in Holt County, NE.

Horse High, Pig Tight, and Bull Strong: Hedgerows Presage Barbed Wire

Hedgerows and fencerows are distinctive rural landscape features. Their composition, form, size, location, and age have always reflected social and natural events. For example, the enclosure landscape of England dates from Parliament's enclosure acts of the 19th century (Pollard et al. 1974), yet many those of Normandy in France are older still. In America, the geometry of the public land survey system that had been gridded onto the Prairie Peninsula of Illinois and Indiana landscape was later adopted along the pre-barbed wire frontier of the 1850's, 1860's and 1870's.

Hedgerows have become an important ecological and cultural artifact in the landscape of southeastern Nebraska (Sutton 1985, Baltensperger 1987). Fencerows predominate in the rural Great Plains, and because they often contain a fence as the most dominant human feature, the term "fencerow" is used. Fencerows (Figure 9.7) are found along field margins, though the plants within them arrived as propagules through the agency of wind or animals. In the summer of 1980, I studied the hedgerow landscape of Pawnee County Nebraska (Sutton 1985), and later the landscape ecology of hedgerows and fencerows in Panama Township, Lancaster County. I recorded extant hedgerow locations, examined their plant communities, and surveyed Panama Township landowners about their attitudes and management produces.

Pawnee County: Hedgerows Enclose the Landscape

Pawnee County, located in southeastern Nebraska was settled before, during, and immediately after the Civil War. Prior to the Civil War, settlers spilling over from northeast Kansas were the first Euro-Americans to lay claim to land in Pawnee County, as did Daniel Freeman 20 miles to the west in Gage County, at what is now the Homestead National Monument of America. After the war, the area quickly became populated with many of Nebraska's most prosperous farms located on the rich bottomlands along the Nemaha River or eventually on the higher Prairie Hills in the northern and western portions of the county (Edwards 1876). (Figure 9.8).

Figure 9.7 Fencerows grow in narrow strips, but differ from hedges in being spontaneously generated and containing multiple species. Watercolor by the author.

Though bottomland settlers had adequate wood for fencing, they quickly imported the Osage-orange for use as a hedge. This was especially true on the uplands. Farmers were given strong economic reasons for planting hedges, since hedges had multiple benefits and were less expensive to create than fences.

Settlement of the prairie Peninsula in Illinois and Indiana spawned an earlier interest in tree propagation. The period horticultural literature devoted a great deal of space to the discussion of the various species of woody plant material useful for windbreaks, fuel, and hedging (Overman 1858, Warder, 1865 Nebraska Horticulture Society 1873, 1880). A typical list of hedge plants for Nebraska included: Osage-orange (Maclura pomifera), honeylocust (Gleditsia triacanthos), buckthorn *(Rhamnus cathartica)*, Russian mulberry *(Morus alba tatarica)*, and white willow *(Salix alba)*. The Osage-orange was probably the most widely planted species, but as later settlements moved north and west from Pawnee County it became less favored largely being replaced by the Honeylocust (Nebraska Horticulture Society 1877). Both the thornless mulberry and white willow, as well as, the slower growing buckthorn fell into disuse; the progeny of mulberry have naturalized in old wire fences, hedgerows, and floodplain forests.

Another widely used hedge plant was the honeylocust. It is native to the wooded lowland areas of the Great Plains and possesses long thorns rising from the stems (Pool 1951). Because the planter was more likely to get a local source of honeylocust plants, survival was better in comparison to the Osage orange at the northwestern limit of Osage-orange's range. The greatest difficulties with the honeylocust were its rapid reversion to a treelike form (unless hedged) and destruction of its roots by gophers (Nebraska Horticulture Society 1877).

Cheaply produced barbwire widely available in the 1880s, spelled the demise of hedge planting and maintenance though not necessarily of the hedges themselves. Barbed wire required less labor to maintain, and the abundant supply of rot resistant Osage-orange could be used for posts. Mr. Greg, a Saunders County, Nebraska farmer expressed the opinion of the day when it came to the continued use of hedging even the Osage orange:

Figure 9.8 Extant Hedges in Clay Township, Pawnee County, NE, in 1979.

"I have some experience in hedge growing– The Osage – and the longer I have done it the less faith I have in it . . . I came to the conclusion that as far as pasture is concerned it is not a success with me. It makes a good windbreak but it takes up a good deal of ground on each side, and I really think we shall come to use the wire fence" (Nebraska Horticulture Society 1880, p. 163.)

The regular care of hundreds of miles of hedge was suspended when farmers simply tacked on the new more efficient barbed wire to the existing hedge plants, or bounded new fields without the benefit of hedge enclosures. The result, in the case of Osage-orange and the honeylocust, was that hedges reverted to trees and the landscape slowly began to change.

The Nebraska Horticulture Society proceedings for 1880, estimated 600 miles of hedge existed in Pawnee County (Nebraska horticulture Society 1880), but with no accurate record of its distribution. In 1982, sets of aerial photographs were reviewed. One set taken in the fall of 1940, reveal 588 miles of hedge; the other taken in the fall of 1979, reveal that the amount had dwindled to 391 miles. By 2017, I tallied only 290 miles (Figure 9.9). In 1880, at the same time barbed wire was generally introduced, Pawnee County reached its maximum hedge mileage. Even after the introduction of barbwire, some farmers may have continued to plant a few hedges and nonetheless, existing hedges used to control stock were not removed -- wire was simply stapled to them. Therefore, hedges revealed in the 1940 aerial photographs should closely approximate the original placement and number of hedges. The decline of hedgerow mileage started with the drought of the 1930's. Some counties west of Pawnee County lost hedgerows to the drifts of topsoil that were left as a calling card of the "Dust Bowl". In Pawnee County, as pictured on the 1940 aerial photographs, the declining hedgerows are readily visible on the dry, south-facing slopes. In 1940, field size had not increased to the point that intentional hedge removal was common, although some harvesting of fuel and fencepost continued to take place. Farmers found that large overgrown hedgerows were simply too hard to remove with the available machinery and tools.

Figure 9.9 Hedgerow removal along a county road in Pawnee County.

That all changed following World War II. Large farms led to land consolidation (Chapter 6) and elimination of division line hedges between separate farms. Larger fields became readily tillable by large machines available after the war. Pasturage was converted to cropland as horses became obsolete. These are also some of the same social and economic forces that currently appear to be affecting British hedgerows (Teeter 1970, Hooper 1974). At the present rate of removal mileage in Pawnee County is trending to 200 miles with the loss of a hedgerow-dominated landscape.

Configuration of hedges can be summarized as follows: the length of the hedges planted ranged from 1/8 to one mile in length with a large portion being one-half mile; the enclosed area ranged from 10 to 640-acres, but the bulk enclosed 40 to 80-acres. Overgrown Osage orange hedges now visually divide the landscape into more or less rectilinear parcels along north to south and east to west property or field boundaries. Hedges were originally maintained an optimum height of five to six-feet, and were allowed to spread more than 4-feet at their base. This served to enclose the livestock but did not obstruct view. Upon reversion to treelike growth however, the view to the distant surroundings was cut off. Roads with hedges on both sides grew into tunnels and added a strong spatial enclosure. This linear feature has diminished where Osage-orange naturalizes and invades poorly managed pastures thereby, creating a savannah-like landscape.

Hedgerows as Anthropogenic Plant Communities: Pawnee & Lancaster Counties

Landscape springs from the synthesis of humans and nature and landscape ecology tries to understand the reality of a landscape as determined by the human nature interaction (Golley 1987; Zonneveld 1989; Golley 1990). Landscape as a coherent unit often results from the directed self-conscious or repetitive unconscious endeavors of humans and nature. Focusing on human created hedgerow and the spontaneous fencerow, I investigated Pawnee and Lancaster Counties' rural landscapes (Figure 9.10) (Sutton 1982 and Sutton 1992). My objective was to analyze and interpret landscape form as result of human activity (regulatory and control domain) within the context of natural parameters, (process domain) and those studies can be seen as a snapshot of larger, complex events in which humans create landscape out of nature.

Figure 9.10 A hedgerow in Southern Lancaster County. Watercolor by the author.

Specifically, in Lancaster County, Panama Township, I investigated technical land management practices, which over time may directly affect a plant community. Finally, at the specific and measurable level, I sought to link the prevalent human attitudes described in specific regulatory and control (disturbance) routines and to further tie those management activities concretely to plant composition and structure. The study's assumptions were: 1) humans act upon their attitudes; 2) repetitive minor disturbances of nature equate with cultural disturbances; 3) plant composition and structure become artifacts of landscape.

Understanding the structure and function of hedgerows has gained the attention of European and North American researchers working in the area of landscape ecology (Forman and Baudry 1984; Forman and Godron 1986; Burel and Baudry 1990; Barrett and Bohlen 1991; Fritz 1991a; 1991b). Petrides (1943) was one of the first in North America to discern the interaction between hedgerows as wildlife habitat. Hedgerows have been studied for decades by European ecologists as unique anthropogenic communities (Bates 1937; Moore et al. 1967; Pollard and Relton 1970; Pollard et al. 1974; Hooper 1976; Willmot 1987). Hedgerow community composition has been both anthropogenic and adventive, drawing indigenous and naturalized species from the surrounding landscape. Community represents a powerful ecological concept because plant communities provide structure, often control ecological functions, reflect gradient changes in the environment, and provide habitat for animals (including people). Conversely, if one knows about a plant community, then one can infer ecological functions, gradients, and interactions (Chapter 5). The concept of community is basic to future probing of landscape structure and function, and should lead to more integrated management of landscapes.

The change to barbed wire for enclosure affects the types of plant materials found in hedges. Routine and time-consuming trimming and plashing, as well as, the removal of undesirable plants ceased with addition of barbed wire. Hedges were attractive places for small mammals and birds and they continued to be sources for the introduction of new plants both native and naturalized. Humans supplied the structure, natural forces the action. To assess the plant diversity in these human induced communities in 1980, I sampled 10 dispersed Pawnee County hedgerows, and in 1990 all hedgerows and fencerows in a portion of Panama Township, Lancaster County. Species presence for each of these 10 hedgerows was determined by walking four, 25-foot transects, recording the occurrence of associated woody plant species In Lancaster County. All hedgerows and fencerows were sampled.

Hackberry (*Celtis occidentalis*) occurred in 100 percent of the Pawnee hedgerows and 75 percent of their transects. Birds, ready consumers of hackberry fruits, enhanced distribution of its seeds in the hedgerow niche. Birds and small mammals also dispersed the fruits of 12 of the most common plants in Pawnee County hedgerows. Two others are dispersed by wind. White mulberry or Russian Mulberry (*Morus alba tatarica*) and Siberian (*Ulmus pumila*), are exotic introductions now naturalized in 80 percent and 60 percent of the transects respectively. Findings were similar in Lancaster County fence rows and hedgerows.

What might the be the role of managing these anthropocentric landscape structures, and were there patterns to plant distributions? Forman and Godron (1986:135) have noted, "Hedgerow vegetation is exceptionally varied, primarily because of differences in hedgerow origin and management." They have also determined other factors come into play such as: 1) the relative importance of trees and shrubs, 2) species present, 3) species dominance and co-dominance, 4) thorniness, 5) physical dimensions 6) presence of human artifacts as swales, walls, or fences. Natural fencerows and purposefully planted hedgerows appear to harbor amalgams of native and naturalized woody plants. Yet, because the local biological, edaphic, and climatic regime with its restrictive moisture gradient disfavors ready growth of woody plants, hedgerows, and fencerows are an excellent place to study changes in woody plant composition and distribution at the margin of their viability.

Closely allied and maybe inseparable from these ecological factors, are those of human actions and interactions within their "agro-cultural" context. For example, the once fire-dominated prairie now converted to cropland, isolates woody plant groups. Management practices such as cutting, mowing, burning, herbicide application, or pruning should radically alter hedgerows and fencerows. Hedgerows and fencerows are strikingly visible plant masses in the space of Great Plains and therefore, provide a dominant visual entity for the study of anthropogenic links between landscape, culture, and structure.

The Lancaster County study had several objectives: 1) describe, interpret, and discuss the woody plant composition and structure patterns, as influenced by ecological and anthropogenic factors, 2) Assess manager/owner attitudes toward the hedgerow/fence landscape as the wider socio-cultural context for ecological and anthropogenic factors, and 3) examine possible links from attitude to management and plant composition and 4) establish a baseline record in time and space of the woody species within several hedgerows and fencerows for future research. It was hypothesized in 1990, approximately 110 to 120-years after their establishment, woody plant species present their density and arrangement would be different in hedgerows and fencerows. For example, Osage-orange influences microclimate differently from fencerows; it was predicted more mesic species and a greater number of interior woodland species associated with it. However, an older, established fencerow of various trees and shrubs might also provide similar microenvironment. Because many of the naturalized and native woody shrubs vigorously regenerate, the eventual loss of Osage-orange protection may lead a hedgerow to the same species composition and structure, as that of a fencerow. However, this last question would need years of plant succession to become more clearly measurable. Furthermore, it was hypothesized that differing management practices between owners in the case of hedges, would result in differences in woody plant structure and composition, and that any management differences may be linked to the owner's attitude toward hedges.

Fencerows are spontaneous and visually patchy (Figure 8.7) and based on observations in the Panama Township study area and elsewhere, fencerows may be more susceptible to ongoing, casual woody plant removal. On the other hand, the dominance of Osage-orange tends to make the hedgerow appear more homogeneous, but results showed species composition, and different densities in fencerows and hedgerows. As might be expected, a wider variation occurred as the species became more rare. Many of the species in both hedgerows and fencerows are members of the deciduous woodland, and reside both as understory and transition between woodland and prairie, or as old-field succession constituents (Bazzaz 1968). Weaver (1965) lists Eastern redcedar and honey-locust as members of the deciduous woodland accompanying shrubs into open areas. Missouri gooseberry (*Ribes missouriense*) and wild raspberry (*Rubus ideaus*), along with woodbine (*Parthenocissus vitacea*), poison-ivy (*Toxicodendron radicans*), riverbank grape (*Vitis riparia*), American plum,(*Prunus americana*), and chokecherry (*Prunus virginiana*) readily inhabit both hedgerows and fencerows. The upland hedgerows of Panama Township, however, are devoid of about half of the typical shrub complement of the deciduous forest. One specimen of coralberry (*Symphoricarpos orbiculatus*),was found, while none were found of Bittersweet (*Celastrus scandens*) and prickly-ash (*Zanthozylum americanum*). Bittersweet has been nearly extirpated from many cropland borders because of its susceptibility to the herbicide, 2,4-D. The upland hedgerows may be distant and disconnected enough from woodlands to prohibit propagule flows.

Because the hedgerow and fencerow create snowdrifts, excess moisture is deposited in and along them (Jenson 1954; Frank et al. 1976; Lyles 1976; Rollin 1983). This, however, is short-lived, intermittent and more than offset by evapo-transpiration. Still, the blockage of wind and disturbance of a dense sod layer, consequently by shade, particularly in hedgerows, offers the chance for initial stages of the succession. When a stream develops a floodplain with wide protecting banks, large fruits such as those of black walnut (*Juglans nigra*), hazelnut (*Corylus americana*), bur oak (*Quercus macrocarpa*), and others are carried up stream by various animals, especially timber squirrels. Animal vectors moving fruits and seeds, especially squirrels were numerous in hedgerows, but because no ready source of large fruits is widely available, these plants (e.g., bur oak) have not appeared. An exception was sample unit where three mature, human-planted walnuts along a hedge have not spread, probably because of unfavorable growing conditions. Many of the less easily dispersed species, large-fruits (autochores), could not be found. This most likely points to the young successional stage of hedgerows and fencerows because these types of fruit are not usually associated with pioneer species (Huston and Smith 1987). The opposite is true of Osage-orange; since its introduction, squirrels and gravity keep new seedlings in close proximity to fruiting trees.

While it is not surprising that fencerows and hedgerows are somewhat different with regards to species composition, density, and structure, it is interesting that analysis showed other strong similarities with a few noted exceptions. All hedgerows and some fencerow woody plant distribution patterns appeared as clusters. This can be explained given the biology of major portion of the woody plants. One would expect fruit dispersal by birds (Smith 1975) to be clustered closely with parent-food source. McDonnell and Stiles (1983) noted what they called "recruitment foci," which received significantly more seed input and thus, lead to a clustered or nucleated spatial structure (Yarranton and Morrison 1974). Each environment, hedgerow or fencerow, can be thought to be limited in biomass by competition for scarce water resources. The relatively high stress environment, and young age (i.e., 1860-1880)) of Great Plains hedgerows would also account for some variance in associated species.

A large number of constituent wind-dispersed seeds (anemochores) would be expected because prairie or open environments, favor wind seed dispersion. This does not seem true for woody plants dispersed by wind; the study found only six anemochores of the 33 total species. Only five hedgerow species were wind dispersed, and they represented a small fraction of the total number of individuals.

However, because of a severe stress gradient, dispersal of plants in Panama Township (and perhaps the Great Plains), hedgerows maybe subject to dispersal rates more in line with that of English snails (Cammeron, Down, and Pannett 1980). Panama Township hedgerows also seems to match the successional models of Huston and Smith (1987), where "the effect of water stress, modeled ... is to slow growth rates and overall rate of successional replacement." They also noted on their computer simulations, "slower build up of biomass ... and higher species diversity."

Each hedgerow or fencerow has its own unique developmental and environmental histories, and hence, are more similar within themselves than between other hedgerows or fencerows, and especially affected by management. Several authors studying birds have made reference to the importance not only of plant composition and structure, but also management of the hedgerow (Linehan 1957; Moore, Hooper and Davis 1967; Murton and Westwood 1974; Wilmot 1980; Arnold 1983; Best 1983; Rands 1983; Shalaway 1983). Management practices can radically alter structure and species composition in hedgerows and fencerows (Helliwell 1975). Consideration of management practices, (or the lack of them), immediately brings us face to face with the impact of human beings. Since hedgerows are anthropogenic, one can approach the concept of plant community where "man [is] a maker of plant communities" (Whitney and Adams 1980). They used several community descriptors, such as species diversity and dominance (importance value) in concert with socio-economic factors to define clear anthropogenic plant communities in Akron, OH.

Management is most likely a disturbance of some type, and may be a primary cause of differences in species composition (Denslow 1980; Noble and Slayter 1980), between hedgerows and fencerows. Management activities importantly have created differing assemblages and structure in hedgerows. The unusual results, indicating little interaction between management and vegetation type (hedgerow or fencerow) when examining species richness, can be explained by the large number of managed hedgerows being grazed and thus, reducing woody species through trampling or browsing. The degree and type of change brought about by differing management activities cannot be addressed in this study because all types of management were pooled when analyzed. Still, there is a noticeable difference in species composition and density between grazed hedgerows and those harvested for posts.

The composition, form, size, location, age, and management of hedges all reflect both social and natural events. Hedgerows occur in the landscape because of human activity, but are subject to natural and social forces. Timing, placement, and type of management add other factors impacting the plant abundance and species content of a hedgerow. Where management is cyclic, however, and more or less predictable, one would expect the hedgerow to more closely resemble natural communities, particularly one with periodic disturbance, such as found at the Vijfheerenlanden willow coppice community in Holland (Dijst et al. 1981).

Landscapes and the plant communities, of which they are comprised, are either natural or anthropogenic. The differences are often subtle but are strongly influenced by management of organisms over space and time The Panama Township study, showed a weak but persistent linkage between attitude, management, and woody plant community structure in a rural landscape. More study material from a wider area could help to strengthen our understanding.

That humans have an impact on their surroundings is not doubted, but the quantity and quality of that impact is largely unknown. The Lancaster County hedgerow study has a number of assumptions and the conclusions are most likely valid for the small segment of a rural landscape, like Panama Township. However, it attempted to quantify a much proclaimed, but poorly documented area of landscape ecology, namely humans and culture, as an ecological force in making landscape. Frequent, repetitive management activities regulate nature into stable or more predictable landscape than might have been predicted.

Relict Rural Plantings: Cultural Landscape Artifacts

Any description and understanding of a cultural landscape must explain the role of plants—both natural and anthropogenic. It begs the questions: Do plants reflect the agency of mankind? Do they indicate a cultural response to the environment? Do they show learning and adaptation and failure and abandonment? In 2017, roughly 150-years of tree-planting experience in eastern Nebraska have resulted in a rural landscape mosaic of spaces and masses of fields and trees. These plantings often provide significant clues as to past land uses within a given farmstead or district. A farmstead dwelling and its accompanying ornamental garden, often undergo alteration (Watts 1963); new houses are occasionally built on old sites and these changes may be reflected in the plantings. The old allee' may lead to the door of a new ranch house or the blank wall of an older home which has had its front door removed (Welsch 1979).

The psychological benefits of spatial enclosure afforded by plants may have been as important as the physical protection (Shelford 1944 p. 135-40). Many settlers' lack of "something to hide behind," drove many nearly mad from the ubiquitous wind, like Rolvaag's character, Beret, in his novel, *Giants in the Earth* (Rolvaag 1929 p. 29). Tree masses brought psychological relief as well as firewood, fence posts, and lumber. A livable Nebraska landscape emblifies the Great Plains landscape and still requires tree plantings. Today, we still need the protection of trees for farms, rural acreages, schools and churches, and small towns. And interestingly we still are learning; a few new additions to the planting palette like Japanese larch, lacebark pine, and black spruce have made tentative appearances and different configurations of windbreaks and planting method have evolved, native trees with better adaptations are moved from other parts of the Great Plains (Bagley and Sutton, 2002).

In an environment hostile to trees, their role in the cultural landscape is significant everywhere and often of greater importance than the more widely studied habitation structures. Tree plantings, especially of coniferous trees, were not confined to the function of simple barriers to Great Plains' winds, but took on some relatively sophisticated design forms referred to as the allee' and bosque. They are man-made though with one important difference: plants respond to the unique regional physical environment, creating an artifact that is the result of interplay between natural forces and man-made form. An analysis of those plantings shows they are as much a part of the cultural landscape structure as barns and houses. Plantings and their integrations and adaptations into the landscape thus, give insight into the changing human and land use patterns of an entire region. In 2017, pioneer plantings were reaching the limits of their lifespan and will soon no longer be there to remind us of their (and our) planted pioneer heritage.

The visual impact of rural planting relicts can change overtime because of political or ecological events (Table 9.1). Timber claims and Kincaid plantings can be distinguished from each other, and from hedges, allees', and bosques on the basis of their shape, size, tree age, and species composition.

Why does all this detailed information presented here matter? First, landscape plantings embody both time and space. Understanding their complete story requires that one must look and not only perceive the vista among the unifying context, but also identify that context and conger up the past. One must also ask, why do things appear as they do? And this is true for both the current as well as historical changes. Secondly, very few people have analyzed or even described the habitat of the ordinary rural citizen or yeoman farmer. References and commentary nearly always refer to that thin veneer of culture that records itself in an often self-conscious, laudatory way. In this chapter, I have described a portion of the cultural landscape of the common man that has become the human and planted face of the Great Plains.

Furthermore, I suggest that the Great Plains landscape as a place and image appears as it does largely due to the contest between human desires and nature's constraints. Presently, its inhabitants show the greatest threat to the cultural, ecological, and visual mosaic that our pioneer ancestors initiated. Large-scale farming has begun to erode the existing patterns in these rural landscapes. In Holt County, the boom of center pivot irrigation sweeps the land, while other areas succumb to fencerow-to-fencerow planting encouraged by short-sighted political rhetoric, farm consolidation, and local tax burdens. The danger is not so much in change itself, since the rural landscape is and has always been a product of change by the introduction of those intent into events. Rather the speed and scale of change, and the impoverishment of what we're able to see of how humans have interacted with the rural Great Plains.

Table 9.1 Summary of Rural Planting Relicts in the Eastern Nebraska Landscape

Study Location	Period	Plants	Intent	Status	Patterns & Forms	Environmental Features
Otoe County						
Ornamental Conifers	1860-1890	8 species	Beautification	2 exotic spp. gone	Allees', Bosques	Original range modified by environment
Pawnee County						
Hedgerows	1855-1880	6 species	Live Fencing	Plant community;	Linear, 1/2 to 1-mile	Most common on upland settled before 1880
				No longer plashed & hedged;	Enclosing 40-80 acres	
				3 exotics naturalized;		
				Extensive removal		
Lancaster County						
Hedgerows	1860-1890	Osage-orange	Live Fencing	Some removal	Patchy recruitment focii	Management affects biomass
Fencerows			Field Boundary	Some removal	Patchy recruitment focii	Anthropogenic
						Animal vectors disperse plants
Holt County						
Timber Claims	1872-1893	8 species	Land Disposal	Forest Habitat evolved	Rectangular blocks	Forest Habitat evolved
			Fuel	Some removal	4-10 acres	Some removal
Kincaid Claims	1904-1914	10 species	Land Disposal	Some removal		Some removal
Shelter Belts	1933-1941	34 species	Wind & Soil	Some removal	Linear, 1/2-1-mile long	Aerodynamic in cross-section;
			Protection			Combined trees, conifers & shrubs;
			Employment			Plants matched to site environment

Settings rendered in plants affect its citizens' sensitivities, moral values, beliefs, and even citizenship (See Morton's quote at the beginning of this chapter.) If tomorrow humans were removed from the Great Plains and nature left again to run an unbridled course, the landscape would continue to change slowly, but, it now would contain new plants in new habitats. It has been and remains a garden on contested ground.

Further Reading

Bagley, W. T and R. K. Sutton (2002) *Woody Plants of the Northern and Central Prairies* Caldwell, NJ: Blackburn Press

Card, F. (1897) Hints on landscape gardening. *Nebraska State Horticultural Society*. 28:84-92.

Cather, W. (1954) *My Antonia'* Houghton Mifflin; New York

Clements, F (1937) *Climate and Life on the Great Plains*. Supplemental Publication 24 Carnegie Institute. Washington D.C.

Cronon, W., 2009. *Nature's Metropolis: Chicago and the Great West*. WW Norton & Company.

Dale E. C. (1948) Wood and water, the twin problems of the pioneer. *Nebraska History Quarterly* 34(2) Summer 87-104.

Downing, A. J. (1859) *The Theory and Practice of Landscape Gardening*. Funk and Wagnalls: NY

Droze, W. H. (1977) *Trees, Prairies and People: A History of Tree Planting in the Plains States*. Texas Women's University: Denton TX.

Edwards, J. (1876) *Centennial history of Pawnee County, Nebraska*. Hassler: Pawnee City, NE.

Ferber, A. E. (1964) What happened to the shelterbelt? *Soil Conservation* 32 February: 160-163.

Freeman, J. F. (2008) *High Plains Horticulture: A History*. University of Colorado Press: Boulder

Finley, R and E. M. Scott (1940) Great Lakes to Gulf profile of dispersed dwelling types. *Geographical Review* 30:412-419.

Hedrick, V. (1950) *A history of Horticulture in America to 1860*. Oxford: New York.

Hooper, M. (1974) Hedgerow removal. *Biologist* 21 September-October:81-86.

Jackson, J. B. (1966) The New American countryside: An engineered environment. *Landscape* 16:16-20.

Jackson, J. B. (1970) The westward moving house. In, E. Zube (ed.), *Landscapes: Selected writings of J. B. Jackson*. UMass Press: Amherst.

Jenkins, M. (1918) Make farm homes attractive. *The Nebraska Ruralist*. 52(5)March 1: 13-18.

Kaul, R (1975) **Vegetation of Nebraska Circa 1850**. Conservation and Survey Division Map. University of Nebraska: Lincoln.

Kaylor, C (1935) Surveys of past plantings. In, *Possibilities of the Shelterbelt Planting in the Plains Region. USDA –Forest Service* pp 39-48.

Kniffen, F. (1965) Folk housing: Key to diffusion. *Annals Assoc. of American Geographers*. 55:549-577.

Lewis, P. (1972) Common house, Cultural spoor. *Landscape* 19(2) 1-18.

Maxwell, E. (1951) Twenty-five years of Clary-McNary tree distribution. EXT Circ. 1728 University of Nebraska: Lincoln.

McIntosh, C. B. (1975) Use and abuse of the Timber Culture Act. *Annals of the Association of American Geographers* 65 September:347-365.

Meredith, M. (1951) The importance of fences to the American pioneer. *Nebraska History*. XXXII:94-107/

Nebraska State Horticultural Society Proceedings (1872) Vol 3.

Nebraska State Horticultural Society Proceedings (1873) Vol 4.

Nebraska State Horticultural Society Proceedings (1877) Vol 8:78-79.

Nebraska State Horticultural Society Proceedings (1880) Vol 11.

Nebraska State Horticultural Society (1901) The Platte Cedar. Bulletin NO. 5 Lincoln, NE.

Olson, D. and J Stoeckler. (1935) The proposed tree plantations—Their establishment and management. In, *Possibilities of the Shelterbelt Planting in the Plains Region*. USDA –Forest Service pp 15-28.

Overman, C. (1858) *Hedge grower's Manual*. Lanphir and Conner: Springfield IL.

Pool, R. (1951) Handbook of Nebraska Bull. No. 32 trees. Nebraska Conservation & Survey Lincoln, NE.

Powell, E. (1900) *Hedges, Windbreaks, Shelters and Live ences*. Orange-Judd: New York.

Reardon, S and D. Dickman. (1977) Cornbelt Conifers. *American Forests* 83(8)8-10.

Riedesel, G (1980) The geography of rural Saunders County cemeteries from 1859. *Nebraska History* 61 Summer 215-228.

Riley, Robert B. 2015 *The Camaro in the Pasture*. U of Virginia Press: Charlottesville

Rolvaag, O. E. (1927) *Giants in the Earth*. Harper: New York.

Scanlon, M (1981) Biogeography of forest plants in the prairie-forest ecotone in western Minnesota. In, *Forest island dynamics in Man-dominated landscapes*. R Burgess and D. Sharpe (eds) 97-124.

Shelford, V (1944) Deciduous forest man and the grassland fauna. *Science* 100 August 18:135-140.

Smith, J. and J. Perino. (1981) Osage orange (*Maclura pomifera*): History and economic uses. *Economic Botany* (35) January 24-31.

Sutton, R.K. (1977) The round peg in the square hole: Center pivot irrigation in the Nebraska landscape." *Landscape* Vol. 22(1): 3-10.

Sutton, R.K. (1982) "The image of a garden: vernacular conifer plantings in Otoe County, Nebraska" *Pioneer America* (14) Winter:93-113.

Sutton, R. K. (1985). Relict Rural Plantings in Eastern Nebraska. *Landscape Journal*, 4(2): 106-115. Retrieved from http://www.jstor.org/stable/43323107

Sutton, R. K. (1992) Landscape ecology of hedgerows and fencerows in Panama Township, Lancaster County, Nebraska. *Great Plains Research*, pp. 223-254.

Teather, E. (1970) The hedgerow: An analysis of a changing landscape feature. *Geography* 55 April:146-155.

USDA (1925) Tree distribution under the Kincaid Act of 1904/ Misc. Circular 16 Washington DC.

Warder, J. (1865) *Hedges and Evergreens*. Orange-Judd: New York.

Watson, D. (1978) Shade and ornamental trees in the Nineteenth Century northeastern United States. PhD. Dissertation University of Illinois.

Watts, M. (1963) *Reading the landscape*. McMillan: New York.

Welsch, R. (1979) Front Door, Back Door. *Natural History* 8(6)76-83.

Welsch, R. (1982) *Of Trees and Dreams: The Fiction, Fact, and Folklore of Tree-Planting on the Northern Plains*. Lincoln: Nebraska Forest Service

Wessel, T. (1967) Prologue to the shelterbelt, 1870-1934. *Journal of the West* 6, December No1-4:119-134.

Westgate, V. (1905) Ornamenting the farm home. *Nebraska State Horticultural Society* 31:239-241.

Winberry, J. (1979) The Osage orange, a botanical artifact. *Pioneer America* 2 August: 1934-141.

Zelinsky, W. (1959) Fences and Walls. *Landscape* 8:3.

10 Placing Middleground: Cather's Divide Landscape

> "Middleground . . . is most critical. Here the linkage between parts of the landscape may be seen. . . . The middleground aspect can often best show whether man-made changes rest easily or uneasily on the landscape. . . Middlegrounds are critical not only because they tend to dominate the view, but also because they may include large acreages." –Burton Litton

Introduction

In the middle distance, a large yellow front-end loader slowly demolishes and piles up an old farmhouse. A century ago it may have winked at a gaily painted barn across the road, but now it falls prey to the sweep of the pivot (Figure 10.1).

It is early June and unseasonably wet and cool. Center pivots pause motionless in the young corn. Low-hanging clouds truncate my view south off the Divide and the wind spits a few raindrops, forcing me into my jacket.

I had pulled to the side of Nebraska Highway 4 for a better look across this undistinguished, yet famous landscape. Before me lies the Divide, a quintessential prairie landscape located just 30 miles due north of the geographical center of the contiguous 48 states. While the Divide flattens on top, it is still a major ridge three to 10 miles wide stretching about 70 miles east to west, separating the Blue, Platte and Republican River drainages in South Central Nebraska.

A treeless transition zone of tallgrass to mixed prairie, the Divide is now in corn and soybeans on its most level parts and patches of pasture in the rougher terrain. Along its broad crest rainwater basins once dotted the landscape, but now filled and farmed, they've become mostly shallow depressions in corn and beans. To the south, hidden behind the low clouds several wooded streams dissect the Divide's slope and lead down to the Republican River.

The Oregon Trail parallels the Divide's northern edge. In 1879, some four years before the nine-year-old Willa Cather arrived on the divide, Per Anderbery of Sweden and Franklin Sutton of Ohio, my father's grandparents, arrived by train then traveled by wagon to settle barely 20 miles to the northwest of my mid-morning stop. This Divide landscape provides the setting for Cather's prairie novels, and for me, reading those novels helps me to begin to understand the landscape of my ancestors and the roots of a place.

Yet, I don't believe Cather can be read by today's resident, and especially by the tourist without a concordance, and in this case that concordance is the landscape itself. The contemporary landscape of Webster County offers the tourist an impression vastly different from what Cather immortalized in her Prairie novels in the early 20th century. The Willa Cather Foundation (WCF) in Red Cloud, NE, has created an official Cather Tour and guide (Figure 10.2) which has evolved over a thirty-year period. It spotlights key sites impacting her novels and tersely and tangentially talks about the landscape milieu of the late 19th and early 20th centuries.

To link Cather and the Divide as it now appears, I'll begin with descriptions of the divide landscape from her novels. Next, I will discuss selected views seen along the route of the official Cather sites tour, the problem of the middleground, and finally, I will suggest within this framework ways for interpreting and understanding the tour.

Figure 10.1 Clearing the Divide in Webster County, NE

Cather's Novels on the Divide

Geography, history, and landscape have traditionally resulted in powerful literary themes (Tuan 1978). The rural Wessex landscape in 19th-century England is embodied in Hardy's *Tess D'Urbervilles*, as is Faulkner's Mississippi in *The Sound and the Fury*. These novelists' evocations of landscape settings have frozen those places in time as surely as a photograph. When millions of us have read descriptions of these places, those places often assume a reality within our minds equal to or greater than the real landscape. David Lowenthal (1975) has written, "the past gains further weight because we conceive of places not only as we ourselves see them but also as we have heard and read about them." Because of Cather's stature as a novelist and because of her use of the landscape as an intrinsic element (some might say character) in her stories, the specific rural landscape of Webster County, Nebraska assumes national and international importance as an artifact of the American pioneer.

Willa Cather's prairie novels (*O Pioneers!* 1913, *Song of the Lark* 1915, *My Ántonia* 1918, *One of Ours* 1922, *A Lost Lady* 1923, and *Lucy Gayheart* 1935) deal with the people on the small stretch of the Great Plains, particularly the experience of settling the area. Charlotte Rohrbach has noted that Cather's description of landscape is accurate enough to label Cather a historian as well as a novelist (Rohrbach 1976).

My Ántonia and *O Pioneers!* plus the other novels, offer rich descriptions of the prairie landscape often quoted nostalgically today as a lament on the passing of that landscape:

From *My Ántonia*:

> All of those same afternoons were the same, but I never got used to them. As far as we could see the miles of copper red grass were drenched in sunlight that was stronger and fiercer than at any other time of the day. The blonde cornfields were red-gold, the haystacks turned rosy and threw long shadows. The whole prairie was like a bush that burned and was not consumed (p. 44).

And elsewhere:

> As I looked about me I felt grass was the country, as the water is the sea. The red of the grass made all the great prairie the color of wine stains, or certain seaweeds when they were first washed up. And there was so much motion in it; the whole country somehow seem to be running (p. 16).

The protagonists in Cather's historical dramas become the immigrants and the prairie landscape itself. This is a key theme of Cather (Danielson 1969). Human character molded by the landscape and the landscape in turn was changed by the humans, their tools-- the plow, the fence, the windmill, and the tree—and a human dream: the garden (Randall 1960, Lauerman 1972, Sutton 1985). Cather plays on this theme when she acknowledges and describes an emerging cultural landscape.

From *O Pioneers!*:

> The homesteads were few and far apart; here and there a windmill gaunt against the sky, a sod house crouching in a low hollow. But the great fact was the land itself . . . [It] seemed to overwhelm the little beginnings of human society that struggled in its somber wastes (p. 15).

Cather's descriptions of this cultural landscape fall into two main categories: the field and the garden. J. B. Jackson (1980), in his essay "Nearer than Eden", calls these categories archetypes and writes, "the garden is where we have to be." Lucy Schneider (1967), echoes this thought, pointing out Cather's unique ability to imbue her garden and orchard settings with a creative and personal quality.

From *Lucy Gayheart*:

> All afternoon Lucy lay in the sun under a low-branching apple tree on the dry fawn colored grass. The orchard covered about 3 acres and sloped uphill. From the far end, where she was laying, Lucy looked down through the rows of knotty twisted trees . . . The orchard had been neglected for years. . . There is something comforting to the heart in the shapes of old trees that have been left to grow their own way. (p. 154)

From *My Ántonia*:

> There was the deepest peace in that orchard. It was surrounded by a triple enclosure: the wire fence, the hedge of thorny locusts, the mulberry hedge, which kept out the hot winds of summer and held fast to the protecting snows of winter. The hedges were so tall that we could see nothing but the blue sky above them, neither the barn roof nor the windmill. (p. 384)

From *One of Ours*:

> Claude took a stick and drew a square in the sand; there, to begin with, was the house and farmyard;, there was the big pasture with Lovely Creek flowing through it; there were the wheat and the cornfields, the timber claim, more wheat and corn, more pastures (p. 389).

The gardens and orchards planted by the settlers are mostly gone now. Excepting for cemeteries those human landscape settings have been replaced by corn and soybean fields; even some pasture has been converted to crops. The industrial agriculture model highlighted in Chapter 7 now covers most of the Divide and Webster County bolstered by the desire for irrigation on a scale unimagined in Cather's time.

Reading the Landscape on the Cather Sites Tour

Many of the points along the rural Cather tour contain elements of the cultural landscape, for example, conserved sites. Others are simply points at which an attempt is made to interpret the landscape presented in the foreground or relate some history. They are all, however, embedded in a working, functional, agricultural landscape. The major interpretive tool for the tour is a WCF brochure. Its tour has been reproduced on Nebraska Department of Roads Webster County map. (10.2) and is largely taken from work by Mildred Bennett and Charlotte Rohrbach and the narrative on the Cather thematic group by David Murphy and Ann Billesbach.

Today the settler's dugouts and soddies are gone and their progeny—large farmhouses and barns—have burned, been abandoned or, as I described in the chapter's opening, are being swept from the middleground by the center pivot. The prairie expanse has been pieced and plotted into corn, beans, and pasture and the relatively large Cather Memorial prairie (Figure 10.3) lies south of the Republican River (Figures 10.4 and 10.5) is the only place to get a sense of its expanse.

Because the tourist interested in following the map to Cather's settings cannot help but compare the landscape of the novels with an extant, dynamic reality, anomalies confront the viewer most often in the middleground. Not enough space exists in this chapter to list step-by-step the Cather tour sites and to provide interpretations. That would be more appropriate as an interpretive design project, but what follow are two main examples.

Willa Cather Memorial Prairie and the Republican River

Starting the Cather rural tour at Willa Cather Memorial Prairie importantly sets the baseline for how this landscape appeared when settled. Managed by the WCF, invasive tree stands have been reduced and the empty middleground stretches in front of the observer.

As one looks over the Republican River, the middleground is floodplain forest (Figures 10.4 and 10.5). In the period of the prairie novels one would have been able to see several miles north to Red Cloud as well as up and down the valley. Originally one could see to and from the river over the top of the extensive riparian wetlands. As a result of the flood of 1935, the Corps of Engineers built a reservoir 45 miles upstream leaving only the natural scouring action of the river. That intervention and the halt to prairie fires have allowed succession of a closed canopy forest in the floodplain. What was once a distant vista is now experienced as a middleground forest

Once Open Spaces Now Cluttered But Devoid of Humans

Scatterings of naturalized Russian mulberry, and Siberian elm along with the aggressive native eastern redcedar, now invade and inhabit pastures, prairie patches, and open spaces. These Eurasian trees, planted for windbreaks (Chapter 9) now protected from fire, clutter middleground open spaces. They distract the viewer from its connecting qualities to the panoramic views from the divide (Figure 10.6). While scattered trees in the middleground present a problem, larger groupings in the creek bottoms and windbreaks provide enough mass to partition the landscape on an appropriate scale. Meanwhile, center pivot irrigation arms lurk everywhere on the Divide (Figure 10.7) as a type of mechanization that Cather would have shunned (Schneider 1967). Webster County is a depopulated area having reached its peak population of 12,008 in 1910 (Cooper-Skjelver 1980). In 2016 it is nearer to 3,800 with 60 percent living in the villages and towns. For example, in the 36 mi.^{2} of Catherton Township in 1890, there were slightly over 70 dwellings, in 1990, and half that and in 2017 less still. Houses have been abandoned, (Figure 10.8) burned or swept away by center pivots. And it is not only houses that have disappeared from the middleground.

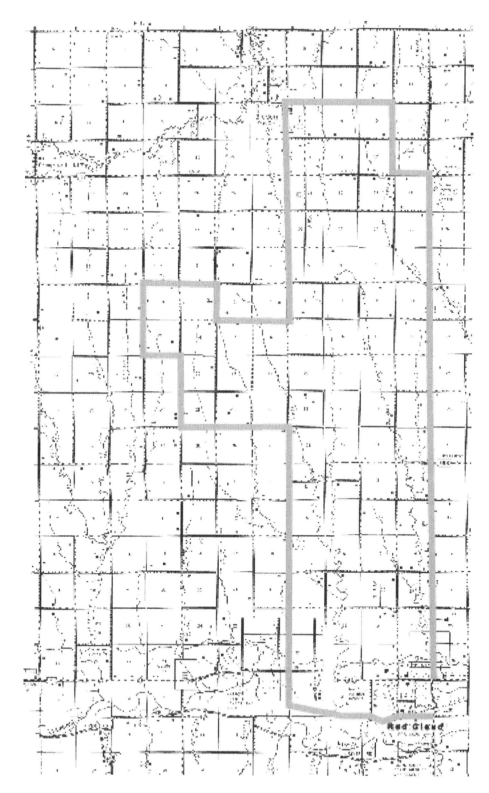

Figure 10.2 Rural tour map of Cather sites in Webster County, Nebraska

Lucia Woods (1973) had difficulty in locating a Webster County Orchard to photograph for her and Bernice Slote's book, *Willa Cather: A Pictorial Memoir*, finally finding a small remnant near Inavale in the southwestern part of the county. Thus, one is left on the tour experiencing a lonely, ghost like milieu.

Because a gap between past and present occurs and especially because of the rapidity of change in rural America, a tourist seeking a specifically Cather experience is, as I have shown, presented with several dilemmas and conflicting images when visiting Webster County due to: the short period of Cather's pioneer settlement, the rather ordinary working landscape that it encompasses, the experience and needs of its residents, and the landscape context versus tourists' states of mind.

The tourist, motivated by historical association with Cather's novels, may expect to see the landscape exactly as Cather described it. In such cases of brief frozen views, the tourist's context is limited. The landscapes in the novel are but snapshots captured and confined consciously by Cather herself to the period 1882-1920. She is, in the words of John Milton (1982), one of those "later pioneers of art—painters, writers, architects, [and] composers of music—who have looked deeply into the landscape for its revealing shapes and forms and spiritual emanations to create new landscapes of the mind."

Lucy Schneider (1967) points out that after the First World War, Cather was far from neutral to the changes emerging in her beloved rural landscape. She was disgusted with the mechanization that was destroying it as a humanized garden. Ann Billesbach, a former curator of the Willa Cather Pioneer Memorial, has pointed out that Cather's trips West became less and less frequent during the 1920's and 1930's and therefore, her knowledge of the later ravages of the Dust Bowl and the Great Depression were not first-hand (Billesbach 1988). The landscape had changed, and she chose not to deal with that change by ignoring it in her novels.

Figure 10.3 Willa Cather Memorial Prairie looking west from the interpretive overlook

Another Cather scholar Jeanette Crain Danielson (1968) notes that,

> Willa Cather does not simply look at the past as a souvenir. She looks at the wasteland of the present only as a cycle in history. The past is not only something to preserve, it is a guide to the future, a part of the present and the future and important in showing man's potential and his place in the universe (p. ix).

So, at the time of her prairie novels, the prairie had all but disappeared and the ideal

Figure 10.4 The Republican River south of Red Cloud, Nebraska, in July 2016

of the garden was falling prey to mechanization. Mechanization is not well suited to the individualized, labor-intensive care of a garden or orchard but responds well to the lack of labor in the depopulated landscape.

Interpreting and Managing Cather's Cultural Landscape

I contend that the middleground surrounding individual sites is critical in providing contextual spaces between them and must be interpreted for the observer. Furthermore, the middleground could be conserved and manipulated at critical junctures where it connects the observer or the special site, to background views. These problems arise because of the tour's sole focus on Cather, a misunderstanding about the mental activity of the tourist, and the sheer amount of middleground.

Since Cather's artistic requirements fixed time in the prairie novels, it does not allow for what Donald Meinig (1979) calls a "cumulative" view of landscape or what David Lowenthal (1975) calls "accretions of occupance." It is precisely that view that a tour must acknowledge in an ordinary working landscape. A working landscape, especially one that requires annual changes of crop covering and ready grading of surfaces, becomes unreal when viewed as something constant.

In agricultural areas such as Webster County, landscape can lose its importance because it is commonplace; it becomes ordinary. Geographers like Meinig and landscape scholars like J. B. Jackson and John Stillgoe recognize the importance of the ordinary or common landscape (Jackson 1966, Meinig 1979, Stillgoe 1982), and I believe that others did as well. Schneider (1967) explained Cather's impetus this way, "Demanding attention in its own right, [the land]

162

serves as a controlling image that gives philosophical meanings to the ordinary facts of life." This accentuates even more strongly Cather's attachment to the uniquely American myth of the yeoman farmer.

This ordinary landscape is the matrix, however, that holds graveyard, barn, orchard, garden, and homestead in their special and spatial relationships. It is important that it provides backdrop, because as Meinig (1979), writes, "All events take place; all problems are anchored in place and ultimately can only be understood in such terms." Robert Melnick (1983), among others, has pointed out in his work on cultural landscapes that we have difficulty in dealing with ordinary landscapes because, it is "the set of components within the larger natural setting which establishes the cultural landscape." This difficulty is further exacerbated by the dynamic qualities of a working agricultural landscape.

J. B. Jackson (1966), an astute reader of ordinary landscapes, remarked, " the [family] homestead has vanished and along with it much of the 19th-century landscape." It has vanished because its residents, particularly those who were major manipulators of landscape, do in fact, disturb and rearrange. They have different rhythms, aspirations, and attitudes that over time, can become discrete and real. A farmer today depends more on the fluctuations of money then fluctuations of weather. Becomes more easily put asunder by hordes of futures speculators then hordes of grasshoppers, is carried more by cash flow than water flow, and arranges and composes his crops more to the tune of farm legislation language, rather than to the call of the soil and the traditions of the past. They are driven by different imperatives and intentions than the tourist. In fact, they may even see a different landscape (Nassauer and Westamacott 1987).

Figure 10.5 The Republican River south of Red Cloud, Nebraska, circa 1900 well after settlement

So whether we agree or not, the psychological and experiential context of the tourist is limited and not easily manipulated as the landscape. That is, tourists are many in number and have little in common except for Cather novels and the incipient immersion in the landscape of Webster County provided by the tour route. Also, a continuum exists between the observer's states of mind and the physical context of observation, and the middleground represents and connects that continuum.

Figure 10.6 A hilltop windbreak spreads Siberian elm and eastern redcedar into an open pasture along Bladen Road

An observer's state of mind on the Cather's divide tour is largely due to a reality of the novels themselves. John Jakle (1987) has noted that the tourist by definition is not a resident and sees things through different eyes; he or she is not privy to the landscape changes or the reasons that initiated those changes. A tourist does not have access to a higher unknowable domain of change because of the brief time for reviewing and experiencing the landscape. Ervin Zube (1982) argues this point in his exploration of southwestern landscape images:

> "Motivations of settlers and explorers, of a new landscape who experiences in a highly purposeful pragmatic and intimate way, are not likely to be the same as those who view it and contemplate the same landscape for relative short time and from a discrete distance and are not committed to that landscape for their future livelihood." (p. 39)

Figure 10.7 A season of irrigation on the Divide has finished with center pivots parked unused and uninterpreted along Bladen Road

On the other hand, David Lowenthal (1975) proposes that, "If the character of the place is gone in reality, it remains preserved in the mind's eye of the visitor, formed by historical imagination untarnished by rude social facts."

So, the tourist's context is limited and it is difficult to experience the sweep of the prairie view from the Divide if one's eyes are distracted by metal barns, porcelain coated silos, center pivot irrigation machines, wind turbines, piles of demolished farmstead, and scattered

Figure 10.8 An abandoned home near the site of the original Cather homestead

trees. In all these tangles, how does a tourist or other thoughtful reader of the landscape reconcile Webster County today with Cather's, prairie novels? How does one resolve the verbal and the visual? Yi-fu Tuan (1978) compares the expansive mind of a novelist to the directed mind of the planner:

> "A novelist is forced to think through in detail the effects of events and initiatives on the densely textured world he [or she] has created. A planner wants to know the impact of a new highway on the community it traverses. The type of mind required to envision all the possible human consequences such a change is that of a novelist." (p. 201).

John Jakle (1987) notes however, "Verbal experience is not the same as visual experience. People respond to space totally for many directions spontaneously, but verbal thought proceeds linearly from concept to concept."(Chapter 1)

Landscape architects also create places but, alas, they must deal with the realities of scale, time, and change. One way that landscape architects create place is to link the existing features with defined paths. For example, a landscape architect laying out trail in the forest, not only has to take into account the engineering factor of slope, the site's natural features, and an ultimate destination, but also how to reveal to the user an understanding of what that specific landscape is all about. For centuries, whether it was the stroll gardens of Edo Japan or the romantic allegorical gardens of England, the sequence, detail, dominant visual features, and distance between vision events, have served the landscape architect as something to mold, direct, and re-create.

Faye Schuett (1983), in her dissertation, "Place, Memory and the Double Life: Experiencing Willa Cather's Novels," uses distinct elements of visual resource analysis in her exploration of landscape as place. The two most useful in connection with the Cather sites tour are what she terms panoramas and close-ups. She calls these objective experience, and they are more easily defined and manipulated by the tour designer or interpreter. The other two, disclosure and reverie, are more subjective. They remain internal to the observer and therefore, less subject to manipulation and biophysical context. According to Schuett (1983):

> "In 'Panorama' place is observed [passively] from afar, surveyed in analytical order and perceived as a whole and static entity. In 'close-up' place is [more active and sensate] observed in proximity, surveyed at random and perceived as a fluctuating and fragmented entity" (p. 28).

Figure 10.9 Ponds, large and small, dot the Divide landscape. Most accrued since the 1930's and were not extant in the late 19th or early 20th Centuries

So, like the basis of several visual resource management models, Schuett finds one has either a background or foreground view of the landscape. Background views [panoramas] are nothing new to novelists (or tourist for that matter) but the use of the foreground [close-up] allowed Cather the possibility of using landscape as a character. The problem faced by the landscape architect and the tourist confronted with reality on the Webster County tour is that panorama and close-up assign no apparent importance to the middleground (which interestingly enough is true of the Cather sites tour; it assigns very little to panorama.) Commonness resides in the middleground and becomes its major expression. It is in large part in a matrix, often amorphous and extensive, and less easily manipulated.

All of the above is true of the Webster County landscape, with one important exception: there exists a designated tour linking specific sites which in turn are embedded in an ordinary matrix. Along a defined path, one has the ability to predict and manipulate the view and the viewer and here the problem of middleground can begin to be resolved through interpretation.

Some work might be done on the middleground, by encouraging good land management. For example, invasive tree removal from native pastures as has been done at the Willa Cather Memorial Prairie. The creation of Cultural Landscape Easements, not unlike Conservation Easements (Chapter 10) might be feasible. Those also might be widely employed to hold off the intrusive appearance of wind turbine farms as happening a few miles east of the tour route. In places like the Pavelka farmstead, careful reconstruction of the triple-enclosed garden detailed in My Ántonia would enhance the visitor experience. So, these various strategies and others would bring the middleground to bear in the process of interpretation.

Conclusion

Cather's prairie novels, while fictitious, were based on a certain and central reality--a distillation of the interaction of settlers with a new land. Unlike Rolvaag (1927), Cather told stories only thinly detached from real people and real places; so, the physical settings can be and are visited and read today in the context of her stories. But they have begun to reach beyond local and regional significance and become tied to the entire settlement area of American Westward expansion. The product of settlement and novel, Webster County and the

Divide represent a cultural landscape formed by the synergistic and symbiotic interaction of humans and nature.

We have seen interest in rural landscapes come and go. For example, the 1990 Farm Bill debate, cross-disciplinary initiatives for rural landscapes for open-space and creation by the National Trust for Historic Preservation, the National Endowment for the Arts and the Natural Resources Conservation Service. This specific study presented here can be of more general use to landscape architects in sorting out apparent conflicts between a working agricultural landscape and the experience of the tourist, especially since tourism is based on literary settings and touted as economic development.

Further Reading

Cather, Willa. (1913) *O Pioneers!*. New York:Houghton-Miflin

_____ (1915) *Song of the Lark*. New York:Houghton-Miflin

_____ (1918) *My Ántonia*. New York:Houghton-Miflin

_____ (1922) *One of Ours*. New York:Knopf

_____ (1923) *A Lost Lady*. New York:Knopf

_____ (1935) *Lucy Gayheart*. New York:Knopf

Cooper-Skjelvar, M (1980) *Webster County: Visions of the Past*

Danielson, J. (1969) A Sense of a Sense of Place in the Works of Willa Cather. PhD. Dissertation Bowling Green State University

Jackson, J. B. (1966) The New American Countryside: An Engineered Environment. *Landscape* 16(1)

Jackson, J. B. (1980) Nearer than Eden. In, *The Necessity for Ruins*. Amherst:UMass Press

Jakle, J. (1987) *The Visual Elements of Landscape*. Amherst:UMass Press

Lauerman, D. (1972) The Garden and the City in the Fiction of Willa Cather. PhD Dissertation Indiana University

Litton, B. (1968) Forest Landscapes, Description and Inventories: A Basis for Land Planning and Design USDA USFS Research Paper PSW 49

Lowenthal, D. (1975) Past Time, Present Place: Landscape and Memory. *Geographical Review* LXV(1):2-36

Meinig, D. (1979) The beholding eye: Ten versions of the same scene. In, *Interpretation of Ordinary Landscapes*. D. W. Meinig (ed) 33-48. New York: Oxford Press

Melnick, R. (1983) Protecting Rural Cultural Landscapes: Finding Value in the Countryside. *Landscape Journal*. 2(2) 85-97

Milton, J. (1982) Plains Landscapes and Changing Visions. *Great Plains Quarterly* 2(1):55-62

Nassauer, J and R. Westmacott, (1987) Progressiveness Among Farmers as a Factor in Heterogeneity of Farmed Landscapes. In, *Landscape Heterogeneity and Disturbance*. M. Turner (ed) 199-210. New York:Springer-Verlag

Randall, J. (1960) *The Landscape and the Looking Glass*. New York:Houghton-Miflin

Rohrbach, C. (1976) Willa Cather: An Historian of Webster County, Nebraska: An Inquiry. PhD Dissertation St Louis University

Rolvaag, O. (1927) *Giants in the Earth* New York:Harpers

Schuett, F. (1983) Place Memory and the Double Life: Experiencing Willa Cather's Novels PhD Dissertation University of Tulsa

Schneider, L. ((1967) Willa Cather's Land Philosophy in Her Novels and Short Stories. PhD Dissertation

Notre Dame University

Stillgoe, J. (1982) *The Common Landscape of America 1580-1845*. New Haven: Yale University Press

Sutton, R.K. 1977. "The Round Peg in the Square Hole: Center Pivot Irrigation in the Nebraska Landscape." *Landscape* Vol. 22 No. 1 pp. 3-10.

Sutton, R.K. 1982. "The Image of a Garden: Vernacular Conifer Plantings in Otoe County, Nebraska" *Pioneer America* Vol. 14 pp. 93-113 winter

Sutton, R. K. 1985. "Rural Planting Relicts in Eastern Nebraska." *Landscape Jour..* 4(2):106-115 winter

Sutton, R.K. 1991. "Not for the Tourist's Eyes Only: Willa Cather's `Divide' Landscape Today." *CELA Conference Proceedings: Selected Papers*. Vol. 3 LAF:Washington.

Tuan, Yi-fu (1978) Literature and Geography: Implications for Geographical Research In *Humanistic Geography:Prospects and Problems*. D. Ley and M. Samuels (eds) Chicago: Maaronfa Press

Woods, L, and B. Slote (1973) *Willa Cather: A Pictorial Memoir*. Lincoln:University of Nebraska Press.

Zube. E. (1982) An Exploration of Southwestern Landscape Images. *Landscape Journal* 1(1):31-40

SECTION 4 INTENTIONAL LANDSCAPES

"Reflective practice is essential to convert knowledge into understanding and, eventually wisdom. Knowledge and understanding are often used interchangeably, but I see them as distinctly different. Knowledge is the acquisition of factual information. It is strictly a mental phenomenon . . . Understanding on the other hand is being able to comprehend the meaning or implication of knowledge. . . . In addition to thinking, understanding is characterized by both an emotional and physical response. . . Where knowledge is static, understanding is dynamic, multifaceted and always carries with it some level of fulfillment. Understanding is an experience that inflates us. . . . ." --Tom Wessels

"The garden has always been an object of love and even a degree of veneration. It is easy to understand why; but one reason for the present outpouring of interest, I believe, is that the garden represents an archetype--one of those images which along with the dwelling, the road and the shrine are seen as essential elements in any desirable landscape. Without the garden the landscape, even the imaginary landscape, is incomplete. As we now visualize it, the garden stands for a particular kind of experience of the environment, essential to the fuller understanding of ourselves; the garden is where we have to be. It is precisely now, when urban existence makes it all but impossible for most of us to relish the quality of a space, when any contact with a garden in particular is out of the question, that the search for the archetype, a rediscovery and confirmation of its existence becomes so urgent." --J. B. Jackson

Intentional creation of landscapes should use both the processes of scientific knowledge and design understanding. When working in prairie landscapes it is essential that designers understand its natural, ecological forces when creating a new place. Conservation of Nebraska's rural landscapes attempt to staunch the flow of sediment and improve the quality of its soils and watersheds. Some of those larger scale techniques can be applied to both rural and urban living.

Gardens (and dwellings, roads and shrines) do not occur without intentions. The gardener and the landscape architect always have some final meaning in mind for their created microcosms of the natural world. Successful designers think simultaneously of space and mass, approach and use, connection and ritual, and form and material. They use an explicit process.

Though often ignored, or at best, taken for granted, public park spaces appear in nearly all of Nebraska's cities, towns, and villages. How they evolved and how they have been and continue to be used reflects community intentions. Such places though memory depositories like cemeteries eschew religious overtones and offer flexibility for many individual and community needs which require open spaces -- athletics, celebrations, contact with nature.

11 Prairie Ecology and Conservation Design

> "This whole effort to rebuild and stabilize a countryside is not without its disappointments and mistakes . . . What matter though, these temporary growing pains when one can cast his eye upon the hills and see hard-boiled farmers who have spent their lives destroying land now carrying water by hand to their new plantations"- Aldo Leopold

Introduction

Years ago after several dry weeks in late summer, southeast Nebraska received three days worth of off-again, on-again rainfall. After the storm front had moved on, I decided to take the family Labrador retriever, Cedar, for a run at Branched Oak Lake, north of Lincoln.

In the welcome sunshine, muddy puddles on the county roads had begun to dry out but the ponds dotting the landscape stood brown, murky and filled to the brim. At the dog training area north and west of the lake, I drove in, parked at the turnaround, and let Cedar out. We continued on foot down the path and over the bridge at Oak Creek where turbid water roiled just below my feet. The low ridge above us had been planted in native grasses and several acres of unplowed prairie flanked us on the left.

As we approached a dam on a small incoming drainage, Cedar bolted and disappeared over the top. Like the ponds encountered on the drive out, this one was very close to full, but because it drained a small watershed covered with native grasses and prairie, its 10-foot depth glistened perfectly clear and clean. You could even see its bottom and in mid-pond, Cedar lazily paddled about. The surrounding prairie provided the micro-structure and filter that kept topsoil in place and the waters clean. It was quite a contrast to the ponds filled with muddied runoff I'd seen earlier.

Another year I am rambling across the rural eastern Nebraska countryside in Cass County. It's mid-May and the corn has emerged only a couple of inches; the soybeans remain unplanted. This time of year always arrives filled with hopes of new growth and change, but the changes aren't always for the better.

The day is sultry and by noon large cumulus clouds darken and portend rain like we've had the last two nights. Up ahead I see something of interest and ease to the side of the graveled road. The land drops away from me, gently sloping through a nascent cornfield toward a creek about a-quarter-of-a-mile distant. Scrambling from my truck with my camera, I survey, then photograph the scene below that has caught my eye. Near the road at the field's high point, about a dozen yards of grass waterway occupy a shallow swale leading into the field. The waterway abruptly ends and plunges into a gash in the earth, five, then six feet deep. This gaping woundscape continues to deepen and widen as it slashes its way toward the distant creek. It doesn't take too much imagination to foresee the gathering storm will be sweeping up more topsoil and dumping its sediment-laden runoff into the stream, and ultimately the Gulf Hypoxic Zone.

Gazing at this example of land abuse, I recall photos of the eroded landscape featuring deep gullies in the Appalachians and Tennessee Valley in the 1930's. Most likely the farmer who does this to his Cass County land pays his taxes and sits piously in church, all the while oblivious to the abuse and earth damage he has himself wrought.

So, are these landscapes intentional ones or cultural ones? Do they represent places of careful design or ones of neglect and malaise? The first had been intentionally left the prairie and expanded to more grasses, but the latter landscape evokes a vandal's ideology. After one hundred years of Cooperative Extension preaching, "Save our soil" and nearly as many years of taxpayer programs to replace some of the structure lost from plowing down the prairie, these scenes occupy too many places. Science tells us Nebraska's landscape (and economy) clings to an undeniably thinning layer of topsoil.

In the 150 years since settlement, the natural soil capital of the Great Plains has shrunk in half in most areas and to less than that in others. In 2016, it is estimated that Nebraska alone suffered $560 million dollars in irreversible soil erosion. Starting with prairie plowdown by pioneers, the trend of simplifying landscape structure has continued unabated and shows 50 years (1885-1935) of uninformed, poor farming methods. Replacement structures have been desultorily applied in an attempt to halt the impacts of unsequestered water churned into soil-bearing runoff. Its premise is that carefully designed conservation structure and active, informed scientific management by farmers with what Aldo Leopold called 'ecological consciousness', would curb soil erosion. Fact is, however, that soil erosion can be greatly reduced and slowed but never entirely eliminated in our annual agriculture. The prairie might be mimicked but can't be replaced.

Though often lost on those interested only in maximum production, the agricultural landscape provides ecological services well beyond provision of crop yields. Those services include: catchment of potable water and aquifer recharge from agriculturally dominated watersheds, providing habitat for indigenous and migratory wildlife, refuges for beneficial insects, sequestration of carbon, recreational open space away from built up urban environments, and living space for both farmers and members of embedded rural communities.

For this chapter, I intend to draw on ideas from several of the previous ones and pull idea strands together weaving them into a broad approach that calls for intentionally replacing structure on our farms and in our cities, that was lost when we destroyed the prairie. I start first, with a few paragraphs on ecology of the prairie (Figure 11.1) connected to some larger thinking and the concepts it evokes. Next, I describe the current conservation practices used to thwart soil loss and conserve water, and finally, I suggest that carefully designed conservation structures and approaches can be applied not only to our farms but also to our cities, and that landscape architecture offers a unique approach to design structure drawing from both design process and scientific method.

Prairie Ecology

Ecology studies the numbers, kinds, distributions, and relationships of living things (biotic) and their non-living (abiotic) context. An understanding of ecological principles is critical before proposing any change in the existing environment. Farmers are, in reality, applied ecologists. However, too often we humans, biased by our finite size and lifespans, initiate many of the changes (many of which cannot be reversed) to the environment, and do so only with short-term goals in mind.

Ecological Structure

The physical contexts of natural and human worlds appear structured, that is they appear textured, patchy, heterogeneous, and repetitious. When determining boundaries between

Figure 11.1 Nine-mile Prairie lies preserved in Lancaster County. Watercolor by the author

several phenomena may overlap and interact. This means we can easily perceive and describe the boundaries of much of the world at our particular human scale of space and time. But that is not the whole story.

Boundaries that delimit identifiable wholes, can be distinct and abrupt (and easily delineated) or wide, slowly changing gradients (and more ambiguous). A boundary can be best thought of as three-dimensional and can be largely based on the energy, material, organisms, and information flowing to, through or along it (Cadenasso et al 2003). However, those phenomena often change when confronted by a boundary; among other things boundaries halt, concentrate, diverge, dissipate, deflect, decay, permute, and co-join. Put simply, boundary structure changes what happens to the flow; structure transforms function.

Understanding ecological structure becomes one of the first things needed in ecological thinking for design, The structure of the world, and its functions are hierarchical and compose into higher, constraining levels of larger and longer lasting phenomena while decomposing into lower levels that support smaller and faster acting phenomena. The landscape's variable structure responds both to disturbances from lower levels and the context of size and constraining events from above. Simplistically, boundaries between levels or discreet structures can be thought of as analogous to valves or filters acting on flows.

What does this all have to do with prairie?

During settlement, Nebraska's pioneers converted prairie structure and its complex perennial plant, animal, and microbe community to agricultural production by simplifying them in space and time. They altered and diverted flows of sunlight (energy), nutrients, water, and organisms across the surface of the prairie and over time annualized the yields. These activities successfully focused flows of energy, as found in a productive system and released, then drew upon the nutrient subsidy stored over thousands of years in the organic matter of deep prairie soils. However, ecological structure resists changes and often modifies functions and events. In the past, periodic disturbances by droughts, fires, and grazing by buffalo, removed or decreased biomass, but nutrients and water largely remained in place, accumulated, and compounded with interest, like a natural bank account (Risser et al 1981). Trampling and disturbance of the soil by bison and prairie dogs allowed rain to be readily absorbed in what Malin (1984) called "… the final stage in the process of natural tillage." These disturbances (11.2) were absorbed by a resilient prairie system without the system undergoing much change.

Prairie Ecosystem

Agriculture shifted a complex prairie ecosystem to a simpler system where production of biomass (e. g. corn and soybeans) supplants a more complex, bio-diverse biome that had accumulated and incorporated over the millennia, a great deal of information about past disturbances such as climate, weather, soils, and associated adapted organisms. That information resides in the genes of its individual native plant, animal, and microbial populations. Complex systems of soil and microbes that recycle above ground and below ground biomass have been simplified so as to redirect the flow of the sun's energy and the soil's nutrients into crop-based biomass. This agricultural production system incorporated (and now requires) large subsidies of water, labor, capital, and macronutrients, especially nitrogen and phosphorus, and be brought in from outside the system.

The prairie only grew and produced biomass as limited by the ambient rainfall and what nutrients could be recycled. Today's simplified structure of the agricultural production system however massively leaks water, soil, and nutrients especially during heavy rainfall. Originally, clear prairie streams fed by runoff from unsullied land cover had names like the Big Blue River, whose now brown and opaque flow belies its namesake. This occurs through boundaries that are poorly defined and structured in space and time.

Larger Concepts

Land use / Land cover

We often confuse and conflate the terms, land use and land cover. Land relates them, but not in the same way. Land use points at the function of land as it interests humans-- how it is used and what output it produces. It is an economic and legal term that defines the activities one might encounter on a parcel of land. Land cover is less abstract and more physical. It defines what covers the surface of a land parcel and implies how that surface would interact with sunlight, water, and other primary flows. One might think of land cover as the horizontal complement to a boundary; it is the boundary at the surface of the earth mediating flows into (and over) it. All land uses have land covers and often the type, amount, and arrangement of a land cover consistently holds for particular land use. For example, commercial urban lands often have impervious surfaces often exceeding 95 percent. However, details about materials and a land use's chosen configuration for its surfaces can be manipulated and lie in the hands of the land designer.

Natural ecosystems have evolved so that their vegetative surfaces attempt to attain the greatest energy absorption and biomass production possible, given their soil and water regime. As noted in Figure 11.2, disturbances often impact and change land and land cover Changing land uses might be considered also as an impact.

Ecologist, Eugene Odum (1969) has suggested a simplified and compartmentalized model (Figure 11.3) of the world's ecosystems/land uses. He also suggests what percent of the earth's land surface each comprises. Placing them into four general categories: 1) Mature Protective-5%, 2) Young Productive-75% 3) Urban-Industrial-10% and 4) Compromise (Hybrid)-10%. He suggests that some movement occurs between the four, but the movement is uneven and most often uni-directional. For example, conversion of Mature/Protective land use is usually a one-way action. Once a prairie is plowed, it is difficult if not impossible to move it back to that category. Once productive farmland is urbanized it is difficult to return it

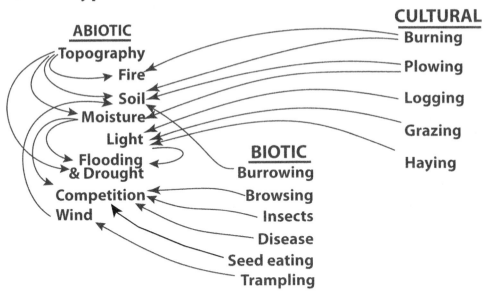

Figure 11.2 Native organisms in the prairie ecosystem have evolved in the face of and interaction with stress and disturbance. This information is stored in their genes.

to production. That is what the dark arrows represent—the ease of conversion—and the light ones depict—difficulty of reassembly. Perhaps the most interesting category-compartment is that of the hybrid. Places occur on earth where perhaps productive intertwines with urban; this happens in the form of gardens, vacant lots and naturalized drainage corridors, which can be purposely designed into that land use. Where 95 percent impermeable urban land cover becomes modified with design of green infrastructure, some structure returns to the land use and its land cover.

Panarchy

The concept of panarchy (Figure 11.4) projects how, over time we can understand the relationships in complex systems like ecosystems and human institutions, and how to predict their organization and operation. By applying panarchy concepts, we can begin to see why some systems seemingly go on forever, while others go off on tangents or devolve into simplified manifestations of their former selves. Panarchy describes the dynamic, hierarchical relationships between small and fast configurations (like annual crops, insects, operating loans, and congressional elections), intermediate systems like forests, prairies, mortgages, and many human institutions, all constrained by large scale and slower moving phenomena like climate, geology, religious teachings, and the US Constitution.

All of these systems are interconnected and linked by revolt and remembrance. Disturbance impacts, (e.g., fire, 100-year flood, bankruptcy, dementia) on a system can be absorbed if it is resilient enough. However, disturbances that exceed a system's ability to absorb them cause a revolt. In that case, excessive loss of information and memory lead to a different, albeit more simplified system. Many such devolved systems carry the germ of remembrance for return to a higher stable state. For example, the genetic information encoded into the plants whose seeds still remain in a site's seed bank after a major disturbance. A number of things

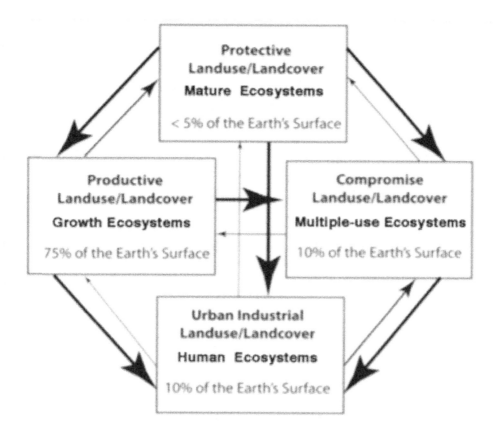

Figure 11.3 Human land uses cycle between four compartments each of which has different impacts on flows of energy, materials, organism, and information. The heavier the arrow the more frequent the change. Only small areas cycle up to protective and the overall trend is toward compromise and urban/industrial land uses. Selection and configuration of land cover within land uses is critical. (Revised from Odum (1969))

such as energy, water, biomass, nutrients, and capital drive these systems through a cycle of release, causing growth paused by constraints leading to conservation, then exploitation, and back to reorganization. This progress sounds orderly, but it's chaotic and often unpredictable. Such a pattern may exist for extended periods until the disturbance that causes reorganization becomes too large or severe. Then the system revolts or remembers and changes level to a new stable state.

Odum's Mature-Protective land use as a large, slow system continually shrinks; little of it remains and more devolves each year. Nebraska's agricultural landscape has paused and teetered on Odum's exploitation phase for 150 years, balanced by subsidies of farm payments, water, nutrients, energy, and vertical (scientific) information.

Conservation Systems: Hybrid Land Use and Land Cover for Productive Ecosystems

Discussed and described below and readily seen and read in the Nebraska landscape, are some of the programs, practices, and structures used to reduce soil erosion. And unfortunately, such erosion represents the greatest output of our productive agricultural landscapes. It occurs

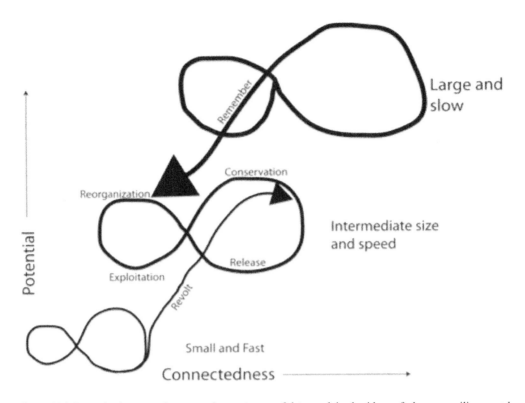

Figure 11.4 Panarchy is a complex, recursive system useful to explain the ideas of chance, resilience and multiple stable states when describing and interpreting ecosystems (and human systems) states and dynamics. This system shares many features of the creative or design process. (After Gunderson and Holling 2002).

Nebraska's prairie topsoil was once as deep in some areas as 24 to 36 inches. In many places now, it is less than half that depth and it continues to erode due to water and wind. The "acceptable" standard by which the Natural Resources Conservation Service (NRCS) assesses topsoil loss is two tons per acre. Two tons per acre means about ½ inch over a 31 by 31-foot area, and if spread over an entire acre it would be about 0.0001 of an inch or the depth of a silt particle. This would mean the loss of one-inch in 10,000 years. While this sounds reasonable and acceptable, the problem is not that simple. Because of a variety of factors, soil loss is not uniform across a farm field and can be quite significant in smaller areas. If the average field size for Nebraska row crops is 125 acres, then losses of .25-inches in just one of those acres means it is eroding at over 40 tons per acre. In Eastern Nebraska, looking at newly planted corn after heavy May rains, it is easy to see 1/10-of-an-inch or more of erosion, even in a no-till field, . (Just remember the Cass County gully and woundscape I described at the beginning of this chapter.) It is estimated that over 70 percent of the sediment in streams and ultimately at the Mississippi River's outlet Gulf of Louisiana, comes from agricultural lands. Additionally, wind erosion leads to scouring and deposition of soil. The Sandhills and in particular the Nebraska's Central Loess Hills, are products of massive long-term wind erosion and deposition following the retreat of glaciers. Water erosion is particularly problematic, however, because runoff can transport soil over long distances.

Since the "Dust Bowl" days of the 1930's, federal aid and technology have attempted to staunch wind and water-caused soil erosion. Since that time, various programs such as the 1950's and 1960's Land Bank, and the later Conservation Reserve Program (CRP), federal and local resources have been aimed at encouraging farmers to remove and protect from production, highly erodible lands. First, using the carrot of paying for idling and covering acres prone to erosion (Land Bank and CRP) and then later with the both a carrot and a stick in the 1990 Food, Agriculture, Conservation and Trade Act (Public Law 101-624 1990). The payment carrot continued, but the stick brought loss of farm payments for things like federally backed crop insurance, Farm Security Administration loans, and disaster assistance, if highly erodible acres were farmed or existing erodible acres in grass or trees were broken out, (Sodbuster) or wetlands were drained for production (Swampbuster).

Today, The Environmental Quality Incentives Program (EQIP) provides cost-sharing and technical assistance for voluntary conservation programs to encourage agricultural producers to farm in a manner where production and environmental quality are compatible. This program has tightly prescribed and geographically targeted goals formed to add landscape structure and promote management practices that conserve, soil, water, and wildlife on agricultural land.

Land Use Decisions

The entire American agricultural landscape has been typed, mapped, and analyzed as to its soil characteristics. This information on soil type, depth, location, slope and so on become important to knowing how a field might be best used, and to determine highly erodible tracts. In order to determine the erodibility potential of a field, NRCS engineers use a general formula called the Revised Universal Soil Loss Equation (RUSLE) (Renard et al 1991)

$A = R \times K \times L \times S \times C \times P$

Where:

- A = Average annual soil loss (tons/ac/year)
- R = Rainfall factor
- K = Soil erodibility factor
- L = Slope length factor
- S = Slope gradient factor
- C = Cropping management factor
- P = Soil erosion BMP factor

R (rainfall), K (erodibility factor), L (slope length), and S (slope steepness) as variables, can be determined from the pertinent soil survey. C (cropping management and P (structural best management practices--BMP's) can be selected based on R, K, L and S to determine A (soil erosion in tons per acre). Another factor, landscape and field context should also be taken into account, though it is not specifically quantified in the RUSLE equation.

Adding Structure with Soil Conservation BMPs

Listed below are best management practices (BMPs) used for productive agricultural ecosystems. They provide some of the needed structure to slow the loss of soil and water. They also can be read as human landscape structures in the landscape.

Cropping Management

Tillage systems such as contour farming, strip cropping (Figure 11.5), no-till, (Figure 11.6) stubble mulching, and cover cropping come from a farmer's decision about how to farm.

Figure 11.5 Strip Cropping 1950, Garden County, NE (UNL-Agronomy and Horticulture Dept.)

These may be based on habit, tradition, knowledge, skill, and/or equipment and can vary from farmer to farmer, field to field, and year to year. Contour farming simply means running the crop rows perpendicular to water fall-line, (i.e. the steepest portion of the slope). As slopes become steeper this simple technique becomes harder to accomplish and more structural treatments become necessary. Strip cropping places different crops in multi-row bands along the contour of the slope, which at minimum are determined by the width of equipment being used. A strip crop pairing that might be used in Nebraska's aglandscape could be corn and soybeans or possibly alfalfa and corn, though mixing a perennial like alfalfa or even an annual like soybeans with corn, complicates management decisions for planting, harvest, fertilization, and pesticide use. Strip cropping is not widely employed on eastern Nebraska farms, though it is found in the western parts (Figure 11.5) .

No-till (Figure 11.6) and its older cousin, stubble mulching, allow erosion. The organic matter in the leaves, stems, and roots begins decomposition and introduces some available nutrients for the next growing detritus to remain on the surface after harvest, and thus reduce both wind and water erosion. No-till reduces equipment passes needed through the field thus reduces fuel cost, wear and tear on equipment, and potential soil compaction. It does, however, require spring application of herbicide to destroy volunteers from last season's crop and emerging weeds. Due to its advantages, no-till has been widely adopted, but it is not a panacea which prevents all soil erosion. Some farmers who think that no-till covers all conservation sins have removed land from the CRP program and now plant and cultivate not on the contour, but up and down hill. Fact is, plant detritus (and soil) does get washed from the field surface in heavy rains and is blown from it in open, dry winters. Cover cropping has begun to gain use on Nebraska farms and much research regarding species, species mixes, timing of planting, and impact on moisture is now occurring. While cover crops also need to be killed by herbicide before spring planting, they do encourage the propagation of mycorrhizal fungi that need

Figure 11.6 No-till cropping requires a spring application of herbicide to control weeds in Cass County, NE

living roots to survive, and if plowed into the field, cover crops can offer an additional source of "green manure" and increased organic matter.

Buffers

Buffers (Bentrup 2008) are implemented as vertical or horizontal boundaries of different plant species that ameliorate the flow of water or wind, and thus decrease potential for soil erosion. Unfortunately, because of high phosphorus and nitrogen fertilizer use, leaching from farm fields along with pesticides attached to soil particles reduces field runoff water quality. The eroded soil from the hilltop soon becomes problematic sediment at its bottom filling terraces, ponds, and reservoirs. Suspended fine particles that do no easily settle out are the main reason for the turbidity of rivers and streams in an aglandscape, and buffers have little impact on them.

Field margins (Figure 11.7) planted to perennial grasses allow equipment to turn around with minimal soil compaction and disturbance. Linear buffers of perennial grasses or shrubs and trees can be planted along the margins of drainage-ways. These riparian buffer strips slow runoff and trap sediment and nutrients. Field windbreaks planted on the south and west sides of fields, buffer and help reduce wind erosion during the dormant season and lower stress on actively growing crops. Windbreaks and shelterbelts also protect human dwellings and livestock during blizzards. It is no wonder that some of the first human structures added to Nebraska's prairie aglandscape were trees (See Chapter 8).

Figure 11.7 Grassed field verge (margin) in foreground, intermittent stream with pond in middleground and farmstead windbreak in background of this Otoe County, NE agricultural landscape.

Conservation Structures

Unlike cropping management systems and buffers, re-establishing physical structure in an aglandscape requires more complex, expensive, direct intervention, and topographic modification. They include terracing, grassed waterways, (Figure 11.8) farm retention ponds and reservoirs for flood control, recreation, and wildlife habitat.

Terraces (Figure 11.9) are of three general types and closely tied to the slope of the field used for rowcrop production. When contour farming occurs on slopes greater than 8% to 10% it can no longer efficiently curb soil erosion. On a 10 percent slope, creating contour terraces are needed. This approach cuts into soil on the uphill side and places it on the downhill side forming stepped slopes with a shallow swale running slightly downhill along the contour. These contour terrace ridges are low enough and swales shallow enough that they can be farmed on the contour. As the slope reaches 18% to 20%, contour farming becomes difficult and depending on the lateral stability of farm equipment used, it becomes dangerous for maneuvering, threatening overturn.

Also, as field equipment gets larger, it no longer fits some terraces, leading farmers to abandon the terraces and thus increase potential for soil erosion. Fitting equipment between the contour ridges also limits its efficiency. The downhill slope is steep enough that it cannot be farmed and best planted to perennial vegetation for stability. Research at The Leopold Center for Sustainable Agriculture, at Iowa State University, has found a biodiverse mix of perennial native grasses, and forbs perform better than simply one species of grass. When fields reach a slope of 45%-50%, even bench terraces do not work well for crop production so use gives way to permanent pasture or hay.

Figure 11.8 A grass waterway in cornfield, Lancaster, County, NE has been cut for hay..

Cutting above the contour and filling below in any terrace formation means that reshaping sloping fields with shallower topsoils exposes subsoil, and thus crop yields become reduced. Bench terraces require the most cut and fill; thus in sculpting them, subsoil exposure is a constant concern.

The shallow trench behind the ridge can be handled in two different ways. First, it can slowly conduct water which collects behind them into a grassed waterway for movement down slope and off the field or into a permanent pond. The second approach requires the addition of occasional small retention basins located at appropriate points along the terrace. These temporary catchments are drained and have their outflow regulated by plastic standpipe inlets (Figure 11.10). The inlets connect to a system of plastic drainage "tiles" that take the place of grass waterways to conduct water down slope and an appropriate outlet. These inlet terraces require a high degree of skill to properly install and are the most expensive structural erosion control measure used in fields. Their high cost mandates careful maintenance and usually requires a cost sharing program.

Grass waterways or permanently grassed swales conduct water from the field and flow along its natural swales and valleys. These engineered structures require careful design that depends on the total area drained, the slope, the length of the slope, and type of soil and vegetation cover. As fields get larger and slopes steeper, grass waterways can be subjected to high quantities of water flowing at high velocities. In appropriate topography and depending on runoff volumes and velocities, grass waterways may have checkdams with stand pipes that deposit the runoff into a pond, though more likely a permanent or ephemeral stream. On shallower slopes draining less area and having a more permeable soil, a grass waterway-like structure may simply spread the water and allow it to percolate into the soil. Use of grassed waterways and water spreaders reduces the area of cropland, so a balance must be struck between adequate flow or no erosion conveyance of runoff versus cropland. Many farmers see grassed waterways as taking up valuable cropland and have eliminated these swales.

Figure 11.9 Permanent vegetation on steep side-slopes of Cuming County bench terraces.

Unfortunately, as described at the beginning of this chapter, water continues to seek its lowest level and routes create severe gully erosion on many farm fields that far exceeds the two-tons per acre threshold.

Ponds and reservoirs store water that can be used for watering livestock, wildlife, and recreation, though these structures must be carefully designed into the surrounding topography and require detailed knowledge of local rainfall, field catchment area, and soils characteristics. If used for stock watering, animal access must be carefully controlled to minimize damage to the shoreline. Maintenance of any conservation structure keeps it functioning in its intended fashion. For example, terraces will collect sediment which needs redistribution through yearly grading and inlet retention areas along terraces are especially prone to filling with sediment. If inlet standpipes become clogged, water may overtop a terrace and cause it to fail. At a minimum, inlet standpipes and bench terraces must be examined each fall and spring and after each unusual storm event. Grassed waterways also need yearly maintenance along their margins, especially where terraces empty into them. Their low point flowline should also be checked for incipient gullies, then regraded and reseeded as needed. Broad, grassed waterways planted to native grasses can be successfully used to grow hay and therefore, do not lead to complete loss of production capabilities. A professional engineer should inspect any dams for ponds or reservoirs, especially its outlets. Excessive silt should be removed and respread on fields. Trees should not be allowed to sprout and grow on the dam itself. Maintenance of conservation structures takes a commitment of time. Unfortunately, many farmers have huge acreages to plant, cultivate, and harvest which allow them to spread their cost per acreage, but encourages them to give short shrift to keeping soil conservation structures functioning.

Whether it was the Prairie States Forestry Project of the 1930's, Landbank of the 1950's, the Farm, Agriculture, Conservation and Trade Act of the 1990's, or the more recent EQIP

Figure 11.10 Terraces can allow ponding using standpipes for water outflow. However, this Jefferson County, NE, field requires annual maintenance for sediment removal to keep terraces functioning.

conservation programs, taxpayers have been partially funding the addition of soil and water conservation project for many years. Trees represent one of the best, long-term conservation land covers, but farmers are reluctant to plant them because trees prove harder to remove when placing land back into production. When commodity prices boom, short-term thinking leads to removing or abandoning conservation structures. Perhaps conservation easements should be placed on conservation structures and held by the local Natural Resource District (NRD) to protect the public's investment from arbitrary removal. Maintenance is a thornier issue.

Conservation Sub-divisions: A New Approach to an Old Idea.

While soil conservationists fight the removal of structures from land under crop production, we know that from the Odum's (1969) compartment model (Figure 11.4) that productive agricultural land gets converted to urbanized uses. One of such uses, conservation subdivisions, could be thought of however, as a hybrid ecosystem, especially if receives careful design attention long before it changes from field to a housing subdivision.

The idea of conservation subdivisions has been around for many years. (Arendt 1996) Conservation subdivisions can be defined as "the clustering of homes or developments to protect environmentally sensitive areas from encroachment." (RBC PDF no date). Conservation subdivisions are usually designed and laid out to be density neutral. That is, they yield a similar number of lots as a conventional subdivision, albeit ones will less square footage. On the other hand, this type of urbanized development in rural landscapes has the advantages of protecting many of the amenities sought out by the homeowner in the first place. It also protects important resources such as existing soil, trees, drainage corridors, and open space. The design process leading to a subdivision plan for review and a legal plat for approval, most often begins with productive farmland that is considered for immediate development.

Below is a new twist to this old idea that the late Walter Bagley and I have proposed. The approach is to push back the beginning of the design process and use conservation easements as a design tool. We suggest it is critical to involve the landowner in identifying and delimiting the features of his or her land to be protected with conservation easements and even planted long before it is sold to a developer. Conservation and Preservation Easements have been around in Nebraska since 1981. Such an easement is defined as follows:

"Conservation easement shall mean a right, whether or not stated in the form of an easement, restriction, covenant, or condition in any deed, will, agreement, or other instrument executed by or on behalf of the owner of an interest in real property imposing a limitation upon the rights of the owner or an affirmative obligation upon the owner appropriate to the purpose of retaining or protecting the property in its natural, scenic, or open condition, assuring its availability for agricultural, horticultural, forest, recreational, wildlife habitat, or open space use, protecting air quality, water quality, or other natural resources." (Nebraska Statues 76-2,111)

As we envision it, the owner or entity with which the easement resides would have it transferred to an "Owners Association," at such time that two-thirds or more of the sub-division lots are built upon. Even with the transfer of easement ownership according to the law, "A conservation or preservation easement shall run with the land and shall be perpetual," and must be approved by the local land use planning authority, such as the county planning commission. For example, current Lincoln/Lancaster subdivision ordinances already require some small intermittent and streams above the 100-year flood plain to be protected and acquired as conservation easements during the subdivision approval and platting process.

Just as the sale of agricultural lands for sub-divisions begins with the rural landowner, the use of conservation easements would also begin with that person as well. The lands to be sub-divided in the future would be analyzed at minimum for slope, soil type and depth, existing permanent vegetation such as perennial grass or woody plants, wildlife habitat, adjacent roads and utilities, existing easements, wetlands, location, quality and quantity of underground water sources, floodplains, areas damaged by erosion or with the potential to be easily damaged. The location of these factors should be accurately mapped as layers on a geographic information system. This inventory will serve as the underpinnings for decisions about areas to include as conservation easements, but also for the location of roads, utilities, and lot lines. So, years before actual subdivision and building occur, a fairly accurate idea of the layout of the subdivision can be established.

Another new, twist deals with the actual design and construction of the subdivision that could be managed by general easements and covenants for the portion of the land not covered by the conservation easement. For example, much of damage to existing and future land quality occurs with site grading and layout of roads and utilities. Engineers needlessly damage large areas of soil by cut and fill when developers ask for potential lots to be graded into walkout basement lots. A good deal of soil loss, by compaction, erosion, and overfill occurs during initial construction. Even Storm Water Pollution Prevention Plans (SWPPP) largely react to development grading but do not limit it. A second wave of soil damage occurs during the construction of individual homes. Unless corralled, most homebuilders run loose on an entire lot; they substitute easy access in all types of weather for thinking ahead to minimize soil loss and compaction. It is not unusual to see homebuilders also staging a job on an adjacent lot. In Lincoln/Lancaster County restrictions now require contractors to implement a mini-SWPPP, though the requirements are minimal and would be enhanced in the development covenants Bagley and I propose. For example, strictly delimited building access zones, weather restrictions, mulching the work areas, and mandating installation of downspout extenders immediately after gutter installation can be important ways to reducing long-term damage that manifests itself long after the contractor has quit the site. This is especially important when in the future extra care (and extra resources) become needed to establish and grow plants on a site with damaged topsoil.

Roadways should be aligned to have little or no ROW grading. Internal roadways, if private roads, have no need to be designed to the specifications used for county roads, but the owner's association would assume upkeep and snow removal responsibility. It is desirable to have utilities placed in a narrow easement adjacent to or within roadways. Roads and deep trenches for utilities that pass near trees can damage their roots, because tree roots spread well beyond their canopies and have the bulk of their roots in the top 8-12 inches of soil. Roads and trenches will terminate tree root spread, though damage may not show until long after the culprit doing grading has left the scene. Boring avoids this type of tree root damage.

Another important feature for an entire sub-division and too often left to individual lot owners is wind protection. Windbreaks should be designed as carefully and extensively as infrastructure like roadways, storm drainages, and utilities. These plantings should look nothing like the utilitarian shelterbelts created for farmland. First, the plantings should be a mixed, multispecies assemblage of hardy, adapted deciduous and evergreen trees, and shrubs in generally linear but not rigidly row-like formations. If possible some or all of these plantings should predate subdivision and use direct seeding or seedlings and heavy mulching for their establishment. Large specimens while immediately and visually satisfying do not establish well, grow slowly and often die prematurely. Shelter planting placement should be carefully located with respect to roads and dwellings to provide winter and summer wind protection but not create problematic snowdrifts or completely block out views.

Rural Lancaster County, NE, has an abundance of existing plantings, many of which harbor weedy and undesirable species. All lots and plantings need a plan and program of annual plant observation, survey and eradication to keep undesirable plants at bay. Plantings in conservation easements should also be designed to withstand heavy deer, rabbit, and squirrel herbivory, but at the same time allow animals shelter and movement. Some plantings may need fencing or other treatments for protection during establishment. A homeowners association should be encouraged to use carefully control hunting for reducing deer predation.

Rain gardens should be required on any building lot and be designed to infiltrate 100 percent of the two-year storm with overflows to be part of a designed treatment train. On larger rural lots it even may be possible to infiltrate 100 percent of the 10-year storm and store the 25-year storm on site. Roadway and driveway drainage should also include bio-swales and, if possible, terminate on the subdivision in wetlands or ponds. Properly and carefully planned conservation sub-divisions should use surface swales and not need bear the expense of underground storm inlet and pipe systems. Water quality at the subdivision outflow(s) can be a real measure of its success as a true conservation subdivision.

Landowners thinking and planning ahead to protect and create conservation areas on their land can enhance conservation sub-divisions' effectiveness. They can do this by using the existing conservation easement as a design tool. In addition to using conservation easements, developer covenants further restrict and control the use, character, and quality of individual lots and subdivision infrastructure. Finally, as an incentive, planning and zoning ordinances should provide density bonuses to developers who use conservation easements and covenants. A portion of the value of a density bonus might go toward endowing the owners association in planting and management of the conservation easements.

Applying Conservation Design to Urban Areas

To survive and prosper, humans require differing land uses in differing quantities and in different arrangements (Figure 11.4) (Odum 1969) beyond agriculture. The configuration or site-plan for various land uses constitutes a designed structure. Layout of a site requires a good deal of thought since its structure will last for a long time. Agricultural land uses, with surface treatments like conservation tillage and conservation structures like grassed waterways, riparian buffer strips, windbreaks, contour plowing, detention ponds, and closed terraces, do not control outflows of water, nutrients, and sediment as well as dense, prairie plantings. So, as agricultural areas urbanize, hard surfaces like roads, walks, roofs, and parking, deflect and concentrate even more stormwater runoff further exacerbating the effluxes of water, nutrients, and sediment. Unfortunately, hydraulic fluid, motor oil, asbestos particles, pesticides, fertilizer, and *E. coli*-laden pet waste, infuse urban runoff.

Landscape architectural design for urban areas offers a suite of soil and water conserving practices to create living, resilient, and locally appropriate infrastructure. These include, green roofs, bio-swales, rain water gardens, home cisterns, and rain barrels, level spreaders, retention ponds, constructed wetlands, wet detention ponds, stabilized natural drainage corridors, and permeable pavements of several types. These BMP (Best Management Practices) replace the need for expensive, highly engineered, buried gray infrastructure and are most often linked in series to filter, cleanse and infiltrate stormwater runoff. Still, even as a city develops and redevelops and installs BMPs, attention must also be paid to minimizing soil erosion.

Drought

So far, the main focus of this chapter has been the intentional design and integration of improving the quality and attenuating the quantity of stormwater for small storms, say, 2-year storms (those at a 50-percent probability of yearly occurrence). But I would like to also point out the important impacts on urban citizens and cities themselves brought about by the lack of runoff--severe drought.

In the summer of 2012, Lincoln and Nebraska suffered a short but nearly debilitating drought. Stories about drought impacts and letters to the editor described anecdotes about brown lawns and wasted water. Undeniably, the drought could be summarized with these facts:

- 1. Global warming, notwithstanding episodic droughts, has been and will be part and perhaps the defining environmental event of living on the Great Plains.
- 2. The 2012 drought was noteworthy in its rapid onset and occurrence during the critical growing season and unusually high temperatures consisting of daily highs and high nighttime lows.
- 3. Even with a new, larger pipeline from the Platte wellfields, potable water will always be a limiting factor for Lincoln.So it is currently investigating accessing Missoouri River water.
- 4. Over the course of a year, the largest use of potable water establishes and maintains our city landscape of shade trees, recreation fields and gardens of all kinds.

Fact one needs no further discussion (unless you are a climate denier), it remains simply the unmitigated background variable that we conveniently choose to ignore during years of ample and timely rainfall between droughts, and in making decisions about Lincoln's land use and development. Fact two, the only way in which the severity of the 2012 drought could have been worse is if we had entered the summer growing season with short supplies of subsurface moisture. Fact three may raise some eyebrows, but the encroachment of the Omaha Metropolitan Utility District on Lincoln's Platte/Elkhorn well fields, and upstream use of the Platte, Loup and Elkhorn rivers for agricultural irrigation, puts Lincoln's water supply quantity and quality at risk. Tjhe city can no longer count on uninterrupted and ample potable water supplies, as emphasized by most of Lincoln's Platte well-field knocked offline in the March 2019 flooding event. Finally, because seasonal, landscape use of water presents the major factor in topping the 65 million gallon a day well-field recharge limit, it must bear the brunt of planning, policy, and ordinance regulation and changes.

Lincoln's Mayor, Chris Beutler, implemented mandatory water restrictions, when in 2012, droughts led to dormant lawns, and declining dying trees and gardens. That Lincoln's landscape remains unsustainable in the face of drought should concern all its residents. What can be done to make it more sustainable and even resilient given drought perturbations and can ideas learned from it be applied to other communities?

First, Lincoln needs to revise its projected expansion and grow by becoming more densely populated. Second, we need to completely rethink how we grade and strip topsoil from developing lands. Topsoil supports plants by supplying nutrients and water. In fact, topsoil is an excellent place to absorb and store water. However, the typical engineered development processes not only remove the ability of a site to store water in the topsoil, but they further compact and disrupt the natural soil structure from infiltrating water into the subsoil and eventually underlying aquifers. Lincoln's older, pre-World War II residential neighborhoods have more intact soil profiles, infiltrate and store more water, and grow plants more easily than those created since the 1940's. The compacted clay subsoil in which most newly developed landscapes are grown, has a lower infiltration rate and hence more runoff.

While many of these newer neighborhoods have home irrigation systems, those systems must be designed and managed properly to make more efficient use of water. Maybe the homeowner should be licensed in order to install and use one. It does occasionally rain during droughts, and we need to make better use of stormwater, infiltrating this runoff to support the growth of trees, and fill cisterns or rain barrels for gardens and green roofs. These green features, in turn, reduce the heat island effect present in a Lincoln dominated by hard surfaces of parking lots, roof-tops, streets, walks, and driveways.

To provide funding for these types of green infrastructure treatments, those narrow self-interest groups who have consistently oppose passage of legislation allowing Lincoln and other Nebraska communities to create stormwater utilities should look to the larger good and let such a bill pass. Stormwater utility revenue, not general funds, should be used for green infrastructure. One of the best uses of such funds would be to plant street trees and retrofit parking lots with shade trees. For example, our current commercial parking space requirements need to be revised downward. Those parking lots sit underutilized most of the time, become super-heated, and generate excessive run off that could be more appropriately directed into groups of tree plantings rather than storm sewers.

The Lincoln City Council should initiate and fund a massive street tree-planting program.

It will be needed as the emerald ash borer kills thousands of Lincoln's trees. Even without the projected borer damage, thousands of gaps in the urban forest canopy have occurred because these leaders have looked on trees as a frill, and not an urban, environmental necessity. A tax on all property owners based on their linear feet of street frontage should be dedicated to funding such a tree planting and maintenance program. Pennies per linear foot would raise ten of thousands of dollars annually, and produce a payback in a cooler Lincoln and with less water and energy demands.

Carefully designing and retrofitting streets and sites to redirect storm water toward their root zones could irrigate trees. This is already happening with sections of the Union Plaza near Que Street with the revolutionary use of Silva Cells™. These cells' underground structures allow roots to grow and develop without breaking up sidewalks and pavement while simultaneously infiltrating stormwater for storage and growth.

Like all issues that impinge on urban environmental conditions, droughts can be planned for, mitigated and integrated with energy use, transportation, housing and quality of life. Perhaps the 2012 drought can serve as wake-up call to rethink how to develop and manage Lincoln's private and public landscapes. The ideas can be transferred to most cities and towns in Nebraska and would positively affect their urban landscapes.

Landscape Architectural Design in the Service of Conservation

Science often brings a deeper and more comprehensive understanding of our ecological context by requiring careful observations over tightly delimited space and/or prescribed time intervals. Scientific process applies vertical thinking (Figure 11.11) with detailed and discrete questions bringing about powerful conclusions concerning under-perceived phenomena and aiding in explaining part of the world surrounding us and how it operates. Though, dogmatic singular reliance on vertical thinking unfortunately often leads to ignoring the larger context.

On the other hand, humans also possess abilities to swiftly observe and act in a heterogeneous, uncertain world, often with incomplete information. This trait aided some of our ancestors to survive in new or unusual environments (Allen and Hoekstra 1992). Indeed, our ability to synthesize wholes from incomplete parts, descriptors, or partial details has shaped human evolution. In turn, our culture has recursively shaped our environment. Humans think best and most creatively when they think, not merely vertically, but also horizontally (Lyle 1985), filling in the gaps, and imagining wholes. Only when creative, horizontal-thinking merges with new conclusions gleaned from vertical thinking can we then truly harness and realize our full intellectual and emotional capacity.

A feature of this horizontal approach creates a design process (Figure 11.11) that has as its focus resolving human needs in light of their physical context and programmatic limitations. The design process is different from, yet complementary to the scientific process (Table 10.1).

Landscape architecture as an environmental design profession has its feet in both design and science. Its practitioners, like farmers, are applied ecologists, but also creative artists. In structuring sites they must be able to flow effortless between two processes: the scientific method to help understand the physical facts and the design process enables an ecological designer to creatively configure a site's land use, land cover, flows and boundaries drawing upon the science of ecology and the art of design. While shown as linear, each process can cycle and begin anew informed by a first iteration.

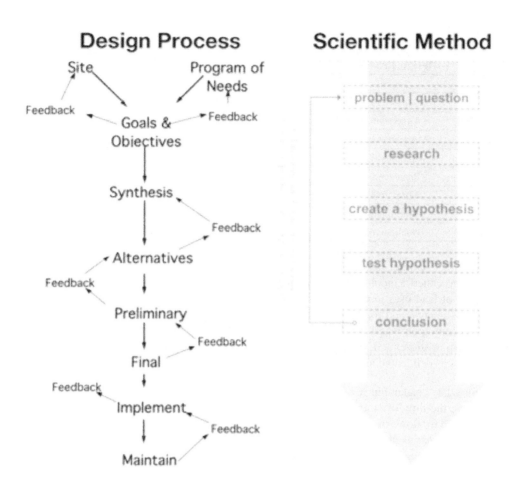

Figure 11.11 The design process enables an ecological designer to creatively configure a site's land use, land cover, its flows and boundaries drawing upon the science of ecology and the art of design. While shown as linear, each process can cycle and begin anew informed by a first iteration.

Designers must be able to gather and use facts about soils, plants, slope, surface and ground water, etc., that inform them of potential starting points in a design process. And they must understand existing land uses, land covers, flows, and boundaries revealed both by facts and by using their imaginations to create new configurations, by placing specific, detailed knowledge about the physical site and its surroundings (the vertical) in context with the proposed uses for and within an area under design scrutiny (the horizontal). The landscape architect must then interpret and imagine in three dimensions and over time how new configurations of land uses, land covers, disturbances, flows, and boundaries might best be configured, reconfigured, and maintained in light of existing and future disturbances. And they must configure sites and cities to meet human needs.

The linearity of the design process followed by landscape architects produces a highly simplified model. Updating this approach allows for and even demands recursiveness (via the feedback loops). Such recursiveness can account for and incorporate hierarchical structure found in CS Holling's model of panarchy in biological systems and in Odum's compartment model, thus, bringing the landscape architect closer to the creative process utilized by both humans and nature.

Table 11.1 Design Versus Scientific Process

Design Process	Scientific Process
Biased	Unbiased
Subjective	Objective
Divergent	Convergent
Many answers	One answer
Complexity	Simplicity
Precedents	Literature Review
Normative	Explanatory
Horizontal	Vertical
Qualitative	Quantitative

For a brief example, consider the Aurora Leadership Center, in Aurora, NE. It sits adjacent to a drainage called Lincoln Creek (Figure 11.12) and lies atop of what was once prairie. The mosaic of land uses in and around the Center, interact with its hard surfaced land cover of roofs, pavements, and topography to impact the flow of water and nutrients into Lincoln Creek. Depending on where you look and how closely you observe, topographic boundaries may be sharp or ill-defined, while the vegetative boundaries are mostly sharply defined, and the land uses as delineated are ambiguous and open to interpretation.

While the Leadership Center's boundaries present a structure partially usable in ameliorating the flow of stormwater runoff, the landscape architect must also structure and bound the land for flows of people, vehicles, wind, sunlight (and shade), and views. The spaces within the boundaries should also fit the kind of activities slated for any portion of the site. Materials, both living and architectural, must be appropriate for the climate, intended use, and its intensity. Perhaps in a more naturalistic site such as found at the Leadership Center, the landscape architect will need to consider the types and needs of wildlife. All of this complexity depends on the designer's ability to interpret and recreate landscape structure as a hierarchy of linked, sustainable, functional, and beautiful spaces.

Summary

This chapter has discussed and framed the concept of landscape structure from the natural prairie, to soil conservation on farms, to urbanizing and urbanized sites. In it the concepts of design process and scientific method have been highlighted as over-arching, complementary approaches to recreating landscape structure resistant to the entropy of soil erosion. Meanwhile, as human activities change the land use and land cover of Odum's four broad ecological land compartments, those changes, in turn, impact the quality and quantity of soil and water leaving those ecosystems. Disturbances to natural and human communities and ecosystems test their resilience and cycle in various stable states predicted by a hierarchical concept called panarchy. Finally, landscape architecture's unique approach to design and structure of sites utilizes and interweaves the imagination from the design process with facts and understanding from science.

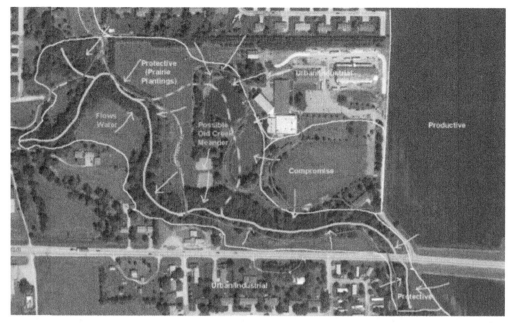

Figure 11.12. Land uses, land covers, flows and interpreted boundaries at the Aurora Leadership Center, Aurora, Hamilton County, NE and their local context. Productive, Urban/Industrial, Compromise and Protective are from Odum Figure 11.3.

Further reading

Arendt, R. 1996 *Conservation Design for Subdivisions*. Island Press Washington D.C.

Allen, T. F., & Hoekstra, T. W. 1992. *Toward a Unified Ecology* New York Columbia Press.

ASLA 2014 http://www.asla.org/design/index.html

Bentrup, G. (2008). *Conservation Buffers—Design guidelines for buffers, corridors, and greenways*. Gen. Tech. Rep. SRS–109. Asheville, NC: US Department of Agriculture, Forest Service, Southern Research Station. 110 p., 109.

Blanco-Canqui, H., & Lal, R. 2008. *Principles of soil conservation and management*. Springer Science & Business Media.

Cadenasso, M. L., Pickett, S. T., Weathers, K. C., & Jones, C. G. 2003. A framework for a theory of ecological boundaries. *BioScience*, 53(8), 750-758.

Christensen, E 1961 *Created Pawns or Creative Partners*. EJC Columbus, NE

Dorren, L., and F. Rey, 2004. A review of the effect of terracing on erosion. In Briefing papers of the 2nd SCAPE workshop, Cinque Terre, Italy (pp. 97-108)(April).

Gunderson, L. H., and Holling, C. S. 2002. *Panarchy: Understanding transformations in systems of humans and nature*. Island, Washington.

Lyle, J. T. 1985. The alternating current of design process. *Landscape Journal*, 4(1), 7-13.

Nebraska State Statutes 76-2,111

Malin, J. C. 1984. *History and Ecology: Studies of the Grassland*. University of Nebraska Press.

Odum, E. P. 1969. The strategy of ecosystem development. *Science* 164, 262, 270.

P. A Risser, Birney, E. C., Blocker, H. D., May, S. W., Parton, W. A., & Wiens, J. A. (1981). *The True Prairie Ecosystem*. Stroudsburg, Pennsylvania: Hutchinson Ross Publishing Co..

Public Law 101-624 1990. Food, Agriculture, Conservation, and Trade Act.

RBC no date PDF Entitled: "Conservation Subdivisions: Ecological, Landscape and Construction, and Legal Applications to Cherokee County, Georgia" River Basins Center, School of Ecology, University of Georgia, Athens, GA http://www.rivercenter.uga.edu/education/etowah/documents/conservation_subdivisions.htm

Renard, K. G., Foster, G. R., Weesies, G. A., and Porter, J. P. 1991. RUSLE: revised universal soil loss equation. *Journal of Soil and Water Conservation*, 46(1), 30-33.

RBC no date PDF Entitled: "Conservation Subdivisions: Ecological, Landscape and Construction, and Legal Applications to Cherokee County, Georgia" River Basins Center, School of Ecology, University of Georgia, Athens, GA http://www.rivercenter.uga.edu/education/etowah/documents/conservation_subdivisions.htm

Nebraska State Statutes 76-2,111

12 Selfish Form, Selfless Nature

"Architects today are obsessed with designing isolated towers leading to disconnected cities where the notion of shared space is being eroded." -Moshe Safdie

"Landscapes are not buildings either: they are more flexible, their interpretations wider, their access broader."-Robert Riley

The land belongs to itself. 'No self in self; no self in things'- Gary Snyder

Introduction

People ahead of me seem to be streaming toward the Nebraska Capitol building. In two's and three's they join a swelling throng at the bottom of the steps for the building's north entry. The steps terminate the south end of Lincoln's newly redesigned Centennial Mall that stretches eight blocks north. It's evening and some folks carry signs referring to 'Black Lives Matter', but I am across the street unable to hear any of the shouts or pronouncements. A couple of Nebraska State Patrol officers guard the north door and bullhorns appear from several people facing the growing crowd. No counter marchers or protesters can be seen and the rally looks to be peaceful.

A group can experience rituals to mark the important religious or even political events. Rituals most often take from the place where they occur and do so in a predictable, orderly, and timely way, extrapolating inward or outward through gestures or body language. Tasked to create form, architects shape buildings to harbor ritual gesture and display body language. Communicating gestures, like experiencing landscape, draws place from ambiguous possibilities. Though in turn, gestures expressed through architectural form reinforce or discourage certain behaviors.

Besides ritual, the layout, structure, and function of intentionally designed spaces affect human relationships, ideology, process, the general environment, and behavior. I suggested in Chapter 11 that productive rural landscapes and urban environments needed intentionally designed structures to overcome loss of soil and to re-establish efficient accommodation and use of stormwater. I also suggested that the design process when applied to questions of site and landscape integrate the vertical power of science with the promise of horizontal creative design. Since cities represent the epicenter of the built environment, their material, forms, and functions seem driven, however, by a sole focus on the ego and adduce the failure of space-making by many building architects and civil engineers.

Below I would like to expand on the example of the Nebraska State Capitol, its grounds and environs as a place that works for people. Then I would like to examine how building architects and much of their current architectural design fails to create useful sites because of a flawed, singular focus on architecture as an object that ignores its adjacent and ancillary spaces. And finally I will use Robert Smithson's dialectic of non-site and site to review standards for an example -- — my design of the proposed Nebraska Veteran's Memorial. I believe my proposed design of that site illustrates how an unbuilt project addresses ritual, site, history, and landscape by downplaying single-minded attention to a built form, but not to the spaces that support it and the people who might use them.

Two State Capitol Buildings

As a comparative example of ritual, form, and political gesture, we might compare the

Wisconsin Capitol and grounds with that of Nebraska. Both states have had progressive leaders, institutions, and citizens. The Nebraska Capitol building in particular was born of the forethought of its citizens and intellectual leaders coupled with the wealth, gleaned from agriculture in a time when price parity ruled. Both buildings lay on four square blocks at topographical high points. These sites, though urban, aptly represent the surrounding milieu. Wisconsin's Capitol building lies in the isthmus between two glacial lakes and Nebraska's sits atop a low prairie rise. Both buildings became urban landmarks with axial path extensions in their larger city contexts. The Wisconsin Capitol has eight entries, four at each cardinal direction and four more at the quarter splits between. Nebraska has just four. The architectural context differs for each—Wisconsin's sports a central dome with wings to the side – and sits as the focus of an urban square, reminiscent of the standard strategic space of many county seats surrounded by commercial enterprises, whereas Nebraska's much taller and slimmer tower sets off askance from commercial activity. Nebraska's Unicameral legislature has seen fit to create a special zoning district around the capitol with building height limits and setbacks as a sub-area plan in the Lincoln/Lancaster Master Plan to maintain a semblance of that distancing.

The space around each building's mass is quite different; Wisconsin's, comprised of a tree-canopied lawn and a wide street parking strip with benches, fountains, and other accouterments, encourages individuals or small groups to form and tarry. Those spaces express enclosure, comfort and, nurture. The Nebraska site spaces are narrower with walkways at twice the distance from the building and street trees are kept at arm's length across very wide perimeter streets. One would be more likely to drive around it than walk. No benches occur and pedestrians are not encouraged to linger, let alone traverse its expansive lawn. Perhaps another way to compare Nebraska's capitol ground with Wisconsin's comes from their local biomes. Wisconsin's has a savanna or forest with groups mingling in shady spaces and Nebraska's expresses wide-open prairie.

From what I have seen of rallies, protests, and general political ritual at the Wisconsin capitol, it mostly moves around the site's center, reminiscent of Buddhist monks' perambulations around a stupa; occasionally protestors even move inside. Site corners become small nodes and the steps there become platforms allowing at least four small to medium rallies at once.

At the Nebraska site, Goodhue's tower commands the territory and the individual. The tower is 432 feet tall and can be easily seen from 15 to 20 miles away. Visitors can circumambulate the tower two stories above the ground on a sort of an outdoor mezzanine, though it is closed in winter and I have never seen a political gathering there. Along this mezzanine Goodhue provided a rich array of bias-relief sculptures carved into the Indiana limestone for decoration and tutelage in civics. The carvings represent the rise of laws and democracy in Western civilization interwoven with mottos and the names of all Nebraska' ninety-three counties. The calm, almost boring landscape consists of a broad lawn, a few carefully placed large shade trees, and evergreen foundation plantings. The grounds' designer, landscape architect, Ernst Herminghaus, kept the exterior rather plain saving a riot of color for the quartet of courtyards. In doing so he conveyed the idea of the stoic farmer-citizen's calm outward demeanor, yet acknowledged an often churning, interior emotion.

The North Steps' broad landing was designed as a small piazzetta with the steps to the north separating it from the street and more steps between it and the front door to the Capitol building. Excepting for the small Abraham Lincoln Plaza at the Nebraska Capitol's west entrance, and unlike the multiplicity of nodes around the Wisconsin Capitol, no other gathering sites exist.

On the piazzetta, citizens pause halfway between the people below and the power above. A nearby motto carved in stone stands out, "The salvation of the state is the watchfulness of the citizen" and it blesses them exercising their rights to free speech and assembly. Perhaps that is why protest groups or political ralliers have traditionally approached and commandeered these North Steps (Figure 11.1). Site elements and spaces mediate citizens' relationships to the Capitol's architectural form and because Nebraskans know the front door presents itself as the place to get attention. When one calls on a neighbor or those in power to redress grievances — you go to the front door.

Form and Space

The Nebraska State Capitol and its grounds have importance like many of our other civic, urban spaces which employed *Homo faber*, the technician, and the toolmaker as their designer. Such a person should possess the skill to create and to wrought a mark on the world, but also the humanity to understand the user. Human dwellings, public buildings, and monuments should attest to that, but something is amiss. This urbanizing world, with its discrete structures on discrete sites, too often departs from a sense of order and no longer suggests or even supports human ritual. Furthermore, out at the fringes, in the exurbs, where shreds of nature lie under pastoral and leafy veils, or further out still ensconced within the vast undeveloped reaches of mountain and forest and plain, built form contrasts violently with site and nature sundering them.

Modern architecture borrows its forms and its materials from industrial technology. But while it may portend power, it touches an unresolved cognitive dissonance in America. Leo Marx's (1964) insightful book, *The Machine in the Garden*, traces this paradox. Western civilization seems, simultaneously seduced by the power of technology (e.g.building or structural mass) and the Arcadian myth of a space occupied by a "natural landscape." This cognitive dissonance shows we've eaten from the tree of knowledge of good and evil yet wish to remain in the Garden. The power of technology predominates and separates culture from nature denying humans their mythic roots (Campbell and Moyers 2011). This denial is perhaps the reason for sensing something amiss. And what's amiss is the lack of fit between architectural masses and forms bereft of nature, natural meaning, or any meaning at all.

What humans have struggled for since their outset, dominion over nature, may soon be consummated. Natural man, or as novelist John Fowles (1979) calls him, "green man," has become technological and urban man with such force, scale, and inexorable success that nature is permanently transfigured and our relationship with it permanently altered. And it is not only tangible nature that has changed. Most importantly our fundamental perception of nature has changed. Today, according to environmental historian, Paul Shepherd (1968)

> "…we live in an avalanche of sensation and excitement with a thousand artificial ways to get pleasure and comfort. Few of them are directly dependent on other organisms and none except gardens are designed as a microcosm of nature…the garden is [has become only?] an abstraction of the natural organic world"

We derive our abstractions from other sources as well. Cultural historian and I dare say deconstructionist, William Irwin Thompson (1988) asserts our "notion of Nature is simply cultural history" because "natural history is a subset of cultural history. Nature is not a state, a place or a ground, but merely the horizon of the dominant culture." Nature seems largely an idea; culture, when it creates (art, architecture or landscape) interprets nature as well as mitigates our place with in it. Kenneth Friedman (1983) points out, "Human beings create art as a cultural act commenting through culture on culture itself."

Figure 12.1. A July 2016 rally for Black Lives Matter at the North Steps of the Nebraska Capitol.

Human separation from and denial of nature has been subconsciously expressed and embodied in built forms. Just look at the rudeness of the deconstruction movement in architecture; its forms are artifacts interpreting culture to what end? Artist, Carolyn Bloomer (1976) declares,

> "The philosophy of an entire society is expressed through its architectural treatment of space… modern glass and steel buildings emphasize simplicity, efficiency and technological power. Each time and culture reveals as well as imposes philosophical concepts of humankind by the way it structures its public and private space."

Architect and theorist, Koolhaus bluntly reproves designers in his own profession, calling modern architectural spaces "Junkspace" which he derides as:

> "additive, layered, and lightweight, not articulated in different parts but subdivided, quartered the way a carcass is torn apart—individual chunks severed from a universal condition."

Traditional or vernacular architecture has borrowed its forms and cues unself-consciously from nature (Rudofsky 1964, Alexander 1977). Dennis Mann (1985) reflects that vernacular or traditional architecture, finds "an awareness of a state of agreement between the buildings and their surroundings."

Still, while being *Homo faber* is part of being human, do we always produce art? Friedman (1983) postulates "the drilling [rig] of an oil company is as much a part of the 'environment' as a tree." Yes, but it certainly is not art. Its creation maybe cultural but the engineers' intents strictly tout, function, and economic gain. It is devoid of any intrinsic meaning. " The viewer must confer all meaning on an oil-rig, because its fabricator intended none.

Since architects, landscape architects, and artists create, we should expect they convey meaning by their "design as introduction of intent into environmental events" (Tatibian 1976). Meaning is crucial to our understanding, evaluation, and appreciation of built forms and intent must be clear and unequivocal if those forms are to be wellsprings of meaning. This is especially true if the designers wish their products to be more than technological objects. Mann (1985) suggests, "Architectural form is self-reflexive; that is, the form itself is the content." No meaning there. The designer only tells us, "What it is." and does not engage us to ask, "What does it mean?" Amos Rapoport and Robert Kantor (1967) have expressed it this way,

> "The problem with much contemporary architecture and urban design is that is has been simplified and cleaned up to such an extent that all it has to say is revealed at a glance. A range of meanings and possibilities has been eliminated… If all is designed and settled there is no opportunity to bring ones own values to the forms…"

Or the obverse according to Gestalt psychologist Rudolf Arnhiem (1951) occurs when ". . . so many people have become blind to the meaning of form that they believe they 'see' when they absorb meaning without form."

Landscape architect and teacher, Patrick Condon (1988), has made a valuable analysis of what he calls "cubist space" and "volumetric space". "Cubist space…is made by placing solids in space; volumetric space is made by enclosing space with solids." Cubist space, like modern architecture, tends to exclude while volumetric space tends to include. This may be why modern buildings tend to ignore their context, while site design and landscape must by its very task define and integrate. By their forms and surrounding spatial relationships the North Entry steps at the Nebraska state Capitol "include" the users. On the other hand, building form as object represents a trophy to architects because it seems more real and tangible than process or space. And while the process of design is an open-ended, messy business, form provides visual stimulus to our senses, potential meaning to the mind and maybe most importantly, satisfaction to the human ego.

Koolhaus (2001) reiterates,

> "When we think about space, we have only looked at its containers. As if space itself is invisible, all theory for the production of space is based on an obsessive preoccupation with its opposite: substance and objects, i.e., architecture. Architects could never explain space; Junkspace is our punishment for their mystifications."

Architects have literally objectified space and at the same time inflated their egos.

Rudolf Arnhiem (1951) states,

> "If we wish to understand the relationship between visual form and the total [human] organism, we must consider the complex interaction of the many forces that make up a person." '

The problem of form, object and space', as I call it, is its very palpability, its perfection, absolute and untouchable, that springs directly from the human ego. It becomes ego displayed as built form … an offspring from the designer's psyche. Ego feeds on novelty for novelty's sake and the recognition that accompanies it. McDonough (1983) associates ego embedded into an urban design profession with an "ideology [that] is manifested in its predilection for statistical studies, surveys, pseudoscientific rationalizations, computer-generated investigations and constant categorizations of humanity…It presumes that the built environment is at its best when it is controlled, stylized, quantifiable and rational." All these left-brain functions intimately intertwine with the ego. The ego has no time for meaning especially when posited in a relational, holistic, subjective and emotional way.

Artist Alan Gussow (1980) however acknowledges the ego's seminal (though not dominant) role in the creative process, "To be an artist in one way is to have a hell of an ego, because it is saying, 'By, god, what you've experienced is worth memorializing; worth making permanent.'...On the other hand to be an artist involved with nature is to be humble since what you create is often a poor imitation of the real thing [nature]."

Mann (1985) says, "The true measure [of architecture] is not in architecture's originality but in its quality." Koolhaus' (2001) concept of 'Junkspace' focuses upon quantity. Ego gets entangled with bigness, not scale and quantity, not quality.

Where is the experience in most built forms made of 'Junkspaces'? Why would ego want input, (other than praise) from someone else like the user or viewer? So we have the problem, reiterated as an endless anarchy of meaningless, built forms, ignoring a natural context and process richly endowed with potential meaning. Koolhaus (2001) is spot-on again suggesting 'Junkspace' usurps your emotions and associations. It co-opts the senses and desires you to experience it as: "rich, stunning, cool, huge, abstract, minimal, [and] historical."

Designers and clients sense something is amiss so to assuage the problem they often apply a balm of green goo, desultory shrubs or barren turf calling it landscape or worse yet, natural. A faux facade which Koolhaus sees and says:

> "Landscape has become Junkspace, foliage as spoilage: Trees are tortured, lawns cover human manipulations like thick pelts, or even toupees, sprinklers water according to mathematical timetables . . . Seemingly at the opposite end of Junkspace, the golf course is, in fact, its conceptual double: empty, serene, free of commercial debris. The relative evacuation of the golf course is achieved by the further charging of Junkspace. The methods of their design and realization are similar: erasure, tabula rasa, reconfiguration. Junkspace turns into biojunk; ecology turns into ecospace. Ecology and economy have bonded in Junkspace as ecolomy"

However design must be process first and last; form and product, second because ever-changing events bring fluidity and impermanence to the built environment and even more so to the landscape. Nature, landscape, and site are fundamentally different from and more dynamic than a building. The Chinese know this because their language distinguishes between ideas for man-made (*wu*) and natural growth, (*wu-wei*), i.e., not made. The wind blows; the sun arcs across the sky; oaks drop their acorns; seedlings sprout in the compost. Even buildings can sprout additions, are remodeled and rehabilitated (Handa 2014).

Others are also aware of this difference. The late sculptor, Robert Smithson's juxtaposition of non-site and site fits the dialectic of building (non-site) versus nature/landscape (site) (Table 11.1). Urban planner, Carl Steinitz (1979) warns against large projects with a "strong concept, fully worked out" as lacking "adaptability" to the complexity of events, both natural and cultural. Landscape architect Lawrence Halprin (1972) urges "imperfect" or "incomplete design" where such "design is to create possibilities for events to happen." The products of design are but points along a cycle of process. Here is where design and nature coincide. Painter Joe Miller ascribes his understanding of creative process to nature,

> "There's a series of events that are one, [but] they are blind to the future and the past, and just carry out the act at that moment. What they do at the moment affects the future but only the next step. Nature has no overall vision of what is to happen" (Gussow 1980).

Table 11.1 Robert Smithson's (1969) Non-Site versus Site

Non-site	Site
Closed limits	Open limits
An array of matter	A series of points
Inner coordinates	Outer coordinates
Addition	Subtraction
Determinate uncertainty	Indeterminate certainty
Contained information	Scattered information
Mirror	Reflection
Center	Edge
No place (abstract)	Some place (physical)
One	Many

Nature as process is open and adaptable. It is selfless.

Most completed design or art objects are static. Environmental artist, Alan Sonfist, created 'Time Landscape for New York,' which Architect, Michael McDonough (1983) describes as, "stand[ing] in contra-distinction to the manmade city around it, making tangible the wilderness that once flourished there and offering the complex processes of the natural environment as an alternative to the monolithic urban imagery." Saarinen (1948) is hopeful for the future, "…mechanization [= urbanization?] of the human mind will turn--when the time is ripe--into humanization of the mechanized mind. Form is bound to follow the same metamorphosis."

The seeming chaos of Nature is just that. It is an illusion. Form and pattern exist, yet to simply extract that pattern from nature destroys its complexity. This is why Fowles (1979) urges "Seeing Nature Whole." One might think of Nature of as a pattern of patterns, a process; what the Gregory Bateson (1976) called a "meta-pattern." In this approach to design, true process can help reunify man and nature by mediating dialectic between form and nature. This occurs as design moves from fixed to fluid, from "non-site" to "site" from building to landscape and from selfish form to selfless nature.

Nebraska Veterans Memorial

A 1999 design competition asked for ideas and a rough budget for a Nebraska Veterans Memorial to be placed on land owned by the Department of Roads along I-80 adjacent to its north Lincoln westbound rest-stop just west of US 77. With this basic information I visited the site and proceeded to think about the features that I thought portrayed what such a memorial might entail as a place.

One of the first things that came to mind was the historicity of such an endeavor and the wars that had impacted Nebraskans. Still a territory at the end of the Civil War, Nebraska posed a distraction of Native American unrest. Its male citizens were minimally involved in the short, Spanish-American War; though two Federalized National Guard regiments went to the Philippines and one regiment helped occupy Cuba. However America's entry into World War I brought major conscription with the Selective Service Act of 1917 and tens of thousands of Nebraska men mustered into military service. The same was true for WW II and to a lesser extent in the Korean, Vietnam, and Gulf Wars.

America's entry in WW I was also its seminal entry onto the world stage. Young men who had only heard of European places from immigrant pioneers ended up there to fight against Germany in the trenches and forests of France. Upon the end of the Great War and the signing of the Treaty of Versailles, November 11 became fixed in American minds as a day to commemorate the brave servicemen and women who had been taken from their quiet lives on the Nebraska plains and sent far away.

For Those Who Served

First, modest goals and objectives were created for the Nebraska Veteran's Memorial (NVM):

Goal: Provide a Place and Space for Ritual and Remembrance
    Objectives: Create a processional space
                            Create an assembly space
                            Tie site to November 11
Goal: Provide a Sense of Nebraska
    Objectives: Use forms, spaces and material found in Nebraska
                            Utilize offsite views
                            Use official state tree, grass and flower
Goal: Provide for Site Function
    Objectives: Universal Access
                            Parking for 30 autos
                            Minimum maintenance
Goal for Future Memorials:
    Objectives: Honor those who served in peace and war
                            Honor both men and women
                            Leave space for future remembrance

A passage from Cather's (1922) Pulitzer Prize novel, *One of Ours*, came to my mind.

> "Claude took a stick and drew a square in the sand; there, to begin with was the house and farmyard; there was the big pasture, with Lovely Creek flowing through it; there were the wheat and cornfields, the timber claim, more wheat and corn, more pastures."

Love of land and the Nebraska landscape had imbued spatial memories into the fictional Claude Wheeler (loosely modeled on Cather's cousin G.P. Cather). In **One of Ours**, Cather taps the cultural landscape of Nebraska both physically and psychologically by projecting it from Claude Wheeler's mind (Cather 1923),

> "The farmer then took the time to plant fine cottonwood groves and to set aside Osage-orange hedges along the borders of their fields."

Below, I describe the design of the NVM and reflect Smithson's concepts of site.

The Memorial as Site

The land and the people upon it bring an important theme to explore in any Veteran's memorial. The Nebraska cultural landscape idioms of cropland, timber claims, square sections, hedgerows, windbreaks, natural streams and so on, might be the material and forms of a memorial since those places, in part, physically represented for what soldiers served and fought (Figures 12.2, 12.3).

Open limits

The crest and hillside selected at the I-80 rest stop allow several points to view out into the surrounding landscape. Because landscape unites the memorial theme and objectives it plays and important role in opening limits beyond.

Series of points

As rituals proceed, they occur at several discrete points: Parking arrival, movement through spaces to the circular node, location of future memorials and views directed to specific points on the horizon.

Outer coordinates

Along with the open limits and off site views, the memorials propose spaces direct the participant to the rising sun's azimuth on November 11, to the Nebraska State Capitol tower, and focus on a small pond, just off site.

Subtraction

Spaces within the memorial result from such proposed features as the subtraction of tree masses for processional paths, open gaps in hedgerows to frame views, the arcing drop outlet for outlining the pond, removal of cottonwoods for interior axes, and spaces carved out for parking autos.

Indeterminate certainty

The cottonwood trees will be planted into a rowed grove (Certainty). Birds will plant the eastern redcedar but the exact location of each will be unplanned and random.

Scattered information

No spot in the memorial contains all the information or is the prime ritual location. A hierarchy of importance will be distributed in time of day and year and in space.

Reflection

The cultural features of pond, path, and parking space, and planted features of hedgerow, cottonwood grove, windbreak, and prairie all reflect those elements presence throughout Nebraska and comprising its landscape. These modifications also accommodate and ameliorate the weather and its impacts on the lives of Nebraskans.

Edges

Physical and implied edges occur within the NVM, at its boundaries and beyond into the surrounding rural landscape.

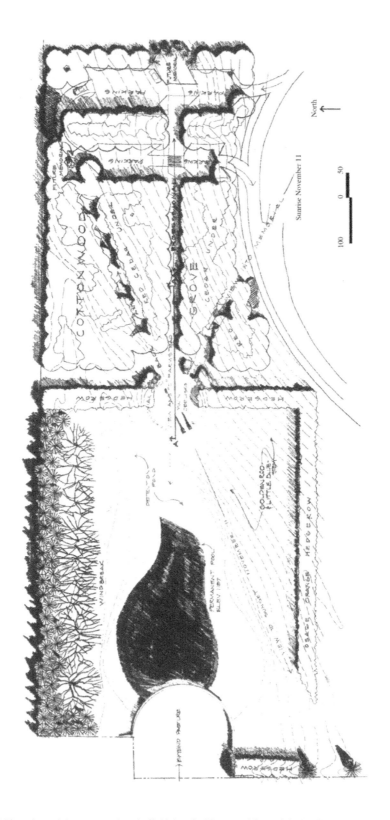

Figure 12.2 Plan view of the proposed, unbuilt Nebraska Veterans Memorial. Design by author

Figure 12.3. Partial sectional elevation along the mail processional from the ceremonial circle into the cottonwood grove. The unbuilt memorial's spaces support the user and the ritual of remembrance and memorialization. Design by author

Some place

While the planted feature might be thought of as abstractions of feature found in the Nebraska landscape, they are sufficiently large and composed of appropriate plants, so as to adapt to the site over time. The site and all of its influences from bird-planted cedars to windbreaks will make this place some place and special.

Many

Just as scattered points occur in the NVM design, many occur for differing memorials and differing locations on the site and off.

Summary

Most building architects' overwhelmingly focus on singular, physical, built form narrows meaning and devalues a user's connection with a place; this often devalues nature herself. Architects' preoccupation with a built, material form must expand outward and go beyond mere function of utility connections, grading and drainage, and auto connections. On small urban sites, perhaps this can happen by using green roofs and green walls. On larger, more generous sites, the conditions of nature, microclimate, plants and pedestrian movement offer potential activities. A skillful site designer understands, probes and engages the site with spaces as well as masses; he or she encourages bonding and ritual from the human user.

Further Reading

Alexander Christopher. 1964. *Notes on the Synthesis of Form*. Chapter 4 Cambridge: MIT Press

Arnhiem, Rudolf. 1951 "Gestalt Psychology and Artistic Form: In, *Aspects of Form*. Lancelot Law Whyte (Ed.) Indiana Press. Bloomington, IN 249 pp p. 206.

Bateson, Gregory 1979. *Mind and Nature: A Necessary Unity*. Bantam NY:NY. p. 128.

Bloomer, Carolyn, 1976, *Principles of Visual Perception*. Van Nostrand Rheinhold. NY. NY 148 pp. p. 65.

Campbell, J. and Moyers, B., 2011. *The Power of Myth*. Anchor.

Condon, Patrick, 1988. "Cubist Space, Volumetric Space and Landscape Architecture" *Landscape Journal* 7 (1): 1-14. p. 1

Fowles, John. 1979. "Seeing Nature Whole" *Harpers*. November pp 48-69

Friedman, Kenneth S. 1983. "Words on the Environment" In *Art in the Land*. Alan Sonfist (Ed.) Dutton NY. NY. 274 pp p. 256.

Gussow, Alan. 1980. In "The Artists and the American Land" Video, Cultural Affairs Unit, Nebraska Educational Television. Lincoln, NE. 60 minutes.

Halprin, Lawrence 1972. *Lawrence Halprin Notebooks 1959-1972*. MIT Press. Cambridge, MA 377 pp. P. 81.

Handa, R., 2014. Allure of the Incomplete, Imperfect, and Impermanent: Designing and Appreciating *Architecture as Nature*. Routledge.

Koolhaas, R. 2002. *Junkspace* . MIT Press.

Mann Dennis Alan. 1985. Between Traditionalism and Modernism: Approaches to Vernacular Architecture. *Journal of Architectural Education* Winter 39(2):10-16

Marx, Leo. 1964. *The Machine in the Garden*. Oxford University Press. NY:NY.

McDonough, Michael. 1983. "Architecture's Unnoticed Avant-Garde" In, *Art in the Land*. Alan Sonfist (Ed.) Dutton NY. NY. 274 pp p. 242

Miller, Joe 1980. In "The Artist and the American Land" Video, Cultural Affairs Unit, Nebraska Educational Television. Lincoln, NE. 60 minutes.

Rapoport, Amos and Robert Kantor, 1967. "Complexity and Ambiguity in Environmental Design" *JAIP*. July 33(4):p. 210

Rudofsky, B., 1964. *Architecture Without Architects: A Short Introduction to Non-pedigreed Architecture*. UNM Press.

Saarinen, Eliel, 1948. *Search for Form*. Rheinhold. NY., N.Y. 3534 pp. p. 27

Shepard, Paul 1968 *Man in the Landscape: A Historical View of the Esthetics of Nature*. Alfred Knopf NY:.NY.

Smithson, Robert 1969. In Lawrence Alloway, "Robert Smithson's Development" In A*rt in the Land*. Alan Sonfist (Ed.) Dutton NY. NY. 274 pp p. 130

Steinitz, Carl 1979. "The Trouble with a Strong Concept, Fully Worked Out" Letter to *Landscape Architecture* November 69 (6) 565.

Tatibian, Jivan. 1976 Remarks at the International Design Conference at Aspen.

Thompson, William Irwin 1988. Remarks at The Land Institute. September 23 Salina KS. (also see Thompson, William Irwin, 1988. **Pacific Shift**. Sierra Club Books S.F. CA. 197 pp.)

13 Pioneers Park: Landscape and Program Dynamics

> "The more successfully a city mingles everyday diversity of uses and users in its everyday streets, the more successfully, casually (and economically) its people thereby enliven and support well-located parks that can thus give back grace and delight to their neighborhoods instead of vacuity."-Jane Jacobs

Introduction

For more than three decades, Pioneers Park was the place to be and be seen by Lincoln's young people. For daylight cruising it beat out circling King's Drive-ins or dragging "O" Street. On the first warm day of spring or the first time young drivers got to take out the family car, the destination was Pioneers Park out of town and then on the outskirts of town. Warm spring Sundays meant hanging out at Pioneers Park and waxing the car, playing a pickup baseball or football game, or having a family picnic. It was Lincoln's shared public place gratefully inhabited by young, old and black and white. As public spaces were meant to be, Pioneer Park let folks mingle and see themselves as part of the same community.

Nebraskans, besides residents of Lincoln, also love their city parks. As public open spaces, parks focus a community's activities, recreation, history, and stewardship. Hence, they often become the repository for community buildings, recreational facilities, attending parking lots and community memorials as well as recreation and ritual. In Nebraska, the 1920's with its economic boom and remembrance of pioneers and the 1930's with economic collapse and government work programs, many communities initiated new public parks and expanded activities in older ones.

Before describing the history and character of Lincoln's Pioneers Park, I would like to compare and contrast it with contemporaneous parks from four other Nebraska communities: Fairbury (McNish Park), David City (Memorial Park), Columbus (Pawnee Park) and Schuyler (Oak Park), all or some of which were built with the help of the WPA (Works Progress Administration) and /or other New Deal programs.

All of these parks except McNish and Pioneers Park have unknown designers; McNish and Pioneers Parks have no major public buildings or stadiums built within them. All, except McNish Park, have public or private golf courses adjoining them. All have some type of focal water feature or features. The parks' sizes, existing layouts, programmatic elements and circulation paths vary widely. Size matters here because larger parks require more maintenance, but with careful and sensitive siting, can absorb additional elements more easily. Pawnee and Memorial Parks have endured major changes, however their newer elements appear unrelated in their form, organization, and use of materials (Figures 13.1, 13.2, 13.3, 13.4).

Pioneers Park

Designed in the late 1920's by Ernst H. Herminghaus, Lincoln, Nebraska's Pioneer Park strongly represents the Beaux Arts style of landscape architectural design, popular in the late 19th and early 20th centuries. As a large municipal park, it became a destination for two generations of Lincoln residents, though accessed almost exclusively by automobile, as it originally lay about a mile beyond the city limits. Its 1993 nomination and subsequent entry on the National Register of Historic Places and selection for a 1999 American Society of Landscape Architects Centennial Medallion attests to the park's significance and relatively intact character.

Figure 13.1 Memorial Park, David City, Butler County, NE. Water, circulation and activities.

Figure 13.2 Pawnee Park Columbus Platte County, NE where memorials and memorabilia line US 81 and flank the park entry.

Figure 13.3 Oak Park Schuyler, Cuming County NE, showing entry to parking and Oak Ball Room. The parking lot to the right is heavily canopied with trees.

Figure 13.4 McNish Park fountain and pavilion suffers from lack of maintenance and irrigation, but has had few incompatible uses foisted on it.

The experience of Pioneers Park really begins about a mile to its east along Van Dorn Street, which served for many years as the main access corridor to this then rural park. Lines of ponderosa pines to the outside and common lilacs next to Van Dorn stretched from about the Salt Creek Bridge (now closed to autos) beyond Coddington Avenue Street to about the location of the park's North Entrance. Coddington Avenue was also heavily planted to ponderosa pine, lilac, and eastern redcedar and borders the east boundary of the park. Those plants hint of the park's planting palette. Recently, an eastward extension of Bison Trail has created a narrow opening in this wall of plantings making the capitol tower visible, and extended the view from the park as one exits the park through the east entrance. In 2020 the southeast corner of Coddington and Vandorn was developed into apartments and the dense planting clear cut.

The context for this very large park is set by varied adjacent land uses including: the Yankee Hill brick factory and clay pit on its southeast corner, the Burlington Northern and Santa Fe railway mainline following Haines Branch Creek along the south border, a recently acquired addition of 230 acres of prairie to the west and northwest, Pioneers Golf Course, and a series of residential lots and acreages to its north and northeast. A new north entry off Van Dorn was added in 1953 to service traffic to Pinewood Bowl. The addition of prairie to the west brings the park's size to about equal that of Central Park in New York City, a place that also initially developed outside city boundaries.

During the 1920's, early Nebraska's settlers were reaching the ends of their lives and many communities sought to honor their pioneering spirit and memory. Inspired by the same feelings and intent, Willa Cather wrote her suite of prairie novels between 1913 and 1935. The park's nucleus created from an initial donation of 500 acres of prairie and cropland came from a former local resident. New York Stockbroker, John F. Harris. He intended for the park to honor his parents and other early Lincoln and Nebraska pioneers. One might wonder why the park design followed the Beaux Arts style (really an amalgam of European style with some naturalistic and some geometric forms) to honor the memory of people who carved a country out of the prairie. Why not use a naturalistic prairie metaphor? I think that design style was appropriately chosen because the human grandeur of the Beaux Arts style fits well with a pioneer's vision of what a humanized landscape might portray. In its essence, the park represents what prairie had become; it symbolized what they had forged.

Landscape architect, Ernst Herminghaus (Figure 13.5), the son of immigrants, (his German-born father was a cigar maker) was not immediately chosen to plan the park, but began his involvement by serving as a consultant to the Lincoln City Council in obtaining master plan proposals. In March of 1929, three plans were submitted; one by P. E. McMillan, a local landscape architect; one by Sonderegger Nurseries of Beatrice and one from Irvin McCrary of Denver. Willie Dunn and Harry B. McNeal of Kansas City separately designed a public golf course (Figure 13.6), proposed as a part of Harris' original program. These two golf consultants had been brought to Lincoln at the urging of Herminghaus. It is unclear why, but after some initial planting in the spring of 1929 none of the three solicited plans were implemented and on January 1, 1930, Herminghaus completed a design for the east 80 acres of the park. Since the submitted plans have been lost, we have no idea what if any ideas Herminghaus gleaned from them in creating his plan (Figures 13.7 and 13.11).

Design Program and Layout

Immediately upon entering the park from the east entry, one experiences its unusually enclosed character and carefully linked spaces. This is no ordinary city park where one

Figure 13.5 Lincoln-born and Harvard-educated Landscape Architect, Ernst H. Herminghaus designed Lincoln's Pioneers Park in the Beaux Arts style.

circumambulates its margins and views toward the inside. Pioneers Park must be physically entered. Upon doing so, the visitor easily becomes involved with its spatial composition and transfixed by its scale. Enclosure afforded by the mass plantings, especially those consisting of conifers enables strong spatial effects.

In its essence, Pioneers Park contrasts with the prairie and plains landscape of Eastern Nebraska. Overwhelmed by ample prospects, Great Plains residents often tend to seek refuge. Herminghaus, familiar with style from both the eastern US and Europe, delivered what the pioneer wished to symbolize: an elegant, settled, and thoroughly humanized landscape. Unlike most any park in Nebraska then or now, the first 160 passive acres sculpt spaces, focus inward, and decompress unimpeded by playgrounds, buildings, parking lots, and all the accouterments

Figure 13.6 Courses such as at Pioneers Park provide recreation and important open space benefits.

and clutter of active recreation. This does not mean the visitor becomes claustrophobic. Sculptures punctuate long internal views and distant vistas to the Nebraska State Capitol orient the user. These distant vistas, carefully controlled and delineated as allees, express the City Beautiful Movement compatible to its Beaux Arts style.

Former architecture professor, the late Linus Burr Smith noted, "Ernst's invitation to enter sets the mood at Pioneers Park... using plantings and spaces as sequence with the skill of a set designer." Two major allees focus outward on the Goodhue Capitol tower some two and one-quarter miles to the east-northeast. As a designed landscape form, an allee's straight, controlled prospect evolved from Mediaeval hunting swaths cut through dense forests (Figures 13.8, 13.9, and 13.10). No forest here, so it needed to be planted.

One internal allee ties together a sculpture of a buffalo near the entry and westward to the originally proposed site for the Red Cloud "Smoke Signal" sculpture. That sculpture was retired to a military crest behind Pinewood Bowl overlooking a meadow and the picnic grounds to the west (Figure 13.12). Evidently, having Red Cloud signaling his warriors to the west made more sense than the chief looking toward the city. The proposed Red Cloud site remained empty of a focal point until Railroad Engine 409 landed there, completely out of context. (Fortunately the engine has been refurbished and retired to Lincoln's Haymarket next to the former Burlington depot.) This key high point in the visual structure of the park still

Figure 13.7 Aerial view of the east portion of Pioneers Park circa 1950.

While Herminghaus was a master plantsman, his desire for a wide variety of trees and shrubs faded in the harsh reality of the Dust Bowl. For practical reasons he used the inexpensive planting palette of species that could be diverted from the Prairie States Forestry Project. We know this because the older trees remained true to the planned massing, but not the species selection. In the end, use of WPA and NYA (National Youth Administration) labor and available windbreak plants won out. Given that many of the conifer tree mass monocultures succumbed to diseases in the 1970's and 1980's, it was perhaps a shortsighted decision. Park restoration in the 1990's incorporated more bio-diversity in line with Herminghaus' original palette. In a 1935 proposal, Herminghaus attempted to display his plant expertise in a design for the "Harris Arboretum" west of the picnic grounds. Though intended to be a layout similar to the Bessey Arboretum, which he knew well from the University of Nebraska Agriculture College campus, it was never planted.

Space becomes defined rather easily in the prairie when one employs large, dense masses of plantings. The location of the park's plantings intertwined with the circulation alignment reinforces the spatial sequence. Topography also plays an important structural role in the park layout and its experience. Arrival at the east entry leads one up slope to the Buffalo Sculpture on a rise displayed against the sky. On gaining this nodal high point and roundabout, an internal allee presents itself, falls away across a pond then rises again to the park's high point, about a half mile to the west. Here, the allees' straight edges strongly emphasize the up and down and contrast with the lay of the land.

After glimpsing this overall layout, one then turns away, proceeds down a road along a route tightly squeezed between trees, by a pond, then around a bend, up deflected vista, finally

Figure 13.8 The eastern vista displays a newly opened view from Bison Circle to the capitol tower.

Figure 13.9. Bison entry circle is enclosed with a wall of Taylor junipers.

arriving atop a broad ridge near the park's high point. The outgoing reverse route seems like an entirely different sequence and experience when, new, previously unseen vistas open up presenting internal and distant Capitol views. I have taken visitors with me going in and out

Figure 13.10. Road leaving Bison Circle revealing evergreens tightly enclosing the space

this road and they swear we were on a completely different route. To the side, well off of the road, bikes and pedestrians move unseen on separate alignments. No parking, playground or other features distract drivers allowing them to focus on the spatial experience and scale shift driving through a giant landscape sculpture.

Along the road, both coming and going, one's focus tends inward to the north so you miss the narrow, higher planted bank to the south needed to screen a gaping crater left from Yankee Hill Brick Company's clay extraction. The park's high point and attending ridge overlay clay of a quality coveted by the company for making their bricks. This unused clay pit wasteland is well known to youths who trespass on part of it adjacent to the park and have dubbed it "Hippie Cliffs."

Site Character and Evolving Program

Pioneers Park drapes across acres of undulating ground sculpted from glaciers and the subsequent erosive work of small drainages. Roger Pabian's (2001) pamphlet on the geology of Pioneers Park offers a detailed description of its parent material, slopes, drainages, and outcrops that underlay the park. In it he notes the erosive action of Haines Branch Creek in creating a level area suitable for the picnic ground, gouged road cuts display glacial till, pond edges incise loess based soils, and an outcrop of Dakota sandstone exposes the slope below the Smoke Signal. Unfortunately, erosion at that outcrop threatened the statue's stability and it has been covered and planted. However, in a city where large swaths of land regularly succumb to civil engineers' unimaginative mass grading plans, the topography of the park remains relatively untouched; the native prairie and even the human planted forests lay lightly on its undulating surface.

The park's North Road remains closed to auto traffic, but also has an inward focus. At one point that road dips unseen to a low point next to a pond in the middle of an allee. On closer inspection, we see Herminghaus has created a small shrub screen of spirea, as a kind of planted "Ha-Ha" like found in many large English gardens sunken to hide fences; here in the park it hides a portion of the North Road.

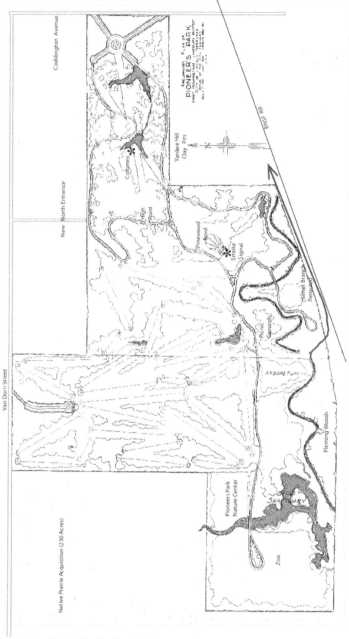

Figure 13.11 Herminghaus' plan for the first eighty acres of Pioneers Park.

Pioneers Golf Course came into being in 1929 before the park, but its design layout of 18 holes fits well into the topography. A 1935 plan by Herminghaus shows addition of nine holes, but as of yet remains unfulfilled. They were to occupy an area, now called Long Meadow, which, instead, has remained as prairie and supplied some of the hay used by grazing animals in the Pioneer Zoo. The course remains separated from the park, has its own entry off Van Dorn, and the boundary between it and the park mutually buffer one another.

Figure 13.12. The Smoke Signal on a slope west of Pinewood Bowl. Its exposed slope and outcrop of Dakota sandstone has been covered with soil.

Figure 13.13 Pinewood Bowl was on the original master plan, but not built until after WW II. A new stage was built in the 1960's.

Pinewood Bowl appeared in the 1935 plan but was not built until 1953 (Figure 13.13.) True to the Beaux Arts theme Herminghaus modeled its stage and setting from the *teatro di verzura* with its planted backdrop at the Villa Gori near Sienna, Italy. As the sophistication and size of productions and audiences increased, the stage was expanded then rebuilt completely and the broad ridge just north of the bowl became designated as a temporary parking lot. Burgeoning crowds and traffic jams after performances also required the addition of a new north entry to the park. It comes off Van Dorn with its own very understated roundabout that now supports a bronze statue of an elk, as a counterpoint to the east entry buffalo. A small, permanent parking lot was added south of the North Entry along the ridge that serviced wintertime sledding to the west. In its flood plain under a canopy of trees, picnic grounds lay with three large group shelters and scores of scattered picnic tables. The creek, prone to flooding, was later relocated and realigned a few yards to the south of the park boundary along the railroad tracks.

The Ager Nature Center and Zoo have also undergone program changes resulting in the addition of a new education building, a restored prairie, a one-room school, and a zoo refocused on native animals including bison and elk. While these activities are not exactly passive, Pioneers Park has not been subjected to absorbing tennis courts, swimming pools, lighted ball fields with bleachers, and parking lots as have many parks which cater to active recreation. Site of new trailhead crosses Haines Branch Creek and will lead to Spring Creek Prairie seven miles to the southwest. (Figure 13.14)

Figure 13.14 Site of new trailhead crosses Haines Branch Creek and will lead to Spring Creek Prairie seven miles to the southwest.

Conclusions

The preceding narrative leads me to conclude that Pioneers Park continues to change in its uses and environment, and those changes will most likely accelerate. Recently it has been designated as the trailhead (13.14) for the Prairie Trail Corridor heading to the south and west

Figure 13.15 Nature Center Building at Pioneers Park

ultimately leading to the Spring Creek Prairie some 6.5 miles away. The Lincoln/Lancaster Comprehensive plan shows that the park will be nearly surrounded by future residential and commercial growth. While Pinewood Bowl is a major concert and musical destination, it was designed into the park from the beginning and temporary event parking is handled well on nearby turf fields.

Stewardship of Pioneers Park has had the attention of the of city leaders. In a revisit of the original master plan in the 1989 Rebuilding Pioneers Park: A Restoration and Management Plan (Figure 14.15), a team of several landscape architects proposed species recommendations and replanting, as well as, calling attention to needs for overall care and protection of the park. While creating a species list for replanting the landscape architects examined six other intertwined issues:

- Roads and Circulation
- Vehicular Parking
- Land Use Adjacencies
- Maintenance
- Equestrian Use
- Winter Activities

How do the Beaux Arts design forms, especially the straight-line geometry hold up to both programmatic and environmental changes? Marc Treib a landscape critic in his article, "The Content of Landscape Form [The Limits of Formalism]" has applied three interacting but separate criteria to understanding the success of large landscape developments such as parks and waterfronts. He suggests, "[W]e might gauge the content of landscape design along three axes: the formal, (which includes space, form and materials); the cultural (which includes history, social mores, and behavior); and the environment (among them ecology, topography, hydrology, horticulture and natural process)." So, at Pioneers Park the Beaux Arts style relates

Figure 13.16. Illustration from *Rebuilding Pioneers Park* detailing aesthetic and maintenance issues.

to Treib's formal axes; Programmatic objectives such as memorializing settlers, providing a community outdoor entertainment venue, and educating about nature fall along the cultural axis; Herminghaus' plant interest and usage overlain on the topography and the park's 80-year long response and adjustment to natural processes such as drought, disease, flooding, and erosion relate to the environmental axis.

Trees are not common in the prairie and the effort to keep the allee edges and conifer tree masses intact have required commitment and funding from the community. The park's renewed emphasis on prairie, the native biome for this place, embraces the open spaces crafted by the Herminghaus' master plan. For example, curvilinear and naturalistic forms of the English garden style that makes up one part of the Beaux Arts style are really quite flexible and can easily support various programmatic changes within the park. The importance of distant views to the essential character of the prairie though, becomes more problematic in the next 25 years when anticipating the park complete ringed by residential and light commercial development. Initially Olmsted handled that type of threat in New York's Central Park by mounding and dense tree planting. And while that might work along Pioneers Park's southern border in the flood plain, it is not applicable to the west and north where the existing prairie grasses lay flat to the topography providing a distant vista. So changing environment and cultural needs will continue to challenge the character of Pioneers Park.

Further Reading

Nebraska State Historical Society (1993) Pioneers Park Narrative Lancaster County, Nebraska, National Register of Historic Places. http://www.nebraskahistory.org/histpres/nebraska/lancaster/LC00-045-Pioneers-Park.pdf

Pabian, Roger K. (2001) *Geology of Pioneers Park Lancaster County, Nebraska.* Circular 14. CSD IANR UNL

Pioneers Park Task Force: Design Subcommittee (1989) *Rebuilding Pioneers Park: A Restoration and Management Plan.* City of Lincoln, Parks and Recreation

Sutton, Richard K. (1986) Ernst H. Herminghaus, Landscape Architect, *Nebraska History Quarterly*

Treib, Marc (2001) The Content of Landscape Form [The Limits of Formalism] *Landscape Journal* (20)2:125-140

SECTION 5 FUTURE LANDSCAPES

"For in thinking about the conservation of environment I gradually came to realize that an environment was not a place; that the words were not interchangeable; and that the difference was critical. There is a great deal of talk these days about saving the environment. We must, for the environment sustains our bodies. But as humans we also require support for our spirits, and this is what certain kinds of places provide. The catalyst that converts any physical location— any environment, if you will—into a place, is the process of experiencing deeply. A place is a piece of the whole environment that has been claimed by feelings. Viewed simply as a life-support system, the earth is an environment. Viewed as resource that sustains our humanity, the earth is a collection of places. We never speak, for example, of an environment we have known; it is always places we have know—and recall. We are homesick for such places; we are reminded of places. It is the sounds and smells and sights of places which haunt us and against which we often measure our present." --Alan Gussow

Future landscapes require imagination, though the closer such visions fit general trends, the more believable they become. Installation of wind power infrastructure is driven by our desire to live more lightly on the earth, but it comes with a cost. Openness and scale, unique features of Nebraska's landscape, change dramatically when enmeshed in tall towers, whirling blades, swooshing blade noise and tangles of transmission lines. I explain the problem and use several fictional scenarios to highlight potential impacts.

After specifically confronting wind energy's relatively new changes to the Nebraska landscape, I suggest an imaginable future with effects of drought expanding into full-blown climate change. I disagree with the landscape observer, writer and teacher, the late Robert Riley when he says, ". . . we can travel through space, but not time, a distant space may be revisited; a past landscape cannot. . ." Yet, Nebraska's wide-open spaces and their innate character represent a quintessential future of our American past. That shared space connects us with our shared past and counterpoints high density and urbanization. Nebraska's open spaces and starry undimmed skys have become a little realized national treasure.

Finally, I share some general concepts that I think might be applied to reading landscape then talk to several people who read landscape into creations they make and share with us every day.

14 Sights (Sites) Worth Saving; Conversations Worth Having

"Wind turbines run off wildlife and spoil hunting in rural areas. They spoil pristine views and tourism." -Nebraska State Senator Tom Brewer

"The new old rural landscape was a place where people worked on the land, earned their living on the land and lived on that land. The new rural landscape is a residence and occasional workplace for people whose livelihood depends not at all on the land."--Robert Riley

Introduction

From 10 miles out, the fluttering horizon signaled our approach to the Flat Water Wind Farm and its 40 turbines scattered just north of the Kansas-Nebraska border in Richardson County. Flat Water provides 60 mW for the Omaha Public Power District and had operated for about two years when James Palmer, a landscape architect and visual resources professional from Vermont, and I visited it. As we drew closer to the slowly rotating wind turbines, their starkly white towers and nacelles stood out against the blue sky. To maximize wind exposure the towers had been placed on hilltops and ridges. The surrounding countryside held no dwellings on the rocky ridges that supported the towers, and on them lush dryland crops had given way to sparse native grasses. Within the wind farm boundaries, individual wind turbine units consolidated their electrical output with lines beneath crushed limestone access roads. An existing nearby 115 kV transmission line provided the final tie-in for power distribution.

At one point on our tour, the county road we followed intersected with another road at a low spot. We paused, got out and surveyed our surroundings. From the hollow where we stood, the tower bases met the hilltops 75 to 100 feet above us adding even more impact to their height. For all his experience with assessment of wind power siting, the four turbines and towers dominating the space around us momentarily took Jim Palmer back. Clearly uncomfortable, he muttered, "These towers just seem to loom over us."

In this chapter, I discuss what I think is the single most important visual impact facing the Nebraska landscape--wind power and its large, visible infrastructure. I start with the most extensive part of that infrastructure, transmission lines and then describe the aesthetic impact of wind power. Next, I use a series of fictional but plausible encounters as wind power might appear in the open landscape, asking whether citizens and their leaders and government is up to (or even interested in) the task of siting wind power so as to minimize visual impacts.

Transmission Lines

Highly visible turbines, blades, and towers represent only part of the wind power development impacts (Figure 14.1). Newly generated electricity needs a network of power lines to move it where it will be used. Occasionally, nearby existing transport infrastructure can be tapped, like at Flat Water, but erecting large regional grid infrastructure from scratch is expensive. The Nebraska Public Power's "r" project, through the Sandhills, originally promoted increased transmission reliability; it now provides a magnet for scores of potential wind farms to transport electricity. It is also a magnet for citizens concerns.

Transmission impacts don't just accrue in rural landscapes. Lincoln, NE, a growing city served by the public power entity, the Lincoln Electric System (LES), also faces transmission reliability issue and has constructed a 345 kV transmission line around its periphery. It also

Figure 14.1 A 115 kV transmission line crosses the Nebraska National Forest in 1979 near Thedford, Thomas County, NE.

upgraded a cross connection between the peripheral lines that runs through the central part of the city. Interestingly, citing visual impacts, that central line was buried, but not so on the periphery north and west of the Lincoln Airport, where it came in contact with historic Nine-mile Prairie.

Nine-mile Prairie rolls across the Nebraska landscape nearly two hundred feet above the city of Lincoln. To the south, east, and north lay areas for future low-rise urban growth most likely before the year 2060. However to the west, urbanization will probably come only in the very later part of the 21st century. Existing visual intrusions on the landscape occur with the water tank to the southeast, former A-bomb bunkers to the north, and a UNL Challenge course to the south. Its higher topographic setting and the extent of the prairie make its visual context a prominent feature of the visitor' experience. Users at Nine-mile prairie include local students, the general public, and regional, national and international researchers, and tour groups. Many come to experience one of the characteristics recorded in early explorers' and pioneers' journals about prairies, namely the prairie's spatial extent and seeming vastness.

A good part of prairie aesthetics generally emerges from the distant views and lack of visual intrusion. Aesthetic conditions connect the viewer to a place providing an important emotional context to the prairie's scientific and physical features. For many viewers, such as children, the aesthetic connection provides the major experience of Nine-mile . They are able imagine in their mind's eye a scene as it may have appeared to a Native American or settler.

Aesthetics

Aesthetics is the study of beauty from which its discussion often brings a snort of indifference from many people -- like it is some sort of wishy-washy, touchy-feely, hogwash. Despite that indifference, questions still remains: Why are certain views preserved? and why do aesthetic assessments that have been carried out across a wide variety of landscapes (grand and common and involving thousands of viewers from wide backgrounds) find that certain landscape features are preferred? In Chapter 2 we discussed the idea of an ecological aesthetics that was more theoretical. The landscape aesthetics in this chapter are more pragmatic and used as a part of Environmental Impact Statements (EIS) and are mostly performed by knowledgeable professionals.

These studies' conclusions provide a wide, almost universal agreement about what makes up our preferred visual environment: Landscapes that appear more natural are more highly preferred. While the towers and lines of a 345/115 kV power transmission line may be objects in and of themselves that possess a rational, regular beauty, they fail in the context of prairie, because they are out of place in a view that focuses upon the vastness of the natural world. Their strongly vertical contrasts overpower the rolling horizontal expanse of prairie. The towers' and lines' scale subvert that singular context. In an urban context with large man-made features such as buildings, roads, billboards, etc. power lines are simply another element in an already visually chaotic, man-made environment. They simply do not fit in a prairie landscape.

Lincoln Electric System Transmission Example

Since the initiation of the National Environmental Policy Act in 1969, major federal actions, which affect the physical, biological, and human environment, have required an EIS that studies alternatives, the consequences and its mitigation. Major interstate power transmission lines are required to complete an EIS. However, Lincoln Electric System's (LES) 345/115 kV line proposal, while of the type and size of an interstate transmission line, did not require either state review (Power Review Board) or an EIS under the Federal, Energy Regulatory Commission. This was problematic, because the environmental impacts for residents in Lincoln and Lancaster County from such a local line are the same as an interstate line.

As noted above the EIS periphery study looked at three broad axes of impacts in the Physical, Biological, and Human realms. Included on the human realm are sociological, historical, economic, and aesthetic impacts. On the biological axis are wetlands, endangered species, etc. For the biological, physical, and human EIS axes of study, the LES study criteria were much more circumscribed and focus only on part of the human axis of the EIS.

Missing from the mostly human axis (and from the corridor weight criteria—Table 14.1) of the LES criteria are interests in aesthetics and historical significance and concern for physical and biological impacts.

The completed corridor selection for the 345/115 kV transmission line project from NW 12th and Arbor Road to NW 68th and Holdrege Street, relied on the criteria shown in Table 14.1 and selected a proposed route based on the total criteria score. However, the criteria were not the only factor used in the selection of the corridor. Flight path restrictions on the height of obstructions adjacent to the Lincoln Municipal Airport were also apparently taken into account, thus creating a precedent for using factors outside the criteria scoring list. So, that

Table 14.1 2005 LES Power Transmission Line Corridor Rating Scale Weight Distribution.

Criteria	Weight
Houses and schools (Economic)	45%
Easement area (Economic)	20%
Restricted O & M access (Functional and Economic)	10%
Route length (Economic)	10%
Buildings (Economic)	5%
Trees (Functional)	5%
Angles (Functional)	5%

criteria process has taken outside factors into account, but has not explicitly or implicitly examined the biological or the visual/aesthetic impacts, as do power line routing studies completed elsewhere in the United States.

Methodology for Assessing Visual/Aesthetic Impacts

What might such a visual/aesthetic impact-study process address? For example, the United State Forest Service and the Bureau of Land Management, as stewards of large public open spaces, have developed methodologies to address visual impacts of power transmission lines. In a three-step process for each proposed corridors, those agencies assess:

- 1) Visual quality of the existing landscape
- 2) Viewer sensitivity to the proposed transmission line and associated ROW clearance
- 3) Visibility of the proposed line and ROW disturbance.

This is an interactive ecological approach (Chapter 2) to landscape beauty in which 1) and 3) above, deal with the objective aspects and 2) deals with the subjective affects on the viewer. The Bonneville Power Administration, no stranger to rural power transmission lines, described in a 2002 draft EIS for the McNary-John Day Transmission Project in Oregon the above activities as:

> "the visual patterns are created by the combination of rural landscapes and developed features in the project vicinity. Visual quality [can be] assessed using the following descriptions. Rural landscapes [are] landscapes [that] exhibit reasonably attractive natural and developed features/patterns, although they are not visually distinctive or unusual within the region. The landscape provides positive visual experiences such as the presence of natural open space interspersed with existing agricultural areas (farms, fields, etc.). Scenic/distinctive landscapes ... exhibit distinctive and memorable visual features (such as landforms, rock outcrops, streams/rivers, scenic vistas) and patterns (vegetation, open space) that usually occur in an undisturbed rural setting but may also be found in an urban setting."

Furthermore,

> "Viewer sensitivity is described as a combination of viewer type, viewer exposure (number of viewers and view frequency), view orientation, view duration, and viewer awareness/sensitivity to visual changes in the project vicinity."

The westward vista at Nine-mile prairie would fall into the category of scenic/descriptive. The types of viewers in the project vicinity would include visitors to Nine-mile Prairie, travelers and rural residents.

Finding and assessing critical viewpoints then assessing whether the transmission line can be seen, and if so how much, determine visibility. While many sensitive viewpoints exist in the corridor, the westward vista from Nine-mile prairies is the most critical (Figure 14.2). That view along with the associated research from 100 years ago and its unplowed state, have recommended the site to the National Register of Historic Places. Once these assessments are done then a description and rating of the aesthetic impacts of a transmission line can be made, and a ranked estimate of the various corridors can be determined. The process, like the existing LES Criteria list, requires judgment from professionals trained in visual impact analysis.

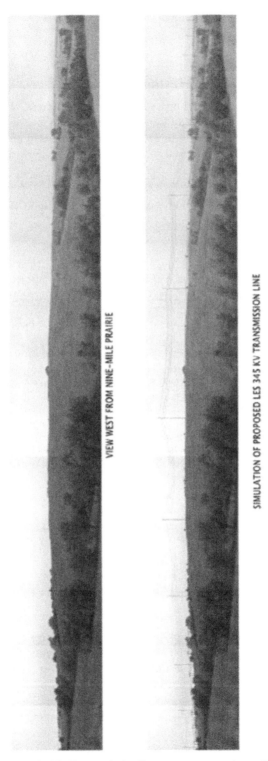

Figure 14.2 Simulation of 345 kV transmission line across western vista at Nine-Mile Prairie

It may also require public assessment of visual preferences or simulations of the proposed transmission line. Visual simulations are very useful in that they can give a glimpse into the future visual quality of a proposed power line and its corridor before it is built. They are completed so the public can view and understand the transmission line's scope and setting and are done so that when a final route is selected documentation exists about the process, the choices made and the alternatives not taken.

Conclusions about the LES Routing Process

The process used with the LES Criteria does not protect important open spaces and vistas in our local landscape -- the ones we see and use everyday. For example, little or nothing on the LES Criteria List keeps a power transmission line out of Pioneers Park or from crossing Wyuka Cemetery (both also listed on the National Register of Historic Places), nothing to keep it from marring the view down the vista to the Nebraska Capitol from Holmes Lake Park, nothing to protect Lincoln's highway entry points, and nothing to keep it from enclosing and disrupting the view across Spring Creek Prairie, Mahoney Golf Course or Wagon Train Lake. The criteria list is biased against protecting natural public open spaces and any rural areas, because by definition an open space has no houses or buildings (50% of the total on the LES Criteria List in Table 14.1). In fact any open space that is now free from the encumbrances of a web of towers and lines can easily and may likely be selected as a transmission line corridor. The existing LES Criteria List is no longer (and probably never has been) adequate for protecting the biological, aesthetic, and historical integrity of our environment. LES updated it criteria and procedures after the Nine-mile prairie concerns.{Note: LES Has since modified its siting process}

Future Landscapes

The impact of wind turbines and their attending transmission network on the landscape is not simply limited to the visual. Whoosh-whoosh of blades—the sound they propagate—was the main reason why the Lancaster County Commissioners in 2016 set (then later rescinded) sound limits that nixed a wind project in a part of the county containing many acreage developments, and a much higher population density than Richardson County.

Transmission lines' and turbine farms' assault our senses of sight and sound making major impacts and changes to Nebraska's landscape. As more and more wind farms come on line, how might we imagine their affect on young people's and visitor's sense of the landscape ?

Sites Worth Seeing

Homestead National Monument of America

Excitedly, Daniel Lopez anticipates his class field trip to Homestead National Monument of America. His fourth-grade class at Crete Elementary School has been studying Nebraska history, especially the Homestead Act, and now it's the time to leave the classroom and see a real place associated with those events. Only recently arrived in Nebraska, Daniel's family moved from Mexico to be with their father who works at a nearby food plant. Along the highway on the bus ride Daniel settles into his seat, tries to ignore his squirming seatmate, and imagines what the pioneers saw arriving here to settle the land. It is such a different one than he remembers of Chihuahua. At Homestead National Monument, his whole class fidgets

Figure 14.3 Simulation of proposed wind turbine farm at Homestead National Monument of America, Gage County, NE.

expectantly as they noisily stream off the bus and head toward Homestead's Heritage Center. Some of the class stays inside to look at the displays, but Daniel and a small group with their class para-professional head out the patio door and make a beeline for the log cabin sitting just a short distance away punctuating the end of the monument's historic hedgerow (Figure 14.3).

Wh-o-o-a! He pauses, taken back; from behind the cabin, actually looming over it, rise spinning wind turbines.

Seated on the bus going home that afternoon Daniel wonders out loud about those gigantic wind turbines. Were these here when Daniel Freeman homesteaded nearby? "No," the teacher had said, "they are a recent addition. But weren't they just like the windmill and farm equipment artifacts kept at Homestead?" Daniel nodded slowly, but he wasn't so sure; they seemed bigger and stood out more.

The Oregon Trail

Annie Leahy liked that she had the same first name as an Oregon Trail game character. In fact, she and her friends from Lakeside Middle School in Millville, NJ spent what her parents thought was too much time playing an online version of Oregon Trail. Yet, she had convinced her parents to include Oregon Trail stops during their upcoming summer trip to her aunt and uncle's house in Portland, OR, on their own 21st Century Oregon Trail trip. They made plans to head west on I-70 then jogged north at Manhattan, KS, following the Blue River and Oregon Trail into Nebraska. Annie was miffed that they missed the Independence, MO trailhead, but now as they swung into the parking lot at Rock Creek Station State Historical Park, near Fairbury, NE, she was really psyched to see a place that preserved the Oregon Trail.

Wait! Just a few steps from where the family parked, she spotted a Conestoga wagon and jumped from their barely stopped station wagon. A long slope rolled out below her like a worn carpet sporting ruts still visible from settlers' wagons. Wagons that had edged their way across Rock Creek, upward out of the Blue River Valley, and at this exact spot onto the open prairie 170 years earlier! She gazed further down the slope, and then came up with a start. The southeast horizon fluttered as a wind turbine slowly spun. Annie was used to seeing industrial lands in New Jersey and in and around Philadelphia. Some how what she saw didn't fit in and seemed to go with the city. Here on the Oregon Trail though, it was an incongruous and unexpected eyesore.

Later Annie and her family left I-80 at Ogallala, NE and ventured northwest through Ash Hollow and into the North Platte Valley, the first place Oregon Trail users saw large rock formations--landmarks dubbed Court House, Jail House, and Chimney. She saw the sunset bathing the valley's clear air and then cobwebs of power lines servicing rows of wind turbines on 240-foot towers atop the 300-foot ridge of the Wildcat Hills. They even dwarfed the 325-foot Chimney-like spire. "Humph!" she complained loudly to her father; he simply said, "You can't stop progress, Annie, and these wind energy farms don't cause pollution." Annie mused to herself, "Well, they already polluted my view of the Oregon Trail, twice!"

Cornhusker Boy Scout Camp

Charlie Atterly is nervous about tonight's ceremony. Would it come off all right? Charlie, an Eagle Scout and leader in the Order of the Arrow from Troop 50 has switched out of his role as a summer councilor at Boy Scout Camp Cornhusker, in Richardson County, NE near the Kansas border and into his role as planner for the "call-out" of new Order of the Arrow members. He knows that it will go okay, but his nervousness stems mostly from the looming towers of wind turbines adjacent to the camp. Tonight's nearly full moon and the darkness should give a sense of mystery as the initiates cross a small lake in canoes, just like in his own call-out experience five years earlier. There is one very big difference now; as if the low whoosh-whoosh of the wind turbines pervading the entire site wasn't bad enough, the scene will be punctuated by the staccato blinking of red, aircraft warning lights mandated by the FAA on each turbine nacelle.

This will be Charlie's last summer at Camp Cornhusker and while a bit nostalgic about it, he's not sure that he really wants to spend another one surrounded by wind turbines. The Council had originally protested turbine placement, but they still sprouted on adjacent, private land. After all, as one of the owners said, "Don't we landowners deserve to get as much cash as we can from our rocky, pasture lands? Besides, the wind turbines don't bother anything."

Charlie shook his head. He disagreed; he felt bothered.

Cather Country

Chinese scholar (not the movie star), Mei Ting knew Willa Cather's prairie novels inside and out, but had never met what some called their main character--the landscape of Webster County, NE. She planned to study that character with a grant from the Asia Foundation to fund her Doctorate in American Studies at Beijing Foreign Studies University. Getting from Beijing to Nebraska was not easy, but after arriving and checking in at the Green Acres Motel, Mei toured Red Cloud. The next day she explored the Cather rural tour route to introduce herself to the landscape that inspired Cather. As Mei's rental car climbed north out of the Republican River Valley toward what Cather dubbed the 'Divide', a long flat ridge separating the Republican and Big Blue Rivers, Mei saw a landscape changed from prairie to one with center pivots, farm ponds, and farmstead windbreaks reclining peacefully on the land; they all looked rather like the "giant gardens rubbing shoulders," as Cather had described. Actual prairie clung to a few rough draws but nothing leaped out at her until massive wind turbines emerged in four or five rows on the northern horizon. As she approaches her destination, the site of Antonia Pavelka's farmstead, Mei became completely surrounded by the wind turbines and felt consumed by their visceral, nearly sub-sonic, whoosh-whoosh. Eight towers loomed within a half-mile, and other more distant towers marched onward toward Bladen, NE.

Mei knows enough American literature and history to understand the impact of the constant wind on plains inhabitants (she's read Rolvaag as well as Cather), but the wind turbine blades seem to amplify the eeriness. She has a feeling that this seemingly quiet, isolated place is evolving into just another machine-dominated setting like she has seen transforming the Chinese countryside. The spate of turbines moves this place well beyond Cather's cycles of history leveraged on the wasteland of present. Ultimately, Mei feels disappointed and cheated, as the panoramic background, Cather's character, now full of wind turbines, seems to rush into the strobe-like flicker changing the intimate space of what was once Antonia's farmyard. Diminished, the scale of the whole 'Divide' landscape has collapsed.

Comeuppance

The preceding scenarios never happened, yet they are plausible fiction. Unfortunately, thoughtless placement of wind turbine farms into Nebraska's scenery represents one obvious, non-fictional thread. Another subtler one is the aesthetic damage inflicted on all the viewers. "Scenery? Aesthetics?" you say, "That's just unimportant stuff, and anyway they're just opinions in the eye of the beholder!" However, aesthetics connects us in a primary and sensory way to the physical world. Devalue that world and you degrade and disconnect its inhabitants. On the other hand, scenery composes generality; it connects some place with every place; it mediates sky, earth, water, and people. It's what we hold in common.

While elected state officials in Nebraska palaver with wind farmer-entrepreneurs over tax subsides and power-line service, Nebraska anticipates the coming of wind power with baited breath. County planning and zoning boards (where they exist—county commissioners where they don't) represent the sole siting and regulatory body anywhere in the process. These appointed boards are usually wont to deny neighbors the dollars gleaned from wind farm leases. Nowhere in the structure of Nebraska's Power Review Board, the public power districts' transmission responsibilities, the state's departments of natural resources and environmental quality bureaucracy, or its tourism or Game and Parks Commission's management, lies authority to stop or mitigate wind turbine development. No legislation about impacts of future tower additions or increases in tower size to approved wind farms, has been discussed let alone envisioned. Wind developers bear no burden of proof as to what they wrought will look like. We never see key observation points or visual simulations and rarely viewshed maps at any public hearing. Wind turbine threats to migrating and resident birds or bats are real, and identified in the recently published Programmatic Environmental Impact Statement (PEIS) for the Upper Great Plains, but it remains to be seen whether the impacts to the scenic, historic, or simple quality of day-to-day rural life (fictionalized above, but plausible none-the-less) will be talked about before another wind farm looms on the horizon.

It seems much easier and more logical to talk about threats to the open Nebraska landscape before wind farms appear. One wonders what citizens might think if they did see visual simulations of proposed turbine placement at key observation points (like from where Daniel, Annie, Charlie, and Mei looked) before such power generators are built, many would think twice about the thousands of miles of expensive, highly visible and weather vulnerable transmission lines needed to service wind farms, poised soon to cover the Sandhills. So, a conversation needs to happen that begins to answer the following tough questions.

What in our vision of the Nebraska landscape is worth saving? What views, vistas, and settings do we cherish and wish to leave unfettered for our children, grandchildren, or visitors? What local landscapes speak about the thread of our contexts for daily living? Which ones help forge a link to the past and thus promote democratic and national identity of our common future in this multicultural nation of immigrants?

Further Reading

Berleant, A 1997. *Living in the Landscape: Toward an Aesthetics of Environment* U of Kansas Press:Lawrence

Bourassa, S. C. 1991. *The Aesthetics of Landscape*. Bellhaven Press: New York

Brewer, T. 2017. Wind Energy Bad for the Sandhills. Editorial *North Plant Telegraph*. Oct 11,2017

Craik, K. H. and E. H. Zube 1976 *Perceiving Environmental Quality: Research and Applications* Plenum Press: New York

Jakle, J. A. 1987. *The Visual Elements of Landscape*. UMass Press: Amherst

Jones, S. R. 2000. *The Last Prairie: A Sandhills Journal*. Ragged Mtn Press/McGraw: New York

Driscoll, E. C. et al 1976. Measuring the Visibility of H. V. Transmission Facilities. Jones and Jones for the Bonneville Power Administration

Kaplan, Rachel and S Kaplan. 1989. *The Experience of Nature: A Psychological Perspective*. Cambridge Press Cambridge

Nairn, Ian. 1965. *The American Landscape: A Critical Review*. Random House: New York

Nasar, J. L. [ed] 1988. *Environmental Aesthetics: Theory, Research and Applications* Cambridge Press:Cambridge

Schaal, H R. 1977. Visual Impact Analysis for Transmission Line Planning Corridors. EDAW for Pacific Gas and Electric.

Santyanna, G. 1955. *The Sense of Beauty*. Modern Library: New York

Tunnard, C. 1978. *World With a View; An Inquiry into the Nature of Scenic Values* Yale Press: New Haven

Walter, E. V. 1988. *Placeways: A Theory of the Human Environment* UNC Press: Chapel Hill.

Zube, E., R. O. Brush and J G Fabos. 1976. *Landscape Assessment: Value, Perceptions and Resources*. Dowden Hutchinson and Ross: Stroudsburg PA

15 Future Landscape: The Eternity of Distance Meets the Illusion of Open Spaces

> ". . . the rutted and powdery two-track stretched to the horizon; the only other road curled off to the left and disappeared into the distance as well. I thought about how we tilled and cultivated the land, planted trees on it, fenced it, built houses on it and did everything we could to hold off the eternity of distance –anything that gives the landscape some sort of human scale. No matter what we did to try and form the West, however, the West inevitably formed us instead." – Craig Johnson

> "There is something about the heart of the continent that resides always in the end of vision, some essence of the sun and wind." – N. Scott Momaday

Introduction

Landscape emerges from the past at the same time that it surrounds us in the present and pulls us into the future. And while we mindfully separate the trinity of time, space, and landscape, they inexorably merge into a continuum. We humans though, have proved adept at suspending time, even if only temporarily, and space only in spots. In turn, the landscape that we see delivers a message as much about us, its human actors, as our world itself.

The future landscape, however, is not a complete unknown, nor are humans ill-prepared for dealing with it. For example, designers must be able to envision a future or they would be unable to design the setting for one. Continuity from moment to moment and from place to place, allows such visions and begets the actions or reconfigurations that follow.

Living in the present, at the edge of history, humans infer and predict the future. Our ancestors became skilled at inferring a future without knowing all the facts. Their success has produced us and that trait resides in our genes. Yet we have always acted with incomplete knowledge about the details and consequences of our actions.

Childhood can be seen as a time for acting and learning about predicting outcomes and consequences. Adults adroitly read physical environments and the actors therein or suffer the consequences. So, those things, actions, and situations that commonly repeat form a pertinent, stable background, and reference for future actions. As declared in the first chapter, form comes from form; its corollary posits consequences of past actions always precede future actions.

Distance

Distance often correlates with the future, but it also has its own physical and spatial attributes and implications. Does distance please or frighten us? How and why does it change? How might one go about understanding what we see of the distant physical landscape? Does it pose harm or opportunity? These are old questions and ones that most likely our ancestors and each intervening generation asked. Commanding their environment as a particular landscape and with their own points of view, structure, and scale, our ancestors could survive, function, and prosper. To do so, they had to quickly describe, interpret, evaluate, and communicate the critical aspects of their habitat. However, their many and varied descriptors really only come to the foreground based on the needs at hand. Because of environmental variety, and necessity based on experience and knowledge, we eliminate unimportant features and reduce options to a manageable few. In other words, we narrow our choices. Those few options could be evaluated—judged as to their usefulness and congruity with social mores or beliefs—then communicated and quickly acted upon.

Humans possess little ability to change time, but readily reshape our surrounding spaces. We do so to accommodate our needs for food, shelter, livelihood, and social intercourse. And we do so mostly at a palpable, human scale. Wherever that scale is too small or becomes too large, humans easily lose connections. This is true for all our senses, but it impacts our highly developed sense of sight most. Sight allows humans to absorb distances and on a clear day in the open Nebraska landscape, we likely see further than we can hear, smell, touch, or taste.

As a part of everyday speech the phrases, 'I see' and 'point of view', attribute sight to ideas, facts, and arguments. References to "point of view" that evince seeing and understanding, though, are personal and anchor not only our bodies, but also the surrounding space. We easily change our location to change our point of view. For example, the real excitement of sculpture arises from our three-dimensional exploration of the spaces and masses created by a sculptor. Likewise, insight gathered from living in our gardens, homes, and communities initiates a kind of sculptural, social participation through which we actualize ourselves and society. When our surroundings draw us in and support our activities, we feel part of a greater whole. Active participation enlightens, involves, and motivates us. When our surroundings lack human scale or do not invite participation we feel estrangement.

Scenic Spaces

An uncluttered view to a distant horizon might have brought despair or resignation to the pioneer traveler trudging the Oregon Trail. But today such an unfettered view from the same place might trigger a visitor's connection to that pioneer as the viewer's imagination cuts across space and back through time. Landscape scenery, unlike scenery back-dropping a stage play, goes beyond mere context and invites awe and participation. Remember, scenery composes generality; connects some place with every place; mediates sky, earth, water, and people.

A cascade of aesthetic actions involves and envelops an observer of scenery who can:

- react to the scene with feelings and emotion
- judge what is seen
- secretly or openly prefer or deny its charms

Scenery and landscape are all about people.

We pay attention to and show interest in a scene that concerns, includes, or limits us (Sauer 1925). We share it as a reality and live in it as a habitat with our fellow creatures and fellow humans (Meinig 1976, Jackson 1984). Pierce Lewis opines, "[Common landscapes] if approached carefully and studied without aesthetic and moral prejudice, can tell us a great deal about what kind of people Americans are, were, and may become." When a scene presents an open, intact, and unified view, it communicates choice, and just as a blank page or canvas invites. Bryn Green (1986) suggests rural open spaces provide choice, and "choice is freedom and freedom is pleasure", capturing in just a few words what I feel is a neglected aspect of what it is to be both human and American. We need and revel in space.

Diverse democracy must share places and the ideas they support. So rural and urban open spaces both hold a key to understanding the human mind and provide a clue to what it means to be an American. To exclude someone as done in gated communities, to relegate some social or racial groups to ghettos, to ignore the economic plight of the rural poor, to sweep the streets clear of homeless people, or ban refugees and visitors based on their religion, hides and stymies assimilation and ultimately social cohesion. Moreover, public open spaces, as Olmsted knew, set the context for social discourse and without that discourse democracy fails. Gertrude Stein (1936) succinctly makes the case for open spaces and the shaping of American experience when she said, "In the United States there is more space where nobody is than where anybody is. This is what makes America what it is." Yet I can't help but wonder as our great open spaces become cluttered with buildings, billboards, and other junk, and our horizons truncated with wind turbine farms and transmission lines, that we become separated from nature, our forefathers in time as well as our fellow citizens in space.

Can rural scenes reveal how we farm as if food mattered and how we rearrange and re-engineer our habitat in line with the values of openness, freedom, and democracy? Just as economic values accrue to the surface of the earth, scenic values also vary in economic potential (Zube 1973). At our best we preserve, plan for, and manage scenery and perhaps let it survive through benign neglect. Though just as the closing of the frontier (Turner and Bogue 2010) signaled a change in American's relationship with their land, our current loss of open spaces and scenery in, adjacent to, and well beyond urban areas starts to damage the linked concepts of past, openness, choice, freedom, and pleasure—those things that I think really express American exceptionalism.

Yet this is all simply talk, just an illusion. Those open spaces with charming or distant vistas of grandeur hark back in time and imbue other more practical viewers with quite different ideas. Those viewers say, "Don't worry about the past, but fear the future." They build economic gains by filling those spaces with things and removing the valuable resources present – ores, fossil fuels, water, soil, grass, timber, wild animals, and even wind. Pragmatists and conservatives most often picture land uses of direct benefit to themselves now, in the present. Unfortunately, the landscape meanwhile staggers and dissembles under the burden of soil erosion, clutter, wind power, economic gains (and losses), land ownership consolidation, rural depopulation, and mounting taxes. Scenery becomes disconnected from a wider democratic ideal and ignores sky, earth, water, and ultimately people.

Future Nebraska Landscapes

Wind Power

We encounter trouble in predicting things when we do not have the experience of similar outcomes or lack the imagination even to guess. Perhaps we find the assumed stable context has significantly shifted or hope against reason that it has not. For example, Nebraska is the only public power state where electrical power is overseen by several geographically distinct, noncompeting and publicly elected boards. In the past, Nebraska had a modest demand for electrical power met mostly by coal-fired, some hydro-electric and nuclear generation within it borders. Public Power's (PP) legal and political structure forestalled seeking to sell power out of the state. That changed with two important and connected actions. First Nebraska PP Districts joined the Southwest Power Pool and the Nebraska Unicameral allowed private, for-profit enterprises to generate electrical power from wind turbine farms for transport and sale outside of the state. The PP Districts would simply supply and create the distribution network of high voltage (115 kV, 230 kV, and above) lines to connect and move the power into the Southwest Power Pool and beyond. This is particularly true of the NPPD "r-project" (345 kV) routed across the open landscape of the southern Sandhills region. Its large, transmission structures are visible for miles, but added to that collection and distribution network, the addition of numerous wind turbine farms appears imminent. These large turbine arrays are destined to fill a large portion of the Sandhills' open vistas with the frenetic whirl of wind turbine blades and a cobweb of transmission lines, thus fundamentally altering its unique "eternity of distance" and limiting our freedom of choice in what we see.

Drought

Predicting the distant future or even near future is difficult because of inherent complexity in a system or community. For example, it is known that the concept of plant succession does not always proceed to a predicted end state, because it contains multiple stable states. Disturbed oak woodlands in the Nebraska landscape do not always return to their former arboreal state but can languish as shrubland.

If stable background variables change in a known way, then it becomes easier to predict what might happen. For example, the small paper birch groves along a portion of the Niobrara River valley in Cherry County represent marooned remnants suited to cooler, moister background variables of the last glacial period and not the current drought prone prairie. The groves are destined to disappear in a hotter and drier climate ushered in by global warming.

So, if I attempt to predict the future landscape of Nebraska, just like plants and peoples who have lived here, I must leap beyond the current physical and social milieu and make some predictions. The first have to do with the relative stability of what we assume to be important environmental variables. Earth will continue to spin around the sun still begetting predictable diurnal and season rhythms. Nebraska's geological foundation most likely will not change barring another ice-age.

But stability of our climate currently stands in question. Greenhouse gas-induced global warming will likely spawn changes in moisture and temperature regimes. Climate scientists predict Nebraska to become drier and warmer south and west of a line from Valentine to Omaha. For short distances along either side of that line, only slight warming and drying might occur and to the north and east moisture may even increase slightly. Though these predictions, in light of the Great Plains' notorious variability, lack surety.

What once appeared as limitlessly prairie soils have lost half their depth (or more) from wind and rain erosion on cropland; in some places farmers till subsoil. Plowshares, chemicals, and cattle herds have turned, polluted, and denuded hundreds of thousand of acres and continue to do so apace. Though, proper soil and livestock management would reduce its loss

While the great drought of the 1930's Dustbowl had its epicenter near the borders of Oklahoma, Kansas, Colorado, and New Mexico, its affects spread widely enough to impact Nebraska. Droughts, even prolonged ones, are not new to the Great Plains (Wishart 2013). But when they occur, plant and human communities stress and change. Plant community structure loosens and members unable to adapt disappear, especially those without deep-rooted resources to tap water. Not surprisingly that idea also could describe drought impacts on human communities. Tightly woven human social groups, just like dense plant structures, resist the change forced upon them by adversity in general, and drought in particular. This is especially true where the two overlap in planted cities, towns, and villages where trees supply shady relief from heat and winds—both symptoms of accompanying drought.

Drought tolerant ponderosa pine woodlands occupy north-facing slopes along the Pine Ridge escarpment. The most important concern with that plant community revolves around the fires favored by drought and potential insect epidemics. These forests create critical watersheds leading to year-round springs and streams that support plants, wildlife, and human communities. Because the bulk of this forest is private, it resides in the hands of many individuals and becomes rife with vacation homes, roads, utility corridors, grazed pastures, and stream corridors, which fragment the forest and heighten potential damage from wildland fires. Complete forest thinning and carefully planned and managed controlled burns on both the public and private forested lands likely might depress, but not eliminate catastrophic fires. It could also slow insect attacks known to favor stressed, older trees. The problem is that management must be aggregated and treated as a whole -- meaning cooperation in crossing property boundaries, fence-lines, streams, and ridges.

Rural landscapes and communities vary in their acceptance, adoption, and preservation of planted landscape structures whether natural forests, village street trees, or rural shelterbelts. The great shelterbelt program of the Prairie States Forestry Project (PSFP) stretched from Texas to North Dakota in the late 1930's (Karle and Karle 2017), but in many Nebraska places those microclimate-ameliorating plantings have been removed, become fragmented, or simply have been left to deteriorate by landowners greedy for a few more acres of corn or soybeans. Southwest Nebraska was not part of the PSFP and possessed only small areas of mostly surface irrigation. So, large-scale additions of planted structure never happened there. Most of such planting occurred adjacent to farm buildings, feedlots, or to form wildlife habitat.

Severe soil erosion during drought damages unirrigated cropland. So, the rise of the all terrain center-pivots fed by aquifers, supports growth of crops. and stabilizes planted structure as long as the aquifers last. The Sandhills of Nebraska might feed the Niobrara, Loup, Dismal, and Elkhorn rivers for hundreds of years and if irrigation capacity is closely monitored, and perhaps hundreds more years if water is carefully metered, and meted out. In areas with surface irrigation the future under prolonged drought becomes less tenable. This is especially true of water originating from the winter snow of the Rockies flowing down the North and South Platte Rivers. It is even truer of the much-litigated Republican River managed by a special state compact between, Colorado, Nebraska, and Kansas. Reducing water for irrigation in southwest Nebraska as mandated by litigation has already replaced irrigated corn and soybeans with dryland wheat and milo. In a mega-drought even those dryland-cropping systems become untenable and soil without plant cover would move with the wind. Likewise, existing native rangeland in the Nebraska Panhandle, northwest tablelands, and the Sandhills could withstand some drought stress, but only with greatly reducing cattle numbers before it too, would blow and move. Sandhills stocking rates would most likely depend more on forage available from wet meadow grazing and haying, than upland ranges.

In addition to stresses on existing Nebraska communities from prolonged drought that will be triggered by greenhouse gas-induced global warming, additional stress will occur with needs to settle refugees fleeing from inundation of many low-lying coastal communities. This migration requires strong social structures to welcome, house, clothe, feed, and educate refugees. Many Nebraska communities sapped of population by nearly a century of out migration do have some extra housing capacity. These communities could quickly initiate growing local human food, but lack jobs, though local food production and community remodeling, or expansion might employ some refugees. Acres of corn and soybeans would need to be replaced by human food gardens and small-scale animal husbandry. Such local production would require intensive retraining and re-adaption for immigrants and would be much different from the existing model of industrial agriculture for world export.

Four Future Scenarios

Leading up to this chapter I have read, interpreted, painted, photographed, mapped, cataloged, described, and pronounced with some detail the physicality and history of Nebraska's natural, unself-conscious/cultural, and parts of its consciously designed landscape. Now in this section I've leapt into the future and am dragging you, the reader, along. What follows are four fictionalized scenarios, because anything describing the future becomes fiction by definition. Written with fictitious (albeit plausible) detail against a reasonably assumed backdrop of landscape and social organization described earlier in this chapter, these short stories emerge from ideas of illusive scenery and fragile open space, freedom and democracy, a potential response of the living landscape to climate and social change, and the eternity of distance.

2025

Galvin Luckey, a Blaine County rancher and ecotourism entrepreneur lives with his family on a 3000-acre pioneer ranch along the North Loup River. Recently, his lowered income from depressed cattle prices has been offset by eco-tourists paying to visit the ranch and view wildlife and open spaces. He is concerned about the balance between property rights and community character impacted by industrial wind turbine farms.

Today, Galvin's long-time attorney, Ed Uttley has come to discuss a potential lawsuit Galvin wants to file against a neighbor, Tim Cutter, who is proposing a 50-tower wind farm. The lawsuit centers on the concept of property rights and Uttley is attempting to school the rancher about them.

Uttley explains, "Owning property brings a bundle of rights, but where private ownership might appear supreme to some individual landowners, it must be tempered by what the community determines as acceptable. So private rights are constrained by public controls."

"Well what about things like vistas to the distant horizon?" Galvin asked. "It's paying more rent now than cows. Even folks just traveling through on the Sandhills Journey Scenic Byway will have their open views ruined by those god-awful wind turbines."

"Vistas may fall under, so-called common property rights where something belongs to everyone, like the air we breathe," replied Uttley. "Those common goods, which we all use, rely on public controls set by a hierarchy of federal, state, and local governments, such as the Clean Air Act, emission standards and regulations for certain chemicals set by the EPA."

"So, maybe uncluttered vistas could be common property?" Galvin half-asked and half-stated hopefully.

"Here is where we might be on to something. Private rights most often, but not always, run congruently with the physical boundaries of a legally owned parcel. Subterranean rights for ores and fossil fuels can be and are detached from the surface rights. Though in, 2009 Unicameral law LB 568 passed and prohibited severing wind rights from a parcel. Though that might cause issues with estate planning and transferring property to heirs," noted Uttley.

He continued, "In Nebraska, by the very actions of the governmental police power of the Natural Resource Districts (NRD), water, especially groundwater, is regulated because it could move out from under a parcel and be sucked into a well on a neighboring land. Also, it is in the public's long-term interest to control excessive use of nitrogen fertilizers, which can impact a town's well water quality. Soil washing off a farm or ranch and damaging another's land through silt deposition is considered a tort in Nebraska. Wildlife also belongs to the people of Nebraska and the Game and Parks Commission set rules governing their harvest and management. Landowners don't own game animals, but do have the right to allow or deny trespass on their land to hunters, anglers, or trappers." Uttley said.

"Law on scenic quality, however, is pretty thin and it is not always considered common property, but it is well-established that the government has the right to control things like billboards," Uttley continued. "Governmental agencies like the State Department of Roads, even allow trees to grow along the roadside in front of them and the "Outdoor Advertisers", as the billboard lobby euphemistically call themselves, can't cut them down. But that is kind of the opposite of what we are talking about here. Your eco-tourists don't want to see power-lines and wind turbines cluttering the horizon and destroying the view. So planting trees along your property line doing the same thing would be counterproductive."

"Absolutely! One of my more frequent visitors called just yesterday and cancelled his reservation for the north cabin, because its back deck now looks out toward the "r-project" line and the front points toward that damn wind-farm Cutter proposes," Galvin affirmed.

"Galvin, I just don't see us winning on the individual merits of just you losing value from ecotourists. We have got to make the case the people in the entire county or group of Sandhills counties stand to lose more than they gain with these visual intrusions," said Uttley.

"I know, I know. I heard a rancher up in Cherry County has complained that an entire way of life is at stake. He envisions and fears giant towers, never out of his view and even being plagued at night by blinking red lights on turbines tweaking the sunsets and sunrises. He claims a distant cousin of his allowed wind turbines on his property for part of the Grande Prairie project over in Holt County. The cousin planned to retire on the ranch and pay his way with wind energy. Only problem is that those turbines are noisy. Their constant whirring drove him off the ranch after only 6 months."

"Galvin, too many people see this place as just a stream of resources flowing directly into their bank accounts and they are strapped by the same cattle prices you worry about. They also feel the same demands for county and state government spreading out services and raising taxes," Uttley said.

"Yeah, I know. One gal who grew-up on a pioneer ranch just like me and thinks she's a real progressive by supporting the r-project and wind power." Galvin snorted. "She even compared the r-project to the REA. Hah! Until NPPD ran that 115 kV line to Thedford back in 1975, there were only smaller, lower voltage lines to towns and ranches. Some ranches even have their own wind power, on 30-foot towers, mind you, that look like windmills for stock tanks. Doesn't seem like she makes a reasonable comparison of 30-foot power poles and towers versus 150-foot towers and 250-foot wind turbines. Wrong by a factor of 10 or even a hundred! You can see those towers from eight to 10 miles off."

Uttley asked, "Was that the same meeting a public power official said that no one likes to look at power lines, but then turned around and in the same breath said 2,500 steel towers along the 250-mile "r-project" right-of-way won't intrude much, because there are already a couple dozen radio towers, and railway signals here now blighting the 18,000 square miles of the Sandhills? That guy doesn't know vertical from horizontal. He's spent so much time looking at aerial photos and plotting power line routes that he thinks the center pivots' footprints and the BNSF tracks strongly impact what we see on the ground. I know you can't see center pivots and tracks from a mile away let alone 10 miles like the wind turbines."

So what do we do Uttley? Galvin sighed.

"I'm thinking we take a clue from Kansas." Uttley said.

"Huh? Kansas is usually clueless." retorted Galvin.

"Well not necessarily, in 2005 then Governor Kathleen Sebelius brought together a group of people proposing with those opposing windpower in the Flint Hills and hammered out a moratorium. The Flint Hills is kind of like Kansas' equivalent to the Sandhills where it's mostly cattle grazing on tallgrass prairies where steers put on a couple of pounds per day weight in the June-July season. In order for the ranchers to keep the cool-season grasses and the previous season's thatch from smothering the nutritious warm-season grasses, they need to burn the prairie-range each spring. Burning doesn't work well around power-lines however, and causes them to arc-out. Building wind power turbines and their accompanying feeder lines would require ranchers to stop burning and make the tallgrass range deteriorate." Uttley related.

"Okay, go on," said Galvin.

"The moratorium still holds and as late as 2016, Kansas Governor, Sam Brownback, who's no fan of governmental or environmental controls, designated the Tallgrass Heartland to save some of the last tallgrass prairie. He even spoke in glowing terms about the moratorium on wind power in the Flint Hills."

"Well, let's get going and save at least some of our Sandhills. We ought to plan for willing ranchers to pledge their spreads to be wind turbine free and then some of its openness can be maintained into the distance and future. I'm going start by proposing the idea to Cutter," Galvin enthusiastically stated.

2040

Elaine Fournier lives in Dawes County just east of Chadron. She works as a forestry management officer and liaison between the Job Corps, US Forest Service, Nebraska Forest Service, and private forest landowners in the Pine Ridge. Elaine is a Native American of the Sioux tribe and was able to attend college using a Starita Scholarship receiving a B. S. degree in Natural Resources Management from South Dakota State University and a Masters in Community and Regional Planning from UN-Lincoln. She now works to initiate and oversee contracts regarding management of a unified forest protection plan for all federal, state, and private forestlands in the Nebraska Pine Ridge.

Enjoying the quiet ride of her hydrogen fuel-cell-powered electric pickup truck, Elaine edged it into Chadron on US Highway 20. The commercial strip looked a bit shop-worn, or more correctly, shop bare. Several unfilled gaps showed where burned buildings had not been replaced in the lackluster economy. The US 20 commercial strip was particularly bare and even oppressive since 25-years ago when the Nebraska Department of Roads had widened it to four lanes, removed dozens of trees, and never replanted any; no space, just concrete.

"Ought to plant some trees now in the building gaps," Elaine thought to herself as she pulled into a coffee shop for a large coffee to go.

"Whew! 7:45 in the morning and it felt like afternoon heat. Should have ordered iced coffee to go instead," Elaine thought.

Each of the five summers she had spent here were hotter and drier. She didn't remember early summer days with such heat and drought growing up on the reservation north and east of here, just across the South Dakota state line.

Back on US 20, Elaine headed west toward Crawford. The Pine Ridge escarpment to the south capped the shallow, wide White River valley and true to its name, that ridge was covered mostly with ponderosa pine. Even from a couple miles away you could smell the scent of evergreen turpenes dispersed in the heat.

She passed the US 385 turnoff to the Black Hills, then drove over Chadron Creek. It, and all the other small streams running north off the escarpment, Trunk Butte, Dead Horse, Indian, Ash, and Squaw came from its forested watersheds and were literally watery life-lines for towns and farmers in between. That water irrigated crops and slaked the thirst of people, and animals, both wild and domestic. Off to the north lay the Chadron airport and its fire air tanker base with two ancient, Grumman Sea Wolf Avenger TBY's, formerly single-engine torpedo bombers completely rebuilt for attacking small fires. Last summer saw them deployed locally on four fires, and they had even been flown and used in the Black Hills. Her own Job Corps camp south of Chadron housed a hotshot team of two-dozen skilled and seasoned fire fighters. No fires yet this summer, but it was early and it was hot.

Along the road an occasional lone cottonwood appeared in the ditch and only near the creek crossings did Elaine see other trees, mostly cottonwood and willow, but some hackberry. Back at Dead Horse Creek, few trees grew at all and the creek's banks were swathed with silvery buffaloberry bushes. When she saw the ghostly barkless remains of dead elm and ash decimated by diseases and insects, it reminded her of the white-man's ailments like small pox, tuberculosis, and alcohol which plagued and killed thousands of her tribe during the last 200 years. Small pox was gone, TB contained, but alcohol ravaged on.

As she moved west, the road came closer to the White River. If she had left earlier and had more time, following the old US 20 road would have gotten her closer to the river and maybe a chance to see some wildlife, but not today. Several cougars had been reported for the region going back 40 years, but they were mostly nocturnal animals. What she saw now were the rocky road cuts the engineers needed to punch through the low ridges, making cuts and fills where the new more southerly US 20 alignment ran. Those cuts showed just how tenuous the soil here was and why it needed careful cultivation and irrigation to nurse hay, corn, and wheat yields from its thin layers.

Ahead in the distance rose Fort Robinson the death place of Crazy Horse, the great warrior and Sioux leader. Its high buttes were clothed in pines. Rounding a left-hand curve she quickly dropped into Crawford and headed south along its eastern edge. Just before the BNSF overpass

Elaine noticed the former machine yard had been cleared and along its trackside a new siding had been built. The rest of the yard contained a small sawmill with several portable mills there as well. Stacks of rough-cut ponderosa destined for use in eastern Nebraska, half round slabs and an ample pile of sawdust all crowded the one-lane road in and out. She noted a new feature; a tub grinder fed logging wastes into several pyrolysis units which produced biochar. Eastern Nebraska farms now used vast quantities of that incompletely burned material, because biochar improved soil tilth, held water, nutrients, and microbes in its tiny pores boosting productivity and cutting pollution. Most of those farms now had less than three inches of topsoil in which to raise crops and the biochar helped, but nothing could replace topsoil.

Turning south on to Nebraska Highway 71, she passed the CENEX station a local hydrogen fuel outlet and headed for the road to the Ponderosa Wildlife Management Area. Elaine thought about the two meetings she had today and wondered if the progress on cooperative forest management was proceeding quickly enough to dampen fire threats. Larry Royster, the local game warden, had asked for a meeting to inspect the thinning work just completed in the upper Fawn Creek watershed. He had mentioned something about a wildlife issue which could only be understood in the field. Elaine was to meet him at his Ponderosa WMA office and they would take both vehicles to the thinning work site. Elaine could then continue on to her second meeting nearby with Dexter Wynn from the Wynn Game Ranch, LLC.

She met Royster, and with him determined which route to take to the place he wanted her to see concerning the work site. Royster led out south, threading the winding road a couple of miles to the top of the escarpment. Elaine hung back trying to avoid the heavy plume of dust, Royster's truck kicked up. As she emerged from the scattered pines and topped out onto the flat, open high plains landscape, hundreds of wind turbines and their slowly turning blades loomed into her view. Thank goodness those things were not covering the White River valley that she saw each day.

Ahead, Royster's tail-lights flared in his truck's dust cloud as he turned down Fawn Road. Elaine followed him along the twisting road down into a denser area of forest to where he pulled over and they both parked. Royster had been pretty tight-lipped about just what he wanted to show her. The Job Corps crews had thoroughly thinned slopes. Elaine and Larry now traversed those slopes on foot starting from the north side of Fawn Road. Thinning operations here left one tree per thirty-five feet and most importantly, the standing pines were limbed up at least eight feet from the ground. That had to be done because while ponderosas will natural thin out lower branches in crowded conditions, the 35 foot on-center spacing would not reduce the lower branches. Low branches make the trees susceptible to transferring a ground fire into their crowns. Downed trees had been carefully skidded and yarded adjacent to Fawn Road, but were now gone. Even the curved and forked logs were taken, not as sawlogs, but to be ground-up and pyrolized for biochar production. Limbs had been piled in larger openings and would be burned this winter. Dark patches of common juniper, creeping Oregon grapeholly, and shunkbush, dotted the hillside with blue grama, green needle grass, and little bluestem filling in. Slow-growing threadleaf sedge clumps would take longer, but all these graminoids benefited from more sunlight. The thinning program had certainly boosted forage production and grazing potential in the Pine Ridge.

After walking for 10 minutes along the hillside's contour on the bouncy, fragrant pine needle duff, they rounded a slight ridge with protruding sandstone boulders.

"Almost there," said Royster. "Just around the this corner."

"So, Larry, you've been pretty mysterious about what you're going to show me," said Elaine. "From what I have seen, the thinning crew has been very careful even with the skidding."

"Here we are; what do you see?" queried Larry, as he abruptly stopped.

Elaine noticed a cave-like depression into the hillside under a rock overhang, and there in the dust appeared a cat track. "Think we've got a cougar den, but it looks abandoned," said Elaine.

"You got it!" retorted Larry. "Question is whether the female has moved her kitts and where to?"

"Look, Larry, I know that for 20 years the Ernie Chambers Cougar Law has given cougars special species status in Nebraska, but we don't even know how long ago that track was made. The person who cruised this stand didn't cover every square foot of it," she said.

"Well, your cruisers need to be more observant about situations like this," suggested Larry. "I don't think you want to have to do an Environmental Impact Statement for each thinned parcel contract."

"Give me a break," thought Elaine to herself. "So where do you think the cat and kitts went?" Elaine said changing the subject.

"Hard to say," replied Larry. "I'm guessing some place quiet, densely wooded, and nearby." Those kitts are old enough to travel, but not great distances. They won't be prowling a 100 square mile area like their mother."

"Okay, look, we're close to finishing thinning in this watershed, " said Elaine. "I will talk to the cruisers and ask them to be "more observant" when they mark areas for thinning. But Larry, you of all people, should realize that cougars hide their dens. They purposely make themselves hard to find."

After leaving Larry Royster where they had parked, Elaine continued down Fawn Road to the flats above the White River then turned west and drove for a couple miles on River Road to Dimple Creek. That small stream was meandering and bubbling by as she crossed the first bridge up Dimple Creek Road. Down here, next to the creek, cottonwood, hackberry, even some small elms towered over mountain birch, redtwig dogwood, black currant and willow enclosing the stream. Further up the stream, the small valley was just wide enough for a few desultory pastures. As the canyon wall closed in and the two-track road became steeper, ponderosa pines crowded the road.

The entire Dimple Creek watershed contained no thinning projects and it supported many dense stands of timber that could easily become crown fires. Even after five years of successful, cooperative forestry management, the Dimple Creek landowners were proving hard to bring on board. Smack dab in the middle of the watershed lay the 1000-acre Wynn Game Ranch, LLC. Elaine was here to talk with and hopefully persuade Dexter Wynn to cooperate on thinning. Getting him on board might move some of the other landowners. Cooperation with neighbors, state and federal land managers was the only way the project could protect the forested watershed and the water it produced. Everyone needed to understand that they were all in it together. Cooperation beats competition.

The road now had a 10-foot high fence along it festooned with large no hunting signs courtesy of Wynn. Dexter Wynn made big bucks catering to trophy hunters looking for the large mule deer bucks and bull elk penned behind the fence in amongst the dense timber. Still Elaine had to believe that hunting in such dense timber was not very easy or productive. The game ranch had had its ups and downs though, especially from the impact of bovine spongiform encephalopathy (BSE) an incurable brain disease and blue-tongue epizootic hemorrhagic disease. Though blue-tongue affected white-tail deer more than the local mulies.

Parked up ahead was a new pickup with South Dakota plates. Wynn lived in Rapid City, so it must be him. As Elaine's very quiet hydrogen electric pickup glided off the road next to the South Dakota pickup. A tall, lean man in pressed and pleated jeans, starched white shirt and grey felt cowboy hat quickly stepped out of some dense brush. He appeared a bit startled.

"Whoa, lady, are you sneaking up on me?" the man asked.

"Not my intention, this truck runs a bit quieter than most. You must be Dexter Wynn," Elaine offered.

"Yes, I am and you must be Ms. Fournier, no doubt. Here to talk about logging," said Wynn.

"Call me Elaine. Well, Mr. Wynn, we remove some carefully selected logs as a part of an extensive cooperative thinning operation; you'd get paid the going board-foot rate with a percentage of it used to support the Pine Ridge Cooperative Forestry Project," replied Elaine.

"Seems like thinning work would disrupt my clients and their hunting, not to mention the problem with crews going in and out of the fenced gates," said Wynn.

"First, we'd work in the off-season, not hunting season. We've had cattle ranchers with the same concern about gates and protocols were worked out to everyone's satisfaction," stated Elaine. "Also opening up the dense stands will benefit the grasses elk graze on. Besides I know that mule deer does seek south slopes with more open canopies and avoid elk. However, on those slopes, the deer choose areas with better plant density for having and concealing new fawns. So, I would suggest you simply plant dense shrubs such as skunkbush, chokecherry, currant, and common juniper on those south slopes to get the same concealed niches amongst ponderosa canopies with less density. Those shrubs also make good winter browse for the mulies"

"Sounds like you have done your homework, Elaine," stated Wynn. "I will definitely give the idea some thought. What kind of a time line are we on here?"

"Right now we are at least nine months out. Earliest we could begin thinning operations is next spring. So that would not interfere with your hunting season," said Elaine.

'I'll be in touch.' Said Wynn.

Elaine shook Wynn's hand, gave him a card and returned to her truck. She got in, turned it around and headed back down Dimple Creek. A couple hundred yards down the road and still next to the Wynn Game Ranch fence, she glanced in her rearview mirror. Elaine smiled to herself when she saw a large cougar gently climbing down from a ponderosa inside the Wynn Game Ranch with a kitt in its mouth.

2060

Jim Heim a Dundy County farmer/rancher lives on a 1200-acre high-plains mixed-agriculture farm near Frenchman Creek north and west of Haigler. His family has owned the place since 1970, when his grandfather moved from Amherst, Colorado to become one of the first center pivot operators in southwest Nebraska. Before that, Jim's great-great grandfather was part of the Rain Belt settlement of the high plains in the 1890's and held on against the droughts which have always plagued the region. The Upper Republican NRD (URNRD) maxed out at 451K irrigated acres in 1997 and has lost acres largely because Kansas pressed for its share of Republican Basin stream flow. In 2012, the URNRD began to buyout irrigation and return pivots to dryland crops such as milo and winter wheat. The water from the first buyouts above Rock Creek was diverted via pipeline down stream.

Recently Jim's operation has shrunk from six pivots to two because starting in 2052 another severe drought cycle impacted the area six out of the last eight years. Four pivots went dry and were abandoned. Cattle were removed from several hundred acres of sandy rangeland and sold, but the range continued to deteriorate along with four exposed pivot sites on less sandy soils. This change has resulted in major wind erosion and shifting dune formations that now threaten the two remaining pivots and the farm's very survival.

The forty-mile per hour wind surging to fifty on occasion had picked up particles of sand and dust which obscured the view of his house a half a mile away.

"So much the better for the lowered visibility," Jim thought. He had not driven his pickup out into the field because he had a project that he didn't want to be seen doing, but it galled him having to sneak around on his own property. He hunched into the southwest wind and moved forward lugging the heavy metal part and his toolbox. Working on a center pivot came easy to him and it was critical work to keep the farm operating.

"The dang Upper Republican NRD wants to shut down much of the ground water irrigation in the Frenchman Creek watershed," murmured Jim to himself. "I'm down to no cows and two pivots. They haven't shut those down yet, but I got a notification that I could only pump six acre-inches from each of them for the entire growing season. Problem is, the drought tolerant crops we were coaxed into planting still need more than that to produce! The university plant sciences department was of little help since most of its researchers were busy working on grants paid for by "Bayer-Sygenta" or "Monsanto-DuPont."

He arrived at the outside edge of the circular field and noted that the first 10 feet in had a 2-3-inch layer of sand deposited on it. The sediment had come, no doubt from the nearby sandy range land, his cattle had once grazed. He had left them there too long after the drought started and now the sand, unprotected by vegetative cover, freely blew onto his fields. That was what he was fighting for now; just to keep his fields from being covered by sand. The secret plan was to defy the URNRD orders and use part of his allotted water to irrigate trees and shrubs he would plant as a field windbreak to reduce the erosion. There was a time back in the 1930's the Federal Government planted miles of windbreaks in Nebraska, but not in Dundy County. Help from them was probably not going to happen anyway with the shortsighted, penny-pinching Republicans still running the House and Senate. It wasn't until 2050 they even contemplated that global warming had a human cause and then it was too late. They call themselves conservatives but give land and soil conservation short shrift.

Last year Jim had constructed physical wooden barriers designed after the permanent snowdrift barriers of which he had seen pictures taken along old I-80 in Wyoming. The lumber came from ponderosa thinning on the Pine Ridge and they had taken him six months to build. Fortunately, he had plenty of labor with displaced Hispanics who moved north as sea levels began to rise and economies deteriorated. . . so much for the much-heralded wall of DJT.

So now in the spring of 2060 he was about to be another step closer by modifying the swing arm corner of his ancient Reinke E2060 to flow into an elaborate system of drip tubing at the base of each carefully planted tree. He figured he need to plant half the pivot perimeter from about 10:30 on the northwest to 4:30 on the southeast. His windbreak design spanned the 50-yards between the wooden barriers and the field edge. First, 50-feet in from the barrier ponderosa pine and eastern redcedar were planted a 12-foot on center. In from that 20-feet came another row of the pine-redcedar combination but offset so that they were staggered from the first row. In another 20-feet he would plant alternating Siberian elm, hackberry, and honeylocust 15-feet on center. Moving in another 20-feet, another row of the same trees. Finally as a fifth row came, a mixture of wild plum, chokecherry, pfitzer juniper, skunkbush sumac, sloeberry, pinyon, and buffaloberry. Each seedling's planting hole would be back-filled with a biochar and compost mixed with the loose soil. A temporary wooden slat snow-fence windbreak would run halfway between each row and parallel with them. The irrigation should get the plants established and work as a water supplement afterwards. In a couple of years the irrigation water could then be devoted to crops if he was still farming.

The part he carried was a manifold he had made in his shop from which 10 drip tube lines would flow. At each 20° position of the parked pivot, he could irrigate five lines to the right and five lines to the left. He spit-out the dirt that sifted into his mouth, then covered his nose and mouth with a bandana. It made him look like the desperate bandito he was but just stealing water. He fit the manifold on to the end of the swing arm corner and clamped it down. It fit like a charm.

Heading back to the house he first followed the pivot arm to its center and from there he could see the house. Probably ought to add to the windbreak around it too. Then he swore under his breath, and thought, "In the nearly 200-hundred years his family had been on the high-plains had industrial agriculture, indeed, any agriculture, become doomed?"

2080

Magdalena Gomez is a 12-year old refugee from the Gulf Coast near Bayside, Texas. She and her mother, father, and brother arrived in Thayer County by train and were deposited at the Belvidere, Nebraska siding in April of 2080 with only a few possessions, the clothes on their backs and little money. In many ways, they resembled the pioneers who came to that region two hundred years earlier.

The Gomez family arrived early on a spring morning. They and four or five other families clustered around the dusty train tracks, breathing diesel fumes and waiting for transport to their new homes. Later in the morning hunger drew the Gómezes onto the town's main street and a short block of low brick buildings with gaps in between them. In a grocery/convenience shop they bought bread and peanut butter, then at a rusty spigot outside filled several plastic bottles with water. Later in the day, a local representative of the National Refugee and Relocation Service (NRRS) arrived and asked the families to gather around. He began in halting Spanish to address the group of about 20 refugees.

"Speak English, so we can understand you!" shouted Clement, Magdalena's father. The

Gómezes' Hispanic features belied their perfect command of English and that Clement's family had lived in South Texas for at least four generations. The NRRS spokesman counted heads, listed, and informed each family in English of when and where they would go next. The Gomez family would be driven to a place just west of Belvidere, but not until evening.

"Maggie, let's go to the grassy area across from the store," whispered her brother, Victor. "Its much nicer to sit on the grass than these sharp stones." So they went there, waited in the shade, and gorged themselves on peanut butter sandwiches slathered with honey they got from a large mason jar. Meanwhile, the spring day heated up and the breeze became a gusty, dusty wind.

Near dusk, an ancient, gray Chevy Silverado arrived and the pickup's swarthy, mustachioed driver helped Maggie and Victor place themselves then their belongings into the truck bed. After watching Maggie's mother, Rosie, and father settle into its cab, Maggie and Victor arranged themselves the best they could to avoid the wind and to cushion the bounce. The truck, running on E-85 alcohol fuel, puttered out of Belvidere into the rapidly enclosing darkness.

Maggie looked out at the landscape around her. It was level in spots and gently rolling in others. Some dark tree stands loomed in the distance, but she saw no lights, no detail, though every once in awhile as seen in the truck's headlights, large mechanical systems with towers and pipes abutted the road. The restless air felt light and dry and seemed very different from the heavy salty sea air on the Gulf Coast.

Maggie felt, scared and excited at the same time. Scared of being thrust into such a new land, but excited to escape the bad situation in Bayside. There, ocean waters had risen slowly in the last several years and flooded the marina then crossed Copano Drive up to 1st Street. Maggie's favorite play area with the blue-roofed gazebo and matching blue playground equipment became inundated and then abandoned. Some said this all came from the collapse of the West Antarctic Ice Shelf, wherever that was. The final blow came from the unusually late Category 3 hurricane aptly named Zephyr. It was the twenty-sixth hurricane of the 2079 Atlantic season arriving in late December between Christmas and New Years. Driven by the storm surge, partially flooded Bayside was washed from the surface of the earth with a fierce finality. Maggie didn't know it, but this scenario would continue to play out for at least another quarter century driving more and more people inland. She and her family were now at their new home in Nebraska, though for them drought would be more defining than flooding.

The Gomez family had first sought refuge on higher ground miles from the initial storm, but with their house gone, they had nothing left. Clement was an apiarist working for the Fennessey Ranch, a skill sought after by NRRS relocation section and duly noted on its refugee database. So, the Gomez family had been fast-tracked (four months!) for relocation to a human food production area just created in Thayer County where the pollinating potential of bees had been deemed critical.

Del Wedell, a farmer and former state senator from Thayer County represents the National Refugee Relocation Service (NRRS) in Nebraska for Jefferson, Saline, Fillmore, Thayer, Clay, and Nuckolls Counties. He is charged with finding places for 124,000 US refugees fleeing from rising coastal waters along the East and Gulf Coasts. Nebraska was charged with accepting 1.25 million total refugees which equaled about a quarter of its 3.1 million population in the 2070 census. The NRRS operated on money from the federal, state, and local governments. This became possible with the final rout and demise of the Republican Party in the elections of 2068 and 2070. Progressive Democrats now held the White House, Senate, and House but it had taken 12 years just to start repairing the damage done to social and environmental programs by the Republicans. Their undoing had started with the decimating drought of the 2050's as pay back for ignoring global warming, which had redrawn the maps of all coastal states. Problem was everyone suffered from the impacts of global warming, not just the Republicans.

As a multi-functional agency, NRRS was developing the capacity and skill to carry out the resettlement mandate such as real estate acquisition (including use of eminent domain if needed), community design and planning, supply of social and medical services, and job training. The focus for rural communities in Wedell's six county-area was agricultural job training and human food production along with housing construction.

This all sounded pretty straight forward in a bureaucratic kind of way, but today Del was worried about the new resettlement area south of Carleton. Land acquisition and planning for a 400-person village was well underway. Last year the land and its pivot had supported 20 families with only a third of the pivot's 133-acres under gardens. The large families, of mostly Hispanic heritage, produced a surplus of sweet corn, carrots, potatoes, and onions. The green beans, peppers, and tomatoes struggled to produce much fruit though. Squash failed miserably because the long-time industrial agricultural landscape was nearly devoid of pollinators. Del got the idea of importing beehives. He then found brought Clement Gomez a Texas refugee and his family to be the village apiarist.

Problem solved, right? Wrong. Jim Hention a neighboring industrial farmer with four center pivots on a section of land had seen the light about the demise of his high input, extensive way of farming, and was now attempting to persuade Clement to work bees for him as he converted corn and soybean fields to gardens for human food crops. Jim viewed himself as some sort of modern day English squire and saw Clement and his family as becoming his peasant workers albeit paid a wage, but without the land ownership promised by the NRRS. Now Del was in the middle of a fight precipitated by a bid to lure Clement into working bees for Hention and not the new village with its growing number of inhabitants.

Del knew that Hention was still sore about not being able to purchase the Willard property just across the road, not to mention the new village springing up just within earshot. The NRRS had snapped up the land in an estate sale from the Willard children who were unable to pay the death taxes. Thank-god Del had not needed to resort to eminent domain in finding land for the initial resettlement villages, one each in each of his six counties. But he knew that the reprieve from that thorny issue would not last long as more refugees flowed in, and willing-seller land became hard to find.

He pulled into Hention's farmyard noting the nicely kept house wrapped in Colorado flagstone just as Jim stepped out his door.

"Hello, Jim." Del said. "Came to talk about the beekeeper."

"Humpf! Don't know why you're bringing all these wetbacks to Thayer County, Del. Then making a big deal when I offered to pay one of them good cash wages to work for me."

"Well, Jim, that is not the way the resettlement program was set up. We are offering these American citizens a chance to restart their lives and help produce the food the country desperately needs. It's a kind of a modern-day homesteading program where they receive full title to their property after 5-years with a promise not to sell for another 10. Because they only get paid after harvest like you do, the cash you are offering sorely temps them."

"So, you steal this good farmland and give it to foreigners!"

"They aren't foreigners! They are American citizens who need help. They'll raise food and pay taxes. No good reason for them to become your wage slaves. Seems to me like you see yourself as a modern-day squire of the manor with peasant laborers. I don't know why you are so adamant about trying to grow horticultural crops anyway. You're not set up for it and know little about gardening. Sure, you have four pivots, but lack the labor that growing vegetables requires. You got an agronomy degree and only know about grasses and legumes – annuals to boot! Seems now that you no longer want to follow the industrial agriculture model of corn and soybeans, you could use your agronomic skills on growing fields of edible dry beans, wheat, pulse, lentils, and oats. Food for people, not gas tanks and cattle. Stay with what you know."

"Still a free country, and Gomez is welcome to make his own decision and get the cash his family needs." Jim declared.

In the end, Gomez was a careful man and ultimately opted to stay with the NRRS settlement, even though cash was tight. He knew that the small intensively gardened land he would own gave him a foothold and a future for his family just like the pioneers who first settled this dry place.

Further Reading

Johnson, C. (2010) *The Dark Horse*. Penguin

Karle, S. T., & Karle, D. (2017). *Conserving the Dust Bowl: The New Deal's Prairie States Forestry Project*. LSU Press.

Momaday, N. S. (1966) *House Made of Dawn*. Harper and Row

Turner, F. J., & Bogue, A. G. (2010). T*he Frontier in American Hstory*. Courier Corporation.

Wishart, D. J. (2013). *The Last Days of the Rainbel*t. U of Nebraska Press.

Zube, E. H. (1973). Scenery as a natural resource: Implications of public policy and problems of definition, description, and evaluation. *Landscape Architecture*, 63(2), 126-132.

16 Reading the Nebraska Landscape

"The land offers us good reading, outdoors, from a lively, unfinished manuscript."-May T. Watts

"Organizing one's perception of the world, whose vastness and complexity is unimaginable, requires discovering areas of order then linking them in coherent patterns that can be recognized readily enough to be useful."—Peter Coyote

Introduction

Like most intriguing landscapes, Lincoln's Wilderness Park changes, but at differing speeds, offering a series of linked, but ambiguous spaces. At least twice per year I led several small groups of students on fieldtrips along its trails to begin reading a landscape. Unfortunately, any narrative assembled from following a series of presupposed steps falls prey to the pre-existing structure of the trail we might choose to follow through the park. Particular spots along the trail offer the best perspectives on certain concepts, such as analysis of stream dynamics and hydraulics, or fluctuations of deer populations and their browsing habits, while other locations provide emotional-sensory aspects like thorny plants or colors, sounds, and smells. So, I warn students that following a trail becomes similar to following the line of argument in a sentence, and it is easy to get locked into a linear, linguistic interpretation and not a holistic experience.

The students taking these fieldtrips, however, didn't seem to mind. Having traveling mini-lectures employs a good deal of interpretation and become novel experiences. The students, by-and-large, enjoy using all of their senses and engaging elemental nature away from a more sterile classroom. Perhaps this is why positive aesthetic experiences often correlate with pleasure. Their sense of enjoyment is important since I believe aesthetic pleasure is ecological and occurs when our senses connect us to the wider world.

For the students, I compared and contrasted reading a landscape with reading a written article. In both cases, I ask the reader to have a questioning mind and be ready to do the work necessary to understand the words or landscape confronting them. First, make connections to what you know but then use both sides of your brain—emotional and analytical. Write about (left side), draw (right side), or photograph (right side) features that seem important to you. Explain why they appear important (left side). Use your imagination to project the place into the future (right side). What and why might changes happen to the landscape in your purview? Describe the forces that might reshape or destroy it. Are some features more immutable than others? Which ones? What makes them so? Why? Finally, after you have done your homework and thought about it some more, discuss the place with others who know it; ask their opinions; shift through their ideas for insights you may have missed.

This approach is quite different from Spirn's (1998) use of a language metaphor in explaining landscapes. Are there rules? Yes, but nouns, verbs, and grammar cannot literally structure landscapes.

In this final chapter I want to reprise and emphasize ideas that I have covered in preceding chapters, then take my own advice and hear about Nebraska from three creative people who deal daily with and draw inspirations from its landscape. I will do so by examining their holistic, creative, syntheses when confronted by landscapes.

Big Ideas Gleaned from Reading The Landscape

In the 15 preceding chapters I have shared my examination of the Nebraska landscape and distilled below some general ideas about it (Table 16.1). Unlike D W. Meinig's "Ten Version Of the Same Scene," (1976) where he suggests and portrays how a person's attitude and unique experience colors what he or she sees in it, and how each of us reacts in our own way to the same landscape, here I provide something different. Each chapter in this book has led to ideas about the wider landscape in general and the Nebraska landscape in particular. I believe some of the identified ideas can be used across a wider range of landscapes. However, as Meinig reminds us, more than 10 versions of the same scene exist. Certainly the Nebraska landscape can and does produce many more than the 15 basic ideas I have listed.

Table 16.1 Some Basic Ideas about Landscape Identified in this Book

	Chapter	Idea
Section 1: Valuing Landscapes	1	Experience
	2	Aesthetics
	3	Values
	4	Scale/Hierarchy
Section 2: Natural Landscapes	5	Structure
	6	Function
Section 3: Cultural Landscapes	7	Change
	8	Artifact
	9	Land Use/Land Cover
Section 4: Intentional Landscapes	10	Pattern
	11	Process
	12	Form/Space
Section 5: Future Landscapes	13	Connection
	14	Distance
	15	Future

Valuing Landscapes

Experience

Experience best starts in the way I used attention and observation in the Japanese garden (Chapter 1). That approach leads to a sequence of description, interpretation, evaluation, and communication. Attention means paying attention: looking and thinking about what is seen.

John Berger in *Ways of Seeing* says unequivocally:

> "Seeing comes before words. A child looks and recognizes before it speaks. But, there is also another sense in which seeing comes before words. It is seeing which establishes our place in the surrounding world; we explain [it] with words, but words can never undo the fact that we are surrounded by it. The relationship between what we see and what we know is never settled."

It is possible to practice reading the surrounding landscape, just as one might read a book. A book, however, distills, and its experience offers only secondary, indirect experience. A walk in the woods is more direct, multi-sensory, and immediate though potentially not as well organized as a book. From such a walk we each supply the chain of thought that directly organizes and links sense and meaning. You authorize your own world. Direct experience first begins with what one already knows and has experienced. Perhaps that is why experience impacts personal happiness more than material things. Experience quickly moves to the task of building-up from and connecting with the familiar.

When experiencing a landscape, ask yourself to note things that catch your attention, familiar or not. Next, look for obvious, existing structures, spaces, paths, edges, nodes, patches, and so on; gather clues about a place's history, ecology, use, extent, and context. Importantly, though often difficult, one should absorb all those details without losing an overall feel for the place as a whole. Guard against the atomization of analysis and thinking solely in snapshots. Devine the landscape's emotional impacts on you. What makes this whole hang together so that you apply the concept of landscape in the first place? What organizes this small sample of the world? What links it to the wider landscape? Identify those features or processes that seem to have meaning to you, both emotionally and analytically. Describe them using many, and if possible, all of your senses. Articulate what they mean to you and why.

Aesthetics

Our connection to landscape involves an aesthetic response which is quite different than a merely sensory one. Aesthetic responses merge intuition and logic. Such responses key on differences that make a difference and that tap our connections with our surroundings. To have an aesthetic response makes us human and makes us part of this world. Gregory Bateson (1979) said it this way: "By aesthetic I mean being responsive to the pattern which connects."

Values

Since we are in and of the landscape we might be judging, our values impact how we interpret and experience landscape. Values help us create meaning about what we see. Those values may be inculcated at an early age by one's family, community, and culture or possibly hard-wired into our genetic makeup. But what and how we value a landscape also shapes our unique experiences, beyond family and culture.

Scale and Hierarchy

Landscapes include, connect, and pre-compose spaces of differing sizes. We experience them hierarchically and relative in scale to each other. Humans interpret landscape scale and in doing so use their judgment based on experience. We just need to remember that we are in and a part of the system which we judge. So scale is not merely size or distance, but synthesizes size in relation to some known, selected or implied hierarchy. Scale is strongly contextual.

Natural Landscapes

Structure

For many people, natural landscapes are those in which the hand of humans plays little, or more likely, no role. I believe that is a problematic position both philosophically and practically which orphans us intellectually and isolates us physically from our supportive context. Nevertheless, the layout and structure of the material world around us first came into being based on physics, chemistry, biology, and a myriad of finite, interconnected, sequential actions and reactions. Based on those influences the landscape's resulting hierarchical structure backdrops, supports, and organizes all life (including humans) and it also suggests to us a structure useful for reading landscapes.

Function

Each structure or meta-structure (structure of structures) we encounter in the landscape has not only a physical dimension but also, a functional one as well. For example, Chapter 11 included a detailed description of a structure called a boundary, where boundaries demark distinctly differing areas that then offer varying impacts to changes or activities nearby. Boundaries such as topographic ridges or shelterbelts modify landscape flows and functions, like wind or water. Aquatic structures such as lakes and rivers impact flows of terrestrial animals that need to cross them but conduct and support aquatic life. Most landscape functions exhibit clues to the viewers about many of the interactions between structure and function present in a landscape before them. Good designers are able to conceptualize and tap those clues, thus interpreting them for the users.

Cultural Landscapes

Change

Robert Riley has said, "Change indeed is at the core of landscape" and cultural landscapes display change by incorporating human structures overlain and entangled with natural ones. These cultural landscapes evolved largely without intention. They were by-products. In Nebraska, farming methods, technology, and the political economy have certainly changed prairie and woodland, but those changes are mostly unintended consequences. For example, the one-mile grid of the General Land Survey system has layered a Cartesian grid structure over a naturally undulating topography, thereby partially changing its structure and function. While the superimposed grid certainly adds complexity to the former natural landscape, its change can also occur through natural functions such as fire and flood.

When thinking about the idea of change in a landscape, we implicitly include the concept of time. Change allows (compels?) one to calculate rates uniting it with the idea of functions, since they are often described at a rate. For example: the flood moved water at 1,200 cubic feet per second through a narrow channel which was unable to contain it; the fire burned the ground layer of 120 acres of dry woodland in one day. Cultural landscapes, whether nostalgic or maligned, do not remain static because human involvement changes and outstrips those of natural changes. Unfortunately, humans seem to accelerate things -- for example, extinction and warming of the globe's atmosphere.

Artifact

We label structures that represent a period or era as an artifact. When singled out, described, and analyzed, landscape artifacts can be categorized as cultural (e.g., hedgerows) or natural (e.g., relict prairies). For example, the silt on a lake bottom is an artifact of upstream soil type, topography, and farm management. So, one might describe it as both cultural and natural, though the management decisions may be an important trigger. The singling out, that is the separation, of an object or structure from its context, may be necessary for analysis and understanding, but such separation from context can mislead as well. As Bateson (1979) noted, description while a necessary tool to understanding any phenomenon, does not explicitly require it be done in a certain way.

Land use/ Land cover

Perhaps two of the most visible aspects of natural and cultural landscapes appear in its land use and land cover. How a particular piece of land is used depends on both political and economic factors, but those become modified by its natural capabilities. Steep slopes and thin, unproductive soil should relegate agricultural land to grazing or wildlife habitat. In fact, the Natural Resources Conservation Service (Klingebiel and Montgomery 1961) has placed all U.S. agricultural and non-urban lands into eight Capability Classes (I-VIII) based on their capability to raise crops and freedom from inherently hazardous conditions. Comparably, urban areas often consist of small parcels with higher monetary value. This makes urban land, since it developed largely for economic reasons, subject to intensive modification. Building codes and zoning regulations heavily control permitted activities and development.

Land cover reflects land use, but can be quite variable. Suffice it to say that agricultural land uses will most likely have natural soil or plant cover, though the amount and kind varies throughout the year. To guard against soil erosion, no till and cover crop management systems on agricultural lands attempt to keep plant or plant litter as the predominant cover. The configuration of land cover is also important. While an urban lot's hard and impermeable surfaces yield high stormwater runoff rates, green infrastructure techniques and structures can slow runoff from large rain events, and in many cases, water from smaller storms can be completely sequestered on site.

Pattern

Pattern repeats similar structure across the landscape. For example, a pattern of hedgerows organized over a large enough area becomes a hedgerow landscape. Shallow, wet prairie depressions fed from small, unconnected watersheds become the Rainwater Basin landscape. Silty pasture slopes with stair-like topography become a "cat-step" pattern in Nebraska's Central Loess Hills landscape. Center pivots assume a packing order (pattern) in areas without delimiting county roads different from those in grid-roaded agricultural landscapes. Un-straightened, that is natural, streams often display repeated looping meanders based on the slope of the stream, the soil type, sediment load and the volume of water carried. North-facing slopes and swale bottoms in mixed and shortgrass prairie landscape often contain grasses from the tallgrass prairie. Identifying these patterns and hundreds more, enlivens reading the landscape and educates the viewer about its structure, organization, and function.

Intentional Landscapes

Process

Intention is a human predilection and condition; nature has no intention and simply is. Intention in the making of landscapes revolves around humans integrating and resolving their specific, identified needs and desires with the actualities of nature. A specific landscape's pre-existing structure and function should be carefully fitted with any human program. This design process best serves landscape change in an open, accessible, logical and repeatable way across a wide variety of landscape types and sizes (Steinitz 1979).

The scientific process rises from logical, detailed observations whose discerned structure has been compared probabilistically. The aim is to describe but importantly to predict change especially to future structures and functions. Scientific process, unlike design process, presupposes no aesthetic intent

Form and Space

The design process while largely rational, results in alternative ways to create form and organize spaces that tap our senses and emotions and offer meaning while concurrently solving land use and configuration problems. Designed landscapes were and are meant to be and do; they should not occur simply as unintended consequences or byproducts of change. Designed spaces must not be leftover scraps, what Koolhaus calls "junkspace."

Connection

Landscape proffers many connections. It links spaces; its artifacts remind us of the past; it reposits nature; it shares with all. It is where we have to be. And connections are what we make in bestowing meaning our world.

Future Landscapes

Distance

Hardened, and mutable structure infuses, organizes, and enlivens landscapes, while visibility at a distance connects us to far away objects and the horizon. Distance links time and space. Distant spaces imply both the future and the past.

Future

Future landscapes and their configurations all have a beginning in the past yet are experienced in the present. Therefore, understanding the pace and type of landscape change in a place can help predict its future. Those predictions show trends, but not specifics and can be taken into account as we (re)design our world. Panarchy reigns.

Beyond Personal Landscapes: Widening the Discussion

Until now, this book mostly discusses personal landscape experience, but even such limited experience can be shared with another person or among those in a group. Only after initially reading a landscape and doing your homework, should one consult with others who have ready knowledge and a different perspective. Ask them questions to widen your context and deepen your understanding.

Describe, interpret, evaluate, and communicate are steps that can be used as a shorthand for reading landscapes. Communication of landscape can take many forms and is necessary to capture and share impressions, connections, predictions and so on. The products of such communication can be examined as concrete evidence of one's experience in it and of it. Creative people in the traditions of art and literature toil to produce and share works with humanity imbued with their unique, but general experiences. Galleries and libraries then collect that work for our examination, learning and pleasure--work that has been painstakingly created and edited. We can access it, but rarely get feedback from its creators about the process of how it came into being and what they think it means.

Nebraska happens to have a cadre of creative artists who experience landscape, examine it, and then respond by creating works related to it. And I am fortunate to have had three of them share with me their approaches, processes, and insights for reading its landscape.

Poet, Twyla Hansen

Twyla Hansen, Nebraska State Poet Laureate (2013-2018) intimately knows the Nebraska landscape. From growing up on a Nebraska farm to creating and managing landscape settings, her experience of landscape and her writings about it, capture common threads. She says that the mechanics of any good, engaging writing start with explaining a central idea and then making that explanation interesting to the reader. Her themes have a strong basis both in landscape and in human emotions and relationships. However, few of her poems are simply one or the other, but intertwine. She recognizes experience by writing about nature's entanglement with humans. To this end, Hansen attempts to interpret raw landscape space in a way that connects it to humans and the idea of place. Thus, a strong sense of place inevitably appears in her poems and most of them have a universal message. Yet that message happens in a particular place. Hansen suggests that physical movement in her experience of real landscapes is important to her writing, "After all, the landscape is constantly in flux and to be in rhythm with it, draws me to move with it, within it, and engage it." Color and other impacts on her senses emerge as key to her involvement with landscape. An inveterate rambler, she frequently treks along edges (roads, paths, creeks, shores, ridges, woods, prairies, etc.) capturing juxtapositions (objects, sounds, shadows, animals, clouds, etc.) In a perfectly ecological statement, she reveals, "It's all happening at the edge." An excellent example of understanding the role which space plays in the landscape in many of her poems, Hansen says, "What you don't say is often as important as what you do."

Following is a short poem used with permission from her 2001 book, *Salt Creek Sanctuary*, set during summer in her garden. It nicely blurs the borders between all our yards and gardens (in Nebraska and elsewhere) by pointing out specific things, activities, and ideas found in hers that reinforce its title, "July".

July

All day from the grove a chorus of cicadas,
In the distance, a thunderstorm flashes

over the city through evening clouds,
and one by one, lightening bugs

signal their luminous abdomens
to the opposite sex. A hot wind

pumping humidity across the low hills,
into trembling leaves of cottonwood.

July crabgrass setting plump seedheads,

> Tomatoes bending under green loads,
>
> a plains toad staking its cool claim,
> under the dog's water dish.
>
> Somewhere in this composed suburb
> a couple will switch off their reading lamps
>
> and turn into the gathering dark to face
> each other. Out in the farmer's cornfield
>
> heated leaves will gradually unfold
> admitting their heavenly gifts.

Connections abound in the stanzas of "July," and not unusually I find some of the big ideas in the Nebraska landscape inhabit her poem. From a thunderstorm to humidity, to a dog's dish and unrolling corn leaves, water or its impacts flow through out the poem's lines. Their spatial connection relies on a hierarchy of scale shown by the back and forth between foreground sounds of cicadas' chorus, visions of lightening bugs, and tactile tremble of cottonwood leaves, plump seedheads and tomatoes against the background of thunder, suburbs, and cornfields. Structures are called out—grove, city, hills, dog dish, composed suburb, and cornfield. And besides connecting, these artifacts also run the gamut from natural to man-made.

While intention seems lacking in the brief description of the retiring couple, on further thought, that lack of intent seems appropriate in lines mostly devoted to naturalistic structures and functions. While the reader should expect Hansen's choice of words to be explicit and concrete, the last two lines that describe leaves "admitting," seems a bit ambiguous. Did the leaves "allow in" water from the mentioned thunderstorm or were the leaves "confessing" a need for water. The ambiguity is a nice landscape touch since all landscapes appear ambiguous and open to interpretation.

Painter, Keith Jacobshagen

Self-described as a Midwest painter, Keith Jacobshagen's roots, education, and home strongly tie him to the central Great Plains. In fact, a good deal of his subject matter comes from the Nebraska landscape that he routinely explores, which is fitting for one who eschews grandiose landscapes of mountain and seacoast. Competent in a variety of media from photography to pastels and watercolors, his major (and very) large images are oil paintings. Jacobshagen, known for his spectacular skyscapes, evolved over the years in reducing his compositions from depicting one-half land to one-tenth land and emphasizing mostly sky. He confesses that some of this interest in sky and his uncanny elevated perspective views came from flying with his father in light planes over the landscape of his boyhood home in Kansas.

Though he has not published or written about his work, (it speaks for itself) he does keep a working journal. In it he records locations and motifs that inform his studio work. The triggering motifs may be captured with words, but more likely with quick thumbnails.

Many of his early landscape paintings were done "plein air" directly in the landscape which necessitated their small size and muted detail. He went back to that approach in 2010 capturing dawn details each day, for a year, no matter his location using oils on a series of

3-inch by 5-inch copper plates. Some of his works include short haiku-like phrases that capture an image's context impossible to recreate with paint: sound, wind, and temperature, nearby animals or other natural phenomena. Not a fair-weather explorer, Jacobshagen directly confronts the Nebraska landscape without regard to weather or season.

"Cooling in July," (1997) (Figure 16.1) deftly expresses the scale and spaces of the Nebraska landscape. Those two ideas lay at the crux of Jacobshagen's ability to distill its essential landscape qualities. Scale and his signature (somewhat elevated) perspective create an aesthetic response which pulls the viewer headlong into the composed space and then beyond into the distance. Inverting our normal visual experience, his exacting distant cloud detail and texture dance on the horizon while the foreground fades to textureless green bands.

Figure 16.1 "Cooling in July" a landscape by Keith Jacobshagen in oils. (Used with artist's permission.)

In fact, that lack of detail invites viewers to bring their own experiences, thoughts, and values to bear. At the base of the painting, details do appear in carefully written notes intentionally scribed on the unpainted canvas.

Detailing the structure of spaces requires masses, but he executes them in such a way they do not overwhelm the spaces. The road, the hedgerow and the horizon only occupy about twenty percent of the composition's area, yet solidly anchor it, providing a required base and grounding its dynamic skyscape. Both near and far land surfaces reflect known activities and display his familiarity with Nebraska's patterns, land uses and land covers. This piece involves the future; its road connects the viewer to the horizon, but also acknowledges in its title, "Cooling in July" – that time brings changes.

Photographer, John Spence

John Spence grew up in Nebraska and spent time working in its rural landscape before he studied architecture then completed both his BFA and MFA in photography. Spence (2005) is strongly committed to knowing his roots and paying attention to understanding Nebraska as a place. The architecture training shows in his devotion to depicting space while adhering to process. He uses various photographic formats, but his 8 X 10 view camera tests that dedication to process in the eight minutes it may take to set up, compose, and expose a scene. Anticipating what will be happening makes that long-time span become even more daunting to accomplish, yet is critical to his work.

Because he understands his analytical bias, Spence (2005) strives for compositions and subject matter which he hopes, "create an emotional response to the place where I am." That means purposely not using icons of the rural landscape like windmills because their familiarity constricts the viewer's range of responses. On the other hand, Spence is not some type of purist or iconoclast. For example, he has discovered the luminous qualities of metal barns which he once shunned but now frequently appear in rural Nebraska.

Spence's photo, "Boone Co., 10-8-87," (Figure 16.2) strongly conveys a sense of both space in its structure and in its details as place. It does so while acknowledging and downplaying many structural features that could very easily overwhelm and diminish the setting as either space or place. In composition, the road draws one's eye to the horizon, but it is minimum maintenance and not a typical Nebraska road regularly bladed by the county maintainer. Adjacent to the road, a tunnel of enormous cottonwoods not only counterbalance the sky but extend themselves, dadoing, subduing, and minimizing that skyward expanse. Those cottonwoods also create a shaded, enclosed, mid-ground space while simultaneously splitting the unpicked cornfields. Tawny corn and colorful fall foliage depict season while the long shadows suggest the time of day. Middleground rarely gets captured in photos of the Nebraska landscape, because such scalar effects rarely present themselves so clearly in Nebraska's broad and open spaces and most photographers lack Spence's compositional skill. In this one photograph, he reproduces the middleground roadway, and foreground detail, yet composes a window to the distant horizon. The scene becomes a spatial trifecta.

With the abandonment of many miles of Nebraska's short-haul rail lines, the image has timeless feel of an artifact. It speaks of John Fowles' (1979) "present pastness." Here railroad tracks stand out, replete with iconic crossing X's contrasting with a neglected road's surface to authenticate a particular time and place. However, for all the commerce to which trains and corn refer, this country crossing remains a by-product of a bygone time. This place claims no intent and came into being from vastly different processes that in Spence's carefully captured view just happen to mesh in time and place.

Further Reading

Bateson, G. 1979. *Mind and Nature: A Necessary Unity*. New York: Dutton.

Coyote, P. 1991. Gary Snyder and the Real Work. *Gary Snyder: Dimensions of a Life*, (ed.) Jon Halper Sierra Club Books

Fowles, J. 2000. *The Tree*. Random House.

Gussow, A., 1972. *A Sense of Place: The Artist and the American Land* (Vol. 1). Friends of the Earth.

Hansen, T. 2001. " July" Sanctuary Near Salt Creek. Lone Willow Press

Klingebiel, A.A. and Montgomery, P.H., 1961. Land-capability classification. Agricultural Handbook. No. 210. Soil Conservation Service. US Department of Agriculture, Washington DC.

Lewis, P. 1983. Learning from looking: geographic and other writing about the American cultural landscape. *American Quarterly*, 35(3), pp. 242-261.

Lynch, K., 1976. *Managing the Sense of a Region*. Boston:MIT Press.

Meinig, D. W. The *Interpretation of Ordinary Landscapes: Geographical Essays*, pp. 33-48.

Riley, Robert B. 2015 *The Camaro in the Pasture*.U of Virginia Press: Charlottesville

Spirn, A., 1998. *The Language of Landscape*. Yale University Press.

Spence, J. 2005. Artist's Statement Animal Science Complex Photographs.

Steinitz, C., 1979. *Defensible processes for regional landscape design*. American Society for Landscape Architects.

Watts, M.T., 1963. *Reading the Landscape of America*. McMillan:New York.

INDEX

A

abandoned homes	24
aesthetics	
and landscapes	35
and Romantics	17
beauty	
admirable	16
ecological	16, 24
enjoyable	16
Conservation Esthetic	18
definition	14, 29
relation to beauty	15
agricultural landscapes	109-110
agriculture	
economic organization	118
indigenous	110
modern	111
Neolithic	110
allees'	22

B

barbwire	145
Bateson, Gregory	8, 18, 24
Berger, John	4
Berleant, Arnold	24, 38
Berry, Wendell	33, 35
Bessey, Charles	65, 132
Butz, Earl	110

C

Cather, Willa	10
books	157
Foundation (WCF)	159
cultural landscapes	163
landscape tour	158
landscapes	158-67
Memorial Prairie	159
catsteps	96, 97
chemigation	112, 125
Christiansen, Emil	118
city edge	39
city-country linkage	40
Clark-McNary Act	133, 140
climate	73
Columbus, Pawnee Park	207
Community Supported Agriculture	40, 43

conservation	
easements	185
subdivisions	184-187
urban soil & water	187-189
crops	
genetically modified (GMO)	113
management	113
protection	113
types	113
crop systems	114
covercrops	115
no-till	115
pasture and range	116
permaculture	116
rotation	115

D

Daisen-in	10
Dass, Ram	6
David City, NE, Memorial Park	207
design	
architectural	196-200
process	189-191
site versus non-site	200
Dunnett, Nigel	25

E

eco-regions	82
ecological	
community	147-151
concepts	175
panarchy	175, 190
plant communities	78
structure	173
Herminghaus, E.H.	210
ethics	14
and aesthetics	36
definition	29

F

Fairbury, NE, McNish Park	207
Farmer's Canal Coop	122
farmland loss	37
fencerows	144, 149-150
fertigation	112, 125
forests	78, 79, 88-92
deciduos	88
riparian	89

upland	89
evergreen	90
cedar savanna	91
ponderosa	92
Fowles, John	10
Furnas, Gov. Robert	132

G

General Land Survey (GLS)	109, 123, 126
geology	67
Gibson, JJ	7
glaciations	66
Goodman, Nelson	4
green infrastructure	188
green roof	25-26
Gussow, Alan	4

H

hedgerows	143-150
layout	147
management	151
species dispersal	150
Homestead National Monument	144

I

irrigation	111
canals	122, 126
center pivot	111, 123, 129, 125-126
costs	123
labor	124
gated-pipe	123
gravity-fed	123
reservoirs	122
sprinkler	123
subsurface drip	123

I

Jackson, JB	110
Jackson, Wes	32
Jacobshagen, Keith	257-259
Janovy, John	15
Johnsgard, Paul	65

K

Kaplan, Rachael & Stephan	37
Kearney Canal	122
Kingsley, GP	122
Kinkaid Act	133, 140-141, 152
species used	141
Kirschenmann, Fred	118

L

Lake Helen	122
Lake McConaughy	122-126
Land	
and human values	
and Utiltarian thinking	31
cover	174
trusts	42
use	174
Land Ethic	
Aldo Leopold	17, 33-35
John Cobb	34
landscapes	
as object	24
as scenery	234
as subject	23, 24
boundaries	52, 173, 190
created	255--259
cultural	21
designed	24, 180-192, 200- 205, 207-220
distance	233
future	
impact of drought	240-249
impact of windpower	235-240,
Great Plains	46, 152
ideas & concepts	251-255
intelligent care of	22
natural	19
natural nearby	37
vivid care	22
object	24
structure	49
values	29
language vs. image	4
Leopold, Aldo	17
Lewis, Pierce	131
Litton, Burton	56
Lopez, Barry	15

M

MacIntosh, C. Baron	132
McConaughy, CW	122
Morris, Desmond	9
Morton, J. Sterling	132, 134

N

Nassauer, Joan	24-25
native vegetation	82
nature and Christianity	31
Nebraska Veteran's Memorial	200-205
program	201
site	201

Nebraska Capitol	194-196
Nebraska National Forest	132
Necker Cube	6
New Lands Act	122
noise	38

O

Oak Canyon Hitchcock Co., NE	66
Ogallala Aquifer	126
depletion	126
water quality	112, 127
Oregon Trail	3
ornamental conifers	134
allee'	139-140
bosque	139-140
distribution	137
planting patterns	138-140
species used	134-137

P

parallax	7
Pfahl, John	7
Piaget, Jean	6
Pioneers Park	207-220
Ernst H. Herminghaus	210
layout	210-215
program & uses	215-218
stewardship & management	219-220
plant communities	78
point of view	7
potential evapo-transpiration (PET)	73
prairie ecology	172-174
prairie	93-101
midgrass	96
loess hills	96
sandhills	98-100
shortgrass	100
tallgrass	
lowland	95, 96
upland	94, 95
Prairie States Forest Program	133, 140-142

R

Rainwater Basin	75
Reclamation Act	122
Republican River Compact	127
rivers	73
Roosevelt, Franklin D	133
Rowe Sanctuary	20
Rulo Bluffs, Richardson Co.	19
rural zoning	42
Ryoan-ji	11

S

Sandhills cranes	20
scale	46-58, 252
and space-grain	52
definition	46
grain and extent	52
hierarchy	47, 51
human model	55
human	55
in landscape ecology	58, 56
distance of view	54
Schuyler, NE., Oak Park	207
scientific method	190
Scottsbluff National Monument	25
senses as a system	5
settlement	66
soil conservation	182-184
buffers	180
grass waterways	182
no-till	179
ponds	183
programs	183-184
strip cropping	178-179
terraces	181-182
urban	188
soil	66, 67, 71
fertility	111, 112
loss on Great Plains	172, 177-178
Spence, John	259
Snyder, Gary	44, 45, 102

T

Thayer, Robert	24-25, 42
Thompson, William Irwin	38
Thoreau, H. D.	9
Timber Culture Act	132, 140, 152
species used	142
woodlots	142
trees	10
as places	10
as symbols	10
meaning	10
on Great Plains	10, 131, 152
planting tax exemption	132
visual impact	152
Tri-County Project	122, 126
Tuan, Yi-fu	3, 6, 36
Twyla, Hansen	256-257

U

urban design	41
urban plant communities	103-105

V

Vandal ideology	32
visual preferences	38
visual ecology	42
visual impacts	223-232
and aesthetics	224
Lincoln Electric System	225, 228
mitigation methods	226
potential examples	228-231
transmission lines	223
wind turbines	231-232
visual structure	49

W

wetlands	78
lakes, fens & marshes	101, 102
Rainwater Basin	102
salt marshes	103
Wilderness Park Lincoln, NE,	250
Wilson, E. O.	37
Wisconsin Capitol	194-196
woodlots	142-143

Made in the USA
Monee, IL
27 June 2023

37661768R00149